# The
# COMMU
# PARTY
# and the

# Auto
# Workers'
# Unions

Jess —
A MUST, for any comrade who gets
as excited about "bulletins" as
you do. Enjoy, and take note!
Yours, in struggle
Hannah Dee X

# The COMMUNIST PARTY and the

# Auto Workers' Unions

## by Roger Keeran

INTERNATIONAL PUBLISHERS

New York

An earlier version of chapter 2 has appeared in *Labor History*, of chapter 8 in *Michigan History*, and of chapter 10 in *Science and Society*.

First Paperback Edition, 1986
International Publishers Co., Inc., New York

**Library of Congress Cataloging-in-Publication Data**

Keeran, Roger, 1944—
    The Communist Party and the auto workers'unions.

    Includes bibliographies and index.
    1. Trade-unions--Automobile industry workers--United States. 2. Trade-unions and communism--United States. 3: Communist Party of the United States. I. Title.
HD6515.A8K43    1986      322'.2'0973      86-142
ISBN 0-7178-0639-1 (pbk.)

FOR CAROL

## About the Author:

Roger Keeran was born in Lapeer, Michigan, and graduated from Monteith College of Wayne State University in 1967. While attending school, he worked for General Motors Fisher Body No. 1 and No. 2 in Flint, Michigan, and the General Motors Stamping Plant in Grand Blanc, Michigan. He received his M.A. and Ph.D. in American History from the University of Wisconsin—Madison. He taught for eight years at the New York State School of Industrial and Labor Relations of Cornell University, and he has also taught at Princeton University and Rutgers University—Newark.

For nearly four years, Keeran served as Education Director of District 65, United Automobile Workers Union (UAW, AFL-CIO) in New Jersey. He is currently Associate Professor and Director of the Credit & Certificate Program of Cornell University's Industrial and Labor Relations Extension at the Center for Labor Studies of Empire State College (SUNY) in New York City. This book received the American Library Association's "Choice Award" in 1981. Roger Keeran's work has also appeared in *Labor History, Michigan History, Science & Society,* and *Industrial Labor Relations Review.*

# CONTENTS

# PREFACE

I began this study ten years ago, while a graduate student at the University of Wisconsin. My interest in the subject came as much from my background as from academic curiosity. I grew up in Lapeer, Michigan, thirty miles north of Pontiac and twenty miles east of Flint, and the home for many who work in the shops of General Motors. In the early 1960s I worked for part of three years in GM plants in Flint and Grand Blanc and joined the UAW. While a student at Wayne State University, I joined the Detroit Committee to End the War in Vietnam and Students for a Democratic Society, and my involvement in campus politics sparked a curiosity about the history of American radicalism. The fusion of my background and this curiosity led me to explore the role of Communists in the history of auto workers' unions in the period 1919–1949. I began the study with few preconceptions. I completed it with an admiration for all of those whose struggles built the union.

I gratefully acknowledge the help of librarians, archivists, and staff of the following institutions: the State Historical Society of Wisconsin, Columbia University Library, New York Public Library, Syracuse University Archives, Archives of Labor History and Urban Affairs at Wayne State University, Tamiment Library at New York University, Martin P. Catherwood Library and the Olin Library at Cornell University, Labor-Management Documentation Center at Cornell University, Archives of the United Mine Workers Union, and "Insurgent Rank and File: The GM Sit-Down Strike of 1936–37" at the University of Michigan—Flint.

I would like to thank the research assistants who aided my work at various times: Scott Buchheit, Chris Farrand, Paula Traffas, Martin Grazier, and Paul Clark.

I would like to thank all of those who generously shared their experiences and ideas in letters and interviews. Their contributions are cited in the notes.

I would like to thank the editors of *Michigan History, Science and Society,* and *Labor History* for having originally published parts of this study.

I would also like to acknowledge a number of friends and colleagues who gave encouragement, criticism, and help along the way: Paul Conkin, Cletus Daniel, Sam and Emma Darcy, David and Doris Herreshoff, David Jacobs, Gerald Meyer, John Najarian, James Prickett, Elsa Rassbach, Barbara Riemer, and William Weinstone.

Joyce Wright typed the final manuscript. For her efficiency, patience, and care, I extend many thanks.

Finally, I would like to thank my daughter, Alice, for giving me much joy and my wife, Carol, for being my most intelligent and supportive critic.

# The COMMUNIST PARTY and the

# Auto Workers' Unions

# I
• • •

# INTRODUCTION

The history of Communists and American labor raises three questions. Were the Communists legitimate (or good) trade unionists? Were they an important influence in the labor movement? Were they good Communists? These questions involve matters that go beyond the history of Communists in the auto industry. Consequently, my work does not provide the last word on them. Yet, raising these questions has a point. It enables me to explain how my views on these questions differ from others who have written about Communists and labor and what assumptions lie behind my work. Finally, it enables me to explain the ways in which the history of Communists in auto refutes some commonly held ideas about Communists and labor. This introduction also discusses several problems of method: the identification of Communists and the reliability of Communist sources and oral history.

Were the Communists legitimate trade unionists? Many writers have argued or assumed they were not. This conclusion rested on an intricate web of ideas about the Communist party and its ends and means. One idea was that neither the Communist party nor individual Communists were free agents. Communists were cogs in a disciplined and monolithic party. The Communist party in turn was part of the Communist International and was therefore the puppet or agent of the Soviet Union. Since the Communists could not respond freely to American conditions, they could not act as legitimate unionists or radicals. A related idea was that the

Communists sought ends that were foreign to American workers and unions. The Communists sought to aid the Soviet Union and to make a socialist revolution, but American workers wanted only immediate economic improvements and American unions wanted class cooperation, bread-and-butter gains, and mild social legislation. Closely related to these ideas were others about Communist means. In order to gain a tool for their political ends, the Communists tried to gain power in the unions. Primarily they tried to infiltrate, control, and dominate the unions. To achieve and hold power the Communists used any undemocratic means available including violence and intimidation. According to this idea, Communist means violated democratic norms and made the Communists untrustworthy unionists.

Examples from the work of journalists, historians, political scientists, economists, and specialists in industrial relations writing between 1938 and 1976 show the constancy and flavor of ideas about Communist illegitimacy. Benjamin Stolberg, whose 1938 book on the CIO served as a sourcebook for many later writers, regarded the Communists as a "disintegrating force in the CIO." He argued that they used "rule-or-ruin" tactics in an all out "attempt to control American labor" for the interests of the Soviet Union. "Stalinism is a danger in the CIO," Stolberg said. "For one thing, it is not interested in American labor as such." Max Kampelman, whose book justified the CIO's expulsion of "Communist dominated unions" in 1949, said, "There is . . . overwhelming evidence to prove that the goal of Communists in the trade union movement is support of Soviet strategy in foreign affairs. . . . Communist unionism, therefore, does not so much represent a trade union philosophy in any meaningful sense of the term as a system of power." In a history of the United Automobile Workers, Irving Howe and B. J. Widick viewed the Communists as "colonial agents of Russian totalitarianism." A study of trade union administration by Jack Barbash reported: "Communist penetration of unions is, as has been said, along with racketeering, a form of union pathology. Communists utilize unions not as institutions with an independent integrity and existence of their own but as vehicles for power aggrandizement in behalf of a foreign government." In 1952, labor historian, Philip Taft told a Senate committee that a Communist was not an authentic unionist because he did not "owe his primary loyalty to the union." "May I empha-

size," Taft said, "that the significant differences between Communist trade-union activity and that of non-Communist militants is
the centrally organized and directed activity of the Communists
and their unswerving loyalty to the Soviet Government." Some recent writers have stated similar views less stridently. In Irving
Bernstein's history of workers in the 1920s, Communists are portrayed as operating on money and instructions from Moscow to
gain "control" and "domination" of the unions in the needle
trades. "Communists in the American labor movement,"
economist Walter Galenson said in 1974, "were committing a
fraud: although professing that their purpose was to engage in collective bargaining to improve wages and working conditions of
union members, they were actually attempting to establish bases
of political power that could be and were used at the behest of the
Soviet Union in times of crisis."[1]

The idea that the Communists were not legitimate trade
unionists because they were agents of the Soviet Union and cogs
in a disciplined, monolithic party is based on a simplistic view of
the Communist party. The party's membership in the Communist
International and support of the Soviet Union did not keep it from
being the main expression of native, working class radicalism during the 30 years after 1919. The Communist party had a dual character. It was a blend of national and international radicalism. The
party was formed mainly by former members of the Socialist party,
who were inspired by the Russian revolution and committed to
making an American socialist revolution. (See Chapter 2.) Many of
those who served at one time or another as leaders of the CP in
Michigan in the 1920s and 1930s originally belonged to the
Socialist party or the Young People's Socialist League. Included
among these were Edgar Owens, Albert Weisbord, Phil Raymond,
and William Weinstone. The Communists saw no conflict between
their commitment to internationalism (and the Soviet Union) and
the interests of American workers. The Communists' ties to an international movement did not keep them from being leading
fighters for industrial unionism in the auto industry. The moral
and intellectual strength that the Communists derived from their
international ties made them better fighters than they otherwise
would have been.[2]

The Communist party's relationship to the Communist International and the Soviet Union was complex, and the idea that the

Communists were agents of the Soviet Union does no justice to it. To be sure, the Communist party of the Soviet Union as the "first among equals" dominated the Communist International. At times, as in 1939 when Stalin signed a nonaggression pact with Hitler, the Soviet Union acted abruptly and independently in a way that forced the American Communists to change their line suddenly and abjectly. (See Chapter 9.) It is equally clear that American Communist leaders at times had an unhealthy deference towards the Soviet Union. Earl Browder, general secretary of the Communist party from 1934 to 1945, once said: "When I was in Moscow, I was like a child." Still, none of this meant that the American Communists failed to take initiatives. In 1934, for example, in a move that foreshadowed the Comintern's adoption of the Popular Front in 1935, the American party dissolved its independent unions and sent their members into the American Federation of Labor. Both William Z. Foster and Browder later insisted that this decision occurred in response to American conditions and was "initiated by Americans in America." Moreover, American Communists participated in the congresses and plenums where the Comintern formulated policies. Here too American Communists exercised initiative. At the Seventh Congress in 1935, the Comintern considered whether the CP should run a candidate against President Roosevelt in 1936. In the end it decided "to leave the matter to the decision of the American comrades." The Americans decided to run Browder for president but to avoid strong criticism of Roosevelt. The "Russian puppet show" image of the Communist party is too frail a caricature to deny the Communists legitimacy as trade unionists.[3]

The idea that Communists could not act as good trade unionists, because they owed their first allegiance to a disciplined party finds no support in the auto industry. The Communist party was a more disciplined party than any other party on the left. In the 1930s this discipline made the party effective and kept it free of the factionalism and splits that divided the Socialists in the 1930s. The party's discipline also aided the struggle for an auto workers' union. It meant, for instance, that the party was able to follow a policy of "concentration," to send party members to Michigan, to place auto workers in key party positions, and to focus the activity of workers and nonworkers on key auto plants. (See Chapter 4.) In the early 1930s as part of the party's concentration on auto, such party members as William Weinstone, Nat Ganley, and Max Salzman came to Detroit from New York. The party placed Bill Allan, a Scottish-born worker with many years of union experience, in charge of Detroit's West Side party organization and Fred Williams, an auto worker and former mine worker, in charge of the East Side. About 1934 the party put the auto workers, Walter Moore, Bud Simons, and Joe Devitt in charge of the Flint party. Concentration meant that the party had nonworkers give help to union organizing and strikes. During strikes, party members who were functionaries, unemployed, or professionals often distributed leaflets, joined picket lines, provided legal defense, and supplied food. Within the auto plants, party discipline enabled Communists to rely on secret and conspiratorial methods, which effective organizing required before the UAW was established.[4]

The idea that Communist discipline prevented Communists from being good trade unionists is based on a distorted and simplistic image of how the Communists acted in the shops and unions. In the mid-1930s Communists in the auto industry worked through two party forms—the shop unit, a group of three or more Communists working in the same shop, and the fraction, the party caucus in the union. Both the unit and fraction had political and union tasks. The units recruited party members, conducted educational discussions, published shop papers, and distributed the *Daily Worker*. They also recruited people to the union and undertook work on particular shop grievances. A party manual described the function of fractions:

> The Party Fraction in a union or a branch of another mass organization meets regularly before the meeting of this organization. At this meeting the members of the Party Fraction discuss and decide how to apply the policy of the Party in the organization; how to introduce the Party campaigns; how to recruit new Party members from the union; how to get new readers for the *Daily Worker*; and what things can be done to improve the conditions of the members of the organization.

Individual Communists were bound to act according to the majority decision of the unit or fraction and the decisions of higher party bodies, but the units and fractions were supposed to enhance the Communists' loyalty to the union and their initiative as union members. "In all detailed questions of the inner life and daily work of the union . . . ," a Party manual said, "the Fraction acts independently on the basis of the policy of the Party." In practice the relations between the party leaders and fractions varied. The party leaders cooperated closely with the fraction in the National Maritime Union but had loose connections with the fraction in the UAW. "In auto," Browder said, "the caucus [sometimes] reverted back to the center for decisions, but most decisions were made in the field." According to Browder, the party did not issue directives to fractions. Instead, usually "all or close Party members," Browder said, "picked up the Party policy and Party line by reading the *Daily Worker.*" On only one major decision of importance did party leaders intervene in the auto fraction. This occurred at the UAW convention in 1939. (See Chapter 8.)[5]

It is important to note that during the Popular Front the Communist units and fractions changed in ways that lessened the separation between Communists and non-Communists. After the UAW and other CIO unions formed, the party became aware that the existence of party units and fractions created mistrust among some workers and made cooperation between Communists and non-Communists difficult at times. To help dispel this distrust the party stopped the publication of shop papers in 1938. Communist units in auto abandoned fourteen shop papers. The next year the party abolished fractions in the unions. (See Chapter 8.) In explaining this decision, Roy Hudson, the head of the party in Michigan, said: "The Party cannot and will not undertake to decide what its members shall do in their unions, but it will always reserve the right to decide who is worthy of membership in the Communist Party." Hudson added that even without fractions, the party expected loyalty to the union from party members. "Anyone who, for instance," Hudson said, "would violate the democratic decisions of his union, or who would associate with and make alliances with reactionary anti-union forces, would certainly find himself called to account." During World War II, the Communists went even further to dispel mistrust by abolishing the shop units for a time. (See Chapter 10.) In short, nothing about the party's structures, functions, and discipline kept Communists from acting as good unionists. By aiding the organization of auto workers in the mid-1930s and in other ways, the party discipline improved the Communists' ability as unionists.[6]

The idea that the Communists' political ends (support for the Soviet Union, class struggle, and socialism) kept them from being legitimate trade unionists is not clear. If it means that the Communists lacked legitimacy, because they held beliefs that other workers did not share, the idea is unreasonable. That would mean that Socialists, Republicans, members of the Association of Catholic Trade Unionists, and others also could not have been good trade unionists. If the idea means that the Communist political ends kept them from doing what good trade unionists do, the idea is wrong. In the auto industry no evidence whatever shows that Wyndham Mortimer, Bob Travis, John Anderson, Nat Ganley, and other Communists were less than effective organizers, negotiators, and grievance handlers. If the idea means that in carrying out the line of the Communist International and the Communist party, Communists acted against the best interests of the auto workers and the auto unions, the point is arguable. Before considering this point, it is necessary to explain the general political lines of the Communist party.

Between the early 1920s and the late 1940s the Communist party went through six periods. From about 1923 until 1928 was a period that the Comintern viewed as the "partial stabilization of capitalism." In this period the Communists through the Trade Union Educational League, headed by William Z. Foster, attempted to "bore from within" existing trade unions for the purpose of getting unions to support American recognition of the Soviet Union, amalgamate the craft unions into industrial unions, and organize the unorganized workers. From the Sixth Congress of the Comintern in 1928 until 1934 the Communist party followed a line known as the "Third Period." This line represented a left turn. It was based on the belief that the capitalist countries were entering a time of crisis and revolutionary upsurge. It called upon Communists to sharply condemn socialists and other reformists as "social fascists" and to form independent, revolutionary unions in some industries. From 1934 until 1939 the Communists followed the Popular Front, a line fully developed at the Seventh Congress of the Comintern in 1935. During this period the Communists saw the main line of struggle occurring between fascism and democracy (rather than between capitalism and socialism). The Communists favored an alliance between the Soviet Union and the United States against fascism (collective security). They abandoned the revolutionary unions of the previous period and entered the AFL and CIO. They worked for unity with socialists, New Deal Democrats, Progressive Republicans, leaders of the trade unions, and other anti-fascists.

From the signing of the German-Soviet nonaggression pact in 1939 until the German invasion of the Soviet Union in June 1941, the Communists followed a line characterized by the slogan, "Keep America Out of War." During this period the party criticized President Roosevelt and trade union leaders who advocated preparation for a war that the Communists viewed as a conflict between rival imperialist powers. From 1941 until the end of World War II, the party followed the line of "Everything for Victory." The party supported the government's wartime policies, the no-strike pledge, class cooperation, and other measures designed to increase production and insure the nation's victory over fascism. After the war, the party again turned left. It saw the country heading toward a period of intense class conflict and the threat of international war and domestic fascism. It opposed the Taft-Hartley Act, the Marshall Plan, and the Truman Doctrine, and in 1948 it supported the Progressive party and its presidential candidate Henry Wallace.[7]

In general the Communist line between 1922 and 1949 did not prevent the Communists from acting in the interests of workers in the auto industry. Rather, the lines helped the Communists to serve the interests of the workers and unions. Some exceptions, however, occurred. In the first period the Communists worked inside the only union of any importance in the auto industry, the United Automobile, Aircraft and Vehicle Workers of America. This union never became an important organization, but the Communists did change it into a union that at least supported industrial unionism, strikes, and racial cooperation. (See Chapter 2.) The party's switch to a line favoring independent unions in 1929 had little effect on the Communists in auto, since there an independent union already existed. The Third Period line encouraged the Communists in auto to do effective organizing among the unemployed (see Chapter 3) and among auto body workers. (See Chapter 4.) It also led the Communists to make apt criticisms of the failure of both the New Deal and the AFL to serve the interests of auto workers. (See Chapters 5 and 6.) At the same time the Third Period had some bad effects. The party's concern with social-fascism divided workers during strikes (see Chapter 4) and led the party to underestimate the favorable effects of the New Deal for the organization of workers. (See Chapter 5.) The Popular Front adopted by the Comintern in 1935 encouraged the Communist efforts to work within the AFL federal labor unions in auto and to forge a united front with non-Communists. (See Chapters 7 and 8.)

For many writers the major evidence that the Communist line clashed with workers' interests occurred in the pact period of 1939–41 and the war period of 1941–45. In the pact period, many have argued, the Communists led strikes in defense industries for the purpose of disrupting war production. Evidence in the auto industry, however, does not back this idea. (See Chapter 9.) During the war, many critics argue, the Communists' support of the no-strike pledge and incentive pay led them to sell out the workers' interests. A close examination of this period, however, reveals that this was a complex problem. During the war the immediate economic interests of the workers were in conflict with what the Communists and most non-Communist CIO leaders saw as the wartime interests of the country. Though the Communists were insensitive to some of the workers' immediate interests, it is false to think that the Communists were faithless to the policies of the UAW. (See Chapter 10.)[8]

During the turn to the left of the Communist line after the war, the Communists in the UAW came into sharp conflict with Walter Reuther. Much of the conflict involved contrived differences that resulted from the power struggle between the leftwing and rightwing groups in the union. Two very real differences, however, were at the root of the conflict. First, the Communists opposed and Reuther supported the development of America's anti-Soviet and counterrevolutionary foreign policy that was reflected in the Marshall Plan and the Truman Doctrine. Second, the Communists opposed and Reuther supported the denial of rights to Communists that was contained in the Taft-Hartley Act and UAW constitution. (See Chapter 11.) Partisans on both sides of these issues believed they were upholding the best interests of workers. Though Reuther triumphed, subsequent events provided some vindication for the Communist position on these issues. By the 1960s the UAW no longer supported American foreign policy uncritically. Victor Reuther, an active collaborator with the State

Department in Europe after World War II, later had second thoughts. He regretted his cooperation with the CIA and criticized the AFL-CIO for engaging in "trade union colonialism" in Latin America and for becoming "quite literally, a disbursement agent for the State Department." In 1959, Congress repealed the section of the Taft-Hartley Act that required union officers to sign non-Communist affidavits. Several writers, including some who had opposed the Communists in the UAW, later argued that the elimination of the Communists had contributed to a decline of democracy, militancy, and critical thinking in the union. In 1963 Paul Jacobs said:

> I submit that we made a great mistake when we kicked the Communists out of the CIO—and, as you know, I was one of those who fought most belligerently to throw them out. I think now that the way the UAW leadership behaved toward its minority was a mistake. We ran scared. That's really why we kicked out the opposition. And when we did it, we really threw the baby out with the bath, because we set up a pattern of conformity; we set up a pattern of refusing to break with traditional ways of thinking. . . . That is why, for example, you can't dignify what goes on at a UAW convention today by calling it "debate." Policy questions are not being debated at UAW conventions. What is being argued about is administrative jazz and union legislative problems. There are no arguments about foreign policy questions or even about domestic policy questions.[9]

The Communist party line guaranteed neither that the Communists would always further the interests of auto workers nor that they would always ignore them. In general, however, the party line aided more than it detracted from the Communists role in auto. Certainly, the evidence suggests no pattern to warrant the conclusion that the Communists were not legitimate trade unionists.

Of all the arguments for the idea that the Communists were not legitimate unionists, the idea that they used undemocratic means to gain and hold power is disposed of most easily. According to Kampelman, the Communists relied on unscrupulous "techniques of group organization and manipulation," including leadership fronts, disciplined caucuses, prepared resolutions, violence, and intimidation. A distinction must be made here between the first of these techniques and the last two. In truth, the Communists did use leadership fronts (alliances with non-Communist leaders), disciplined caucuses, and prepared resolutions. The mastery of such simple techniques helped them gain influence in the UAW. These techniques, however, were neither uniquely Communist nor undemocratic. They were common techniques that Communists and non-Communists used. James Prickett showed that many writers condemn Communist methods as insidious by simply describing commonplace political behavior in loaded language. "For example," Prickett said, "non-Communists win union elections, but Communists 'capture' a union. Non-Communists join unions; Communists 'infiltrate' or 'invade' them. A non-Communist states his or her position; a Communist 'peddles the straight party line.' Non-Communists influence or lead groups; Communists dominate them. A non-Communist political party passes resolutions or makes decisions, but a Communist party invariably issues 'directives.'" Moreover, the most undemocratic maneuvers in the UAW were the efforts to expel Communists and their allies from the union and to deny Communists the rights of other unionists. President Homer Martin's expulsions in 1937–38 and the anti-Communist amendment to the UAW Constitution in 1941 naturally stemmed from non-Communists and not from Communists. (See Chapter 9.)[10]

The use of violence and intimidation is altogether different than the use of caucuses and prepared resolutions. In the auto unions no instance of Communist violence and intimidation against their opponents has come to light. Several times, however, anti-Communists used violence and intimidation. Dramatic episodes of threats and violence against Communists and alleged Communists occurred in 1950, 1952, and 1954 (outside the period of this study). In 1950, after Roy Webb, a founder of Nash Local 75 in Milwaukee, had signed a public letter calling for the withdrawal of American troops from Korea, he was thrown down a flight of stairs. The fall broke Webb's back. About the same time groups of workers manhandled Communists and alleged Communists and expelled them from auto plants in Detroit and Flint. In 1952 the House Committee on Un-American Activities (HUAC) held hearings in Detroit at which witnesses including UAW staff members testified on Communist activity in the auto plants. Excerpts from *Labor Action* for March 7 and 11, 1952 conveyed the violence that resulted:

In one auto plant, the wife of a man named as a Stalinist was tormented and driven from the plant. The newspapermen were there with photographers, egging on the workers for "some action shots."

The aftermath of the first week of hearings by the House Committee on Un-American Activities was a violent flurry of un-American activities typical of a vigilante-democracy.

All week long, the hatred, prejudices, and passions inflamed by the sensational anti-Communist stories in Detroit's daily papers exploded into mob rule in many auto shops.

Seven persons named as Communists were fired, one was forced to quit, and ten were marched or ordered out of plants.

Among the plants where trouble took place were Midland Steel, Hudson, DeSoto, Metal Products, Dodge, Cadillac, Briggs, and Chrysler.

What was especially tragic about the Chrysler situation was the vicious anti-Negro sentiments, the obscene anti-Negro comments, that spread throughout the plants. An effigy of one Negro was hung up. In other plants, workers came in with ropes, just as in the deep South.

In another plant, where the local union president is Jewish, vulgar, anti-Semitic signs were posted or scrawled on bulletin boards. It was a week of hate and fear and violent anger.

In 1954 when the House Committee held another series of hearings in Michigan, more violence against Communists and alleged Communists occurred. In auto the Communists were the victims rather than the perpetrators of violence and intimidation.[11]

The most persuasive evidence that the Communists were legitimate trade unionists was their backgrounds and actions. The leading Communists in the automobile industry were workers and unionists of long standing. Wyndham Mortimer, the leading Communist in the UAW, was born in a Pennsylvania coal mining community. His earliest memory was "walking behind the parades of striking miners." He went to work in the mines at the age of 12 and joined the United Mine Workers at the age of 16. By 1936 Mortimer had been a worker for 40 years and an auto worker for 20 years. In the early 1930s he organized an independent union in the White Motor plant in Cleveland. The union soon became AFL federal labor union 18463. Bob Travis quit school at the age of 16 to work in a forge. By 1936 he had been an auto worker for a dozen years and had helped organize federal labor union 18384 in the Toledo Chevrolet plant. Nat Ganley quit school in New York after the eighth grade and became a painter and a member of the International Painters Union (AFL). After coming to Detroit in 1933, he worked as a punch press operator in the auto industry and as an organizer for the Trade Union Unity League before helping to organize UAW Local 155. John Anderson, a native of Glasgow, Scotland, became a skilled tool and die maker in the auto industry in the 1920s and helped to organize the Mechanics Educational Society of America in the Ternstedt plant in 1933 before working with Ganley to organize Local 155. Before Bud Simons became the rank and file leader of the GM sit-down strike, he had worked in the early 1920s as a farm laborer and harvest hand in Indiana, Kansas, and the Dakotas, a ranch hand in Texas and in the late 1920s and early 1930s as an auto worker at Studebaker in South Bend and Hayes Body in Grand Rapids. As a farm laborer he had joined the Industrial Workers of the World, and as an auto worker at Hayes he had joined the Auto Workers Union affiliated with the Trade Union Unity League (TUUL). Bill McKie was born in Carlisle on the border between Scotland and England. At the age of 12 he became an apprentice sheet metal worker. Before he became the first president of Ford federal labor union 19374 in 1935, he had been a member of the National Sheet-Metal and Braziers Union of England, Scotland, and Wales for over 30 years and a Ford worker for 8 years.[12]

In the 1920s and 1930s Communists in auto were the main voices on behalf of industrial unionism and class struggle. Their ideas—that auto workers needed a single union organized on an industry-wide basis (rather than many unions on a craft basis) and that the auto workers needed strikes (rather than government intervention or employer cooperation) to gain a union—proved apt and progressive. The ideas met the needs of auto workers and pointed to the path that the auto workers eventually took. Moreover, the Communists led the way in putting those ideas into practice. They built local unions. They led strikes. In the auto industry the Communists were not merely legitimate, they were experienced and often outstanding unionists.

For many writers, the idea that the Communists were not legitimate trade unionists had a correlate in the idea that the Communists achieved influence in the CIO only because of the unusual mood of the times, the CIO's "need for experienced personnel" and the "tolerance" and "emotionalism" of the labor movement in the 1930s. "The Communists' movement alone,"

David Saposs said, "would not have entrenched them so solidly within the CIO; the attitude of the organization's key leaders aided them, both directly and indirectly." In the national office of the CIO, where John L. Lewis hired Lee Pressman and Len De Caux, and in the Steel Workers Organizing Committee, where Philip Murray hired scores of Communist organizers, this idea was true. In the UAW, however, clearly the Communists achieved influence because they were there at the beginning and helped build the union from the ground floor up. Similarly, Sidney Fine was misleading, when he stated: "The Communists, by boring from within, were able to gain positions of power inside the UAW, and they were able to play an important part in the GM sit-down strike." The Communists gained influence not by "boring from within" the UAW but by building it. (See Chapters 5 and 6.)[13]

How important was the Communist influence in the labor movement? This question can be separated from the question of Communist legitimacy. David Saposs, who thought the Communists were not bona fide unionists, believed their influence was important. "From 1935 to 1950," Saposs said, "the covert branch of the Communist movement particularly was phenomenally successful in the trade unions." Other writers, particularly some writing since 1960, saw the Communists as legitimate trade unionists but have dismissed their importance. The different views reflect changing popular concerns. During the Cold War writers stressed the danger of Communists, whereas writers in the more recent period, when the Communist party was weak, have stressed the unimportance of Communists. I disagree with both.[14]

Several arguments have supported the unimportance of the Communists. The Communist party was small and had little political support among workers. During the Popular Front, the Communists simply acted like other good trade unionists. The important influence in the success of the CIO came less from Communists than non-Communists, particularly the CIO leaders and organizers, John L. Lewis, Sidney Hillman, John Brophy, Adolph Germer, and Powers Hapgood, and such state and federal officials as Michigan Governor Frank Murphy, President Roosevelt, and Senators Robert Wagner and Robert LaFollette. The unimportance of the Communists was first stressed by journalist, Edward Levinson in 1938. "Communist influence in the C.I.O.," Levinson said, "is a figment of imagination. [John L.]

Lewis's opposition to Communism is well known. The large C.I.O. unions—miners, steel workers, rubber and needle trade workers—have no trace of Communist influence in their ranks. In the auto union, the Communists are an active faction, but their party is . . . opportunistic and self-effacing." More recently, the historians Irving Bernstein and Sidney Fine have said similar things. In his study of labor in the 1930s, Bernstein described the Communists as competent unionists in agriculture and in the radio and electric industry and elsewhere, but he dismissed their importance generally. "The size and importance of this Communist penetration [into the labor movement] have been clouded by myth, exaggeration, and nonsense. . . . In the late thirties the issue was not very important. The Communists faithfully adhered to the Popular Front line and worked with non-Communists for trade-union objectives. . . . At bottom, the Communist Party never became a mass movement and failed almost totally to convert American workers."[15]

In a study of the GM sit-down strike, Sidney Fine said that the Communists played "an important part" in the strike and that they and their "fellow travelers" and sympathizers "were prominently involved." Fine, however, gave major credit for the strike outcome to others. The CIO made an "important" contribution, and Lewis's assistance toward the end was "crucial." Socialists played a "very substantial part" as did civil libertarians, clergymen, and students. "Finally, and enormously important in determining the outcome of the strike," Fine said, "was the assistance rendered the UAW during the sit-down by federal and state officials." Fine thought that Governor Murphy's action was "the single most important factor" in bringing the strike to a successful conclusion.[16]

The lack of a clear definition and measure of Communist influence clouds the question of its importance. If Communist influence means the ability of the Communists to persuade workers of their ultimate ends, the need for a socialist revolution, then Communist influence was as small in auto as the number of party members suggests. If Communist influence, however, means the ability to persuade workers and others to adopt attitudes or take actions on immediate political and union issues, then it was a force to be reckoned with. Two easily overlooked characteristics of the party contributed to its influence in this second sense. First, though the party was small, its influence reached far beyond its membership. Second, the Communists had certain qualities by virtue of their experience and organizational connections that enabled them to play a role in building the UAW that could not have been easily duplicated by others in the mid-1930s.

### Communist Party Membership, 1930–1949[17]

| 1930 | 7,500 | 1938 | 54,000–75,000 |
| 1931 | 9,300 | 1942 | 50,000 |
| 1932 | 14,500 | 1945 | 65,000 |
| 1933 | 18,500–19,200 | 1946 | 52,500 |
| 1934 | 23,500–23,800 | 1948 | 55,000–60,000 |
| 1935 | 26,200–35,400 | 1949 | 54,174 |
| 1937 | 40,000–43,000 | | |

### Number of Party Members in Steel, Metal, Mining, and Auto, 1928–1942[18]

| | 1928 | 1930 | 1935 | 1939 | 1942 | 1943 |
|---|---|---|---|---|---|---|
| Steel | — | 331* | 700 | 2,000+ | 852 | — |
| Metal | 851 | 331* | 1,250 | — | 1,648 | — |
| Mining | 1,200 | 314 | 1,073 | 1,300 | 289 | — |
| Auto | 407 | 750 | 550 | 1,100 | 629 | 1,200 |

*Combined membership in metal and steel.*

During the 1930s the Communist party never had over 75,000 members and never over 1,100 members who were auto workers. It is impossible to say how non-Communist workers in auto and elsewhere viewed the party, but probably no more than a third so much as viewed it as a party deserving the rights accorded to others. Opinion polls in the late 1930s showed that only 35 percent of the people thought that Communists had the right to publish literature and hold meetings, only 16 percent thought they had the right to hold public office, and only 15.4 percent of CIO members thought the government should not restrict the Communists in any way. In Middletown (Muncie, Indiana), where a half of the factory workers were in the automotive industry in 1935, Robert and Helen Lynd found no sharp differences between the business class and the working class in their attitudes toward communism. The Lynds found the following common attitudes:

That socialism, communism, and fascism are disreputable and un-American. That socialists and communists believe in dividing up existing wealth on a per capita basis. "This is unworkable because within a year a comparatively few able persons would have the money again." That radicalism makes for the destruction of the church and family, looseness of morals, and the stifling of individual initiative. That only foreigners and long-haired troublemakers are radicals.

In 1936 only 16 people in Middletown (less than 1 percent) voted for the CP. A radical labor veteran in Middletown said: "A few of us are socialists. Even if we wanted to, as very few do, we would not be communists, because the Communist party can't be on the state ticket, the trade unionists have no use for it, and you can't get over a lot of other things for labor if you brand yourself as too radical."[19]

Though Communist numbers were small and the ceiling of public tolerance for Communists was not very high, the Communists still had influence that well exceeded party membership. Part of this influence was due to the immense number of people who passed through the party. Morris Ernst and David Loth estimated that 700,000 people passed in and out of the party during the thrity years after 1932. James Prickett gave a "reasonable minimum estimate" of onetime party members as 500,000 and onetime members in basic industry (steel, metal, mining, railroad, and auto) as 100,000. A reasonable estimate of onetime party members in the auto industry would be 14,000–20,000. Part of the party's influence was also due to people who for various reasons never joined the party but sympathized and worked with it. Some party officials estimated that the number of party supporters was ten times larger than the number of members. Historian Bert Cochran has suggested that party membership figures would have to be multiplied by "three or more" to get an accurate picture of Communist influence.[20]

Robert Alperin and James Prickett explained why many who left the party continued to work with it and why many who worked with it never became members. Alperin found that the people who left the party "generally were not in disagreement with its program," and that most remained party supporters. Many reasons short of total rejection caused people to leave the party. Some left the party because membership in it meant a distraction from other political activity. Some were temperamentally unsuited to the demands of party life. Some feared repression or the loss of jobs. Some had personal conflicts with party members. In spite of the party's efforts to root out "white chauvinism," some blacks experienced racism on the part of white Communists. Some people disagreed with a particular part of the party line. Some were turned away by the "life of the units," the lack of encouragement, guidance, and discussion. Some failed to understand the necessity of a Communist party. During the mid-1930s, party members often were so busy with mass struggles that they failed to recruit. As the party expanded rapidly in the 1930s, the organization lost many potential members simply by failing to process application forms and by neglecting to assign new recruits to party units. Where such circumstances kept some people from joining the CP and kept others from continuing as members, they did not keep such people from continuing as party supporters. These supporters formed a Communist milieu that far exceeded the numerical strength of the party. "While the American Communist Party," Prickett said, "never attained the mass popularity of the French and Italian parties, it is highly inaccurate to view it as 'ignored by the working class.'"[21]

Not only the size but the quality of Communist influence made it important. During the Popular Front, the Communists' cooperation with non-Communists and support for John L. Lewis and President Roosevelt often obscured their differences from non-Communists. However fine, the differences were clear enough. In 1936–37 the Communists in the UAW had advantages that others lacked. The Communists had experience. They knew how to organize workers, to avoid company espionage, to put out a newspaper and a leaflet, to conduct a strike, and to wage a legal fight on radical terms. Through the party and such related organizations as the International Workers Defense, the International Workers Order, and the National Negro Congress, Communists had contacts with ethnic and native American workers who could be trusted, and they had supporters outside the plants who could be mobilized to aid strikers. During the organizing that preceded the GM sit-down strikes and in the strike itself these qualities enabled the Communists to play a crucial role, particularly when it came to making decisions as to how the union should respond to spontaneous strikes, government injunctions, spies, threats of violence, and back-to-work movements. Clearly these decisions did more to determine the outcome of the strike than Governor Murphy's refusal to cut off welfare payments to striking workers and his refusal to send troops to evict the strikers. Moreover, it was likely that Murphy's refusal to send troops was influenced by the knowledge that the union would resist a forced eviction and that a bloodbath in Flint would sully Murphy's reputation as a pro-labor New Dealer. Moreover, as important as the Socialists, liberals, the CIO organizers, and John L. Lewis were in the sit-down strike, the Communists exercised the key influence over the basic organizational and tactical questions that were so vital in de-termining the strike's outcome. (See Chapter 7.)

Bert Cochran recently added a new wrinkle to the argument over the importance of the Communists. Cochran diminished the importance of the Communist leaders of the General Motors sit-down strike of 1936–37 by stressing the importance of the spon-taneous actions of the workers. Cochran argued that the union was too chaotic in 1936 to allow for any "well-planned strategy." Cochran maintained that the union made no definite decision in advance to strike GM, had no organizing schedule, no strike dead-line, and no strategy for shutting down Flint Fisher Body No. 1 and Cleveland Fisher Body. In truth, there was a great deal of spontaniety and no exact deadline existed. Nevertheless, the spon-taneous outbreak of the strike did not negate the existence of a strategy, preparations, and a general deadline. "The whole pol-icy," John Brophy told Adolph Germer in December 1936, "is to move towards a climax in January in the event that General Motors refuses to confer and negotiate on a broad scale." Moreover, the evidence indicates that the Communists prepared for the strike, had a general deadline, and after the outbreak oc-curred, gave it form and direction. (See Chapter 7.)[22]

Because of the large circle of party supporters and the special quality of Communist contributions, Communist influence surely had importance in auto, more importance anyway than many writ-ers have allowed. Communist influence, however, was superficial and fragile. It lacked the solid foundation that a large and commit-ted party membership would have provided. It rested on less than fully committed supporters, on alliances with non-Communist union leaders, and on the Communist occupancy of union offices. It also depended upon the Communists' experience in trade union struggles, experience which non-Communists soon acquired. Of course, these limits underscored an impressive paradox of Communist history in auto, namely that a few did so much. These limits, however, also gave the Communists an Achilles heel. They helped to account for why the attacks on the Communist party after World War II so easily scattered supporters, broke alliances, and tumbled the fragile scaffold of Communist influence in the UAW and elsewhere. (See Chapter 11.)

Were the Communists good Communists? In the past few years historians associated with the New Left have raised this question and have answered that the Communists were not good Communists because they failed to fight for socialism. "The Communists," James Weinstein said, "became part of the mainstream of mass unionism but abandoned any struggle for an independent class politics. . . . Socialism did not emerge as an issue because the Communists never put forth a serious socialist position for which to argue as an alternative to the New Deal." Similarly, James Prickett argued: "The Communist Party . . . failed to provide a radical alternative to the New Deal. . . . Communists were superb liberals, but poor Communists." Relatedly, so the argument goes, the Communists failed to build a base for independent political action and for their own party. Their failure made the Communist party vulnerable to attack in the late 1940s. Their failure also meant that the Communist effort in building the CIO simply aided "liberal politicians and corporation leaders in adjusting the social system to the changed needs of the corporations." From an anarchist point of view, Jeremy Brecher argued similarly that Communists and other political leftists of the 1930s did "little to clarify the possible revolutionary significance of mass actions or to develop their more radical potentialities."[23]

The question of the worthiness of Communists as Communists transcends not only the history of Communists in auto but also the subject of history. Since the question involves a definition of a good Communist, it is political as well as historical. And since it involves what might have resulted had the Communists acted differently, the question is speculative as well as historical. Still, the question is an important one, and the history of the Communists in auto has some bearing on it.

The Communists never abandoned the struggle for socialism. Even during the Popular Front (1935–39) and World War II, when the party held that the immediate struggle was between fascism and democracy rather than between capitalism and socialism, it continued its agitation for socialism. In the party's view, the fight against fascism and war and for industrial unions and social legislation did not replace the goal of socialism but were the necessary preconditions of a fight for socialism. In a report to the Central Committee of the CP in 1936, Browder said that organizing people into struggles against the "most reactionary manifestations of capitalism," such as fascism and war, was "the quickest and most direct road to socialism." Before workers would have an interest in socialism, they had to become convinced of its necessity through their own experience in struggle. Before they had the capacity to win socialism they had to first have organization. "Everything that organizes and activizes the working class and its allies," Browder said, "is progress toward socialism; likewise, everything that weakens and discourages the forces of reaction goes in the same direction. This is the fundamental conception that underlies the revolutionists' understanding of the fight for the People's Front."[24]

Throughout the 1930s, the Communists conducted education about socialism. Their agitation on behalf of the Soviet Union, for example, taught what socialism could mean concretely. Discussions on the lack of unemployment in the Soviet Union, and on Soviet education, health care and industrial production conveyed a practical sense of what socialism could mean in the United States. The party also conducted general education about socialism. Max Gordon, a Communist organizer in upstate New York from 1936 to 1942, later said:

> Many activists in unions and other organizations often did experience tension between their activity and socialist advocacy. . . . But the party organizations operating through the many members not in that position did propagandize for socialism by way of regular sales of the party press, which carried socialist materials, party shop papers, pamphlets, leaflets, lectures, etc. Scores of pamphlets dealing with socialism, in some cases issued in hundreds of thousands of copies, were published during the late thirties. They included cheap mass editions of the Communist classics (*The Communist Manifesto* at five cents, for example), numerous penny pamphlets on the American Communist Party's fundamental aims; a series of nickel pamphlets describing what a socialist America would mean for workers in specific industries, for blacks, farmers, youth, women, professionals; pamphlets dealing with housing and health under socialism, etc. In addition, every party program and election platform, as well as every

political report, linked the question with the party's contemporary activities. As of 1936, some sixty-five party bookshops in forty-four cities sold Marxist literature, with emphasis on socialist materials. There were nearly a dozen Marxist educational institutions in operation; they were not confined to party members.[25]

Naturally, it is difficult to say how much of the party's education about socialism reached the auto workers. UAW Local 248 in Milwaukee, however, provided an example of what Communist supporters did to bring a broad education to workers. The leadership of Local 248 was sympathetic to the CP and believed the workers needed an "education toward socialism." (See Chapter 11.) In many ways Harold Christoffel and the other leaders of the local encouraged the workers to acquire such an education. They had the Communist People's Book Store set up literature tables at the union's educational classes. They promoted the *Daily Worker* and the *Midwest Daily Record*. They supported the Communist Book Find Club. They publicized the courses of the party's Abraham Lincoln School in Chicago. And they invited Communist and other leftwing speakers to address meetings and educational classes of the local.[26]

Most socialist education took place outside the shops. Particularly during strikes, like the GM sit-down, the Communists avoided open propagandizing (except for selling the *Daily Worker*) for fear of dividing the workers and providing ammunition to the employers and journalists, who were anxious to exploit any signs of Communist revolution. (See Chapter 7.) Yet, this caution did not prevent individual Communists from discussing socialism with their fellow workers. In a response to Jeremy Brecher, historian David Montgomery said:

> Brecher's contention that Leftists of the '30s were so enamored of the CIO and the New Deal that they waged no struggle for socialist consciousness among their shopmates is a popular notion in the student Left today, but it rests on no evidence whatever. Many an older worker could tell him quite another story. What does he think the men talked about for 41 cold days and nights in Fisher Body Number 2? Neither he nor I has discovered the answer to that question, but my own experience in a sit-down strike 17 years later suggests that they had far more in mind than simply the militant and dramatic tactics on which our historical accounts have riveted their attention.[27]

To point out that the Communists conducted agitation and propaganda on behalf of socialism does not, of course, mean that they could not have done more than they did. They undoubtedly could have done more to advocate socialism, to build the party, to press for independent political action, to act independently of Lewis, Hillman, and Murray, and to criticize President Roosevelt. One indication that the Communists could have done more was the way in which many Communists later scored the party's caution. Weinstone, Michigan party leader during the sit-downs, said, "We were at fault in not making our Party known, because we failed to come forward as Communists. . . . That was a bad mistake." Weinstone and other Communists later regretted the party's tailing CIO leaders at the 1939 UAW convention. (See Chapter 7.) They also regretted several of the party's policies during World War II. (See Chapter 10.) Still, it is important to see the party's actions in historical context. From 1920 to the present the Communist parties of all Western countries, including the United States, faced a common dilemma. They have been revolutionary parties in non-revolutionary situations. Consequently, they had two choices: they could continue to act as revolutionaries and face almost certain isolation, or they could plunge into reformist activity and risk the necessary compromises. All things considered, the Popular Front represented the best solution to this dilemma that the American Communist party or any other party ever found. The party made an important contribution to the mass struggles of the 1930s, it gained the closest thing to a mass base it ever had, and it greatly widened the audience for its socialist message.[28]

It would be a mistake to assume that the Communists could have spoken more forcefully for socialism or acted much more openly as Communists than they did without having endangered their position in the UAW and CIO. The Communist position was insecure. Len De Caux, who worked in the national office of the CIO, said: "Everyone in labor or progressive politics played footsy with the communists at some time or in some way. A rule of the game was that the communist player should not proclaim his communism." As if to illustrate what happened when that rule was violated, CIO lawyer, Lee Pressman, said: "An organizer on the staff once came to Lewis and told him that he was a Communist and Lewis fired him. He [Lewis] was not going to be sucked into acknowledging their presence and giving them endorsement. As long as they followed CIO policy and stuck to trade unionism Lewis would leave them alone." In the UAW from 1935 to 1949, the Communists faced a steady stream of attempts to prevent their membership in the union, to expel them from positions, and to bar them from offices. Under these circumstances, the Communists were as good as they could have been.[29]

Summing up the discussion to this point: Three generalizations have a key place in the scholarship on the Communist party and labor. The Communists were not legitimate trade unionists. They were not an important influence in the labor movement. And they were not good Communists. My work does not disprove these generalizations. In the study of Communists in auto, however, I find no evidence for them. The history of Communists in auto points to a different view: the Communists were legitimate and often outstanding trade unionists and good Communists, and they made an important, even crucial, contribution to building the auto union in the 1930s.

Three methodological problems require attention: the identification of Communists and the reliability of Communist sources and oral history. Any study of American Communists confronts the problem of how to identify members of the Communist party and how to distinguish actual members of the party from close supporters and casual allies. The reason for this problem is the habit of Communist secrecy. The American Communist party has never enjoyed full acceptance and citizenship. Membership in the party has always entailed certain real or potential risks—the loss of friends, income, influence, or worse. Outside of party functionaries who had the security of paid positions, only a few Communists openly identified themselves. The party's records that contain information on membership are unavailable to researchers. Many of those who were active in or around the party in the 1930s are now dead. Others have refused to discuss either their own relationship to the party or that of their friends. Many Communist writers have also avoided such details. They have instead lumped Communists with other left-wingers or progressives. In the official history of the CP, William Z. Foster referred to Wyndham Mortimer and Bob Travis as "left wingers." In a popular history of the GM sit-down strike, Henry Kraus barely mentioned the Communist party. In an autobiography written thirty years after leaving the UAW, Mortimer identified only one auto worker as a Communist and said nothing about his own relationship to the party. Paid informants of Congressional committees and anti-Communist writers have left a voluminous record of alleged

Communists and their activities, but this record is often unreliable. To paraphrase Malcolm X, those who say don't know, and those who know don't say.[30]

Because of these difficulties, I have used the word Communist carefully. I have identified individuals who were open Communists. I have identified others as Communists when open Communists or others who were not antagonistic to the party so identified them. When doubt existed about a person's membership, even a person closely identified with the party, this has been indicated. As noted before, the Communist party was surrounded by a circle of close supporters, who numbered many times the number of party members. The party and its circle of supporters represented a coherent milieu. I use such phrases as "the Communists and their close supporters," to refer to this Communist milieu.

In terms of determining the party's influence and an individual's political attitudes and behavior, membership in the party milieu was probably as important as membership in the party. The Communist milieu was a coherent group of people who considered themselves communists, who trusted each other, and who shared a common vocabulary, a common subculture, and many common aims. Members of the milieu used the party language— progressives, Left and Center forces, white chauvinism, Trotskyite, social fascist, opportunism, sectarianism. They belonged to the party-related mass organizations such as the National Negro Congress, International Workers Order, International Labor Defense, American League Against War and Fascism, American Writers and Artists Congress, and American Student Union. They read the party-related press that included the *Daily Worker, Michigan Worker, Midwest Daily Record, New Masses, Fraternal Outlook*. Ethnic members read *Glos Ludowy* (Polish), *Uj Elore* (Hungarian), *Morning Freiheit* (Yiddish), or others of the thirty-one daily foreign language papers. Working class members of the party milieu were often distinguished from their fellow nonpolitical workers by a wider acquaintance with culture, both middle class and proletarian. They often read the novels, poems, and essays of Michael Gold, Howard Fast, Richard Wright, Langston Hughes, or Mike Quin. They saw the plays of Clifford Odets and such Russian films as "Potemkin," "Alexander Nevsky," and "The Road to Life." They listened to the music of the Almanac Singers,

Earl Robinson, Woody Guthrie, and Paul Robeson. The more serious among them attended party lectures and classes and read the pamphlets put out by the Workers Library and such books as George Seldes, *Facts and Fascism,* and A. B. Magill and Henry Stevens, *The Perils of Fascism.* All of this and more gave the Communist milieu a coherent and distinctive character and distinguished its members from Socialists, Trotskyists, New Deal Democrats, and other trade unionists.[31]

In this study I have relied on many Communist sources. These include the *Daily Worker, Michigan Worker, Communist, Political Affairs, Party Organizer,* shop papers, press releases, pamphlets, books, leaflets, reports, and minutes. They also include William Z. Foster's history of the CP, Henry Kraus's history of the GM sit-down strike, the memoirs of Wyndham Mortimer, John Williamson, Al Richmond, and Len De Caux, and a biography of Bill McKie by Phillip Bonosky. The historian David Shannon has suggested that Communist sources pose a special problem of reliability, and "one must exercise more than usual scholarly caution about veracity." Shannon provided no reasons for this caution, and one can only assume that he believed that Communists exhibited a "more than usual" tendency to lie. This is unconvincing. Communist sources are much like any official sources, whether of unions, governments, businesses, or non-Communist parties. Official sources sometimes exaggerate their groups' strength, influence, and accomplishments, ignore or justify mistakes, failures, and embarrassments, and impute cynical and outlandish motives to opponents. Scholars using official sources must discount the self-serving, probe the meaning of omissions, and use external verification, internal consistency, and common sense to seek out the truth. Communist sources are no different. They require typical not "unusual" scholarly caution.[32]

In one way, however, Communists sources do pose a special problem. With rare exceptions, only the published record exists. Most minutes of Communist meetings, unpublished reports, and correspondence are unavailable to the researcher. Consequently, much about the internal debates of the party remains unknown. It is impossible to reconstruct the differences in opinion within the party and the nuances of change in the party line. It is also impossible to know the details about the relations between the leaders of the party and the party members in the auto unions. Yet, the published record contains a rich storehouse of information. Since the *Daily Worker* and other publications provided the party's main channel of communication, the most essential information about the party is there.

In this study I have used oral history interviews. These include interviews done by Jack Skeels for the Archives of Labor and Urban Affairs at Wayne State University, the interviews by Neil Leighton and the staff of the "Insurgent Rank and File: the GM Sit-down Strike of 1936–37" at the University of Michigan—Flint, the interviews at Columbia University, an interview of Henry and Dorothy Kraus done by Elsa Rassbach, and interviews I have done myself. Peter Friedlander, whose book on the emergence of a UAW local relied heavily on oral history interviews, pointed out that "if certain problems are to be explored at all, they must be investigated through the use of oral history techniques." Oral history is a particularly helpful tool for understanding the history of Communists. As rank and file workers in general, Communist workers have seldom written autobiographies or had biographies written about them. As the big losers in the political contests of the 1940s and 1950s, Communist workers have often had their history ignored or distorted by the victors and other partisans. Oral history can help fill these gaps and correct these distortions. Yet, oral history has its limits. "Memory," Friedlander said, "is a treacherous thing." To insure the reliability of an interviewee's memory, I have relied whenever possible on verification by the written record and the memories of others. I have also looked for internal consistency in the interviews. Where such verification is impossible, I have treated information provided by interviews much like that provided by memoirs and autobiographies. Where an interview provided a new piece of information, and one uncontradicted by reliable sources, I have often used it, letting it stand as our best available knowledge, until other scholars find reason to either supplement or replace it.[33]

# II
# ...
# THE AUTO WORKERS UNION

The automobile and the automobile industry symbolized the prosperity of the 1920s. The automobile became the most coveted consumer item in a market flooded with new gadgets. For George F. Babbitt, the hero of Sinclair Lewis's 1922 novel, "his motor car was poetry and tragedy, love and heroism." For most of the business class in Middletown, Robert and Helen Lynd discovered "ownership of an automobile has now [1925] reached the point of being an accepted essential of normal living." By 1929, when the industry produced 4,800,000 automobiles, one person in five owned a car. The automobile industry shared the prestige of its product. For many capitalists, the industry—and particularly Henry Ford's policies of high output, low prices, and high wages—symbolized the vitality of what *Fortune* called the "new capitalism." Fordism became capitalism's answer to Marxism. For many workers, too, the industry symbolized the promise of a good life. Hoping to capitalize on the Doctrine of High Wages that Henry Ford had advocated in his book, *Today and Tomorrow* (1926), and the five-day workweek that Ford had initiated in 1926, droves of young men, like Walter Reuther, left their rural homes for Detroit.[1]

Besides the shimmering Ford flivvers and the Pierce Arrows, besides the glittering promises of Fordism and the new capitalism, the auto industry harbored another, harsher reality in the 1920s. This was the reality inside the shops, a reality of speedup, industrial accidents, long hours, monotonous work, tyrannical work rules, capricious foremen, wage cuts, seasonal unemployment, and the open shop. Such conditions spawned attempts by auto workers to unionize. Leading these attempts in the late 1920s, the Communist party and the Communist-led Auto Workers Union waged an almost single-handed effort to bring an industrial union to the auto industry. Though unsuccessful, the Communist effort highlighted the plight of auto workers and the obstacles to organization, and it also laid the basis for the successful union struggle of the 1930s, in which the Communist party would play a major role.

The Communist movement in America began in 1919 almost completely isolated from the nation's 343,000 automobile workers. From the beginning of the movement, nearly insurmountable objects blocked Communist influence among auto workers. For the first several years sectarian revolutionary policies, factional divisions, and government persecution saddled Communist activity. The overwhelmingly foreign-born composition of the Communist movement restricted its access to the auto workers, two-thirds of whom were native-born. The employers, churches, and newspapers constructed a barrier of anti-Communist propaganda between the Communists and the average worker. In spite of these obstacles, the Communists managed to recruit a small nucleus of auto workers in the 1920s. Most remarkably, while this nucleus never exceeded 500 workers, it developed a considerable influence. By 1929 the Communists had established party units in a dozen or so auto shops and issued a dozen shop papers. They also established important links with foreign-born auto workers through fraternal and cultural organizations. They led the only industrial union of auto workers and participated in the most important auto strikes of the 1920s. In these ways, not only did the Communists achieve a base for themselves and establish the groundwork for their widespread influence in the 1930s, but also, as a United Automobile Workers' veteran later noted, they "helped pave the way for industrial unionism" in the auto industry.[2]

For the first several years, the Communists' liabilities loomed much larger than their assets. The left-wing Socialists who bolted from the Socialist party (SP) to form the Communist movement in 1919 were themselves divided into two warring factions, the Communist Labor party (CLP) and the Communist party (CP). Over 90 percent of the combined membership of both parties consisted of foreign-born people. The intense ideological struggle that the early Communists waged with the reformist leaders of the SP, their exuberant indentification with the Russian Revolution, and their belief in the revolutionary potential of the postwar strike wave produced an extreme, revolutionary rhetoric among early Communists that further retarded their appeal. Members of both Communist parties belittled "reform palliatives" and insisted on "only one demand: the establishment of the Dictatorship of the Proletariat." According to Charles Ruthenberg, an early leader of the Communist party, only a half-dozen original Communists "knew anything about the trade union movement." On top of these liabilities, the Communists faced government repression. The persecution culminated in January 1920 in a series of raids directed by Attorney General A. Mitchell Palmer against Communists and other radicals. The raids led to the arrest of thousands of Communists. As a result, for two years the Communists retreated into an "underground" existence of limited public activity, and their membership declined from 40,000 to 10,000.[3]

In spite of everything, the Communists showed a certain vitality. In May 1920, a group from the CP led by Charles Ruthenberg joined with the CLP to form the Communist Party of America (CPA). In June 1921, the CPA formed an open, legal arm—the American Labor Alliance, and in December the Alliance joined with the Workers' Council, which was composed of socialists who had recently left the SP, to form the Workers party. Soon another large group of former Socialists including the large and active Finnish and Jewish federations joined the Workers party. The Communists eventually abolished the underground organization, and in 1925 they changed the name of the Workers party to the Workers' (Communist) party. In the early 1920s the Workers party attracted to its ranks some of the most active members of other left-wing groups. These included: Alexander Trachtenberg, J. Louis Engdahl, and Moissaye J. Olgin, former Socialists who were part of the Workers' Council; William D. Haywood, the exiled leader of the IWW; Boris Reinstein and Caleb Harrison of the Socialist Labor party; Otto E. Huiswoud, Richard B. Moore, and Cyril Briggs of the black socialist journal, *Messenger*; and William Z. Foster, the leader of the 1919 steel strike and head of the Trade Union Educational League.

The Workers' party represented what Communists called a

"party of a new type," a party of committed revolutionaries, devoted to the principles of Marxism-Leninism, pledged to lead the working class in its immediate economic and political struggles, and committed to a long-term struggle for socialism. The Workers' party differed from both the Socialist party and the Industrial Workers of the World (IWW). Whereas in general the Socialist party confined its activity to electoral campaigns and political education, eschewed alliances with non-Socialist groups, and avoided sharp criticism of Samuel Gompers and the American Federation of Labor (AFL), the Communists engaged not only in electoral and agitational activity but also in the day-to-day economic struggles of workers. They also tried to cooperate with non-Communist groups and openly criticized the narrow craft unionism of Gompers and the AFL. Whereas the IWW had confined its activity to organizing an independent revolutionary union outside the AFL, the Communists disavowed "dual unionism" and tried to transform existing unions. The Communists operated within the Trade Union Educational League (TUEL), which, under the leadership of William Z. Foster, tried to organize workers around the demands of amalgamating existing craft unions into industrial unions, building a labor party, supporting the Soviet Union, and organizing unorganized workers.[4]

The particular vagaries of Communist factionalism left the Communists especially isolated from auto workers. Nearly half of the country's 343,000 auto workers lived in Michigan, which contained twelve of the seventeen largest automobile companies, including the three giants, Ford, General Motors, and Chrysler. Michigan accounted for 75 percent of all automobiles built in the United States. Before World War I, the Socialist party had a thriving branch of 6,000 members in the state. It published eleven newspapers in such industrial centers as Detroit, Flint, Grand Rapids, Kalamazoo, and Saginaw and elected mayors and other municipal officers in eight cities including Flint and Kalamazoo. In 1919 Michigan Socialists constituted one of the so-called left-wing branches that deserted the SP to form the Communist party. The Michigan Socialists, however, were misfits. Led by Dennis E. Batt, a machinist, and John Keracher, a shoe store owner, they had developed a unique political sect that rejected any compromise with capitalism, dismissed the importance of all struggles for "immediate demands," and insisted that educating the workers to

Marxism provided the only path to socialism. This "educational brand of Communism" had no appeal at all to the orthodox members of the CP, who expelled the "Michigan Mensheviks" in less than a month. With a few allies in Buffalo and Rochester, the Michigan group then formed the Proletarian party, which established a "Proletarian University" in Detroit and maintained an independent, localized existence until the 1940s. Consequently, the Communists inherited little of whatever influence the Michigan Socialists had among auto workers.[5]

In 1919 a single union of significance existed in the auto industry, the independent United Automobile, Aircraft and Vehicle Workers of America, also known as the Auto Workers Union (AWU). It had begun as an industrial union affiliated with the Knights of Labor. In 1891 the union entered the AFL as the International Union of Carriage and Wagon Workers. As the number of automobile workers expanded from 12,000 in 1904 to 76,000 in 1909, many carriage and wagon workers transferred their skills to the auto industry. Reflecting the occupational shift, the union in 1912 broadened its jurisdiction and changed its name to the Union of Carriage, Wagon and Automobile Workers. By 1916 the union's industrial structure embraced some 13,000 members, mostly skilled tradesmen—trimmers, painters, woodworkers, upholsterers, and sheet metal workers. The union's interest in the auto industry angered various AFL craft unions, such as the International Association of Machinists, which also claimed jurisdiction over certain automobile workers. In deference to the interests of the craft unions, the AFL conventions of 1915 and 1916 ordered the AWU to drop "Automobile" from its title. When the AWU refused, the AFL suspended it. Thus, in April 1918 the AWU became an independent union claiming 23,000 members.[6]

William Logan, head of the union, and Ben Blumenberg, John Martin, Charles Dickenson, Hal Richards, and Arthur Rohan, five of the union's seven organizers, belonged to the SP. Though the union made "no claim as a revolutionary organization," the leadership openly proclaimed its Socialist sympathies. In the union's paper Logan argued that the public should "own in common all things it uses in common." The union's paper, the *Auto Worker*, carried articles from such Socialist journals as the *New York Call* and the *Milwaukee Leader* and from the pens of Eugene Debs, Scott Nearing, James Oneal, Max Hayes, and Oscar Ameringer.

The paper frequently ran articles sympathetic to the Soviet Union. The union ardently defended industrial unionism. "As long as there are industries that are owned and operated for the benefit of individuals and for profit," Logan declared, "just that long there will be a growing demand for the industrial union." While it ridiculed the organizational failures of the IWW, the union's leaders acknowledged that "certain of its plans and principles have always appealed to us." In May 1920 the Auto Workers Union sent a delegate to the Socialist convention, and the next issue of the *Auto Worker* ran a front-page picture of the Socialist presidential candidate, Eugene V. Debs, under the headline: "Socialists Nominate Old Friend of Auto Workers."[7]

Logan and the other AWU leaders had no sympathies with the SP's left-wing or early Communists. In the spring and summer of 1919 the *Auto Worker* carried many articles by right-wing but none by left-wing Socialists. The union leaders regarded left-wingers as those who "shouted the loudest and talked the reddest." In 1919 a union spokesman noted that some left-wingers worked in the automobile industry and derisively added that "one of them once made an application for [union] membership." After the foundation of the CP and CLP, Logan advised auto workers to keep their eyes on the immediate practical tasks before the union, "instead of waving the bloody shirt of revolution." At the same time the *Auto Worker* published a right-wing Socialist satire of the Communists entitled, "M'ass' Action of the R-R-R-Revolutionary Prowling Terriers." Purporting to give instructions to would-be Communists, the article advised:

> *Don't* change your underwear. Fresh underwear will make you comfortable and therefore inclined to tolerate the present damnable system and dampen your revolutionary fervor.
> *Don't* take a bath. This is but a petty reform.
> *Don't* wear a necktie. It will attract too much attention and thus distract the revolutionary proletariat away from their revolutionary goal of the dictatorship of the revolutionary proletariat.[8]

At the time of the emergence of the Communist movement in 1919, the Auto Workers Union was enjoying the most heady advance in its thirty-year history. Sharing in the general postwar upsurge in union activity, the union struck plants in Detroit, Flint, Milwaukee, Grand Rapids, and New York City. In 1919 the AWU grew to over 45,000 members with thirty-five locals in Detroit, Toledo, Cincinnati, Flint, Pontiac, Buffalo, Chicago, and New York City. The union's "strongest and largest" local was Detroit Local 127. It had units in fifteen automobile companies in the Detroit area and scattered members in half a dozen other shops. Before the 1920 recession, Local 127 had a weekly paper with a circulation of 50,000 and a membership of between 30,000 and 35,000; it was growing at the rate of 1,000 members a month.[9]

In 1920 the tide turned against the union. The Justice Department round-up of radicals ordered by Attorney General A. Mitchell Palmer and a new open shop campaign linked strikes and unions—particularly industrial unions like the AWU—with foreigners and radicals and created a crippling public atmosphere for union activity. In Detroit the Palmer raids netted 827 persons "who believed in communist or anarchistic doctrines," and the Immigration Department subsequently deported 234 of them. An open shop drive in the early 20s spawned twenty-three employer open shop associations in Michigan. The Employers' Association of Detroit adopted the motto, "Detroit is Detroit because of the Open Shop." Employers and unionists alike soon regarded Detroit as the paradigm open shop city. Henry R. Leland of the Cadillac Motor Car Company told a meeting of the American Plan Open Shop Conference in Detroit that the city's many millionaires had the open shop to thank for their success. No unionist would have disputed his claim.[10]

The economic recession and open shop campaign had disastrous effects on the union. In January 1921, a headline in the *Auto Worker* announced, "Michigan Workers Walloped by Depression and Reaction." The paper reported that 300,000 men were out of work in eleven industrial centers of Michigan, and 65 percent of the work force in Detroit was unemployed. Unemployment drove people from the industry and the union back to the farms and small towns of Michigan and the states to the south, diverted much of the union's energy and resources to welfare activity, and increased the apathy and vulnerability of those union members who remained employed. In its weakened condition the union lost support. It could not protect its members from the wage cuts and the worsening conditions produced by the economic downturn. This became painfully evident when the union struck the Fisher Body Company in February 1921. The strike dragged on until

April and ended in a complete rout for the union. The AWU secretary later recalled that "losing that strike" had the effects of "an awful tornado." He said, "The union never did recover after that strike." By 1922 "Depression and Reaction" had reduced the union to only 200 or 300 members in its former stronghold of Detroit and to only 800 members nationally.[11]

Meanwhile, the Socialist leaders of the AWU remained hostile to the Communists. The *Auto Worker,* for instance, announced the formation of the Workers' party with an editorial entitled "Saved Again." With heavy-handed sarcasm the paper reported that the Workers' party convention included "the brains of the coming revolution," and the convention's resolutions "announced the downfall of capitalism, the bankruptcy of business and the end of the interests." The auto union's paper reported that the convention disposed "of a few minor matters such as the dangers of Capitalist Imperialism, Militarism, the Disarmament Conference" and then "devoted several moments to the formation of a real revolutionary party for the revolutionary revolutionists." The convention offered to American labor "a class conscious fighting organization with a set of 'fighting leaders'" who were "guaranteed to be staggering around with a load of brains heavy enough to cause flat feet." The paper closed with this advice: "Remember these leaders are the type who will take a foot if given an inch. Better give them the foot first." As late as May 1922, the *Auto Worker* referred to the Communist party as a "self-constituted and lippy" organization of "fatheaded fanatics" who needed "an adult dose of croton oil to take the pressure off their brains." That, however, was the last time the AWU leadership openly criticized the Communists until 1924.[12]

Sometime in 1922 the Workers' party assigned Edgar Owens, an alternate on the Central Executive Committee of the party, to head the party organization in Detroit. From this date the Communists began to build their own party organization in the auto industry and to gain influence in the Auto Workers Union. Though crippled by arthritis, Owens was an effective public speaker and an able organizer. He hardly resembled the AWU image of the "fatheaded fanatic." At the age of 43, Owens had already served as an organizer for the Socialist party of Illinois and district organizer for the Communist Labor party. Owens had been a victim of the Palmer raids of January 1920 and as the result of a raid by government agents of a Communist meeting in Bridgman, Michigan, in 1922, Owens had served a brief term in prison. Soon after his arrival in Detroit, Owens met with William Logan, head of the Auto Workers Union. Owens explained that the Workers' party trade union program favored industrial unions, organization of the unorganized, support for the Soviet Union, and formation of a labor party. Owens also made Logan a proposition. If Logan would permit Owens to work for the AWU, Owens promised to bring twenty–five or thirty Communists into the union as organizers. Since, as a Communist auto worker later recalled, the union was merely "a shell of the old organization," Logan readily agreed to Owens's suggestion. This meeting marked the real beginning of Communist activity in the automotive industry.[13]

After meeting Owens, Logan expressed a guarded sympathy for the Communists. The *Auto Worker,* which Logan edited, began carrying favorable articles on the Soviet Union and the Trade Union Educational League. In January 1923 Logan devoted three editorials to the Workers' party. The first criticized the Conference for Progressive Political Action for excluding the Communists at a recent meeting in Cleveland: "The Workers' party was flattened out by the steamroller in a way that made it obvious that the Conference had little stomach for a free and frank discussion of whether or not a frankly revolutionary body should be allowed an opportunity to present their views." The second editorial defended the party against newspaper attacks on its affiliation with the Communist International. It called the articles "another batch of propaganda" aimed at discrediting those who advocated the recognition of the Russian government. Since capitalism was international, why should workers not "have a headquarters with an international program." Logan avoided favoring the Workers' party over the Socialist party, but he made clear in the third editorial that he regarded the two parties as "the two most prominent movements that stand for fundamental, revolutionary changes in society." Since tactical differences and mutual antagonisms arising from their past histories foreclosed any unification of the two parties, Logan proposed that auto workers adopt an impartial wait-and-see attitude. "A great deal that is now theoretical," he concluded, "will have to prove its worth as time goes by."[14]

By entering the AWU Owens began to implement the Communist trade union policy of working within the established unions and building a "united front" with "progressive" trade unionists. Owens' most difficult problem was getting other Communists to join the Auto Workers Union. In the early 1920s wage workers constituted the overwhelming majority of party members, but only 5 percent of the membership belonged to trade unions. Many Communists were unskilled, industrial workers, for whom no union existed. Moreover, the majority of Communists were foreign-born; uncomfortable with the English language, many confined their political activity to their foreign-language federations. A Communist who moved to Detroit in the early 20s later recalled that getting the foreign-language members to abandon their preoccupation with the politics of "the old country" and to attend to the American political and trade union struggles posed a major problem for the Workers' party in Detroit.[15]

On March 9, 1924, Edgar Owens devoted a meeting of the Detroit Workers' party to this problem. He told the gathering that the party's Industrial Commission expected all Communist auto workers to join Local 127 of the Auto Workers Union, and he had William Logan explain the aims and program of the union. Arthur Rohan, who later replaced Logan as head of the AWU, recalled that after this meeting "some very hard workers who were Communists" joined the union.[16]

Between 1924 and 1930, Detroit's Communists acquired a significant influence in the auto industry, an influence all the more astounding for their small numbers. They established small organizations of Communists in nearly a score of auto plants. They also assumed control of the Auto Workers Union, a rather easy accomplishment, since the union had become nearly moribund under Socialist control. They issued a dozen shop papers and the union newspaper, through which they regularly reached thousands of auto workers. They recruited auto workers to the AWU and participated in the most important auto strikes of the decade. Communist recruitment and agitation in the industry helped to prompt the AFL to launch its only organizing campaign of the 1920s, though the effort proved utterly feeble and inconsequential. Five aspects of the party's work accounted for its ability to wield an influence beyond its small numbers. The first was the organization of the party itself. After 1925 the Communists, unlike the Socialists, based their organization primarily on the organization of Communists at the workplace. The second was the social basis of the party. Though the largely ethnic composition of the Workers party kept it from having easy access to native-born auto workers, the ethnic fraternal and cultural organizations in which Communists were active provided the party with an access to ethnic auto workers. The third was the commitment to immediate economic struggles. Communists participated in the strikes of workers, even when those strikes occurred without previous organization and with little chance of success. The fourth was the party's united front policy. Though often applied unsuccessfully, the united front policy committed the Communists to cooperate with nonparty workers in immediate struggles. The fifth was the ability to marshal outside resources. In its organizational and agitational efforts the Communists consistently drew upon the valuable assistance of such nonworkers as journalists, lawyers, and the unemployed. All these factors contributed to the party's influence.

In September 1925 the Communists reorganized their party and changed its name to the Workers' (Communist) party. The party replaced the quasi-independent language federations inherited from the SP with "language fractions," or caucuses of party members located in the same city who spoke the same language. The basic party structure became the shop nuclei or shop units of three or more members working at the same place of employment, and street nuclei of members unattached to the shop cells. To complete the reorganization in Detroit, the party sent in a new District Organizer, Albert Weisbord, in 1927. Weisbord's father was a Russian-Jewish immigrant who manufactured accessories for men's coats. Weisbord had gone to Harvard Law School and served as national secretary of the Young People's Socialist League. After graduating from Harvard in 1924, Weisbord had joined the Workers party and worked for a year in a textile mill, and the year before coming to Detroit he had led a strike of textile workers in Passaic, New Jersey. During Weisbord's year and a half in Detroit, the Workers' (Communist) party grew to 600 members, including 350 members in 12 shop units. With units in the Chrysler, Murray Body, Briggs, Buick, Packard, and Durant Hayes-Hunt plants, the Detroit party possessed more members organized into factory cells than Pittsburgh, Cleveland, Chicago, and Kansas, the other major industrial districts of the party. In 1928, when less than 10 percent of the 10,000 party members belonged to shop nuclei, nearly half (300 of 700) the Detroit Communists belonged to factory cells. Outside of the Detroit District, a shop nucleus of eight members operated in the Cleveland Fisher Body plant, and another of three members functioned in the Cleveland White Motor Company.[17]

The Communist shop nuclei tried to act politically in the shops by spreading the party program, building groups of sympathizers, and encouraging industrial unionism. Typically, the nuclei would meet twice a month to discuss these tasks and to conduct "educationals" on such questions as "The Backwardness of the American Working Class" and "Work Among Women." Overwhelming obstacles, however, stood in the way of effective political work. Any attempt to reach the workers in a plant pitted the nuclei against what one Communist called the "fierce espionage system" of the company. Beyond that the nuclei had to face the demoralization occasioned by their limited numbers and isolation. A typical auto nucleus consisted of only a dozen or so Communists scattered throughout various departments in a shop containing thousands of workers. Many nuclei members could speak no English; in one unit "half of them [the nuclei members] speak English with difficulty, some not at all." In many cases, Communist workers hesitated to join the union; in one case an auto shop nucleus of twenty-five members contained only three union members until the head of the nucleus applied pressure on the slackers, after which "a few more" joined the AWU. The irregularity of employment and the fluctuation in party membership deprived the nuclei of a stable base of experienced workers; the drudgery of daily factory work exhausted nuclei members; and the relative economic and political stability of the 1920s deprived members of any sense of imminent crisis or high political purpose. Such conditions were demoralizing. "We had meetings," Vera Weisbord said, "that included men with drawn, grim faces who came in so exhausted by the day's toil on drill, punch press or assembly line that they had to struggle to keep awake. They would refuse to remain later than ten o'clock." In one auto industry nucleus operating in a plant of 15,000 workers, only six of twenty-five members regularly attended nucleus meetings, and the nucleus reportedly led "an isolated life, unknown to the workers in the plant, without influence, without contact."[18]

In spite of the obstacles, the auto shop nuclei exercised a certain influence. The main activity of the shop units was the publication of the shop papers—small, crudely printed four-page sheets costing a penny that appeared weekly, monthly, or (in most cases) irregularly. Communist workers and their sympathizers provided the news about shop conditions that went into the papers, and they also surreptitiously distributed the shop papers within the workplace. Communists not employed in the shops did the actual writing, editing, layout, and printing, as well as the distribution at the plant gates. Written simply and directly in prose "understandable by the average worker," the papers were designed to serve as the "mouthpiece of the Communists, shedding light on the economic and political problems of the workers, raising slogans for the betterment of their conditions." Also, the papers were to serve as an "instrument for extending the circles of sympathizers gathered around the group in the factory." To a remarkable degree the papers accomplished these ends.[19]

In April 1926 the Ford shop nucleus published the first auto shop paper, entitled the *Ford Worker*. The first issue announced: "May this little missive . . . create the determination and unity needed in the effort to put our class in its rightful position, that of a ruling class instead of ruled. We aim to bring about a condition where the exploitation of man by man shall cease." The *Ford Worker* achieved the widest circulation of any of the Communist shop papers. The Detroit party claimed a circulation for the paper of 20,000 in 1927, though Jack Stachel, a leader of party trade union work, estimated the paper's actual readership as close to 6,000. Other shop nuclei initiated their own versions of the *Ford Worker*: the *Dodge Worker, Fisher Body Worker, Workers' Bulletin, Briggs Worker,* and *Chrysler Worker*. Each had a circulation of between 100 and 3,000. Except for a few papers such as *Red Motor* and *Sparkplug,* published by the nuclei in the Cleveland White Motor and Fisher Body plants, respectively, most of the auto papers appeared in the Detroit area. Although well over a dozen shop papers appeared in the auto industry in the years following 1926, probably no more than eight existed at any one time.[20]

The shop papers contained droll anecdotes, bits of doggerel, and sermonettes on unionism. Accounts by workers of their deplorable conditions provided the paper's mainstay. The descriptions covered wage cuts, speedups, layoffs, unhealthy and dangerous working conditions, confusing and inequitable piece rates, tyrannical work rules, and arbitrary and prejudicial foremen. The workers' complaints ranged from quibbles to demands for basic human dignity. One worker wrote that his foreman had removed the cuspidors from his department while forbidding workers to spit on the floor. A Ford worker wrote: "The dirt and filth is awful! In some places it is an inch thick on the floor . . . there is no ventilation system worthy of the name. The men are compelled to work in these filthy, dusty rooms that are a menace to their health. During the hot weather we go home covered with cotton dust, grease and sweat. . . . On this second floor there is nothing to carry the dust away so it settles over everything. We breathe it into our lungs and we eat it during lunch period. We are not allowed to sit on the stock to eat, so like pigs and dogs we eat on the floor." Such simply worded complaints, so authentic and so compelling, conveyed an uncanny emotional power, a sadness, a bitterness, an anger that auto workers alone understood. Many of these stories ended with the conclusions of a Dodge worker writing of the colds and rheumatism that the men in his department contracted from having to work while standing in water: "This is the price we pay for working in an Open Shop."[21]

While the fear of reprisals forced the shop nuclei to operate secretly, the shop papers openly proclaimed their Communist origins and consistently raised political issues beyond the immediate grievances of the workers and beyond the papers' immediate purpose of pushing unionism. The *Dodge Worker,* for instance, announced in its first issue: "This little paper is edited and printed by the Communists working in the Dodge Bros. plant. . . . It is our aim to speak in behalf of the exploited workers in this shop, to point out some ways through which we can improve our conditions and put an end to the system of exploitation." The shop papers backed the idea of a labor party, supported Sacco and Vanzetti, and appealed to auto workers to vote for the candidates of the Workers' (Communist) party. Moreover, the papers consistently advocated the goal of socialism, not abstractly but concretely, by lauding the accomplishments of the Soviet Union and asking auto workers to support the Soviet Union and oppose the anti-Soviet policies of the capitalist countries.[22]

The employers naturally did their utmost to discredit and suppress the papers. The Employers Association of Detroit accused the papers of "magnifying supposed grievances" and "charging management with wrongs that never existed or for which they were never responsible." In and near the shops foremen and plant guards seized copies and harassed distributors. Employers fired workers suspected of writing for the papers. At the Ford Motor Company, the watchful eyes of Ford's Service Department and the Dearborn police made the distribution of the paper an act of daring. At shift changes Communists from outside the Ford plant came to the gates, distributed the paper for five or ten minutes, and then disappeared into the crowd before the servicemen discovered their presence. Nevertheless, the servicemen frequently seized the papers, and the Dearborn police often arrested the distributors—so often, indeed, that they arrested one distributor, Sarah Victor, three times in one afternoon.[23]

In spite of the attempts of the employers to suppress the shop papers, the papers reportedly went "like wildfire" among the workers. Robert L. Cruden, a radical labor reporter who worked in the Packard plant in Detroit in the late 20s, claimed that even though the papers made "somewhat overdrawn" criticisms, they were "very effective" and widely read. "The very fact that their grievances are worth publishing," Cruden noted, "gives the workers an immense amount of confidence." Similarly, Reinhold Niebuhr, a careful observer of the industrial scene in the city of his parish, expressed a grudging admiration for the shop papers: "It is rather significant that the rising tide of resentment among Ford workers has no avenue of expression except through the communistic weekly sheet, the *Ford Worker*. This paper which is sold surreptitiously in the vicinity of all Ford plants, boasts a weekly circulation of ten thousand copies though the actual number of Communists is hardly one-tenth of that figure in the whole city [of Detroit]. The paper is crude enough in its temper, but it fills its pages with specific instances of injustice rather than with the usual communistic propaganda." Niebuhr warned the readers of the *Christian Century* that if respectable labor leaders did not soon organize the automobile workers, "the revolutionary radicals who are now the only spokesmen of the discontent of Ford workers will gain an influence out of all proportion to their qualities of leadership."[24]

While working in the Detroit auto shops in the late 1920s, Frank Marquart, who later became educational director of United Automobile Workers Union (UAW) Locals 600 and 212, encountered the Communist shop papers. As Marquart recalled, "Those papers had the smell of machine oil about them. They fairly bristled with live, on-the-spot shop reports, exposing flagrant health hazards in the paint shop, describing brutal acts of this or that foreman toward the men under him, citing facts and figures about speedup on specific job operations, revealing how workers got shortchanged by a bonus system no one could ever figure out." The auto workers whom Marquart encountered loved these papers. "The paper gave them a visceral reaction; it spoke to them about the experiences that impinged on their nerves, muscles, and brains. The paper said what they felt!" The papers particularly impressed Marquart by the way in which they "publicized the employers' discriminatory practices: the way Negroes were confined to the dirtiest and meanest jobs," particularly in the foundaries and toilets. "I can credit those papers," said Marquart, "for making me conscious of the fact that Negroes have special problems as a minority group, apart from the general conditions of wage workers." As for the impact of the papers on workers in general, Marquart opined, "I do know that those papers played a significant role in preparing auto workers' minds for the union thrust that was to come in the days ahead."[25]

While the ethnic composition of the Communists hampered Communist effectiveness and isolated the nuclei from native-born workers, it also provided an avenue of influence to the foreign-speaking auto workers. Foreign-born workers constituted a substantial portion of Detroit auto workers. Poles and others had settled in Detroit before 1910, and large groups of Russians, Yugoslavs, Greeks, Lithuanians, and Finns came to Detroit (often from other parts of the country rather than from Europe) in 1913–14 to capitalize on Henry Ford's offer of a five-dollar-a-day wage. By 1930 only New York City (33 percent), Cleveland (26 percent), and Chicago (25 percent) equalled or surpassed Detroit (25 percent) in the proportion of foreign-born in their population. With the possible exception of the Syrians (50 percent of whom worked in mercantile firms), the Greeks (many of whom owned small stores and shops), and Italians ( many of whom were construction workers), most of the foreign-born workers in the Detroit area found employment in the auto industry. Though the extent of Communist influence among foreign-born auto workers is impossible to determine, the Communists participated in the benevolent, educational, and cultural organizations of nearly all major ethnic groups. Though the Communist influence on ethnic workers was small compared to the influence of conservative, nationalistic, and church-related organizations, it was large compared to the influence of any other radical party.

The 300,000 Poles in the Detroit area were the largest foreign-born group. They lived mainly in Hamtramck, where Poles constituted 80 percent of the population in 1930. Many Poles worked in the Dodge plant in Hamtramck. In the Polish community Communist influence found expression in the five local branches of the Polish Mutual Aid Society, the Communist Mixed chorus, "Harmonia," and the Polish Workers Educational Association. Among the 50,507 Russians in the Detroit area, many of whom worked at Ford and many of whom sympathized with the Russian Revolution, the Communists exercised influence through the Russian Consolidated Mutual Aid Society, the Russian Cooperation Society, and the Russian Working Women's Club. In 1930, 26,304 Hungarians lived in the Detroit area; many worked in Ford, Briggs, Chrysler, and Dodge. In the largest Hungarian settlement in the southwest section of the city called Delray, the Workers' (Communist) party represented one of the three most prominent political clubs, and the Communist newspaper, *Uj Elore*, represented one of the three most widely read Hungarian national dailies. Detroit Rumanians numbered 16,301 in 1930; large numbers of them worked in the Ford plant in Dearborn. The Communists had contacts with the Rumanians through a large Communist-sponsored chorus of young Rumanians called "Flacara" (Flame). Some of the 15,000 Ukranians in Detroit belong to such Communist-affiliated groups as the Ukranian United Toilers and the Ukranian Toilers of America. Among Detroit's 12,300 Lithuanians, the Lithuanian Workers of America, a "Communist split-off" from the Lithuanian National Alliance, represented a major benevolent group. The Lithuanian Communists had their own hall and were "very active in forming educational groups and promot[ing] many lectures, concerts, and dramatic performances." They were one of "the real centers of Lithuanian life." Though only about 9000 Finns lived in Detroit, most worked in the auto plants and the Finnish community contained a strong element of Communist supporters. After the Russian Revolution, Communist Finns took over the most active organization in the Finnish com-

munity, the Finnish Socialist Club. Under Communist leadership
the Communist Workers Club provided a full program of cultural
activities, plays, lectures, and dances. Moreover, the Finnish
Workers Club on Fourteenth Street became a regular meeting
place for the Communist Party, the Auto Workers Union, the Unemployed Councils and other Communist-related groups. The
Communists also had strong ties with a number of groups in Detroit's Jewish community. These included the *Morning Freiheit*,
the Jewish Workers Club, the Jewish Workers Schools, and the
Jewish Women Councils. After 1930, the Communists had another
channel of influence to Detroit ethnic workers through the International Workers Order, a fraternal association specializing in low
cost insurance, which had a least four branches in Detroit by
1932.[26]

As the Communists became active in the auto industry,
conflicts erupted between them and the Socialist leaders of the
union. Differences arose first over the election of 1924 and later
over union strike policy and control of the union itself. In the
election campaign of 1924 the Communists opposed Robert
LaFollette, the candidate of the Progressives, whom they
criticized as a "failure," a "reactionary," a "menace," a "tool of big
business," an "enemy of labor," and the "candidate of political
gangsters." Such criticism annoyed AWU president, Logan. "The
program of the Workers' party," he said, "has its merits and the
party has its quota of able, honest, and conscientious men and
women, but the party is not so immaculately clean either in its
theories and practices and personnel that it can afford to brand
those who disagree with it as traitors of the working class and as
crooks and job hunters." Logan endorsed LaFollette, who he said
was doing his "best to usher in better government."[27]

The Communists and Socialists also disagreed over union
strike policies. Logan and the other AWU leaders shared the AFL's
aversion to strikes. Lester Johnson, secretary of the union, later
recalled that the union organizers "did not want strikes" because
walkouts "created a lot of work" and "took away dues." Logan had
a special antipathy for the spontaneous, unauthorized strikes, the
only kind to occur in the industry after the decline of the union.
Logan repeatedly advised the workers that organization should
precede action. "Why put the cart before the horse?" he asked.
The Communists took a more activist approach than did Johnson

and Logan. They favored assisting the spontaneous strikes and using them as an opportunity to educate the strikers and enlist them in the union. When half a dozen departmental walkouts occurred in the Fisher Body plants during the summer of 1926, the Communists proudly claimed that they were "among the first to start the row and down the tools."[28]

Relations between the Communists and the Socialist leadership of the AWU continued to deteriorate after the Communists began seeking union office. This move occurred in 1926, after the party's Trade Union Committee recommended that "all members of the party who are eligible to join the unions in the Auto industry shall be distributed proportionally with a view to capture the machinery of both the Auto workers and machinists Locals in the various Automobile centers." In order to keep the Communists and other young activists out of office, the Socialists resorted to several bureaucratic maneuvers, including a change in the union's constitution to restrict eligibility to office to those who had been members of the union for at least a year. In 1926, however, after a year in the union, a tireless and passionate young Communist named Phil Raymond challenged Lester Johnson for the post of union secretary. The son of Rumanian and Palestinian immigrants, Raymond had grown up on the lower east side of New York City, where he had listened to radical soap-box orators and read the Socialist tracts of Oscar Ameringer and Eugene Debs. Converted to socialist ideas, Raymond joined the Young People's Socialist League and later the Socialist party. When the Socialist party split, Raymond entered the Communist party. In 1924, after several jobs in the East, Raymond came to Detroit and began working at the Kelsey Hayes Wheel Company. With a little union experience and a great deal of energy and oratorical ability, Raymond defeated Lester Johnson by one vote and became the first Communist officer of the AWU.[29]

After Raymond's election, the Communist influence and numbers grew. According to Johnson, the Socialists soon "saw the handwriting on the wall." They tried changing the union's constitution to make the Executive Board the governing body of the organization, instead of the Board of Administration, which contained elected representatives from the shop units. "All that did," Johnson acknowledged, "was to stave off the time." Within a year or so, the Communists had three or four members on the Executive Board. Feeling their positions threatened, the Socialist officers accused the Communists of faultfinding and of using the union for propaganda purposes. By 1927 most of the Socialists in the union gave up the struggle for control. "The way the thing was operating," Johnson recalled, "I just ceased to be active." Johnson left the union and entered law school. The head of the union, William Logan, and the secretary, Charles Dickenson, resigned. The union combined the offices of president and secretary into the post of executive-secretary, to which it elected Arthur Rohan. Rohan stayed in that position until 1928 or 1929, the only Socialist in a leadership increasingly Communist.[30]

By the early 1930s all key union leaders either belonged to the party or had close connections. Phil Raymond became head of the important Detroit Local 127 and editor of the *Auto Workers News*. After Rohan left the union to take a position in the sheriff's office in his native town of Racine, Wisconsin, Alfred Goetz, an automobile machinist, became the leader of the AWU. In 1932 Goetz became Michigan's organizer of the Communist Unemployed Councils. For a while A. B. Magill, a writer for the *Daily Worker*, edited the *Auto Workers News*. John Schmies, a machinist at Briggs in the late 20s, a secretary of the Detroit section of the TUEL in 1929, and District Organizer of the Communist Party in Detroit in the early 30s, became a member of the Executive Board of the AWU. Philip Frankfeld, the District Organizer of the Young Communist League (YCL) in 1929, and Leo Thompson, another leader of the YCL, became AWU organizers.[31]

The main objective of the Communists in the auto industry was what William Z. Foster called "the greatest and most pressing task now confronting the working class"—the organization of the unorganized. A report of the party's Trade Union Committee in July 1926 recognized that the problem of organizing auto workers was "a difficult one" for a number of reasons: the indifferent "attitude of the general labor movement represented by the A.F. of L.," the "prejudice of the craft unions" toward unskilled and semiskilled workers, who constituted the majority of the auto work force, the prevalence of foreign-born workers, the existence of the employers' "army of spies, intimidating and threatening these workers with deportation," the "considerably higher" wages paid to auto workers in comparison with other unskilled and unorganized workers, the "Ford welfare institutions and the myth of his fairness to Ford workers," and finally the existence of "a large group of workers who can be named migratory workers who wander from one industry to another." Because of the difficulties presented by the industry, the Communist party decided that its "immediate tasks" should include not only an effort to "stimulate the drive for organization among auto workers" but also an effort to "bring pressure to bear" on the International Association of Machinists (IAM) "to become the dominating force in the drive for organization." To further these ends the Trade Union Committee decided to spread its program for an auto drive within the IAM and to conduct a demonstration at the AFL 1926 convention in Detroit "demanding this body get behind the drive." In 1927 the Trade Union Committee reemphasized the need "to immediately build and strengthen the Auto Workers Union, throwing into this work all our available Party and left-wing forces in the city of Detroit, and also to try to secure the support of the local labor movement."[32]

In trying to prompt the AFL to organize auto workers, the Communists were clearly bucking the tide. The leaders of the AFL more or less ignored this task. In the 1920s they retreated, barred Communists from their unions, repudiated the Brookwood Labor College (a progressive school for unionists set up by A. J. Muste in Katonah, New York, in 1921), abandoned independent political action (after an unenthusiastic endorsement of Robert LaFollette's presidential bid in 1924), and directed much of their resources into union banks and insurance companies. The AFL shied away from aggressive organizing and embraced a policy of labor-management cooperation. William Green, who assumed the leadership of the federation after the death of Samuel Gompers, believed that unions should "see that management policies are efficient" and that the "best interests [of workers] are promoted through concord rather than by conflict." AFL strikes and membership declined precipitously in the 1920s. By the end of the decade union membership had fallen from 5,047,000 to 3,442,600, from 19.4 percent of the nonagricultural work force to 10.2 percent.[33]

The Communist strategy came the closest to realization in the automobile industry. Largely because of Communist agitation, the AFL started an organizing campaign in auto, one of only two AFL organizing efforts in the 1920s. The Automobile Committee of the Machinists reported in 1924, "As a result of our indifferences in the past, dual organizations have come into existence in answer to the need of the men in this industry for the protection of their rights. The natural tendency of working men is evident by the rapid growth of such dual organizations, such as the auto and aircraft workers, for the protection of their mutual interest." The committee warned: "Their success is a serious menace to the very existence of our organization." After the Communists began issuing shop papers and moving into the leadership of the AWU, James O'Connell, head of the Metal Trades Department of the AFL, picked up the Machinists' cry. In 1926 he expressed concern to the department over "would-be leaders attempting to sow seeds of dissension and build up a semblance of an independent organization" in opposition to the "legitimate" trade union movement. "Of course," he said, "this state of affairs is largely due to the ultra radical element whose inspiration, advice and instructions come from a country far from our shores. While no real progress has been made by this radical element to weaken or destroy our movement, we must not take it for granted that their activity has by any means ceased."[34]

At the AFL convention in Detroit in October 1926, O'Connell introduced a resolution calling on the federation to start an organizing drive among the automobile workers. The delegates had much reason to favor this resolution out of fear that the Communists would beat them to the punch. The Communists in Michigan lacked the resources to start a big campaign among auto workers. Earlier that year, however, Communists in Passaic, New Jersey, and New York City had led major strikes by textile, fur, and ladies garment workers. Though only the fur strike ended successfully, the strikes showed that under the right conditions a small number of Communists could do much. The Executive Council's report to the convention bristled over "groups which advocate communist principles and theories." Such groups were handicapping "both organizing activities and the solidarity of the trade union movement." No one could say that the unorganized workers in the nation's third largest industry would remain immune to Communist agitation. The delegates unanimously passed O'Connell's resolution, and the *New Republic* declared that "everything" the convention accomplished was "insignificant beside the] resolution to unionize the automobile industry."[35]

The Communists had every reason to view the AFL move as a

hostile gesture designed to thwart the Auto Workers Union. Since 1923, when Samuel Gompers and Matthew Woll had launched a drive to defeat the TUEL program within the Illinois Federation of Labor, the AFL leadership had pursued a relentless policy of squashing Communist efforts on behalf of amalgamation, a labor party, and the recognition of the Soviet Union. They had expelled known Communists from local unions and national conventions. The Communists, nevertheless, continued to oppose dual unions and to favor work within the Federation. In Detroit, for instance, the Communists managed to establish tenuous relations with Frank Martel, head of the Detroit Federation of Labor, with whom they cooperated in meetings to mark Lenin's death, to greet visiting Soviet flyers, and to support Sacco and Vanzetti. Although the Communists ceaselessly criticized the AFL, they kept the criticism within fraternal limits. While the Communists devoted their energy to building the independent Auto Workers Union, the shop papers advised their readers to join either the AWU or the International Association of Machinists. "No matter what differences we have among ourselves," the *Ford Worker* said, "we must have a united front against the bosses." Thus, the Communists declared that they were "pleased to hear" of the federation's intention to organize auto workers. Phil Raymond wrote Green that the AWU would "render all assistance possible" to the effort and asked him "under what terms and conditions" the AFL would lift its suspension of the Auto Workers Union.[36]

The AFL soon showed that it had little determination to organize the automobile industry and no intention of welcoming the AWU back into its ranks. Green, who often made clear that he wanted "no relations or dealings with the communists because there is something in their creed that makes them unmindful of certain standards of ethics and mutual consideration that we call good manners," informed Raymond that the AWU could only return to the AFL as a federal labor union. Since this meant that the union would have to relinquish control of its funds and strike decisions to the national federation and relinquish its members to any international union that claimed jurisdiction over them, Green's reply was tantamount to a rejection.[37]

The AFL organizing campaign never got much beyond the stage of passing the convention resolution. In 1927 Florence Thorne of the AFL national office asked William Chalmers, a scholar knowledgeable of the industry, the best basis on which to organize auto workers. Chalmers responded that the AFL campaign might "experience some slight difficulty because of the Auto Workers Union," whose "organizers have made many speeches to the men . . . many [of whom] have responded to the general philosophy of unionism." The internal deficiencies of the AFL, however, proved a more decisive obstacle than the AWU. Rivalry among the eighteen international unions that claimed jurisdiction in the industry prevented concerted action. In June 1927, Green appointed AFL staff member Paul J. Smith to head the auto drive. Though Smith and a few organizers established a headquarters in Detroit, the highly touted drive consisted of little more than a couple of feeble and futile efforts to sell Henry Ford the idea of union-management cooperation. In July 1927 and again in February 1928 Smith reported to Green that efforts to organize the industry had produced nothing.[38]

The AFL's organizing fiasco afforded the Communists an opportunity to assail the federation's incompetence and conservatism. William F. Dunne accused the federation of "surrender" and "conscious reaction"; Foster charged that the leadership had gone completely over to "class collaboration" and was concerned only with the protection of "their group interests as a bureaucracy." The federation's failure also meant that the Communists in the auto industry had to resume building "fires under the reactionary leaders."[39]

In 1927 the Communists increased their efforts. Commenting on the state of the industry, Reinhold Niebuhr wrote in June: "There is no question that discontent among the workers is rising to a pitch which augurs an evil day for the industry. . . . The time would now seem ripe for a real organizing effort." Niebuhr hoped that someone besides the Communists would do the job, but he recognized that the AFL lacked "the energy and resourcefulness to tackle the problem." Moreover, the Socialists in Michigan were "generally defunct," and the Wobblies (IWW) were "few and demoralized." Thus, as a writer for the *Daily Worker* put it: "The party must be the driving force in the whole movement. . . . There is no other group that can go through with an aggressive organizing campaign."[40]

The AWU tried to reach the auto workers by three channels: a newspaper, recruitment meetings, and strike support. Since the

*Auto Worker* had ceased publication in 1924 during the downturn of the union's fortunes, in April 1927 the Communists launched the *Auto Workers News*. Phil Raymond later explained that the paper's main purpose was to develop "some feeling of confidence on the part of the workers themselves." The Communists' *Auto Workers News* differed markedly from the earlier *Auto Worker*. The Socialist paper was sixteen pages long, cost fifteen cents, and contained a variety of analytical news articles written by professional journalists and the union's officers and organizers. The Communist paper was four pages, cost only a penny, and contained short, simple articles that workers often wrote or dictated and that dealt with shop conditions and protests. Though the price and content of the *Auto Workers News* may have appealed more to the unskilled workers than did the *Auto News,* the appeal made no difference in the kind of workers attracted to the union. A contemporary observer noted: "The greatest degree of union activity has arisen not from the lowest paid groups in the industry, but from groups that might almost be called the aristocracy . . . [and] the history of their agitation does not make it appear that it is from the lowest paid workers that the greatest support of Communist organizational activities will come."[41]

The first issue of the *Auto Workers News* reported on a fire that killed twenty-one workers in the Briggs Manufacturing Company, a body plant notorious for its hard and dangerous working conditions. The paper dismissed the conclusions of the Michigan Department of Labor and Industry that the blaze was "an act of Providence" and placed the blame on the company for failing to provide an adequate ventilation system to dispose of the inflammable fumes arising from the lacquering process. The *Auto Workers News* accompanied the report with a poignant verse entitled "Bodies by Briggs":

> Bodies by Briggs, this cinder heap
>    of things that once were men,
> Bone of our bone, our brothers, they
>    slain in that flaming den;
> Such is the tally of wealth and greed thru
>    all of mortal ken,
> Death marks the score in the worker's
>    blood using a golden pen.[42]

In many ways the content of the *Auto Workers News* resembled that of the Communist shop papers. Most articles dealt with shop conditions, the worst of which existed in such body shops as Briggs and Murray. Often the paper made jokes aimed at Briggs. The *Auto Workers News*, for example, told of a reckless aviator, who when asked if he feared death, replied, "What, afraid of being killed? Why I've been working at the Briggs Mack Ave. plant for two years!" The paper frequently contained accounts of the workers' complaints against speedup and of the related complaints against industrial accidents and the bonus payment systems. A Chevrolet employee working eleven and a half hours a night wrote: "Hell has no terrors for the workers who can stand a few nights of it. The place is a mad-house. Straw bosses are continually yelling for more production, more production." A woman worker at Briggs reported: "We're on piece work and the rate is so low we gotta work like blazes to make anything. Naturally, we have to tie up the safety guards. Gee, it makes me sick to see all the cute young girls get their hands [cut] off . . . I go to work every night fearing that before morning my finger will be off." Another Briggs employee wrote: "We are rushed in our work so much and many of the punch presses are just rattle traps that there always is someone getting hurt. And when we come to the first aid we generally find a line up and have to wait our turn. Every day the floor becomes as bloody as a slaughter house."

Headlines of industrial accidents studded the paper's pages: "Another Victim of the Speed-up System," "Six Workers Killed in Ford Rouge Plant," "Ford Speed-up Maims Workers." The uncertainty of employment also ranked high as a source of complaint. Workers railed against layoffs, short work weeks, and the substitution of poorly paid women workers for men. A typical headline read: "Human Scrap Pile Grows, Old Employees Are Thrown Out of Work." The tyranny and favoritism of foremen provided another common grievance. A Briggs worker used the *Auto Workers News* to castigate a foreman on Line 1: "During my two years of working under him I have never heard him address me or any other man in a friendly spirit. When he wants something done he stands about 300 feet away from a person and yells at him as if he were a dog."[43]

Like the shop papers, the *Auto Workers News* went beyond a concern with the immediate shop grievances and raised political issues. The paper printed articles on the Soviet Union, particularly on improvements in the conditions of Soviet workers. The paper also called upon auto workers to support the Gastonia strikers, Sacco and Vanzetti, and Communist candidates for local office. The union focused special attention on the plight of women, blacks, foreign-born, and young workers. For a while the *Auto Workers News* ran a special Women's Column, and it fought the practice of hiring women at substandard rates. "Girls must have a chance to earn a decent living," the union argued, "but one of the demands of the Auto Workers Union must be: 'Equal pay for equal work.'" In a similar vein the union protested against employer practices of paying black workers less than whites, of giving blacks "the hardest and dirtiest work," and of trying to keep the workers divided by arousing "suspicions and prejudices." The union's special appeal to black and ethnic workers differed sharply with the union's behavior under Socialist leadership. Under the Socialists the union had contained no black workers; the union's president had referred to the Chinese as "Chinks," and the paper had carried "niggah" jokes. In contrast, under Communist leadership, the union declared: "All workers must get together—men, women, young workers, all nationalities, all races, for their own protection."[44]

In a short time the *Auto Workers News* achieved a wide readership in the plants and became the butt of employer hostility. In *Conveyor* (1935), a novel about Detroit auto workers in the late 1920s, the hero, Jim Brogan, first encountered the *Auto Workers News* while witnessing a couple of policemen assault its distributor outside the plant gates. His reaction doubtlessly typified that of many workers. "He read the . . . paper carefully. Evidently most of it was written by workers like himself, for it had none of the smoothness of the regular newspapers. But it had the goods just the same. There wasn't any doubt about that. This was one paper that knew what it was talking about." Robert Cruden, an AWU member who attached ventilators to Packard bodies, claimed, "Every issue . . . was greeted with enthusiasm." The employers failed to share this enthusiasm; in Detroit, Flint, Pontiac, Lansing, and Toledo they tried to prevent the paper's distribution. The employers' enmity achieved such intensity that workers dared not distribute or read the paper openly in or near most plants. Often, the union relied on women, including a sympathetic group of physicians' wives, to sell the paper at plant gates. Within the plants interested workers developed ingenious schemes for the surreptitious circulation of the papers. Cruden recalled, "At lunch we'd sneak behind bodies and read and discuss it." In its first year the *Auto Workers News* achieved a monthly circulation of between 12,000 and 18,000.[45]

Conditions inside the auto plants made open union activity nearly impossible. The long shifts and monotonous, tiring, and often dangerous work absorbed and deadened a worker's attention. Robert Cruden reported that terrific pressure existed "to work swiftly, for if a body went through unassembled there was trouble and plenty of it." By the end of his eleven hour shift, he functioned "in a semi-conscious state." The danger of injury and the surveillance of foremen and straw bosses riveted an employee's mind to the job. The knowledge that layoffs and rehiring often depended upon the whims of the foremen created a constant pressure on the workers to work hard and avoid trouble.[46]

The prevalence of company espionage systems also discouraged open union activity. The authoritarianism of the Ford plant was atypical only in its extremity. By the 1920s Henry Ford had a "service" department unofficially headed by Harry Bennett and manned by an assortment of mobsters, boxers, and ex-convicts to oversee his employees. Ford not only prohibited talk of unionism and politics in his operation but also discouraged any conversation whatever. Bill McKie, a Scottish-born AWU activist, called this "the Ford Silence." McKie's biographer described McKie's first day at Ford's in 1927: "The shop, except for the triumphant grind and screech of the belt, was as quiet as a church. No human voice was raised here. No man spoke to fellow man. For the eight hours they ran along this never-ending line they gave up the power of speech." Another Ford worker described the regimentation and intimidation as "worse than the army." Under such conditions no AWU member could engage in open recruitment.[47]

Since organizing within the shops was so forbidding, most proselytizing occurred at shop gate meetings. As workers on their lunch break streamed from the plant or hung out of the shop windows for a breath of fresh air, Phil Raymond, Alfred Goetz, or some other union organizer would mount a soapbox or a car hood, distribute membership cards, and discuss the merits of unions and the specific demands of the AWU: a wage increase; a minimum wage of forty dollars a week; an eight hour day and five day week; the right to organize; the abolition of all discriminatory practices against women, Negroes, youth, and old workers; the abolition of night work for women, the establishment and enforcement of safety and sanitary regulations; an end to speedup; and unemployment insurance financed by the state and employers and administered by the unions.[48]

This agitation had no appeal for the fainthearted. Police officers regularly broke up the gatherings and arrested the speakers. Sometimes the workers jeered and ridiculed the organizers. Many regarded the union spokesmen as "Reds from Russia." Occasionally workers heckled the organizers and advised them to "Get a Job!" Nevertheless, Raymond and his colleagues persisted, and their efforts were effective. William Chalmers, a student who attended many AWU meetings to gather information for a thesis, concluded that the "attentiveness of the workers at such meetings" and "the discussions among workers that followed" showed that these soapbox orations "caused the thoughts of the workers to turn to a more critical appraisal of the employers' activities."[49]

The AWU also sponsored gatherings in the homes of sympathetic workers, the halls of nationality groups, and the union office. Raymond tried to reach foreign-born auto workers through their social and fraternal clubs, a technique UAW organizers later used successfully. This tactic reflected the necessity of recruiting workers some place where, as Raymond noted, "they could be protected from being immediately victimized" by the employers. Frank Marquart, later an educational director of the UAW, recalled that he and a group of fellow workers often attended AWU meetings in the late 1920s. Although Marquart and his friends sympathized with the union, they never joined. Nevertheless, Marquart claimed that at these forums "I first became introduced to radicalism" and "I was promptly converted to industrial unionism."[50]

Besides using the newspaper, shop gate meetings, and forums, the Communists also relied on strike support to spread the message of unionism. Even without a union, the auto workers frequently walked off the job to protest wages or conditions. The vast majority of these outbreaks occurred in the oppressive body plants. Generally a wage cut or a reduction of piece rates caused the walkouts, and they usually involved only one or two departments. While these spontaneous walkouts extracted concessions from the employers, they seldom had the organization or solidarity necessary to prevent the firing of prominent leaders. In the period 1926–30, the AWU recorded over fifty spontaneous strikes. Though the Communists initiated few if any of these, they became involved in over a score of them. The AWU aided the four most important auto strikes of the late 20s—those at Briggs Meldrum in 1927, Fisher Body Plant No. 18 in 1928, and Graham-Paige and Murray Body in 1929. The Graham-Paige and Murray Body strike involved more workers than any walkout in the industry since 1921. Where the AWU lent its assistance, either the union had volunteered its help or the strikers had asked the AWU for help, sometimes after failing to obtain aid from the AFL. The AWU helped the strikers to organize mass meetings, formulate demands, select strike committees, establish picket lines, write leaflets, and obtain legal aid. The AWU organizers impressed on the workers that a successful walkout demanded racial solidarity and such aggressive tactics as mass picketing. Also, Raymond and other organizers frequently urged the strikers to broaden their demands to grievances beyond those that prompted the immediate protest and to strengthen their protest by appealing for support from unemployed workers and employees in nonstriking departments. Occasionally the AWU assistance helped turn spontaneous outrage into a sustained and successful struggle, but almost as frequently strikers won gains without the help of the union or even lost strikes in spite of AWU aid. The union signed up hundreds of members during the course of these strikes, though most passed from the ranks after the immediate crisis had subsided.[51]

In 1929 William Green wrote to Paul Smith, an AFL organizer at Nash: "The appalling indifference of the [auto] workers themselves is a difficulty that seems to be insurmountable." The indifference Green perceived had numerous causes: the relative prosperity and easy credit of the 20s; the militant anti-unionism of the employers and the government; the inexperience, diversity, and transiency of the auto workers themselves. While the Communists disagreed with Green about the insurmountability of the problem, their failure to organize the auto workers in four years of intense activity bore testimony to the difficulty. The auto workers, Raymond recalled, regarded the Auto Workers Union—even after years of activity—"like a fire department" that they could ignore except for those occasions when they needed to call on it for help.[52]

Nevertheless, by the end of the 1920s, the Communists had established their presence in the automobile industry and had spread the idea of industrial unionism to large numbers of unskilled auto workers. In 1930 the CP had 400 members in the industry. Only in the needle, building, and metal trades and mining did the party have more members. By April of 1928, the Detroit District achieved a membership of 570, of which 95 percent were "proletarians and their wives." The party had formed twenty–two shop nuclei in the district. Of these, fifteen nuclei containing 210 members operated in "the most important automobile plants in Detroit." Also, the party claimed to have sixteen language "fractions" that were "representative" of the foreign-speaking population of the city.[53]

Through the *Auto Workers News*, strike support, and shop gate, household, and fraternal society meetings, the Communists had spread the idea of industrial unionism and built up a rudimentary union structure in certain shops. Though the union never divulged exact membership figures, AWU membership reached several thousand by 1929, and the locus of membership apparently shifted by that time from New York City, which had the largest local in 1927, to Detroit. On January 31, 1929 an AWU conference in Detroit attracted 60 delegates, allegedly representing between 5,000 and 10,000 workers in Detroit, Pontiac, Flint, and Cleveland. About 35 delegates represented such fraternal and benevolent societies as the Lithuanian Working Women's Alliance, the Supreme Lodge of Lithuanians in America, and the Bulgarian Educational Club. At the time of the next AWU conference on August 24, 1929, the union reportedly was active in Detroit, Pontiac, Flint, Grand Rapids, and other auto centers, and membership was "being steadily increased." By that date, Detroit Local 127 had organized its membership on the basis of departmental, shop, and city committees, and the 57 delegates to the conference represented 37 shop committees. After observing the AWU first hand, William Chalmers wrote: "The Communists . . . have made a profound impression on the workers of the industry through their continuous and strenuous activity. It is they, not the American Federation of Labor, who have constantly urged the workers to organize, who have addressed impromptu meetings . . . who have led spontaneous walkouts and strikes . . . and who have aroused the opposition of the employers. . . . [If] the industry is going to be organized 'from the outside' in the immediate future, it will be the Communists who will be responsible."[54]

Communist activity in the years before 1933 provided a unique optic through which to view the auto industry. Their failure either to build a stable union or to stimulate a real AFL recruitment drive provided a sharp focus for both the difficulties of organization and the passivity of mainstream labor. Equally of interest, Communist strike support and shop papers pierced the veil of the industry's vaunted welfare capitalism and high wages and exposed the manifold grievances of the workers in the shops. Moreover, the effort of Raymond and his colleagues had a transcendent importance. Both the party and the union recruited and gave practical organizational experience to workers who later became active in the drive to form the UAW. Also, through the shop papers, shop gate meetings, and fraternal societies, countless auto workers who never joined the CP or AWU became aquainted with radical ideas. These workers became conscious of shared grievances. They learned of socialism, and they encountered the idea of an industrial union. In these ways, the Communists did more than anyone in the preunion days to lay the foundation for a successful auto union.

# III
### • • •

# WORK OR WAGES:
# ORGANIZING THE UNEMPLOYED

The economic depression of the 1930s hit no industry harder than the automobile industry. Between 1930 and 1933, the auto workers of Detroit and other cities responded to the depression's economic hardships with organized protests directed against employers, landlords, and local government officials. In three important ways, these protests served as a prelude to the unionization of the automobile industry, which began in a sustained manner in 1933. First, since the auto industry had spearheaded the prosperity of the post-World War I era, the prostration of the industry and the struggles of jobless auto workers was significant. It underscored the collapse of the widespread illusion that American industry in the 1920s had entered an epoch of increasing profits and wages. Second, since the Communists organized the major unemployment protests of auto workers, they gained their first widespread influence in the industry as well as prominence in the subsequent union struggles. Third, by providing many auto workers with their first experience of organized struggle, the unemployment protests helped to lay the groundwork for the strikes and organization that soon established the United Automobile Workers Union.

In the 1920s the American automobile industry symbolized the dynamism of a new, reorganized capitalism—a capitalism capable of avoiding the cyclical economic crises of the past, of achieving unending expansion and prosperity, and of providing both continuous profits and high wages. Detroit was the "City of Tomorrow." In 1929, after a visit to Detroit, Mathew Josephson declared: "All of the industrial leaders whom I saw voiced their optimism and their intense satisfaction over the present state. Nowhere in the world or in human history were great masses of human beings lifted to such a scale of well-being and mechanical comfort." The economic collapse of 1929 shattered such illusions by creating massive unemployment among auto workers and causing cuts in wages and hours for those who remained employed. The depression fostered a level of conflict between workers and employers unequalled since the early 1920s.[1]

With the general economic downturn in the autumn of 1929, auto employment fell precipitously. Because of the industry's concentration in a few cities and because these cities depended almost completely on the auto industry for their economic well-being, the auto workers suffered uncommonly from the crisis. In Toledo, for example, economic life centered around the Willys-Overland plant. In March 1929, the plant manufactured 42,000 cars and employed 28,000 persons; by fall the company had cut back production and had reduced its work force to 4,000. By the first of the new year, 30 to 40 percent of the city's male population was jobless. After touring Willys-Overland early in 1930, *Survey* investigator, Beulah Amidon, remarked that the plant reminded her of

the old desert towns left in the wake of a mining rush. There was the same sense of suspended life, as I moved among silent, untended machines or walked through departments where hundreds of half-finished automobile bodies gathered dust while they waited for the next cleaning or finishing process. The effect of sudden paralysis was intensified by the infrequent groups of workers, almost lost in the vast, dim spaces, going about tasks that seemed very small and futile in the midst of the elaborate equipment for mass production, for an unending stream of assembled, tested, finished cars rolling out of the factory doors.

The following years brought no respite. In the spring of 1932, Willys employed only 3,000 persons; most of the city's 1,000 automobile parts plants sat idle. Mauritz Hallgren, a frequent contributor to the *Nation*, reported that "one fifth of Toledo is on the dole"; another authority called the desperation, "the worst the city has ever faced."[2]

During the first years of economic crisis, Detroit, the center of the auto industry, suffered the highest jobless rate in the nation. The Ford Motor Company, the largest of the city's auto firms, reduced its payroll from 128,142 persons in March 1929 to 100,500 in December. Worse lay ahead. In April 1931, only 84,000 Ford employees remained at work, by August only 37,000, and half of these worked three days a week. As the number of employed plummeted, the number on relief soared. In October 1929, the Department of Public Relief cared for 156,000 persons, by April of the next year, 728,000. During the winter of 1931 the municipal lodging houses fed 12,000 men daily and lodged 5,000 nightly. In February, the city received 211,000 applications for relief; by spring the applications were arriving at the appalling rate of 500 a day. The corrupt and inadequate relief system left many citizens hungry. In late 1931, two adults could obtain only $3.60 for food, with a small additional allowance for each child. That year the Department of Public Welfare dropped from the rolls 900 families whom it deemed insufficiently needy; the average income of those dropped from the rolls amounted to $1.56 a week. In the fall of 1931, a physician at Detroit's Receiving Hospital claimed that an average of four persons a day entered the hospital too weak from starvation to survive.[3]

The absence of any federal system of social welfare meant that the unemployed had to rely on either their own meager resources or the overtaxed benevolence of local, private charities. In Flint, over half the employed population of 83,000 worked for General Motors (GM), which had branches of Chevrolet, Fisher Body, Buick, and AC Sparkplug located in the city. Though the Flint Chamber of Commerce refused to say how many were unemployed, a large number of workers lost their jobs in November 1929, when General Motors (GM) slashed production to one-seventh of normal. Neither GM nor the city government assumed any responsibility for the jobless. The entire burden of relief fell to such private agencies associated with churches or with the Flint Community Fund. The Methodist Church, for example, fed as many as 1,200 people daily. Even in 1931, when the city established the Flint Relief Commission, funding still came from private contributions.[4]

Faced with such conditions, many unemployed workers showed a readiness for radical, if not always political, solutions to their troubles. In Detroit unemployed workers broke windows and looted grocery stores at night. Others entered chain stores, ordered all the food they could carry, and left without paying. Children snatched bundles of groceries from the hands of unwary shoppers. In Centerline, near Detroit, the police accused Communists of having incited a group that raided the market of the C. F. Smith Company. A jobless Detroit auto worker later recalled that in order to feed his family, he regularly snatched milk from the porches of the luxurious homes in Rosedale Park and stole corn from farmers' fields and peddled it door to door.[5]

The employers cut back wages and hours causing even auto workers who remained employed to suffer from reduced incomes. In the fall of 1931, Ford and GM led the auto firms in wage cuts of over 10 percent. Between 1930 and 1932 the decline of wage rates in the industry varied from 4.7 percent for certain women laborers to 20.4 percent for certain skilled craftsmen. Henry Ford, the symbol of high wages, reduced the earnings of his employees from between $8.00 and $9.60 a day to between $6.00 and $6.40; Walter Briggs, the industry's symbol of ruthless exploitation, slashed the wages of some male employees to ten cents an hour and of some female employees to four cents. Rueful Briggs workers said, "If poison doesn't work, try Briggs." From a survey of 111 auto workers conducted between August and October 1931, the Labor Research Association reported that of the 90 persons who had worked in the last year, most had employment for only a few days a week, and their annual earnings had fallen to $757, compared with $1,639 in 1929. During one year of part-time employment, Wyndham Mortimer, a drill operator in the White Motor Company and later vice president of the UAW, earned only $53.65. "Everybody I knew," he remembered, "was working part-time or not at all."[6]

In anticipation of a general crisis in capitalism, the Communist International turned sharply to the left in 1928. In Moscow in March 1928, a meeting of the Red International of Labor Unions (RILU) that included American representatives decided that "the vital and immediate task" of the TUEL was "to become the leading organization struggling to organize the unorganized." A. Lozovsky, General Secretary of the RILU, urged the Americans to quit "dancing a quadrille" around the AFL and to form new unions, where necessary, to reach the unorganized. Later that year the Sixth Congress of the Communist International declared that after a period of partial stablization, the capitalist world was entering a "Third Period" characterized by economic crisis and revolutionary upsurge. In order to lead the masses in this new period, Communists had to discredit the "social fascist" leaders of traditional unions and Socialist parties and had to organize the workers into "united fronts from below" and into "revolutionary industrial unions."[7]

The new line of the Communist International had major repercussions on the American party. Because of the recent expulsion of Communists and others from the United Mine Workers Union and the International Ladies Garment Workers Union, some sentiment already existed in the TUEL for the creation of new unions. In March 1928, Foster, the head of the TUEL, said, "The organization of the great unorganized masses remains our central task and it must be accomplished either within or without the old trade unions." Jay Lovestone, the general secretary of the party, however, strongly resisted the new line. As a result, he and several hundred of his followers were expelled in 1929. A Secretariat composed of Max Bedacht, Robert Minor, William Weinstone, and Foster assumed the party leadership after Lovestone. Earl Browder replaced Bedacht as administrative secretary in 1930 and was elected the party's general secretary four years later. As part of the changes in 1929 the party adopted a new name, the Communist Party of the United States of America. The same year, the TUEL changed its name to the Trade Union Unity League (TUUL) and placed its main emphasis on organizing new unions in unorganized or partly organized industries. For Communists in auto, the new emphasis produced no dramatic changes, since they already had an independent union. The depression ended any immediate prospects that this union had for successful organizing in the plants.[8]

In 1929, as the coming economic crisis led to cutbacks in production and employment, AWU activity first increased slightly then plummeted sharply. Early in the year the size of the *Auto Workers News* expanded beyond the already large 1928 circulation. In August, Raymond reported that the union was "working in Detroit, Pontiac, Flint, Grand Rapids, and other auto centers," and that union membership was increasing "steadily." As the economic crisis deepened, however, union activity temporarily diminished. AWU organizers found themselves jobless, along with many of the workers they hoped to recruit. In January 1930, union leaders complained that "the lack of organization in the shops" impeded recruitment and the union was failing to "register many permanent organizational gains." The Pontiac local deteriorated from 93 members to less than 15. In Cleveland growing unemployment wiped out all but one of twelve locals, and AWU locals in Grand Rapids, Michigan, and Oakland, California collapsed leaving the union with only "a few contacts."

At an AWU conference on March 8, 1930, attended by 32 delegates representing 1,000 workers, Raymond explained the "difficult problems" confronting the organization and admitted the union's present inability to recruit "substantial numbers of the unskilled" and the "little headway" made in bringing "Negro, women, and young workers into the union." Though the immediate circumstances offered little hope for optimism, Raymond reassured the delegates that "the present period" represented "the best time for organization," since "workers know that conditions are just as bad in other shops, and the only possibility of improvement is through organization."[9]

Meanwhile the Communist party, like the AWU, suffered from the initial blast of the depression. In 1929, the party claimed an overall membership of between 12,000 and 14,000. Ten percent of the members belonged to shop nuclei. By early 1930, the membership dropped sharply to 6,145. Unemployment played havoc with the Communists' central goal of building cells at the work place. Of 6,167 new members recruited to the party between December 10, 1929 and February 28, 1930, most had no jobs. In some districts 75 percent of the new recruits claimed no work place. So inauspicious were the conditions for organizing in the plants and so weak was Communist activity in the plants, that the shop nuclei failed to recruit a single member in late 1929 and early 1930. By September 1931, 25 percent of the party lacked employment. Nine months later the party returned to its former strength of 14,000, but only 94 Communists—less than 1 percent—held jobs in "large factories." In November 1932, the proportion of jobless in the party had increased to 40 percent.[10]

The Detroit district possessed a higher percentage of proletarian members than the party as a whole; consequently, its proportion of unemployed members probably exceeded the party's national average. Communist activity in the auto plants declined sharply until the fall of 1932. In March 1928, 43 percent of the Detroit Communists belonged to auto shop nuclei, but by June

1930 the figure dropped to 21 percent. In 1928 Detroit Communists issued a dozen auto shop papers, but in February 1932 only one appeared, and in April none at all. Though diminishing the opportunities for agitation in the shops, the economic downturn created fresh opportunities for Communist agitation among the growing numbers of the desperate and the hungry.[11]

Though several Communists attempts to organize the unemployed in the 1920s were unsuccessful, the scope of unemployment and the depth of suffering in the winter of 1929–30 made another attempt imperative. Under the aegis of the Trade Union Unity League (TUUL), Communists launched a drive to organize jobless workers into groups eventually known as Unemployed Councils. The Unemployed Councils raised two central slogans: "Don't Starve, Fight!" and "Work or Wages!" The councils had two thrusts: first, to convince the jobless that they should overcome ethnic and racial divisions and unite to struggle against the effects of the depression; and second, to convince people generally that the responsibility of providing relief for the unemployed must rest on the government and the employers. To accomplish this the councils focused agitation on the demand for federal unemployment insurance. In 1929, Detroit Communists shifted their energies from organizing the AWU to organizing Unemployed Councils. Wherever the unemployed gathered—in parks, on breadlines, at factory gates, outside flophouses, soup kitchens, shelters, welfare organizations and relief offices—organizers searched out recruits.[12]

Early in 1930, Communists in the auto centers conducted a number of small demonstrations demanding relief for the jobless. In January, Phil Raymond led a group of 200 unemployed persons to the city hall of Pontiac to demand a meeting with the mayor. When Raymond tried to make a speech on the steps of the building, the police arrested him. On January 29, Fred Beal, the Communist leader of the textile strike of 1929 in the Loray mill in Gastonia, North Carolina, addressed a meeting of 200 people in the Wolverine Hall in Pontiac. Following his speech, the police arrested him. On February 24, George Kristalsky, the Communist candidate for mayor of Hamtramck, led an unemployment demonstration in that largely Polish city which was located within the boundaries of Detroit; the same day other Communists held a similar protest meeting in downtown Detroit's Cadillac Square.[13]

These protests served as a prelude to a call by the Communist party, the Unemployment Council, the Trade Union Unity League, and the Young Communist League for nationwide unemployment demonstrations on March 6, 1930. The demonstration call demanded relief for the jobless, a seven hour day, and a five day week, as well as unemployment insurance financed by employers and the state that would be administered by committees of workers. During the first days of March, Communists distributed leaflets and copies of the *Daily Worker* throughout Detroit's working class neighborhoods.[14]

On the appointed day, thousands of people answered the call in every major American city. In Detroit, despite police warnings to avoid the demonstration, between 50 and 100 thousand people gathered on the streets and sidewalks of the downtown area. Police Commissioner Harold Emmons mobilized the entire Detroit police force of 3,600, including 36 mounted police, 160 motor cycle police, and one armoured riot car. At one o'clock, a group of young Communists standing in front of the Majestic Building pulled signs reading "Don't Starve, Fight" and "Work or Wages" from under their coats, while other Communists began to address the crowd gathered in Campus Martius Square. At that moment the police moved to disperse the crowd. A wild melee ensued. In the words of one witness, "at point after point mounted policemen in groups of three, four, and five rode onto the sidewalks and charged straight into the crowds of orderly, peaceful people." The force of these attacks pushed people through the plate glass windows of stores along Woodward Avenue. Policemen seized placards and knocked their bearers to the pavement. A lead pipe thrown by a demonstrator felled a policeman. For two hours the fighting raged. Finally, to clear the streets, police ordered the drivers of city buses and street cars to go through the crowd that remained.[15]

Demonstrations likewise occurred in other auto centers. A riot, comparable to Detroit's disturbance, took place in Cleveland after the Mayor informed 10,000 to 25,000 demonstrators that he lacked the power to adjust their grievances. A three hour riot in Milwaukee led to 47 arrests and four injuries. In Grand Rapids, 1,500 people held a peaceful protest. Auto workers in Hamtramck, Kalamazoo and Toledo also demonstrated.[16]

In Flint, where the party contained only 22 members, a crowd, estimated by the Chief of Police Caesar Scavarda at 15,000, turned out for the demonstration. Phil Raymond, John Marr and

Leo Thompson, Detroit's AWU leaders, conducted a march from the Chevrolet factory to the city hall. Scavarda later explained to Representatives Carl Bachman and John Nelson of the House Committee to Investigate Communist Activities how he managed to keep the Flint demonstration peaceful.

> MR. SCAVARDA. Yes, Sir. The demonstration in the way the Communists wished, did not take place, due to police preparation, although thousands of persons congregated on the streets in the vicinity of the city hall. As a result of the police preparation, all known and admitted communists in the city were apprehended and locked up.
> MR. BACHMAN. How many were arrested?
> MR. SCAVARDA. Six all told. . . . There was no trouble during the demonstration and the people were kept moving. There was nobody there to lead the demonstration; the leaders were all in jail.
> MR. NELSON. What charge did you make against them that you might arrest them?
> MR. SCAVARDA. There was not any charge.
> MR. NELSON. You just arrested them?
> MR. SCAVARDA. That is all.
> MR. BACHMAN. Why, you arrest them for disorderly conduct, do you not?
> MR. SCAVARDA. Well, possibly that would be a good excuse.[17]

With even fewer scruples and greater efficiency than Scavarda's, the Pontiac chief of police did not wait for the demonstration before making arrests. A week before March 6, his police raided a meeting in a private home, arrested 15 Communists, and placed them in the jails of 15 nearby townships. Consequently, when several thousand people gathered in downtown Pontiac on March 6, no organizers appeared to address them.[18]

The events of March 6 provoked varied but extreme responses. At one extreme, Republican Hamilton Fish warned the House of Representatives that Communists threatened the internal security of the country, and on his recommendation the House established the body, later known as the House Committee on Un-American Activities, to investigate American Communism. At the other extreme, the Detroit Federation of Labor claimed the Detroit protest merely represented the invention of "the fertile brains of the headline writers of the daily newspapers." Similarly, the newspaper editors in Flint and Detroit called the demonstrations a "fiasco" and dismissed the "scores of thousands" who turned out as "curious sightseers," people out to "see the fun," and "mostly gullible folk of limited mentality."[19]

For the Communists, the March 6 demonstrations had two important consequences. First, demonstrations focused national attention on the plight of the jobless. Writing in *Scribners*, Louis Adamic pointed out that the protests had made a front page issue of the unemployment problem, which most newspapers and persons of importance had previously ignored. Second, the protests represented a high-water mark of Communist political influence. The response of auto workers to the March 6 call represented a degree of influence unequaled by the CP in the preceding decade of activity. Using hyperboles that their recent success made understandable, the Communists stated that the demonstrations, "like a thunderstorm clearing the air," had dispelled the illusion of the wellbeing and complacency of the American wage workers and had established the Communist party as "a recognized power; a major, American political factor."[20]

After March 6, Detroit Communists intensified their activities among the unemployed. Phil Raymond, Alfred Goetz, John Marr, Leo Thompson, Nydia Barker, and other Communists active in the AWU formed Unemployed Councils in Detroit, Hamtramck, Lincoln Park, Pontiac, Grand Rapids, and other automotive centers. In Ecorse, outside of Detroit, black Communist, Clarence Oliver, organized a Council composed largely of blacks formerly employed by Ford. In Hamtramck, the Unemployed Council cooperated with several Polish fraternal clubs and used their facilities for biweekly meetings. Lincoln Park's Unemployed Council converted some southern workers with previous Ku Klux Klan allegiances. By 1931, Detroit Communists had created at least 15 Unemployed Councils with a total membership of at least 1,500.[21]

On March 29–30, 1930, representatives of the Detroit Unemployed Councils attended the First Preliminary National Conference on Unemployment in New York City. John Schmies, a German-born auto worker and District Organizer of the CP in Detroit, chaired the conference. The conference adopted a platform for the Unemployed Councils that demanded federal unemployment insurance, federal appropriations for relief, no discrimination because of race, religion or sex in the rehiring of workers, exemption from taxes and mortgage payments for the jobless, and fair distribution of available employment. The Detroit councils later added a demand of their own—free milk for babies. On July 4–5, 1930, worker representatives from Detroit joined 1,320 delegates in Chicago to establish the Unemployed Councils of the U.S.A. The Detroit Unemployed Councils also participated in such national demonstrations as Unemployed Insurance Days on February 25, 1931 and the National Hunger March on December 7, 1931.[22]

On the local level the Unemployed Councils sponsored numerous demonstrations for improved relief. In April 1931, several hundred followers of the Unemployed Councils held a protest at Detroit's city hall, where a delegation to Mayor Frank Murphy demanded better food for the municipal lodging houses and more courtesy from police toward lodging house guests. On the day before Thanksgiving 1931, the Young Communist League led a march of several thousand people to the employment office of one of the Briggs plants, where they demanded jobs and unemployment insurance. The next year the Communists led a demonstration of 10,000 unemployed workers to the Briggs plant on Mack Avenue. When a committee approached the plant to present their demands, 100 policemen stormed out of the plant gates and flailed people with their clubs, while a group of mounted officers rode into the demonstrators. A writer for the *Nation* declared that the police "put down" the protest "with a show of brutality virtually unprecedented in this depression." Such dramatizations of the plight of the jobless auto workers were commonplace in Detroit in the early 30s.[23]

The Unemployed Councils also concentrated on open resistance to evictions of impoverished tenants. An unemployed Detroiter, who had formerly worked at Packard, Kelsey Wheel, Chevrolet and Ford, explained to Edmund Wilson the Communists' procedure: "When there's an eviction about to take place, the people notify the Unemployed Council, and the Communists go around and wait till the sheriff has gone and then move all the furniture back into the house. Then the landlord has to notify the authorities again, and the sheriff has to get a new warrant, and the result is that they never get around to evicting people again. They've got the landlords so buffaloed that the other day a woman called up the Unemployment Council and asked whether she could put her tenants out yet." This auto worker claimed that Detroit Communists had "practically stopped evictions." Bill McKie, who joined the CP while working at Ford's, recalled a tenant who spurned the assistance of the Unemployed Council and attempted to dissuade a deputy sheriff from evicting him by standing on his front porch wrapped in an American flag. Only after this ploy had failed, did he accept the more direct solution of the council. On one occasion, a group of occasion, a group of Communists resisted the eviction of a Polish family so actively that the process required over 100 officers and 19 constables to cordon off an entire residential block. Council organizers also developed the skill of bypassing disconnected gas and electric services. The Detroit Edison Company discovered cases of restored gas and electric service where someone had left a tag behind giving the time and place of a Communist meeting. Such initiative prompted Communist leader, Earl Browder, to praise the Detroit district as the only one in the party to have "really systematically approached" eviction fights.[24]

Of the numerous struggles engaged in by the Unemployed Councils, one assumed an importance above all others, for it resulted in what became known as the Ford Massacre. In February 1932, the Unemployed Councils scheduled a hunger march on the Ford plant in Dearborn for March 7. The plan called for presenting the Ford Motor Company with a list of 14 demands, including demands for: jobs for unemployed Ford workers, a seven hour day with no reduction in pay, a slowing down of "the deadly speed-up," free coal for the winter, free medical service for employed and unemployed Ford Workers at the Ford Hospital, the end to job discrimination against Negroes, relief and medical services, the abolition of the Ford Service Department, and the right to organize. To build support for the march, the Unemployed Councils held a meeting in Detroit the night of March 6, at which TUUL leader, William Z. Foster, addressed several thousand workers.[25]

Even though Monday, March 7, was a cold, blustery day, 1,300 men and women, including some who had lucklessly come to Ford's that morning seeking work, gathered at Fort Street and Oakland Road on the western outskirts of Detroit, two miles from the Ford plant. Alfred Goetz, chairman of the Michigan Unemployed Council, and Joe York, a former auto worker and current district organizer of the YCL, led the crowd down Fort Street across the Baby Creek Bridge. Seventy Detroit police officers stood by watchfully but did not interfere. At Miller Road more people joined the demonstration, swelling its number to 3,000. Goetz hopped on the back of a truck and spoke briefly: "We are not going to the Ford plant to create a disturbance. We are going to present the pressing demands of the workers. But we are going to the Ford plant, and if we are attacked, we will know how to defend ourselves." The demonstrators then proceeded five abreast toward Dearborn. Their banners read: "We Want Bread, Not Crumbs," "Tax the Rich and Feed the Poor," "Fight Against Dumping of Milk While Babies Starve," "All War Funds for Unemployment Relief."

At the Dearborn City line, a brief confrontation occurred between the demonstrators and 50 Dearborn policemen. Charles Slamer, the acting chief of police, demanded to know who the leaders were. From the marchers, the cry went up, "We are all leaders." Slamer then ordered them to stop or be shot. When the protestors pressed forward, officers fired teargas. This gas scattered the front lines, but a swirling wind soon cleared the air before the gas had any effect except to anger its intended victims. In the next instant, a hail of stones and clumps of frozen mud forced the police into a ragged retreat down Miller Road. At the next intersection, firemen tried but failed to hook up their hoses to a fire hydrant, and as the marchers overtook them, they joined the police in backtracking toward the Ford factory.

At Gate 4 outside the Ford complex, policemen, firemen and Ford servicemen prevented the marchers from entering to present their demands to the company's management. Firemen began pouring streams of icy water onto the marchers, who replied with a barrage of stones. According to a worker who was there, "Suddenly the cops began shooting into the crowd with revolvers. . . . The cops seemed to have gone mad and shot left and right into the unarmed crowd. And the workers stood their ground. They continued [to] throw rocks with considerable effectiveness." When the shooting stopped, three men—Joe DeBlasio, Coleman Leny, and Joe York, the nineteen-year old District Organizer of the YCL—lay on the ground dead or dying. To avoid panic, Goetz hopped on the back of a car and began speaking. He said that the bullets were Ford's answer to the demands of the employed and unemployed workers, and he took a vote to leave. While Goetz spoke, a car containing Harry Bennett sped out of the employment office and stopped near the demonstrators. As Bennett emerged from the car waving either a white flag, teargas gun, or revolver, a rock from the crowd hit his head and tumbled him to the ground. The police then aimed a fusillade of 200 to 300 shots at the retreating workers, killing a sixteen-year old boy named Joe Bussell and wounding scores of others. By four in the afternoon, the fighting was over. The demonstrators had smashed most of the windows in the Ford employment office and injured 15 policemen; the police and Ford servicemen had wounded as many as 60 demonstrators and had killed four.[26]

The Dearborn authorities, the Ford Motor Company, and Detroit Prosecutor Harry Toy immediately placed the blame for the bloodshed on the Communists. The Dearborn police charged that the demonstrators had fired first. The Dearborn Public Safety Commission "commended" the police for their "cool judgment." A Ford official asserted that the Company had "no responsibility, since none of its men were involved." Meanwhile, Prosecutor Toy ordered the police to arrest all injured demonstrators and to chain them to their hospital beds. He also issued warrants on charges of criminal syndicalism for the arrest of William Z. Foster and several local Communist leaders, including John Schmies, Detroit District Organizer of the CP. By the end of the day, policemen had jailed 60 suspected Communists and, in search of the fugitive Communist leaders, had raided the headquarters of the CP, the AWU and several fraternal societies.[27]

After the March 6 demonstration two years before, public officials, labor leaders and the press had unanimously criticized the Communists and congratulated the police, but this time public opinion was divided. The *Detroit Free Press* held that "professional Communists alone" were "morally guilty of the assaults and killings." Speaking in Detroit, Joseph W. Sharts, a member of the National Executive Committed of the Socialist party, declared, "I have never noticed the Communist leaders conspicuous where the shooting begins. They spur others on and then disappear." The *Detroit News* called the incident a "tragedy" for which no one bore blame. The *Detroit Times* accused the police of having "changed an orderly demonstration into a riot with death and bloodshed as its toll." After conducting its own, independent investigation, the Detroit Federation of Labor declared that no evidence existed to substantiate police claims that the demonstrators had arms. It blasted the police action as "wanton and disgraceful," and "an indictment not only of its system, but of the leaders of this community." Roger Baldwin of the American Civil Liberties Union declared that the manhunt for Foster only served "to divert public attention from the crimes of those sworn to guard the public peace." Detroit Mayor Frank Murphy, whose police had joined the Dearborn forces in the midst of the fighting, wired the YCL that he was blameless, since the murders occurred outside his jurisdiction. The diversity of opinion reflected the growing social and political divisions in the city.[28]

Though "forced into hiding" by the police raids and threat of arrests, the party leadership immediately mobilized a response to the killings. Maurice Sugar, an extremely capable lawyer connected with the International Labor Defense, took charge of the legal defense work. The party organized a mass protest rally in the Arena Gardens for the following Friday night, at which over 5,000 people heard speeches by a brother of one of the slain men and by representatives of the YCL, the Unemployed Councils, the International Labor Defense. The Communists also arranged a protest funeral for the four dead men. Their bodies were laid in state in Ferry Hall, where several thousand workers came to express their sympathy. Above the coffin hung a huge red banner with a picture of Lenin, one side bore the slogan, "Ford Gave Bullets for Bread," and the other side, "Police Bullets Killed Them." Joe Bussell's mother told mourners, "He was a worker's son, and I am proud that if he had to fall, he fell fighting for the workers." On Saturday, 20,000 people participated in a funeral march down Woodward Avenue. After observing the scene from the thirteenth floor of a downtown building, Oakley Johnson wrote in the *Nation:*

> Witnessed by several thousand spectators, the procession came slowly toward Grand Circus Park, the band in front playing the "Internationale," a massed square of workers carrying a huge red banner with the slogan in white letters, "Smash the Ford-Murphy Police Terror." The funeral cortege of a score of automobiles came next, and after it, as far as I could see up Woodward Avenue, workers in mass formation, carrying banners.

Later that day, the four men were buried in a common grave in Woodmere Cemetery overlooking the Ford factory.[29]

Before 1933, the Communists unquestionably achieved their widest influence among auto workers through the struggles of the Unemployed Councils. In the week after the Ford Massacre, for example, the YCL received 40 applications for membership, and for a time, young men on the north side of Detroit reportedly greeted each other on the street with clenched fist salutes. Moreover, in the three months following the massacre, the party in Detroit recruited 450 new members, and in the first nine months of 1932, over 920 new members. As always, the party recruited many more people than it retained. Still, by August 1932, the Detroit party had 800 members, a gain of 230 since 1928. These numbers, however, were but a small reflection of the thousands of people that the Communists drew into eviction fights and unemployment demonstrations. In May 1931, a year before the dramatic confrontation at Ford, Mauritz Hallgren, writing in the *Nation*, estimated that the Communist party had 30,000 sympathizers in Detroit.[30]

Two major reasons accounted for the leap in Communist influence in the early 1930s. First, unemployment and its accompanying difficulties shook many jobless workers' confidence in the existing social and political system. A survey of unemployed workers revealed that nearly 25 percent of them (four times as many as employed workers) felt that "a revolution might be a good thing for this country." Second, for these radicalized people, the Communists had answers, a program, and a plan of action. At a time when leaders of labor, business, and government manifested complacency, confusion, and paralysis in the face of widespread suffering, the Communists proposed concrete actions—demonstrations and eviction fights—on behalf of a concrete program such as unemployment insurance and federally financed relief. Moreover, in the theory of socialism and the experience of the Soviet Union, the Communists offered a long-term resolution to the problem of capitalist economic crises.[31]

These reasons for Communist influence were discovered by three writers who visited Detroit in 1931 and 1932—Charles R. Walker of *Survey*, Mauritz Hallgren of the *Nation,* and Edmund Wilson of *New Republic.* Each noted the radicalization of unemployed auto workers and the appeal of Communist ideas and activism. When Walker visited the city, he found despairing auto workers, who had come to Detroit years before to take advantage of the high wages, but who, in 1931, faced endless unemployment, foreclosed homes, and dissolving families. Such workers expressed extreme bitterness toward "the 'big shots'—meaning all presidents of banks, the heads and high officials of the automobile companies, and of course Mr. Ford." Walker discovered that "masses of starving workmen" who had trusted in the city for relief the previous winter were now "turning to other sources of leadership and hope":

> I attended a meeting of unemployed workers on the outskirts of Detroit in the local schoolhouse. The speaker was telling about Soviet Russia. A little man behind me kept shouting in my ear: "They've got a better system than we've got." I turned around and looked into a strong American face. "Are you a Communist?" I asked. "Hell, no," he said, "I'm a Roman Catholic; how can I be a Communist? But they've got a better system than we've got."

Similarly, when Hallgren visited Detroit shortly after the Ford Hunger March of 1932, he discovered that the Communists had made "deep inroads" among Detroit workers, who were "impressed by the vigor and promptness" with which the Communists organized "demonstrations against wage-cuts, reduction in relief expenditures, and the dictatorship of the bankers." Wilson made comparable discoveries. An unemployed, Scottish-born auto worker told him: "What we ought to have here [in Detroit] is a revolutionary movement geared into the particular needs of the American worrukers [workers], and I will say quite frankly that if it isn't the Communist Party, I don't see any other elements in the country who will supply it."[32]

Though the Communists continued to organize the unemployed, this activity had decidedly less importance after 1932 than before. By June 1933, the CP reported that unemployment activity in Detroit had begun "to slump" and by the fall of the year the party reported that the city's Unemployed Councils were "completely out of existence." Several circumstances contributed to this decline. Because the unemployed workers typically had less stable lives and less permanent grievances than employed workers, the Unemployed Councils possessed less viability than unions. Moreover, as the depression wore on the initial shock and anger of many of the unemployed gave way to despair and resignation. Others found hope or illusions in Roosevelt's New Deal. Moreover, in 1933, Communists and others who had been active in the unemployed struggles began to turn their attention again to the shops, where early in the year a sudden outburst of spontaneous strikes and the AFL's decision to launch an organizing drive presaged the coming struggle for unionization.[33]

# IV
### • • •
# THE BRIGGS STRIKE

Before the formation of the UAW, the high point of Communist union activity in the automobile industry occurred in the Briggs strike of 1933. The Briggs strike and several related auto strikes occurring at the same time represented the most important walkouts of auto workers in the pre-union era. Occurring early in 1933, the strike wave indicated that a mass, rudimentary sentiment for unionization among auto workers existed before the passage of President Roosevelt's New Deal labor legislation and before the AFL initiated a drive to organize the industry. During the decade preceding the 1933 strikes, the Communists represented the most active union force in the industry, and the AWU prepared and led the walkouts. The 1933 strikes, thus, underscored the importance of Communist influence in the preunion era of the auto workers' history.

As part of the switch to the Third Period line, the Communists' Auto Workers Union affiliated with the Trade Union Unity League. On August 24, 1929 in Detroit at a conference attended by fifty-seven representatives of thirty-seven shop committees and addressed by William Z. Foster and Jack Johnstone, the AWU selected delegates to a convention to form the TUUL. This convention took place in Cleveland on August 31 and September 1, 1929. The 690 delegates to the convention elected Foster as general secretary of the TUUL and the auto worker, John Schmies, as assistant secretary and treasurer. The convention declared that the TUUL's "main task" was "the organization of the unorganized into industrial unions independent of the A.F. of L." The convention favored a "militant strike policy" and adopted the central slogan, "Class Against Class." Its program included the slogans: defend the Soviet Union, fight against capitalist rationalization, organize the unorganized, for the seven-hour day, five-day week, for social insurance, for full racial, social and political equality for Negroes, organize the youth and the women, defeat the misleaders of labor. In spite of the enthusiasm with which it was formed, the TUUL had little immediate affect on organizing in auto. An AWU convention in Detroit on March 8, 1930 drew only thirty-two delegates representing 1,000 workers in five cities. This was a smaller conference than six months before.[1]

The depression made it impossible for the Communists to implement the TUUL trade union program. Indeed, the massive unemployment in the auto industry nearly wiped out the gains the Communists had made during the 1920s. Reports in the *Party Organizer* indicated that the auto shop nuclei nearly disappeared. In October 1931, when a Fisher Body plant shut down in Cleveland, the shop nucleus of ten members "Dropped all activity for two months." In 1931, a Communist working in "a large automobile factory" in Detroit reported that he "was the only party member" in his department. A Communist working in a Fisher Body plant reported that in December 1931, when the plant reopened after a shutdown, the nucleus had only three employed members. By early 1932, the auto nuclei were issuing only two shop papers, *Spark Plug* (Fisher Body in Cleveland) and *Ford Worker* (Detroit). Similarly, unemployment reduced the membership and activity of the AWU. In July 1932, John Schmies, head of Party District 7 (Detroit), declared, "Until lately the Auto Workers Union, you might as well say, did not exist. Whatever attempts were made to build the union were a flop."[2]

Outside the plants the Communists had remained active. Between 1929 and 1933, besides organizing the unemployed, Detroit Communists also ran candidates in local and state elections. In 1930, for example, Phil Raymond ran for mayor of Detroit on a platform that opposed evictions and favored the Workers Insurance Bill, full equality for Negro workers, and the right of workers to organize without police interference. Also, the YCL engaged in such activities outside the shops as forming a sports club to involve young workers in baseball and boxing. The party also continued to sell the *Daily Worker;* between November and December 1930 the number of subscribers to the paper in Detroit rose from 752 to 860. In November 1932 the Communists began publishing the *Michigan Worker,* a bimonthly and later weekly newspaper. The only major union activity in which the Communists became involved occurred in 1930, when the AWU supported a spontaneous strike of workers in the Fisher Body No. 1 plant in Flint, Michigan.[3]

The Fisher Body strike began on the morning of July 1, 1930, when 200 metal finishers in the Fisher Body Plant No. 1 walked off the job to protest a reduction of piece rates. Although the union had followers and sympathizers in the Flint plants, no party or union member initiated the walkout. By noon, however, Communists from Detroit arrived and began circulating leaflets calling for a meeting at Tilden Hall. At the meeting, Raymond led a discussion on the ways to organize and spread the strike. He urged the 200 workers present to use militant mass picketing and to form "a fighting unit of workers to overwhelm the government and the capitalists." With the help of AWU organizers, the workers developed plans to broaden the protest. The next morning the original strikers marched through Plant No. 1 disrupting work, persuading many of the remaining 7,400 employees to join the strike, and forcing the company to close down the entire operation. When the swelled ranks emerged from the factory, Nydia Barker, a young Communist, who later became a recording secretary of the Detroit DeSoto local of the UAW, and Henry Albertini, an Italian-born Communist and former Wobbly, led a march through the streets to the nearby Buick plant, where workers on their lunch break swelled the crowd to nearly 18,000. When Barker and another Communist, William Siroko, attempted to address the gathering, Flint police arrested them. Strikers and sympathizers then proceeded peacefully to the Dixie Dance Hall outside the city limits, where Jack Stachel of the International Labor Defense and representatives of the TUUL spoke to the strikers, signed up members for the AWU, and arranged for mass picketing the next day.

At 5:00 the next morning picket lines began assembling before the gates of Fisher No. 1. The crowd grew to hundreds and then thousands, spilling into the streets and blocking traffic. This time blood flowed. Backed by Michigan state troopers, the Flint police charged, on horse and on foot into the crowd, dispersing it, in the words of Police Chief Caesar Scarvada, with "a considerable amount of violence." Scarvada's men arrested 11 people including three Communists—Phil Raymond, Steve Miller, and Louise Morrison. That night the police raided the local offices of the AWU, confiscated its records, and arrested two members of the YCL.

On the following day, a Sunday, the strikers held a picnic. The police raided the festivities and arrested four Communists. Undaunted, the strikers and the few remaining Communists planned more mass picketing for Monday. Outwitting police efforts to prevent them from congregating, between 7,000 and 8,000 people gathered at the Fisher No. 1 gates at the beginning of the first shift. Again the police moved in. They dispersed the picket line and chased some of the picketers as far as the Oakland County line which was eighteen miles from the plant. By the end of the day, half the workers returned to the job. On Tuesday, the remaining strikers called off the protest. The AWU effort failed. Despite the Fisher Body Company's promises to refrain from reprisals, it dismissed the local strike leaders.

The experience, daring, and energy of the AWU organizers failed to compensate for the union's limited numbers and resources, and the lack of previous organization among the workers. Nor could the union surmount the solid wall of opposition from the employers, press, and police, who shared the belief of Fisher Body Manager, A. B. Whiting, that the "entire trouble" resulted from "foreign agitators and Communists," and this justified any expedient to crush the uprising. During the strike, the Communists failed to enjoy even elementary civil liberties; the police arrested them for offenses no more insurrectionary than attempting to speak in public. After the strike, police chief Scarvada proclaimed that thwarting Communism required him to "violate the law" and that, if necessary, he would "continue to do [so]." Despite these handicaps, the AWU recruited over 350 people during the course of the conflict. Six years later, the workers of Fisher Body No. 1 spearheaded the great General Motors sit-down strike.[4]

In 1931, with the encouragement of the Communist International, the CP developed a policy of "concentration" designed to focus the party's activity on "the most decisive industries"—mine, steel, textile, marine, and auto. As "areas of concentration," the party selected Cleveland, Chicago, Pittsburgh, and Detroit. At this time the mass unemployment had so decimated the party's shop nuclei that less than one percent of the party's 14,000 members worked "in large factories." The strategy of concentration was designed to overcome this "isolation of the Party from the decisive masses of the American proletariat." Cleveland Communists selected the Fisher Body plant as a focal point, and Detroit Communists directed their efforts toward the two most notorious auto plants, Ford and Briggs. As part of this policy, the Communists soon sent William Weinstone, Nat Ganley, Max Salzman, and others from New York to Detroit, and the Communists in Michigan placed auto workers in charge of the party sections in Flint and on the east side and west side of Detroit. In 1932, a slight upturn in production enabled the Communists to rekindle their activity in these plants.[5]

The Communist efforts in 1932 shared much in common with their efforts in the 1920s. The shop units continued to publish shop papers. Though in each month during most of 1932 only one or two units managed to put out a paper, two new papers appeared in the summer of 1932, the *Ternstedt Workers Bulletin* and the *Young Ford Worker.* As more Communists became active in the shops, more papers appeared. By 1935 there were 14 auto shop papers, and between May 1935 and January 1936, twelve shop units in Michigan put out 22 different issues. Besides putting out shop papers, the units engaged in other activity. John Mack, in one of the Briggs plants, described the typical operation of his unit. The unit consisted of ten members in a department of 700 workers. It met once or twice a week. "In our meetings we discussed what we did in the last week, what contacts we met, the experiences we had and what successes and what mistakes we made. We would discuss methods of approach [to other workers] and plan our work for the following week." The unit made a list of all the workers in the department, decided whom to ask to join the party and whom to ask to buy the *Daily Worker,* party tickets, and pamphlets. In one year the unit sold $325 in *Daily Worker* subscriptions, 350 tickets for party affairs, and 100 pamphlets. Mack reported, "We have gained our sympathizers' confidence, who feel that we know what we are doing, and that we take our work seriously, not exposing ourselves or them [to company reprisals]."[6]

Besides recruiting party members in the shops, the nuclei also tried to set up shop committees or rudimentary union structures and to involve the workers in struggles around their immediate grievances. Often even tiny units produced an astounding amount of agitation. In a Fisher Body plant, a unit of three Communists sold pamphlets and pasted stickers on walls and machinery. In conjunction with a street nuclei of non-workers, the unit held weekly shop gate meetings and distributed literature at the gates. It also passed petitions in the shop for unemployment insurance and for the freedom of Tom Mooney, a labor organizer, who was convicted on perjured testimony of having thrown a bomb that killed eleven people at a Preparedness Day Parade in San Francisco in 1916. The unit then visited the homes of the petition signers, where the Communists discussed "unsatisfactory conditions" with the workers and tried to recruit them to the nucleus. Between December 1931 and March 1932, the nucleus recruited twelve new members. This nucleus then led a short strike in a department of 30 piece workers and succeeded in winning the removal of an overbearing straw boss. According to a nucleus member, "The victory caused the workers from that department to look upon our comrade [who led the protest] as their group leader."[7]

The extent of nuclei activity was all the more remarkable for the obstacles they faced. According to a Communist at Ford, religious beliefs and racial prejudices kept many workers from joining the Communists. This problem was compounded by the political inexperience of many Communists in the shops. Many Communists reportedly lacked the ability to answer workers' questions "about the activity of our Party, about the Soviet Union, about capitalism and Communism." Even sympathetic workers had trouble with the party slogan, "Every evening to Party work." The rigorous demands of party life contributed to yet another obstacle, "the wife question." According to a Communist at Ford, "There is much trouble on this. When we already thought we had a member in our unit, suddenly the wife shows up, and he says the wife does not allow him to read the *Daily Worker*. The wife does not allow him to join the union or the Party. . . . The comrades working in the shops must be absolutely clear as to how to handle this problem and get the worker into the organization despite the wife, or help him convince his wife to join."[8]

The main obstacle to party and union work in the shops remained the companies' espionage systems. The *Party Organizer* contained numerous reports of workers dismissed for political or union activity. The threat of detection increased after the Ford Massacre of March 1932, when the Ford Service Department "fine-tooth-combed" the plant for radicals, and "many of the most militant workers were fired from the shops." Fear of detection and dismissal forced Communists to adopt a conspiratorial mode of operation. The party advised nuclei members to identify themselves as Communists only to "sympathetic workers." It admonished young Communists who advertised their beliefs by "going-without-hats" and affecting "a certain type of careless dress and get-up." Ingenious methods of agitation evolved to circumvent the espionage network. Max Salzman, a Communist in charge of organizing at the Ford Rouge plant, reported that the Communists there painted signs on viaducts leading to the plant, stuck leaflets to machines moving along the conveyor belt, distributed tiny flyers disguised as Christmas seals, and installed rolls of toilet paper containing leaflets inside company bathrooms. Also, on several occasions outside supporters distributed between 10,000 and 15,000 leaflets on streetcars and highways leading to the Ford plant. Although the conspiratorial mode dominated nuclei activity in the shops, whenever a crisis situation demanded action, the nuclei members had to be prepared "to appear in their true colors before the workers even at the risk of arrest and dismissal."[9]

The Briggs Manufacturing Company provided a natural choice for Communist concentration. The body workers were the most militant group within the auto work force because body building had originally required highly skilled labor—mill hands, framers, panelers, molders, metal finishers, trimmers, painters, and stripers; these workers had enjoyed high wages, independence and pride. By 1933, the body workers still contained the most skilled craftsmen in the industry, including the highly skilled tool and die workers, but the mechanization of the 1920s had deprived other skilled body workers of a privileged position. Consequently, an observer noted in 1933: "The body workers, with high wage traditions behind them fiercely resist the downward trend of wages. They have not lost the independent spirit they had when they were skilled workers and therefore invariably take the initiative in resisting worsening conditions." The highest concentration of body workers existed in Briggs, the largest independent manufacturer of automobile bodies, frames and stampings. Briggs built auto bodies for Chrysler, Hudson, Graham-Paige, and above all, Ford, which obtained 43 percent of its auto bodies from Briggs. The Briggs Company had four plants in Detroit—Vernor Highway (also known as Waterloo), Highland Park, Mack Avenue, and Meldrum Avenue—and employed over 10,000 workers. In spite of the depression, Briggs made substantial profits in 1932 and 1933.[10]

The Briggs plants had notoriously bad working conditions. On April 23, 1927, a fire originating in the painting process had destroyed a large building at the Harper Avenue plant and had killed 21 workers. The workers, who referred to Briggs as the "butcher shop," complained about dangerous working conditions, low wages, speedup, and dead time (periods of production stoppages for which the workers received no wages). A fact finding committee appointed during the 1933 strike by Detroit Mayor Frank Murphy found such complaints "in many respects well-founded." The workers also complained about company "rackets"—the sickness and accident insurance, the welfare fund, and the sale of tools and identification badges. The cost of these items was deducted from the workers' paychecks by the company. A leaflet issued during the strike showed a photostatic copy of a worker's paycheck, which because of dead time and deductions amounted to only forty-nine cents for two weeks employment. Briggs workers also complained about the arduous work and long hours, sometimes as long as sixteen hours a day. According to one worker, a typical Briggs worker went home "completely exhausted" at the end of a day's work, "threw himself on the bed, laid down and rested, maybe ate his supper, and went to bed again, and could perform no social activity whatsoever in the course of the week."[11]

In November 1932, the Communists began the concerted agitation at Briggs that eventually led to a strike. At the end of the month they held the first meeting of the AWU at Briggs Waterloo, a plant employing about 500 highly skilled body workers. Only two workers showed up. Another meeting a week later attracted four workers. At these meetings discussion centered on the plant's recent wage cut as well as other grievances, and members composed a small leaflet to pass from hand to hand in the shop. On December 18, AWU members distributed small, typewritten slips of paper to other workers asking them to organize and fight against low wages, long hours, speedup, and layoffs. At the beginning of January, when the Waterloo unit of the AWU learned of a wage cut at the Briggs Mack Avenue plant, it decided to call a clandestine meeting of carefully selected workers to mobilize sentiment against an anticipated cut at the Waterloo plant. Twenty-eight workers attended this meeting on Monday, January 9. These workers decided to organize a strike, if the wage cut materialized. They also set up a shop gate meeting for the following day. At noon the next day, Phil Raymond, head of the AWU, gave a brief speech outside the plant on the need to organize a strike if Briggs again cut wages, and then according to previous plans a waiting car whisked him away minutes before the police arrived to disperse the gathering. That night 60 Waterloo workers attended a union meeting that developed plans and elected a strike committee to initiate a work stoppage, if the company tried to cut wages.

At 11:30 Wednesday morning, January 11, the company announced a 20 percent wage cut. The strike committee immediately notified all floors to stop work, and the workers walked out. That afternoon a mass meeting of strikers, chaired by Phil Raymond, added new members to the strike committee, including three officials of the AWU and a representative of the Communist-led Unemployed Councils. The participants at the meeting drew up a list of demands, elected a twelve-man negotiations committee, and established a picket committee. Nearly all the day and night shift workers joined the walkout. On Thursday, the strikers picketed, distributed leaflets at the other Briggs plants, and held a mass meeting in the evening. On Friday, the negotiations committee reached an agreement with the management that a mass meeting of strikers voted to accept. The Briggs management agreed to rescind the wage cut and to take back all workers without discrimination for strike activity. At the ratification meeting, strike leaders called upon the workers to join the AWU, and 178 did so on the spot. *Federated Press* reporter, Joe Brown, called the strike, "A clean cut victory." While noting that the majority of the strikers did not belong to the AWU and that members of the Industrial Workers of the World (IWW) and Socialist party had participated in the strike, Brown declared that "the A.W.U. is entitled to credit for taking the initiative." Brown also noted that the Waterloo victory had an "electric" effect on other auto workers and proved "that strikes could be won even during a depression."[12]

Although the local newspapers carried no reports of the Briggs

Waterloo strike, news of the victory spread to other plants and helped trigger a series of strikes in January and February. On Friday, January 20, one week after the Waterloo settlement, between 900 and 1,400 of the 3,000 workers in the Detroit Motor Products plant engaged in a spontaneous walkout in response to a wage cut ranging from 15 to 35 percent. A mass meeting of strikers summoned Phil Raymond and the AWU to lead the strike. Raymond used the same tactics as he used in the Briggs Waterloo strike. After a three-day walkout, the company agreed to rescind the wage cut, to eliminate dead time, to recognize grievance and shop committees elected by the workers, and to rehire strikers without discrimination. Joe Brown declared, "If that is not a victory, a definition of the word 'victory' would be welcomed."[13]

At the same time a short strike occurred at the Hayes body plant in Grand Rapids. The Hayes plant, a body supplier for Continental Motors, had a small coterie of AWU members who operated through the existing company union. Raymond had visited the AWU members early in the year and helped them organize a confrontation with the management that secured a 10 percent wage increase. According to Raymond, "Everybody knew who engineered the whole thing. Soon after that there was a mass entering of the union." The day after the Motor Products strike began, 450 Hayes workers conducted a strike against a wage cut and eventually won another 10 percent wage increase. At the time of the Hayes strike AWU workers included Bud Simons and Walter Moore, men who helped lead the General Motors sit-down strike of 1936–37 in the Fisher Body 1 plant.[14]

After these walkouts, AWU members in the Detroit Hudson plants began to create strike sentiment. To avert a strike, Hudson closed its plants on January 30. When the plant reopened on February 7, Hudson fired two union men, "Curley" and "Bodycotee." The dismissals sparked a walkout of 3,000 workers in the body plant. Though the strike was spontaneous, the workers summoned Phil Raymond and other AWU representatives to a mass meeting. According to Joe Brown, a dispute arose among the strikers over Raymond's leadership after Raymond attempted "to put over C. P. Propaganda." According to Brown, the CP propaganda consisted of nothing more than a statement in which Raymond said, "We must have solidarity between the workers both white and black." The dispute arose when a striker from Arkansas interrupted Raymond to say: "We don't want any of that nigger lovin' stuff." The dispute over Raymond resulted in his stepping aside the next day, but it resulted in neither a rejection of the Communists nor the union, since the strikers then chose as their leader, John Schmies, district organizer of the CP. According to Brown, the "Auto Workers Union had control of the strike from beginning to end." Eventually some 4,000 workers in both the main and body plants became involved in what Hudson vice-president, Max F. Wollering, called "the first walk-out in the history of the Hudson company." After five days, the company agreed to demands for a wage increase, relief time, new stock and tools, and no victimization of strikers. In spite of the fact that Hudson refused to rehire the two dismissed workers, the strikers nonetheless accepted the company offer as a victory and returned to work. Three hundred and fifty strikers joined the union.[15]

The high point of the strike wave occurred during the third week of January, when 6,000 workers in the four Detroit Briggs plants went on strike and 4,000 workers in the Murray Body company turned a lockout into a strike. This series of strikes began on Sunday, January 22, when metal finishers in two departments at the Briggs Highland Park plant walked off the job. About 30 representatives of the metal finishers went to the Finnish Hall in Detroit where the AWU was holding a conference "to fight against wage-cuts and speed-up and for jobs and relief." The delegates met with Raymond and asked for the assistance of the AWU in organizing a walkout to demand, among other things, a basic minimum rate of fifty-three cents an hour, and the abolition of dead time. The conference pledged its support to the metal finishers, and the union advised them to return to work the next day and to bring the rest of the plant out on strike. On Monday morning the metal finishers at Highland Park led a walkout of between 2,000 and 4,000 workers. Anthony Gerlack and John Mack of the AWU rented a hall and organized mass meetings at which the strikers elected a 45 man strike committee, drew up a list of demands, and prepared picket lines. Meanwhile, AWU members at the Mack Avenue plant stirred up strike sentiment there and on Tuesday morning led a walkout of between 4,000 and 6,000 workers. A mass meeting of Mack Avenue strikers selected Phil Raymond to lead the strike. That night the two groups of strikers selected a joint strike committee. The strikers demanded the abolition of the rackets, dead time, and the bonus system; the institution of a forty cents an hour minimum wage, a nine hour day and five-day week, and time and a half for overtime; the recognition of shop and grievance committees; and no victimization of strikers. By the end of the week workers at Briggs Waterloo, Briggs Meldrum, and Murray Body joined the strike. While an improvement of wages and conditions soon ended the Murray strike, the Briggs strike defied early resolution.[16]

Several circumstances differentiated the Briggs strike from the other walkouts and resulted in its lasting longer, becoming more bitter, and ending less successfully than the others. The Briggs strike followed several successful strikes and involved many more workers than the earlier ones. Also, unlike the other strikes, the Briggs strike was less a response to such specific grievances as a wage cut than it was a response to general discontent. Thus, encouraged both by the recent victories of other workers and by the magnitude of their own walkout, the Briggs strikers were determined to fight for a list of far-reaching demands. Since the great number involved in the strike would have made a wage settlement costly and agreement to the strikers' demands would have been tantamount to union recognition, the Briggs management became determined to resist the strike.

Both sides drew hard lines. During the first week of the strike, Briggs promised to eliminate dead time and to reinstitute a guaranteed minimum hourly rate for piece workers. The workers, however, rejected this offer as insufficient and insisted on the satisfaction of their other demands as well. Then Briggs declared that the strike was Communist-inspired and refused to meet with the strikers "for any purpose whatsoever." Briggs informed the Mayor's fact finding committee that it would "never" change its "position that all grievances must be heard individually through the foremen or through designated company officials when the men had returned to work. No opportunity for workmen's representation would ever be given." Briggs's position, of course, reflected the prevailing attitude among auto manufacturers, and the company's adamancy may well have reflected its dependence on Ford. Department of Labor conciliator, Robert Pilkington, believed that orders from the large firms were "contingent upon the Briggs Company's successful resistance to any plan of settlement that might involve union recognition in any form." Briggs treasurer, Judge William F. Connolly, declared: "In a city this size, there are so many men unemployed we should have no serious difficulty in obtaining capable workmen. . . . [We] will not allow the Communist-led strikers to hang Philip Raymond's red flag on the Briggs Manufacturing Company. Should we allow these people to continue with their strike, it would be another victory for the Communists. Our position, we feel, is more or less that of a lead-off man in a baseball game. We felt this strike would continue right down through the automobile industry."[17]

During the first week pressure mounted on the strikers. Henry Ford announced that the strike was "the biggest surprise" of his career, and in a move that the strikers perceived as an attempt to turn public sympathy against them, Ford closed plants around the country, laying off 150,000 workers. The Detroit *Free Press* accused the strikers of "depriving" these "men and women in other plants of the means of livelihood." Hundreds of policemen, deputy sheriffs, special deputies, and state troopers patrolled the Mack and Highland Park plants and arrested strikers for yelling at scabs. On Friday, January 27, Briggs announced that the strikers had until Monday to return to work; at that time Briggs would begin hiring new workers. Detroit's "radio priest," Father Coughlin, urged the strikers to return to work. In spite of the pressure against them, the strikers held together for the first two weeks.[18]

Because of their ability to call on outside resources otherwise unavailable to the strikers, the Communists played a particularly important role early in the conflict. Besides the initial AWU organizers—Raymond, Gerlack, and Mack—Communists John Schmies, Andrew Overgaard, John Anderson, Bill McKie, Nydia Barken, and Will Parry aided the strike committee in various ways. All had previous organizing experience with the AWU and Unemployed Councils. The Communist Unemployed Councils played an important role in influencing the unemployed not to scab on the strikers. During the first week of the strike, the Unemployed Councils issued handbills and called a mass meeting of the unemployed to support the strike. On Monday, January 30, the day on which Briggs planned to hire new workers, the Unemployed Councils helped mobilize massive demonstrations at both the Mack Avenue and Highland Park plants. Of the 10,000 people who turned out at the Mack Avenue plant, nearly half marched with the Unemployed Councils on the south side of Mack Avenue.

They carried banners with such inscriptions as "The unemployed won't scab on the strikers" and "The unemployed will help to win the strike." At the Highland Park plant, where the strike committee and Unemployed Councils led thousands in mass picketing, Joe Brown observed, "Strikers holding solidly. No evidence that the unemployed will scab." The Communists also helped the strikers obtain legal aid. On the second day of the strike Raymond put the strikers' Legal Defense Committee in touch with Carl Dunning of the International Labor Defense (ILD). The ILD contributed $48.50 to the strike fund, offered the strikers assistance in soliciting local liberals for contributions, and supplied the services of the Detroit labor lawyer, Maurice Sugar.[19]

Even though the AWU, the Unemployed Councils, and the International Labor Defense represented the most active, visible and well-organized groups, a variety of other political and labor organizations also became involved in the walkout. Frank Cedervall, an IWW member chosen by the strikers to give daily "pep talks," later recalled: "Everyone was in there paddling his oar trying to get members. . . . Every shade of radical of every possible opinion was there." Four Wobblies, Leon Pody, John W. Anderson, John Oneka, and Cedervall belonged to the strike committee at the Highland Park plant. They organized a relief committee that acquired "enormous quantities of food stuffs" for the strikers. A few members of the Socialist party and the Proletarian party also participated in the strike. During the strike's second week SP leader, Norman Thomas, addressed a rally outside the Highland Park plant and helped obtain a $100 donation to the strike committee. Besides the political radicals, the Detroit Federation of Labor "endorsed" the strike, and skilled workers belonging to the Metal Finishers Union, the International Association of Machinists, and the independent Dingmen's Welfare Club (made up of workers who removed imperfections from auto bodies) joined the walkout. Followers of A. J. Muste's Conference for Progressive Labor Action became particularly active at the Mack Avenue plant, where they eventually assumed control of the strike committee. Led by George Cornell, this group formed the short-lived American Industrial Association for Briggs workers in the spring of 1933.[20]

Given the array of forces on both sides, a complete victory by the Briggs strikers was probably unachievable. Such a victory would have been tantamount to union recognition, and neither

Briggs nor the large auto firms on which it depended were pre-pared for this. Moreover, a huge pool of potential scabs existed; according to the Mayor's Unemployment Committee at least 175,000 jobless workers lived in Detroit at the time. During the second week of the strike, Briggs began hiring new employees, and by the end of the second week the company had reportedly enrolled 3,000 workers at the Mack Avenue plant and had enough production to begin limited deliveries. Though strikers attempted to dissuade scabs and once swarmed over three trucks leaving the plant and destroyed their contents of floor panels, the strikers failed to prevent the increasing use of scabs or subsequent de-liveries of products. Moreover, the Detroit Federation of Labor provided nothing but verbal support, and the AWU lacked suf-ficient material resources to sustain a long strike.[21]

Though the obstacles facing the strike made an unqualified victory improbable, the strike might well have ended more hap-pily than it did, had not redbaiting attacks against Phil Raymond and the other strike leaders divided and weakened the movement. From the start, opposition to the AWU as a "Communist union" emerged among some workers. Slim Darrow, the head of the picket committee, represented the major spokesman of this view-point. Raymond tried to assuage such misgivings by assuring the strike committee that he was present not as a Communist but as an organizer. "I emphatically deny," Raymond told a Detroit *News* reporter, "that the industrial disturbances now going on at the Briggs and other Detroit automobile plants is [*sic*] Republican, Democratic, Socialistic, Communistic or of any other political character. . . . The ranks of the Auto Workers Union is [made] up of men of all political and religious creeds. We make no discrimina-tion. Of course we have a lot of Communists, just as we have a lot of Democrats." For a week, the strike committee resisted the anti-Communist aspersions of Darrow and others. In a statement to the press, the strike committee declared: "Briggs officials are not fighting the Communists in this case, because we are not Communists. We called upon Phil Raymond only as an organizer of the automobile workers' union and it is only in this capacity that he is acting." When the local press erroneously reported that a strike meeting had excluded John Schmies, the strike committee announced: "We know he [Schmies] is a Communist but he is part of us and we will work with him. . . . Raymond, Gerlach and the

Auto Workers union are part of the strike movement and the union is leading the strike."[22]

Soon sentiment turned against the Communists. In the second week of the walkout, after the police had arrested Raymond on a charge of criminal syndicalism, the Mack Avenue strike committee eliminated him from the leadership. Then the leadership removed all known Communists from strike committees. On February 8, the strike committee announced: "We have definitely eliminated the Communists and their allied organizations in general and Phil Raymond, secretary of the Auto Workers' Union in particular, from among us. We believe that if the officials of the company will meet with representatives of the men and discuss the differences with fair and open mind, the strike can be settled within a few hours." From that point on, non-Communists George Cornell, Earl Bailey, and Robert Darrow, assumed charge of the strike.[23]

Three developments explained the removal of the Communists. Most importantly, at the beginning of the second week of the strike, a sudden barrage of outside attacks against the Communist leadership occurred. These attacks implied that the Communists represented an obstacle to a settlement. On Monday, January 30, an editorial in the Detroit *Free Press* warned the strikers "to guard against exploitation by professional agitators who thrive through the fomentation of industrial trouble." The same day a Briggs spokesman charged that the strike was "Communist inspired, Communist planned, and Communist led." The next day, Briggs told Pilkington, the Department of Labor mediator, that it refused to deal with a strike committee that was "Communistic," and the press reported that Pilkington was "seeking to find a committee which is not." At the same time the Detroit Federation of Labor announced that the strikers' "greatest mistake" consisted of "permitting the Communists to inject themselves into their movement." Such outside pressure turned the strike committee against the Communists. According to Raymond, the non-Communist members of the strike committee began to think that if they got rid of a few people, the Briggs management would deal with them.[24]

The second source of anti-Communist sentiment was the variety of radical and labor groups involved in the strike. Socialists, Wobblies, and others criticized the Communists for involving the unemployed in the picket lines, and for raising the issues of black and white unity and unemployment insurance. According to one strike participant, "In their endeavors to prove that the C. P. members have no race prejudice, they [the Communists] lean over backwards at times." The same participant noted that unemployment insurance "was not a demand of the Briggs' strikers." Since such Communist behavior hardly warranted the exclusion of Communists, criticism of the Communists stemmed in part from ideological differences and sectarian jealousy.[25]

Anti-Communist sentiment derived from a third source, the Communists' own mistakes. In some ways, Raymond and the other local Communists acted too opportunistically. Andrew Overgaard and Jack Stachel were probably at least partially correct when they asserted that Raymond and the others erred in trying to defuse the redbaiting by passing themselves off as "hired experts," instead of attacking the redbaiters and "bringing forward the Auto Workers Union as the organization that organized the strike." Yet, even more damaging than such opportunism was the party's sectarianism. The party's Third Period orientation produced a mistrust of "social fascists" and an arrogant attitude among some Communist leaders that mitigated against an effective united front during the strike. After Norman Thomas addressed strikers at the Highland Park plant, the AWU issued a sectarian leaflet that attacked the Socialist leader and that claimed the company wanted to use Thomas's "fine talk to help break the strike." The Communists made another sectarian error at a major mass meeting attended by 3,000 strikers in Danceland auditorium at the end of the second week. The Detroit *Labor News* claimed that "practically the only speakers were active Communists" and "none of the regular leaders of the strike" addressed the meeting. Several sources also reported that in addressing the meeting, Communist leader Earl Browder gave the party credit for the walkout. According to the *Labor News*, this meeting, and particularly Browder's claim, alienated many strikers from the Communists; another observer stated that afterwards "the strikers who had been wavering or who had supported Raymond lined up with Darrow." In this way, Communist sectarianism during the strike aided the anti-Communism outside and inside the strikers' ranks and led to the removal of Communist leadership.[26]

The redbaiting significantly weakened the strike. It furthered the belief that the removal of the Communists would facilitate a settlement. This proved illusory. After the purge Briggs favored the strikers' demands no more than before. The redbaiting divided the strikers and deflected attention away from the main enemy toward mutual suspicions and recriminations. Soon after the Communist purge, the joint strike committee split apart, and the strikers at Highland Park, where the Communists had enjoyed the greatest support, returned to work. By eliminating the Communists, and consequently the AWU, the Unemployed Councils, and the International Labor Defense, the strikers lost experienced organizers, valuable outside support, and inexpensive legal aid. Since Briggs's ability to hire new labor from the vast pool of unemployed provided an indispensable asset for the company, the loss of the organized support of the Unemployed Councils represented a particularly telling blow. Soon Briggs had enough employees to resume partial production. The workers at Highland Park, Waterloo, and Meldrum ended their walkouts by the end of February; the Mack Avenue strike dragged on with ever-diminishing numbers until May 1. Though a complete victory might have been impossible at this time, the redbaiting and its consequences explained why the strikes obtained no more concessions than those won the first week.[27]

The Briggs strike represented the peak of AWU strength in the auto industry. The union recruited 4,000 workers during the strike wave and achieved a total membership of nearly 5,000. The union, however, failed to retain most of these members after the walkout. By July 1933, the AWU had shop locals in Briggs Waterloo, Motor Products, Hudson Jefferson, Hudson Gratiot, Ford, Murray Body, Dodge, Chrysler, and Chrysler Jefferson, but total union membership had slumped to 1,500. Probably the redbaiting attack on the union that occurred during the Briggs strike partially accounted for the union's failure to hold new recruits. Beyond this, union leaders also admitted that they failed to bring the union forward sufficiently during the strike and that they had engaged in sectarian and "clumsy methods" of work that had antagonized other workers. A Communist in the AWU said that in some shops the term Bolshevik had come to mean "someone who makes himself a nuisance."[28]

In spite of the prominent role Communists played in the 1933 strikes, few auto workers joined the party. As the result of a party recruiting drive during the first nine months of 1933, the party as a whole reached a total membership of over 20,000, a greater number than at any time since the Red Scare of 1920, but at the same time the Detroit district of the party recruited less members (389) than in a comparable period the year before (924). Less than 40 of the new recruits worked in the auto industry. Party initiation fees and dues payments during the strike wave actually showed "a very sharp decline" over preceding months. The most likely explanation for this decline was that the most active party members were devoting their time and energy to the strikes rather than to party recruiting. One party member also blamed the opportunism of Communist leaders, who tried "to keep the face of the Party covered. . . . The whole atmosphere in the strike was one of 'Don't mention the Party.'" At the end of the strike, the party could claim party units of between five and fifteen members in only nine shops.[29]

The Briggs and related strikes of 1933 represented the most serious manifestation of auto worker protest that occurred in the preunion era. These strikes indicated that the objective conditions of the depression and the subjective activity of the Communists and other leftists were creating a mass sentiment for unionization before the appearance of New Deal labor legislation and AFL organizers. The strikes also demonstrated that, even in the depths of the depression, the workers could win significant concessions. These concessions were not confined to the struck plants either. As a contemporary observer noted: "The epidemic of auto strikes last spring resulted in an improvement in the conditions in other factories that did not strike. The series of strikes brought the orgy of wage cutting by the auto barons to an instant and complete stop." In the end the most remarkable aspect of the Briggs and related strikes was not that they failed to achieve complete victory, not that the Communists were purged, not that the Communists failed to win permanent gains for themselves and their union, but rather that the strikes occurred at all, that they were led by Communists, and that they represented an early step toward complete unionization.[30]

# V

### • • •

# TOWARD AN INTERNATIONAL
# INDUSTRIAL UNION OF AUTO
# WORKERS
# (I)

Until 1933 the Communist AWU was the only active union in the automobile industry. Then the situation changed markedly. Beginning with the Briggs and related strikes early in the year, the auto workers entered a period of strikes and rebellion that would last until 1937. As A. J. Muste noted: "Early in 1933 hell began to pop. Strike followed strike with bewildering rapidity. The long-exploited, too long patient auto slaves were getting tired of the game." The inauguration of President Franklin D. Roosevelt in March 1933 and the ensuing New Deal legislation created an atmosphere somewhat more conducive to unionization than had been the case under the previous Republican administrations. Roosevelt's National Industrial Recovery Act (NIRA) of June 16, 1933 with its declaration that "employees shall have the right to organize and bargain collectively through representatives of their own choosing" provided an apparent sanction for unionization. Soon the industry was alive with organizers. Auto companies launched company unions. The AFL and the IWW began organizing drives. Within the next couple of years such independent unions as the Mechanics Educational Society of America, the Associated Automobile Workers of America, and the Automotive Industrial Workers Association came into existence. Out of this welter of organizational activity, a single industrial union emerged in 1936—the United Automobile Workers Union (UAW).[1]

Even though the Communists represented only one of the

96

many organizations bidding for the auto workers attention, they played an important and unique role in the drama leading to the UAW. In 1933–34, a number of choices faced auto workers and those attempting to organize auto workers. Should organization proceed by company or real unions, by AFL or independent unions, by craft or industrial unions, by one or several unions, by reliance on government intervention or by direct action against employers? Here resided the Communist importance. The Communists understood what was necessary to organize the auto industry, and for the first year under the NIRA they were virtually alone in advocating the course auto workers eventually followed to successful unionization. The Communists repudiated company unions, craft unions, and reliance on government intervention. Instead, they advocated a single, united, industrial union, controlled by the rank and file and geared to struggle with the employers. Between June 1933 and June 1934, the Communists not only carried on a relentless campaign of propaganda and agitation on behalf of these ideas, but also demonstrated the practical vitality of these ideas by helping to build several of the most important auto locals and leading several of the most important auto strikes.

In June 1934, soon after President Roosevelt signed the NIRA and William Green, AFL president, announced the AFL's decision to initiate an organizing drive in the auto industry, the Communists unleashed a barrage of criticism against both actions. At an AWU conference on June 24 and 25, Phil Raymond denounced the NIRA as a "vicious recovery bill that aims to force us into an organization that the bosses choose for us." The *Michigan Worker* warned that the AFL would use the statute "to smash the struggles of the workers."[2]

At an Extraordinary Party Conference in New York City on July 7, 1933, the Communists further elaborated their critique. Speaking for the party's politburo, Earl Browder argued that the New Deal constituted "a policy of slashing the living standards at home." While it was "incorrect to speak of the New Deal as developed fascism," nevertheless "in the labor section of the New Deal are to be seen the clearest examples of the tendencies towards fascism." Browder maintained that the aim of the NIRA was to establish "government fixed wages, compulsory arbitration of all disputes with the government as arbitrator, [and] abolition of the right to strike and independent organization of workers. These things are to be achieved through the industrial codes worked out by employers and given the force of law by the signature of Roosevelt, supported when and where necessary by the American Federation of Labor and the Socialist Party, who have already entered wholeheartedly into this pretty scheme."[3]

Reflecting the general weakness of the party's ultra-radical Third Period orientation, the Communists obviously misread the fascist danger in the New Deal and AFL policies. While the NIRA may have represented certain corporatist ideas, Roosevelt, unlike Hitler and Mussolini, was unprepared to destroy existing trade unions, outlaw strikes, or impose compulsory arbitration. By exaggerating the menace of the NIRA, the Communists at first failed to appreciate that the mere passage of the statute, along with the AFL's organizing drive, provided a certain impetus to legitimate unions. Nevertheless, the experience of auto workers soon justified the Communist skepticism of the NIRA and AFL. As subsequent events revealed, the Roosevelt administration was too solicitous of the interests of the auto manufacturers, and Green was too solicitous of the interests of the hidebound craft unionists, for either to do much in the way of furthering an auto union.

In July and August 1933, Hugh Johnson, head of the National Recovery Administration (NRA) supervised the formulation of a NIRA "code of fair competition" for the auto industry. As part of its assault on the NIRA, the AWU submitted a code to the NRA hearings. The AWU code called for a "drastic" cut in hours and substantial wage increases. The AWU proposed a seventy-five cent minimum hourly wage, a thirty-hour week and a guaranteed annual wage of $900. The AWU code also called for: employee-elected committees in all departments to regulate production schedules; a policy of no discrimination against women, Negro, and young workers; a social insurance system financed by the federal government; an employer-financed plan for unemployment, sickness, disability, and old age; the right of workers to elect shop and departmental committees; and the right of workers to engage in strikes and mass picketing. The AWU realized its code had no chance of acceptance, but the proposals served as a standard against which to measure the final code's provisions.[4]

The actual preparation of the auto code fell almost entirely to Johnson and the National Automobile Chamber of Commerce (NACC), and the final code approved by President Roosevelt on

August 26 conformed completely to the NACC's wishes. In the code hearings and discussions, Johnson failed to consult any auto worker union. Claiming to represent thousands of auto workers, William Green had testified at the code hearings, but even his modest recommendations for a sixty cent minimum wage, a thirty-four hour week, a simplification of the bonus system, and no qualification of Section 7(a) were ignored by Johnson and the auto manufacturers. The final code set minimum wages at forty-three cents an hour and maximum hours at forty-eight a week. Moreover, Johnson permitted the auto manufacturers to include in the code a special "merit clause," qualifying the right-to-organize provisions of 7(a). The merit clause reaffirmed traditional open shop practices in the auto industry. It provided that "employers in this industry may exercise their right to select, retain, or advance employees on the basis of individual merit, without regard to their membership or nonmembership in any organization." The auto code contained no provisions for social insurance, unemployment insurance, overtime pay, call-in pay (payment for being "called-in" to work and then sent home), changes of the bonus system, the election of shop committees, the right to strike, or labor representation on the code authority. The auto magnates were pleased. *Automotive Industries* regarded the code as "the first victory of industry over organized labor under the Industrial Recovery Act." Though having failed to affect the final outcome, Green avoided criticism of the code. The Communists did not. Phil Raymond called the code "a slavery pact" and "a vicious attack on the living standards of auto workers." Not only did the wage provision "not raise pay," but it provided "an open incitement to wage cuts." The "infamous" merit clause gave "the companies the right to hire and fire at will."[5]

In the summer and fall of 1933, the AFL organizing drive among auto workers fully justified Communist criticism. In launching the auto drive, President Green failed to abandon the cautious policies that since 1924 had characterized his leadership of the AFL. The former coal miner from Coshocton, Ohio remained a prudent and faithful steward of the craft union tradition of Samuel Gompers and a genial, mild-mannered tool of the craft union interests on the AFL Executive Council. Even as he entered the unfamiliar territory of mass production workers, Green continued to oppose industrial unions, strikes, and independent political action and to favor cooperation with the employers and government. Green's decision to launch the auto drive was apparently motivated by pressure from John L. Lewis, the powerful head of the United Mine Workers Union, who told the AFL president that Section 7(a) of the NIRA would be "absolutely meaningless" unless the leaders of labor "boldly and audaciously" used the statute as "the weapon for a great organizational attack." Though Green initiated the auto drive, caution and ambivalence rather than boldness and certainty marked it from the outset. As one observer noted, the AFL leader approached the organizing task like a timorous suitor; he "felt about the automobile industry as an old and impotent man feels about a young and desirable woman. He wants her, yet he is afraid."[6]

The personnel, resources, and tactics that Green employed in the auto drive all reflected his fear of moving too rapidly and antagonizing the craft union interests, the employers, and the government. For the job of recruiting a half million auto workers scattered across the country, Green assigned William Collins and three full time assistants. Collins, who established headquarters in Detroit in June 1933, lacked vigor, ability, and knowledge of the industry. One journalist described him as "a middle-aged Sunday school teacher," another as "heavy-set" and "flannel-mouthed," and a third as "an old-fashioned AFL organizer, who could be relied upon not to display too much energy." In his first speech after arriving in Detroit to take charge of the auto drive, Collins announced that there was "no place" for the Communists in the AFL. To allay craft unionist fears of industrial unionism, Green decided to induct the new recruits into federal labor unions, temporary locals under the control of the AFL Executive Council. Later, the federation could assign federal labor union members to the appropriate craft union. The federation leaders believed that difficulties with employers could be solved by submitting them to the NRA Compliance Board or to the National Labor Board (NLB) established by Roosevelt in August 1933. Both Green and Collins believed that Section 7(a) provided sufficient leverage to organize auto workers and improve their conditions without resorting to force. Frank X. Martel, head of the Detroit Federation of Labor, summed up this orientation in June, when he declared: "Under the new law, I do not believe it will be necessary to have strikes to gain improved conditions."[7]

On a number of occasions in the fall of 1933, Communists clashed with AFL organizers over federation policies. The first of

these clashes occurred when the federal labor union at the Bower
Roller Bearing Company in Detroit walked out on September 18.
It charged that the company had discriminated against unionists in
a recent layoff of 143 workers. While AWU members urged the
workers to rely on "militant struggle" to win reinstatement of the
unionists, Collins prevailed upon the strikers to rely on the NRA
Compliance Board. The board reached a settlement the following
day. The company agreed to give preference to qualified, former
employees in future hiring. This, however, fell short of the strikers' demands for reinstatement, and John Schmies branded the
settlement "the first act of treachery and sell-out . . . by Mr.
Collins."[8]

An even greater debacle than the Bower strike occurred when
federal labor unions in the Ford plants in Chester, Pennsylvania
and Edgewater, New Jersey engaged in a strike at the end of September. A company decision to reduce the work week from five
days to four without raising the daily wage prompted the walkout.
Led by Sam Reed, AWU members joined the picket lines and distributed leaflets urging the strikers to persist in their mass picketing, to assert rank and file control over the strike, and to spread the
walkout to other Ford plants. Though New Jersey AFL organizer,
Hugh V. Reilly, reluctantly sanctioned the strike, he provided no
material assistance to the strikers, neglected picketing, tried to
prevent Communists from joining the picket lines, and squelched
a rank and file attempt to send a car caravan to Detroit to spread
the strike to other Ford workers. Like Collins, Reilly chose to rely
on the NLB and NRA Compliance Board, both of which proved utterly incapable of inducing Ford (which refused to recognize the
NIRA) to reach a settlement. Even though the Compliance Board
determined that Ford had used an illegal lockout, had refused to
bargain, and had discriminated against unionists in hiring, the
Justice Department refused to prosecute the company. In January,
the workers ended the strike in defeat, and the demoralized Chester workers abandoned their union and returned the AFL charter.[9]

A similar pattern of events occurred during a federal labor
union strike at Nash. On November 9, a reduction of piece rates
led to a spontaneous walkout of 200 workers at the Nash plant in
Kenosha, Wisconsin. A lockout of the plants' 2,000 workers followed. The Communists, who had both a shop nucleus and an
AWU unit in the plant, immediately began agitation for a mass
strike. At a meeting of strikers, called by AFL organizer Paul

Smith, on the night of the walkout, the local Communist leader, Dalton Johnson, urged the strikers to conduct a mass strike, to elect a broad rank and file strike committee, and to demand a 35 percent increase for all workers as well as the abolition of the gang system. Smith denounced Johnson as an outsider and ignored the AWU's suggestions. Following typical AFL practices, Smith failed to orchestrate a strike and simply relied on John A. Lapp of the Chicago Regional Labor Board to mediate a settlement. The final settlement, ending the dispute on November 21, contained the company's agreement to bargain with shop committees, but it also continued the controversial new piece rate for a trial period. The Communists, who remained active on the picket lines throughout the course of the strike, denounced this as a "shameful settlement" that failed to contain "one single demand which was originally put forward either by the workers or by the A. F. of L. leadership itself." A Communist observer noted: "The fact that our comrades at the strike meetings took the floor at every opportunity and pointed out to the workers the burning issues and exposed the A. F. of L. leadership, has created a great deal of sympathy inside the shop for the Auto Workers Union and the Party."[10]

On November 14, 4,000 members of a federal labor union at the Edward G. Budd Company in Philadelphia began a work stoppage. This union sought to force the company to bargain with it, instead of with a newly established company union in the plant. As in the other strikes of the time, the AWU appealed to the strikers to elect a rank and file strike committee, draw up their own demands, and eschew arbitration. The AWU also criticized the AFL for failing to have AFL machinists join the strike. The AFL, however, again relied on the intervention of the National Labor Board. After months of effort, the NLB failed to devise a solution acceptable to both sides. At the end of March 1934, the federal labor union called off the strike in defeat. Shortly afterwards, the Budd federal labor union collapsed.[11]

By early 1934, the failures of the AFL organizing drive had lent legitimacy to Communist criticism. Between July 1, 1933 and February 15, 1934, the Detroit AFL headquarters had spent only $5,692 on organizational work and had managed to recruit only a few thousand auto workers. While Collins bragged to the auto manufacturers that "I never voted for a strike in my life. I have always opposed them," the auto manufacturers defied Section 7(a) with impunity. They fired unionists, employed private detectives and spies, established company unions, and refused to recognize or bargain with the federal labor unions. On January 31, 1934, Collins reported to the Executive Council that employer intimidation was so great that he could no longer persuade workers in Detroit, Flint, Lansing, and Pontiac to attend meetings. The fledgling federal labor unions in Michigan were, in his words, "destroyed."[12]

At the same time the Communists took up an oppositional role toward the AFL auto drive, they became involved in conflicts with the leadership of a newly formed organization of auto tool and die makers, the Mechanics Educational Society of America (MESA). Between 1929 and 1933, the average annual wages of these highly skilled workers had dropped from $2433 to $623, a greater percentage of decline than for unskilled auto workers. Moreover, due to the stresses of the depression, most jobbing shops had initiated a contract system of payment that forced the workers to bid against each other for jobs and forced wages to as low as at twenty cents an hour. Such impoverishment led to the formation of MESA in February 1933. The original goals of MESA were to upgrade the skills and training of tool and die makers. The dominant personality in MESA was its national secretary, Matthew Smith, an English-born, independent socialist, who had immigrated to the U.S. in the 1920s. After the passage of the NIRA, Smith took the lead in transforming the educational society into a trade union. In July 1933, MESA launched a recruitment drive in Detroit, Flint, and Pontiac and soon claimed 5,000 members. In Smith's vision, MESA had as an immediate task "to temper wage slavery" and as an ultimate goal "to function in a planned society as a national instrument of production, cooperating with a recast distributive system to make a Brave New World."[13]

The Communists first gained prominence in MESA during a massive strike of tool and die makers in the fall of 1933. The strike began on September 22, in Flint, where nearly 2,000 workers, representing about 19 percent of the tool and die makers in the city, walked off their jobs in GM plants. The walkout followed futile discussions with the GM management, at which MESA had demanded a thirty-seven and a half hour week, the abolition of Saturday and Sunday work, and a pay raise from the prevailing $.80 to $1.50 an hour. Within a week, tool and die makers in Pontiac and Detroit joined the walkout. The union held mass meetings, established mass picket lines, and on October 12 conducted a solidarity parade of 10,000 workers down Woodward Avenue in Detroit. The walkout involved about 14,000 workers and affected 57 jobbing shops connected with the Automobile Tool and Die Manufacturers Association, 60 independent shops, and every major auto plant in Detroit, Pontiac and Flint except Ford and Graham-Paige.[14]

The Communists soon realized that MESA represented a positive step in the organization of auto workers and began to play an early role in building the organization. They became so active that Elizabeth McCracken, Matt Smith's personal secretary, surmised that MESA "had most of the Communists in Detroit as members." According to Federated Press reporter, Joe Brown, "a number of the several hundred members of the Auto Workers Union" belonged to MESA and "played an active role in the [1933] strike." Early in the walkout the AWU issued leaflets and held solidarity meetings at plant gates and workers' halls to generate strike support. A flyer issued to Chevrolet production workers contained the headline: "Support the Striking Tool and Die Makers/Don't Scab!!" It read: "We members of the Auto Workers Union Chevrolet Branch, wholeheartedly SUPPORT the STRIKE of the Mechanics Educational Society in their struggle and call upon every rank and file member of the A.F.L. and I.W.W. and Unorganized to build [a] UNITED FRONT against Company Unions and Reactionary forces." A leaflet of the Briggs Highland Park Local of the AWU declared: "This struggle is our struggle. By all means we must join and support them."[15]

Two Communists played particularly prominent roles in the strike. John Mack, an AWU member and participant in the Briggs strike earlier that year, became a member of the Flint strike committee. John Anderson (not John W. Anderson, the Wobbly), who the next year ran for governor on the Communist ticket, became a strike leader in Detroit. A scrappy Scotsman, who had immigrated to the U.S. in the 1920s, Anderson first became politically active with the Unemployed Councils and then with the AWU during the Briggs strike, where he had handled legal defense. He later explained that he joined the CP because "those guys were in the forefront of the fight, and if there's one guy I admire it's a guy whose willing to lay it on the line for what he believes." During the MESA strike, Anderson single-handedly organized a walkout of his fellow tool and die makers at Ternstedt. Afterwards, Anderson built Local 7 into one of the largest locals in Detroit and became the most popular opponent of Smith within MESA. When Smith expelled Anderson from the union the following spring, Local 7 voted to reinstate its Communist leader.[16]

Since Matt Smith, unlike Green and Collins, had no reluctance to strike, the Communists' conflict with the MESA leadership assumed a somewhat different aspect than their conflict with the AFL. During the course of the walkout the Communists berated Smith and Jay J. Griffen, chairman of the joint strike committee, for their reliance on government mediation, their alleged undemocratic procedures, their neglect of the Ford workers, their refusal to unite with the AWU, and their failure to involve unemployed workers on the picket lines. The main point of difference, however, centered around the craft union orientation of Smith and Griffen and the industrial union orientation of the Communists. While Smith and Griffen confined the strike, as well as the union, to skilled tool and die makers, the Communists (as well as IWW, SP and Proletarian party members) argued for involvement of production workers as well. When the MESA leadership refused to take such steps, John Schmies, Detroit district organizer of the CP, accused "Griffen and his clique" of blocking "every militant move to win the strike."[17]

Early in October, after NLB representative, John Carmody, had failed to induce the manufacturers to reach an agreement with the union, MESA leaders agreed to let the Communists try to broaden the strike to production workers. Toward this end, between October 12 and 16, the union sponsored a series of mass meetings chaired by John Anderson. At a meeting on October 13, David Jones, Communist candidate for mayor of Dearborn, Frank Cedervall of the IWW, John Mack of the Flint strike committee, Paul Grow of the MESA rank and file committee, and Jack Fisher and Phil Raymond of the AWU called for a general strike, a united front of MESA, AFL, AWU and IWW, and a concentration on shutting down the Ford plant. Raymond declared: "The time has come to tell King Henry I of Dearborn to join the Czar of Russia." At this time the Communist party issued 40,000 leaflets calling for a general strike. On Sunday, October 15, nearly 10,000 people attended a MESA mass meeting on Belle Isle. According to an observer, however, this number represented "only strikers and sympathiz-ers," and widespread support for a general strike failed to mate-rialize. The effort was probably doomed from the start because most production workers were still unorganized and had had no previous contact with MESA. Moreover, the AFL refused to recog-nize or support the MESA walkout. Additionally, it was the end of the production season in Detroit, an inauspicious time for produc-tion workers to have any leverage. The lack of workers leverage was amply illustrated by a concurrent IWW strike then fizzling at Murray Body.[18]

On October 18, MESA leaders attended an NLB hearing on the strike in Washington. It was a futile exercise. Only one employer representative appeared, and the board merely advised the union to resubmit its demands to the manufacturers. The Communists denounced the "Smith-Griffen gang" for creating the "illusion" that "the NRA would win the strike for the tool and die makers." After the hearings, disillusioned and demoralized strikers turned to violence. On October 30, in what auto workers dubbed "the wild ride of the die-makers" 2,500 strikers in a huge motorcade attacked eight jobbing shops. They overturned cars, burned blueprints, and shattered windows. Smith and others accused the Communists of instigating the violence, but the Communists blamed Smith and Griffen. The party maintained that the violence failed to constitute "the kind of militancy calculated to win the strike." At the same time, the Communists said the union must either reinvigorate the strike at key plants or else conduct "an or-ganized retreat." The union leadership apparently reached the same conclusion, for at the beginning of November, MESA began reaching informal agreements with most of the struck plants. Though these agreements fell far short of the union's original de-mands, they did abolish the contract system and other "glaring evils" in the jobbing shops.[19]

In several ways the strike served to extend Communist influence. It indicated that even without a treasury, and experi-enced organizers, MESA, by striking, did more about establishing a union and winning gains than the AFL by its studious discourage-ment of strikes. Joe Brown observed: "It was very significant to find that many of the Communist phrases concerning the bureau-cracy and dishonesty of the Federation officials were accepted by the rank and file of the tool and die makers. This was true, although a great majority of these same men were definitely anti-Communist in their position." Though the Communist effort to unite the production workers and the tool and die makers failed at this time, Communist insistence on the desirability of this end, along with the failure of the tool and die makers alone to wield sufficient power to effect a completely successful strike, did much to shape the future attitude of the rank and file. According to Joe Brown, MESA members had entered the walkout "imbued with a lofty craft psychology," but "during the strike they rapidly learned of their common interest with the production workers and their attitude slowly changed until the sentiment for industrial unionism found no opposition."[20]

Even though in 1933 the Communists appeared wherever auto workers were organizing or striking the membership of the AWU declined. This paradox was quite understandable. The combined activity of the AFL, MESA, IWW and company unions in the latter half of 1933 overshadowed the Communists' AWU and detracted from its earlier appeal as the only active union in the industry. In October 1933, John Schmies reported that while the AFL and other unions were "making deep inroads among sections of automobile workers," the AWU "has not only not gained in membership, but has actually declined all the way down the line." A report on AWU membership in the spring of 1934 indicated a total of 885 members. Of these, 275 members worked in the Detroit area: 70 at Ford, 55 at Budd, 50 at Chevrolet, 45 at Murray, 30 at Hudson, and 25 at Dodge. Outside Detroit, the union had its greatest strength in Hayes Body in Grand Rapids (300), Commercial Body Shops in Philadelphia (200), Nash in Kenosha (40), and Willys Overland and Chevrolet in Toledo (45). At this time the Communists also had active members and supporters in such plants as Motor Products in Detroit and White Motor and Fisher Body in Cleveland, but they operated in AFL locals rather than in the AWU.[21]

The growth of the AFL and independent unions and the stagnation of the Communist revolutionary unions led the Communist party to shift its emphasis away from the unions of the TUUL. A directive of the Political Bureau in January 1934 urged the strengthening of opposition work within the AFL and independent unions. The Political Bureau's directive recommended that Communists in the "Federal unions in the steel and automobile industry" oppose "the Roosevelt law," the worsening conditions, and the "treacherous and splitting tactics of the trade union's bureaucracy." The directive also urged support for higher wages, shorter hours, union recognition, the right to strike, and trade union democracy. Increasingly, the AWU operated more as an opposition caucus within the federal labor unions than as an independent union.[22]

The dissatisfaction of federal labor unions over the flourishing of company unions, employer discrimination against unionists, and failure to achieve recognition or improved conditions forced Collins to threaten "aggressive action." Consequently, on February 6, Collins advised the federal labor unions to demand a 20 percent wage increase. A meeting of federal labor union officers in Lansing on March 4, 1933, selected four plants to make wage and hour demands on their employers and to strike if satisfaction was not forthcoming. Collins, however, had no intention of backing his threats with force. On March 1, he had already asked for NLB intervention. When Conciliator James F. Dewey came to Detroit and promised hearings on the dispute, Collins got the strike postponed. At the hearings on March 14 and 15, union representatives presented their case concerning company unions, discrimination, and the failure of employers to negotiate. At this time they asked for elections to determine employee representatives by majority rule. Afterwards, to give Hugh Johnson time to arrange a settlement, the union again postponed strike consideration, this time until March 21.[23]

The AWU greeted the strike threat with enthusiasm. On March 10, the union issued a call for "United Action" to "prepare for strikes" and to "build one powerful union in [the] auto industry." The AWU declared: "We must place the interest of all auto workers above the interest of any particular group of workers." A short time later the Auto Workers News published a comprehensive statement on the state of the industry under the NIRA. The statement denounced the auto code for endorsing the open shop and claimed that "fully 50 percent of the automobile workers have been forced into company unions." The statement showed that the profits of General Motors, Chrysler, and Packard had increased under the code, while real wages had declined. The statement also contained reminders of the continuing discrimination against Negroes in the industry and the victimization of union members. It also reminded workers of the cases where the intervention of the NRA

Board failed to help strikers. The AWU statement said: "Workers in the automobile industry have found thru bitter experience that they cannot depend upon government agencies or the A. F. of L. officials to safeguard their interests." After the Washington hearings ended inconclusively, the AWU announced in leaflets to auto workers: "The promises and hearings in Washington have gotten us nothing. The manufacturers refuse to yield. . . . NOW IS THE TIME TO STRIKE AND WIN!"[24]

The production season in the auto industry peaked in March. Knowledge of this, coupled with Collins's threats and the Washington hearings, intensified strike sentiment everywhere. On March 19, Collins said that only "the direct intervention of the President" could avoid a walkout. The next day, Roosevelt intervened. Hence, a day before the strike deadline, Collins and his assistants again prevailed on the federal labor unions in Michigan to delay strike action. During the following days, Roosevelt met separately with representatives of the manufacturers and the union, and on March 25, he announced a general auto settlement. The settlement contained nothing about wages or hours. It settled no cases of discrimination but referred such cases to an Auto Labor Board (ALB) to be created for that purpose. The ALB, however, could act on discrimination cases only after a local had submitted a list of its members. The settlement failed to grant union recognition or to provide for representation elections governed by majority rule. Instead, it only proposed a scheme of "proportional representation," that required the employers to meet with all employee organizations, including company unions. The settlement also failed to provide a seniority system based on length of service, a demand the union had sought. Instead, the settlement proposed a complicated prescription for seniority based on marital status, length of service, skills, and performance. Donaldson Brown of GM acknowledged that the employers were "tremendously happy" with the President's settlement. Collins wired the federal union in Flint: "Tell the men to go to work. It's the biggest victory they have even won."[25]

The Communists appraised the settlement quite differently. An AWU united-front conference in Detroit greeted the announced settlement with the cry of "sell-out." Subsequent union flyers claimed the settlement represented a victory for the manufacturers but a "complete betrayal" and a "doublecross" for the workers. The Communists quite accurately pointed out that the settlement failed to satisfy any of the union's original demands. Moreover, in some respects, the settlement worsened the workers' position. Proportional representation "put the Presidential seal on the company unions." The seniority clause made "efficiency" (or submission to speedup) "a condition for holding the job." The requirement that the unions release lists of members presented the danger of blacklisting and more discrimination than currently existed. The union charged that the settlement again exposed AFL officials as betrayers and again indicated that the only course was for "all workers, of all unions [to] join together in one united front for the fight against the manufacturers." The AWU newspaper, flyers, and such Communist shop papers as *Ternstedt Worker*, *Red Motor* (White Motor) and *Sparkplug* (Cleveland Fisher Body) spread these ideas widely through the industry.[26]

However vitriolic, the Communists response to the auto settlement expressed the feelings of many in the industry. Matt Smith said the settlement was "a farce to put it mildly." Detroit labor lawyer, Maurice Sugar, wired Frank Martel that he would express exactly what he thought of the settlement, "but profanity is prohibited in telegrams." Leonard Woodcock, future UAW president, was with Flint unionists in the Pengelly Building when Collins's "victory" telegram arrived on March 25. According to Woodcock, the men felt a "deep sense of betrayal," and Woodcock witnessed "men simply tearing up their membership cards and throwing them on the floor," until the "floor was littered, covered with these torn-up cards." In Cleveland disillusioned auto workers burned their AFL membership cards.[27]

In seeking to avoid a confrontation with the auto companies, Collins believed that the union, which had recruited only 32,000 of the 470,000 workers in the industry, had insufficient strength to win such a contest. Many auto workers, besides the Communists, disagreed. In the wake of the March settlement, a number of strikes occurred in defiance of Collins's wishes. With the exception of a walkout at Motor Products, all of these strikes occurred outside the Detroit area, away from Collins's restraining influence. They involved Nash workers in Kenosha, Racine and Milwaukee; Fisher Body workers in Cleveland, St. Louis, Kansas City, North Tarringtown, and Flint; and Auto Lite and other parts workers in Toledo. Although these walkouts produced only mixed results, the locals that struck invariably became the strongest locals within the AFL auto network. This was true as well for locals outside the Detroit area, like the South Bend Bendix local and the Cleveland White Motor local that won concessions by threatening to strike. Nonideological unionists, such as Homer Martin in Kansas City and Carl Shipley in South Bend, led most of these locals, but in Toledo radical members of the American Workers Party (AWP) and its affiliate, the Lucas County Unemployed League, played a major role. The AWP, an outgrowth of the Conference for Progressive Labor Action, was headed by A. J. Muste, a Dutch-born minister, pacifist, socialist, and head of Brookwood Labor College. Communists were very active in Motor Products, Nash, Toledo Auto Lite, and Cleveland's White Motor and Fisher Body.[28]

Between April 5 and 7, workers shut down the Motor Products plant in Detroit in a dispute over a wage cut. The Motor Products local contained a Communist-organized rank and file opposition that had been critical of AFL policies, and when Collins had tried to dissuade workers from a strike on the night of April 4, members of the local had "booed and howled down Collins." A Communist shop paper declared the workers were "sick and tired of the 'wait and delay' policy of the A. F. of L." The AWU supported the walkout; Communists Phil Raymond and David Jones were arrested on the picket lines and charged with inciting to riot. After the intervention of the ALB, the union and management reached a settlement that granted, among other things, a restoration of old piece rates, payment of fifty cents an hour for dead time over an hour, and a 10 percent wage increase for skilled and semi-skilled workers.[29]

During the Toledo auto strike of 1934, Communists and Musteites (members of Muste's AWP) played a major part in turning a rout of the workers into a partial victory. The conflict began on April 11, when Federal Local Union 18384 began a strike that within several days involved workers in three interlocked auto parts companies, the Electric Auto Lite Company, Bingham Stamping and Tool Company and Logan Gear Company. The walkout occurred after the three firms failed to fulfill a promise to reach an agreement with the local by April 1. Among other demands, the union sought a 20 percent wage increase and a promise of union security. Only a small minority of the workers in the three plants joined the walkout, and the companies continued to run production in spite of the strike. William Green believed that the strike was ill-advised and offered no assistance. Within a couple of weeks the strike looked hopeless. These circumstances probably accounted for the local's reliance on radical assistance, and for the radicals' ability to achieve the influence they did.[30]

From the beginning of the walkout Communists and Musteites offered their support and joined strikers on the picket lines. But Communist denunciations of the Musteites as "'left' social fascists" and Musteite suspicions of the Communists prevented effective cooperation between the two. Of the two groups, the Musteites had the larger following in Toledo and exercised greater influence during the walkout. The Communists had only a small following in Cleveland. According to Ohio district organizer, John Williamson, only three or four party members worked in the Auto Lite plant, and they were old, foreign-born workers. The party suffered from a "complete isolation from organized contact with the strikers prior to the strike." Similarly, the "very small and inactive" AWU local "played no role during the strike." The Communists did, however, have an active Unemployed Council in Toledo, and through its activity the party carried on considerable agitation and supplied volunteers for the picket line.[31]

The radicals aided the strikers by helping organize the walkout and by generating strike support. Early in the walkout, after Thomas Ramsey, the local AFL organizer, had warned the strikers to have nothing to do with Communists and had failed to establish picket lines, about 30 workers from the Bingham and Auto Lite plants sought advice at the Communist party office. Williamson and the local party organizer, Kenneth Eggert, gave the workers "some idea on how to take the situation into their own hands." Bob Travis, a leftist in the Toledo Chevrolet plant, helped the Auto Lite strikers arrange picketing, and party women established a soup kitchen. To build support for the walkout, the Communists also issued 16 different leaflets (a total of 105,000 copies) and held seven shop gate meetings as well as perhaps a dozen other strike support rallies at which Earl Browder, William Patterson, William Weinstone and other party leaders spoke.[32]

The radicals' major contribution was their defiance of court injuctions. On April 17, in response to an application by Auto Lite and Bingham, Common Pleas Judge Roy Stuart issued a restraining order that limited picketing to 25 persons at the two Auto Lite gates and at the Bingham gate and that prohibited picketing by the Lucas County Unemployed League, the Lucas County Unemployed Council, and all other nonunion people. Judge Stuart followed this act with a similarly worded temporary injunction on

May 14 and a permanent injunction on May 15. To enforce the injunction, Lucas County Sheriff David Krieger appointed 150 special deputies, paid by Auto Lite and Bingham. On May 5, in a letter to Judge Stuart, Sam Pollock of the Unemployed League condemned the initial restraining order as a curtailment of "the rights of all workers to organize, strike and picket peacefully" and promised that the league would "deliberately and specifically" violate the order. The Musteites and Communists then mobilized their followers among the unemployed to bolster the picket lines. Roy W. Howard of the Scripps-Howard newspapers noted with amazement that the unemployed "appeared on the picket lines to help striking employees win a strike, though you would expect their interest would lie the other way—that is, in going in and getting the jobs the other men had laid down."[33]

Defiance of the restraining order rescued the walkout from certain defeat. On May 15, deputies arrested 107 strikers for violating the May 14 injunction. The next day 46 were arrested. On May 17, over 200 strikers and sympathizers stormed the jail; the following day a similar crowd demonstrated in the corridors of the courthouse as Judge Stuart opened hearings on the contempt charges. After this, the picket lines grew. On Monday, May 21, 1,000 picketers demonstrated at Auto Lite. They stoned several carloads of scabs leaving the plant and scuffled with strikebreakers. On Tuesday, 4,000 picketers and spectators appeared, and on Wednesday, 6,000. That day tensions rose. A bolt thrown from a window in the Auto Lite plant struck a young girl on the head. Deputies "unmercifully" beat up an old man. Then, after strikebreakers turned a hose on the picketers, a major riot broke out between the strikers and the scabs, police, and deputies caught inside the plant. A Toledo Communist described the scene: "The police and Deputy Sheriffs were helpless. The entire neighborhood was seized by the workers. The Communist Party and the YCL members played an active part in organizing squads in different streets around the plant and charged the police and the plant and when necessary retreated in an organized way. Hand to hand fighting with police took place, with the workers getting the upper hand. The economic struggle developed into a political struggle, into class war."[34]

The siege of the plant continued through the night until the next day, May 24, when Ohio Governor George White sent in the National Guard. The National Guard used bayonets, tear gas, vomiting gas, and bullets to disperse the crowd. Guardsmen's bullets killed two strike sympathizers. Fighting between the guard and demonstrators raged all that day. The next afternoon fighting again erupted between the guardsmen, who then numbered 1,350 (the largest peacetime mobilization in the state's history), and an estimated crowd of 20,000. On May 26, yet more fighting occurred. Strikers and their supporters pitted bottles and bricks against tear gas and bayonets. When the violence finally ebbed, radical condemnations of the "murderers" and calls for a general strike flowed. At a Communist-sponsored rally on Sunday, May 27, William Weinstone, who had recently replaced John Schmies as district organizer for Detroit, declared: "Only by establishing a rule of workers in place of a rule of the capitalists can prosperity and freedom for everybody be won." The rally raised two slogans: "You Can't Make Auto Parts With Soldiers" and "A General Strike to Support Auto-Lite Workers."[35]

By May 28, 95 of the 103 unions affiliated with the Toledo Central Labor Union had expressed a readiness to support a general strike. On that day, however, William Green informed Otto Brach, head of the Central Labor Union, that he did not believe it "necessary for the organized workers in Toledo to engage in a sympathetic strike." Though Green and local federation leaders ended the threat of a general strike, the picket line violence effectively closed the Auto Lite plant, provoked the intervention of Department of Labor mediators, and hastened a strike settlement. The written settlement on June 4 yielded a company promise not to discriminate against union members, a 5 percent wage increase in all three plants, as well as a unique preamble to the agreement repudiating "the tactics of Communists." While Brach called the agreement "a splendid victory," the *Daily Worker* stated: "The strikers victorious on the mass picket lines, were defeated by the maneuverings of the AFL leaders who succeeded in their strategy of splitting them up and blocking a general strike for their demands." Both appraisals contained some truth. Clear to all, however, was that in the most dramatic confrontation of the NIRA period, Auto Lite workers, defied the AFL no-strike policy, relied on outside radicals, and won one of the few signed agreements in the industry and established one of the strongest auto locals in the AFL.[36]

The most important example of the Communist help in building a strong and militant local occurred at the White Motor plant in Cleveland. There the leading Communist unionist was Wyndham Mortimer. Mortimer, the son of an English immigrant coal miner, had begun work as a trapper boy in the mines of Pennsylvania at the age of twelve. Later, as a young man, Mortimer worked as a rail-straightener in the Lorain steel mills, as a brakeman on the Pennsylvania Railroad and the New York Central Railroad, and as a conductor for the Cleveland Railway Company. While on these jobs Mortimer had belonged to the United Mine Workers Union, the Brotherhood of Railway Trainmen, and the Industrial Workers of the World. In 1908, after hearing a campaign speech by Eugene Debs, Mortimer joined the Socialist party. He studied not only the popular writings of Kate Richard O'Hare and John Spargo but also the classics of Marx and Engels. In 1917, Mortimer joined White Motor, a leading manufacturer of trucks and buses. In the years that followed, Mortimer gained a respected standing in the plant as an outspoken and intelligent socialist, unafraid of opposing his employer. During the early years of the depression, Mortimer joined the Communist-oriented Small Home and Landowners League in Cleveland, and by 1932 he belonged to the Communist party. At that time, this diminutive, 48 year-old father of two children became the leader of an attempt to establish a union at White Motor. His experience, convictions and ability suited him well for the task.[37]

After deciding to organize a union, Mortimer and several friends first sought help from Harry McLaughlin, Executive Secretary of the Cleveland Federation of Labor. When McLaughlin informed them that "no one can organize that bunch of hunkies out there," the White Motor men proceeded alone. With proceeds from a suit raffle, Mortimer had membership cards printed, and the nascent organization began to recruit members and hold meetings in a Slovenian Hall on St. Clair Street in Cleveland. During a recruitment campaign in the summer of 1933, Mortimer sought assistance from John Williamson, district organizer of the Communist party, who put the White Motor leader in touch with Phil Raymond. In August, Raymond addressed a meeting of the White Motor union, which then decided to affiliate with the AWU and the TUUL. By November, an AWU member claimed that the union had organized 90 percent of the plant and was trying to create an organization "controlled by the rank and file" that would be "a real fighting weapon and not a debating club." About that time, at the White Motor gates, representatives of the Cleveland Metal Trades Council began distributing leaflets that called on the workers to choose between the AFL and AWU, between Franklin Roosevelt and Joseph Stalin. According to Mortimer, this appeal created "confusion and disruption" in the plant. When Mortimer learned that some union members preferred AFL affiliation to independence, he called a meeting of the union and recommended, for the sake of unity, that the members dissolve the AWU local and join the federation. "A few days after the mass meeting," Mortimer recalled, "several carloads of workers, all leaders in the TUUL union, drove down to the Metal Trades Council, and we all signed applications to join the federal union."[38]

In establishing Federal Local Union No. 18463 at White Motor, George McKinnon, a Cleveland AFL organizer, appointed as officers, men "from the most conservative elements in the plant." Though excluded from the major offices, Mortimer became chairman of the grievance committee. In that position, he and his loyal supporters among both Communists and non-Communists set the tone for the local. In so doing, Mortimer had the help of the CP's Hungarian-language newspaper, *Uj Elore,* which called meetings of the Hungarian-speaking workers to win them to the union and to the party's policies. He also had the aid of the Communist nucleus at White Motor, which among other things regularly published *Red Motor,* a shop paper filled with critiques of AFL leaders and policies. Soon Mortimer and his supporters had distinguished the union as one of the most militant, independent, and successful locals in the industry.[39]

Confrontations with AFL leaders and the White Motor management repeatedly marked the early history of Local 18463. Soon after assuming the chairmanship of the grievance committee, Mortimer led the union in successfully resisting an attempt of certain craft unions to claim jurisdiction over skilled workers at White Motor. Mortimer also engineered work stoppages on Saturday and Sunday until the company agreed to pay time-and-a-half for Saturday and Sunday work. In December 1933, by a vote of 1,087 to 78, the union threatened to strike unless the company granted it a wage increase, improved conditions, and recognition. Though the management succeeded in convincing the union that it could not afford a general wage increase, it did agree to certain wage improvements and adjustments. White Motor also agreed to deal with the elected representatives of the employees, including those of the federal labor union.

At the end of February 1934, the union again voted overwhelmingly to strike unless the company granted a 20 percent wage increase. On February 27, George Lehman, the appointed president of the local, wired William Green that "the men were condemning the AFL and you in particular. The men are sure they can whip [the] co [*sic*] into shape." Green wired back the same day: "Urge you take no hasty action on strike. . . . must be sure of success before undertaking strike." White Motor averted a strike by raising the minimum rate of common laborers from 43 to 51 cents an hour, the rate of semiskilled from sixty to 67 cents, and the rate of highly skilled workers by five cents. When asked if Green had authorized a strike, Mortimer, the head of the strike committee, allegedly replied: "Hell no! We did not expect him to. We took the right in our own hands. We had enough of his telegrams telling us to do nothing." After this, the White Motor union emerged as one of the few with a signed agreement.[40]

As in earlier periods, Communist influence in 1933–34 stemmed from factors other than their numerical strength. Four circumstances, in particular, enabled a small number of Communists to exercise a disproportionately large influence: the policy of concentration, the ability to draw on nonauto workers for support, the conformance of many Communist ideas to the objective needs of unionization, and the lack of significant rivalry from other left-wing groups. Throughout the auto industry, the Communists possessed no more than several hundred members. In 1934, District 7 (Michigan), for example, contained only fourteen shop nuclei of 183 members. The District had only 166 party members in AFL unions and only 250 members in revolutionary unions. Nevertheless, by concentrating their efforts on key industries, cities, and plants, the Communists maximized their impact. In 1933–34 Communist concentration points included the Nash plants in Kenosha, Racine, and Milwaukee; the tool and die, Briggs, Ford and Murray shops in Detroit; and the White Motor and Fisher Body plants in Cleveland. Communists inside the shops amplified their influence by utilizing outsiders. During the Toledo strike, and elsewhere as well, party functionaries and unemployed workers manned picket lines, organized rallies, distributed literature, and sold the *Daily Worker*. In Detroit, the small number of Communists actually in the shops and unions could rely on the support of the District's six full-time functionaries and some of the 1,300 party members in street nuclei.[41]

Communist influence also stemmed from the correspondence of their ideas to the aspirations of auto workers and to the requirements of unionization. The ideas of industrial unionism, unity of all auto workers, aggressive strike action, and rank and file control provided a more realistic blueprint for unionization than the AFL's craft unionism, avoidance of strikes, reliance on government mediation, and control from the top down. The Communists' ideas were, of course, not theirs alone. Nor were their ideas any more reflections of Marxist ideology than the AFL's ideas were reflections of business, unionist ideology. Rather both sets of ideas derived from experience; for the AFL, from a decade or more of isolation from industrial workers, and for the Communists, from a decade of efforts to organize workers in auto and other industries. The failure of the AFL to make much headway after a year of effort, naturally turned the minds of many auto workers toward the ideas propounded by the Communists and other radicals. Industrial relations researcher, Marjorie Clark, credited the "continued communist and I.W.W. agitation against the Federation" for having "created very real distrust in the minds of many automobile workers" against the AFL leadership and policies.[42]

Communist influence at this time also derived from the almost complete lack of influence in the auto industry of other left-wing groups. The Trotskyists, Proletarians, Socialist Laborites and other tiny sectarian groups had only a handful of followers among auto workers. The Musteites never achieved a following among auto workers outside of Toledo, and their influence in that city ebbed after 1934. During the summer and early fall of 1933, the IWW exercised considerable influence among auto workers in Detroit. They established a regular six-day-a-week radio program on station WEXL in Dearborn, distributed some two million pieces of literature and held regular shop gate meetings. They also established a new, large office for their Metal and Machinery Workers Industrial Union No. 440, which the *Industrial Worker* later described as a "lavish front for the growing union." During September and October 1933, however, in what a local IWW leader, Frank Cedervall, later described as "a tragic error in the history of the

IWW," the Wobblies led an ill-timed strike at the Murray Body plant. The strike failed utterly. In the wake of defeat, the IWW organization in Detroit collapsed.[43]

By 1933–34, the Socialist party had almost completely lost the influence it had had among auto workers in the early 1920s, when Socialists led the United Automobile, Aircraft, and Vehicle Workers of America. Even though during the early years of the depression, the SP underwent a revival in which its membership jumped from the 1927 low of 7,793 to the 1934 high of 20,951, the Socialists remained an insignificant force among auto workers. In 1933, the Socialist party had only 537 members in Michigan. Important in accounting for the SP's limited influence among auto workers was the party's policies and composition. Until the SP's Detroit convention in June 1934, the so-called old guard, led by Morris Hillquit (until his death in October 1933), James Oneal, Algernon Lee, and Louis Waldman, determined party policies, and they supported the AFL leaders. At the party's convention in 1932, the old guard defeated a resolution, sponsored by the militant caucus, that called for Socialists to "stimulate and press the organizing of workers, especially in the basic industries, along industrial lines." In 1933, Norman Thomas acknowledged that the old guard's tendency "to tie up blindly to the A. F. of L. leadership no matter what happens" played into the hands of the Communists. Even though most of the party's new recruits in 1933–34 sided with the militant caucus against the old guard, the new members consisted mainly of middle class and college-educated youth rather than workers. Noting the bankruptcy of the Socialist party in auto at this time, Joe Brown observed: "The local leadership refused the suggestion of [Norman] Thomas that they go into the A. F. of L. With a leadership that was largely 'intellectual' and a membership quite largely from the unemployed, I don't believe they shall become a factor in organization." Consequently, until the formation of the UAW, the Communists experienced little rivalry from Socialists.[44]

During the first year of the NIRA, Communist activity produced mixed results. Several of the most distinctive features of the party's Third Period orientation had questionable or even negative consequences. The party erroneously perceived that the New Deal contained fascist tendencies that would lead to the outlawing of strikes and imposition of compulsory arbitration; it consequently underestimated the fillip that New Deal legislation would give to union organization. The party's reliance on revolutionary unions proved ill-conceived; the AWU floundered and most workers who joined a union preferred the AFL or MESA. It is important to note, however, that two years before the Seventh Congress of the Communist International changed from the Third Period to the Popular Front, John Anderson and other Communists had already joined MESA, and Mortimer had led the union at White Motor into the AFL. Mortimer's move in 1933 attracted criticism from Joe Zack, the party's trade union secretary in Ohio. Early in 1934, however, the party confirmed the wisdom of Mortimer's move by stressing the need to work within the reformist unions. The party soon expelled Zack for refusing to accept the new emphasis. Party attacks on Wobblies, Socialists, and Musteites as social fascists aroused little noticeable sympathy among workers and precluded effective united fronts in such situations as the Briggs strike. Overall, however, the Communists produced more positive than negative results. Even the mistaken aspects of the Third Period had a positive side. The skepticism with which the party viewed established political and labor leaders enabled Communists to expose the egregious deficiencies of the New Deal and of AFL and MESA policies. The Communists made their most effective criticism in action; they demonstrated the effectiveness of their ideas by putting them successfully into practice. The Communists helped to organize strikes, recruit union members, and determine the aggressive policies of the strongest and most effective AFL and MESA auto locals. Beginning in June 1934 the Communists began to parlay their local influence into a national movement that demanded an international union of auto workers based on the ideas of industrial unionism, rank and file control, and militant strike action.

# VI

• • •

## TOWARD AN INTERNATIONAL INDUSTRIAL UNION OF AUTO WORKERS

## (II)

Beginning in 1933, the Communists played a key, though hardly solitary, role in a struggle to secure a single, international, industrial union for automobile workers. For the most part this struggle occurred within the federal labor unions. The struggle took the form of a rank and file movement initiated and led by Communists and aimed at forcing the AFL Executive Council into granting an international, industrial charter to the federal labor unions. Beyond this, the movement also advocated rank and file control, the right of auto workers to determine their own leaders and policies, and a militant organizing drive. It opposed the policy of conciliation and cooperation pursued by the AFL. Outside the federal labor unions, Communists in the AWU (until it disbanded in December 1934) and in the Mechanics Educational Society of America (MESA), pushed similar ideas. This movement for an international did a great deal to shape the character of the UAW that emerged in 1936.

During the first year of the AFL organizing drive in the automobile industry, the Communists repeatedly advanced ideas of unity and cooperation among the various unions in the industry and of the need for the immediate establishment of a single, international union. In February 1934, a typical AWU statement declared that the auto workers "must all find a common understanding for unity against the companies and against the labor misleaders who are trying to split our ranks." This idea answered a real need. The local federal labor unions required a central body to deal with the national employers, to coordinate organizing efforts, and to gather and disseminate information needed for local bargaining. Reflecting this general need, non-Communist unionists also raised the idea of formal cooperation between federal labor unions. In September 1933, the St. Louis Chevrolet and Fisher Body local called for cooperation among the federal labor unions, and in December 1933, the local convened a conference in Detroit of representatives from several federal labor unions to consider the idea of forming a national council. In April 1934, Carl Shipley, president of the Bendix local, wrote to William Green to suggest the formation of a national executive committee, and on June 3 in Chicago, the Bendix local held a conference with representatives of eight federal labor unions that endorsed a proposal for a central body for auto unions.[1]

In response to such pressure, as well as to the disillusionment of auto unionists over the March settlement, William Green and William Collins called a National Conference of United Automobile Workers Federal Labor Unions. On June 23 and 24, 137 delegates from 77 federal labor unions met for the conference in Detroit's Fort Wayne Hotel. The purpose of the conference was to approve a national council that would serve Collins in an advisory capacity. Before the conference met, Collins composed the bylaws of the national council. He proposed that it consist of 11 elected representatives, who would meet at his behest and aid him in recruiting auto workers and gathering statistics. At the opening session of the conference, Green stated that federal labor unions, then containing 18,000 members, remained too small and immature to sustain an international union. He assured the delegates, however, that the federation had a "firm intention" to establish an international "just as soon as the workers have demonstrated their ability to sustain themselves as an integral part of the trade union movement." The AFL President also reiterated the federation's determination to develop "a cooperative relationship" with the employers and to direct industrial disputes away "from the field of conflict to the council chamber where the law and rule of reason can settle labor's problems." For the Communists and others disillusioned with the AFL, this was just more twaddle and delay.[2]

The Communists viewed the Detroit conference as an opportunity to reiterate their criticism of AFL policy and their call for industry-wide unity. In an "Open Letter" distributed to the delegates on the first day of the conference, J. Wilson and Phil Raymond of the AWU said: "The no-strike policy of the AFL leadership has proven to be disastrous. In following their advice— placing all dependence upon the NRA, upon arbitration, and upon the good will of the employers—the auto workers were led from defeat to defeat. As a result, low wages, speed-up, discrimination against union members, unemployment, [and] the growth of company unions still continues [*sic*] in the industry and is [*sic*] now being intensified." The letter went on to blame the AFL for stopping a general auto strike in the spring, for putting over the Washington agreement, for impeding strikes in Cleveland, Tarrytown, St. Louis, Flint, Toledo and other cities, and for approving the Automobile Labor Board. Wilson and Raymond declared that the "demand of the hour" was for "a united fight of the rank and file of all unions in the industry for the improvement of conditions" and for "a united industrial union of all auto workers, including the member[s] of all unions and crafts in the auto industry, with control lodged in the hands of the workers in the shops."[3]

Within the conference itself, the Communists Wyndham Mortimer of White Motor and Sophie Kushley (formerly Nydia Barken, an AWU organizer) of Ternstedt's led a loosely organized rank and file caucus composed of about 25 delegates from Cleveland, Tarrytown, South Bend, Flint, Kenosha, and Detroit. The rank and file caucus opposed Collins's proposal for a national council and introduced its own resolution calling for the immediate establishment of an international, industrial union. The caucus demanded that an international include the AWU and MESA and be controlled by the rank and file. The caucus also demanded that an international have as its purpose the struggle against the employers and company unions. Two other groups also opposed Collins's plan. A group of delegates from the Studebaker and Bendix locals and the Chrysler Jefferson and Kercheval locals proposed that the AFL Executive Council promptly establish an international. The Hudson local, led by Arthur Greer, favored the formation of a National Executive Council that, unlike the council envisioned by Collins, would have full authority to guide the auto unions, would select its own chairman, and would develop the procedures and program for establishing an international union.[4]

Tension between the AFL organizers and the dissidents dominated the conference. Thomas Ramsey, an AFL organizer from Toledo, attacked the AWU open letter and accused Communists of trying to disrupt the union from inside and outside. Dissidents criticized the quality of AFL organizers, and, in an expression of displeasure, ordered the organizers to leave the floor and sit on the platform. Dissidents also attacked the financial setup of the federal labor unions and objected to the Automobile Labor Board, with which the AFL was cooperating. Mortimer proposed electing a chairman for the conference and accused Collins of highhandedness for ruling this motion out of order. Another delegate introduced a resolution supporting the Communist-backed Workers' Unemployment Insurance Bill; Collins ruled it out of order with the remark, "We want no Communist bills here."[5]

On the afternoon of the second day, a major confrontation occurred over whether to endorse an international union or a National Council. Green repeated his belief that the auto workers were unprepared for an international and that a National Council would constitute a step toward an international status. Green also insisted that the "rights of the craft unions must be respected as far as it is possible." Mortimer attacked the National Council proposal on three grounds: (1) Green would appoint the council's chairman, (2) the council would have only advisory powers, and, (3) the council would meet only at Collins's behest. Mortimer argued that the auto workers needed a union where the rank and file had authority, because his own union, which the rank and file controlled, was growing, while unions which AFL organizers controlled were losing ground. He further argued that only an industrial type union would have the strength necessary to fight the company unions and the corporate attacks on workers' living standards.

Despite such arguments, the conference rejected the opposition resolutions. As a vote on a National Council neared, Mortimer leaped from his seat and charged to the platform. "Brother Chairman," he shouted, "I want to speak in opposition to this resolution. It does not meet the needs or desires of the auto workers. What we need is an international industrial union of all automobile and parts workers." Mortimer later recalled that Collins responded by slamming his gavel and shouting: "Sit down! I know who you are speaking for. Every time I hear the words 'international industrial union' I know where it comes from. It comes straight from Moscow." Over Mortimer's protest, the conference approved a National Council and elected 11 members to it. Though losing, the dissidents registered a strong protest. At least 50 of the 137 delegates, voted against the National Council. After the vote, 24 delegates led by Arthur Greer, bolted the conference, and several weeks later they formed a separate union, the Associated Automobile Workers of America (AAWA). About half of the dissidents remained, and before the conference adjourned Mortimer collected their names and addresses. "We used these," Mortimer later recalled, "to good advantage in the period ahead."[6]

After the June conference, the White Motor local initiated a movement for an auto international. First, in the summer of 1934, Mortimer organized the Cleveland District Auto Council (CDAC) consisting of the nine auto locals in the area—White Motor, Fisher Body, Hupmobile, National Carbon, Baker Rau Lang, Bender Body, and Willard Storage Battery. With Mortimer as president, the Cleveland District Auto Council became the center of the dissident forces. The Council collected monthly contributions from its constituent locals and published the first UAW newspaper, the *United Auto Worker*. Henry Kraus, a graduate in mathematics from Case Western Reserve and an aspiring writer close to the Communist party, edited the paper. The CDAC began sending bundles of the *United Auto Worker* to the auto unionists Mortimer had met in Detroit; before long the paper reached a circulation of 65,000.[7]

In August 1934, the CDAC held a conference of the nine Cleveland auto unions. The conference issued a manifesto criticizing the AFL's passivity, its reliance on government intervention, its capitulation to the March settlement, and its separation of the auto locals. The manifesto contained all the criticisms the Communists had made. To this familiar litany the statement added a protest against the AFL's June conference and the "rubber stamp" National Council. The manifesto concluded: "The only way to bring about the correction of the present evils is through the adoption of a policy of aggressive struggle against the employers, the establishment of militant leadership in the unions, and the unification of the federal local[s] into an International Union within the A.F. of L. based on the principle of industrial unionism and rank and file control." A short time later the CDAC invited other federal labor unions to attend a Conference for an International Union of All Automobile and Auto Parts Workers in the American Federation of Labor to be held in Cleveland, September 16, 1934.[8]

Green quickly perceived that the Cleveland Auto Council posed a serious threat. He believed that Communists were behind the CDAC. Following the CDAC meeting of August 18, Green issued a statement that Communism was "not so much concerned with economic improvement" as "political revolution" and that its purpose was "in direct conflict with the philosophy of trade unionism and the American Federation of Labor." Shortly thereafter, Green urged all local AFL officers to "take decisive and drastic action to expel from membership therein every known [or] proven communist and communist propagandist." At the same time, the National Council, the Cleveland Central Labor Council, and the Metal Trades Council denounced the CDAC and ordered it to disband. The Metal Trades Council referred to the CDAC as the "Kremlin." The National Council, composed of AFL loyalists, declared that the Cleveland auto locals had established the CDAC "without authority from their own local unions or from the American Federation of Labor." Asserting that the Cleveland locals would utilize the CDAC for "communist propaganda," the National Council urged Cleveland unionists to withdraw from the Cleveland Council and to remove the Communists from their organization. According to a Flint unionist, Collins was "extremely hostile" to the Cleveland Auto Council's call for a conference, and attempted to prevent Michigan locals from linking up with the Cleveland group.[9]

The CDAC rejected the order to disband and proceeded with plans for the September 16 conference. Fifty delegates from 36 locals (mainly in Michigan, Wisconsin and Ohio) answered the call. Such Communists and Communist sympathizers as John Anderson, Fred Williams, Bud Simons and Joe Devitt came from locals in Detroit and Flint. Several Socialists, including Walter Reed of Flint, attended. Twenty-five members of the Associated Automobile Workers of America also showed up, but the conference refused to seat them, because it wanted to protect itself from the charge of dual unionism. Moreover, some Communists believed that Greer's organization was simply a "disguised company union." In its main business the conference called for an international union organized on industrial lines, controlled by the rank and file, and dedicated to an effective struggle against the employers. To keep the pressure on the AFL, the meeting decided on another conference in Michigan on November 10.[10]

Though Collins dismissed the September 16 conference as "simply a part of the destructive methods pursued by Communists in their efforts to disrupt and destroy trade unions," certain changes in AFL policy and personnel in the fall of 1934 represented a concession to rank and file agitation. In September, Green renounced the March auto settlement and the Auto Labor Board. In October, the AFL Convention in San Francisco authorized the Executive Council to issue an international charter to the auto unions. The resolution, however, had two serious limitations. It failed to grant the prospective international complete jurisdiction in the industry, and it demanded a "provisional period" in which the AFL would supervise the union's affairs and appoint its officers. The same month William Green replaced William Collins as the AFL's national representative in auto with Francis Dillon. If this move was designed to appease auto workers disgusted with Collins's lack of vigor, the substitution promised little improvement. Rose Pesotta described the new appointee as "the cartoon prototype of a union official, pot-bellied, always with a large cigar." Soon after assuming his new position, Dillon revealed attitudes identical to those of his predecessor. "We do not seek strife or trouble," Dillon declared, "but wish to carry on our work and negotiations with management in an orderly business-like way. . . . We hope that out of our work in the coming months will come a better mutual understanding with management and the possibility of solving mutual labor problems by round table discussions on a cooperative basis."[11]

Neither the decisions of the AFL convention nor the appointment of Dillon satisfied the rank and file movement. On November 10, when the movement, now calling itself the Committee for the Promotion of an International Industrial Union in the Auto and Parts Industry, convened its Michigan conference in Pengelly Hall in Flint, the participants triumphantly assumed credit for the AFL Convention's decision in favor of an auto international. Sensing·their growing authority among the auto workers, the 43 delegates from 18 locals denounced the convention for failing to promise the rank and file complete control over their prospective international, particularly over the selection of officers and the conduct of finances. The meeting demanded that the Executive Council of the AFL call a constitutional convention of auto workers that would have "full power" to exercise "the full rights of any other international union." The conference stressed that it did not want just an international, but an international that had an industrial form and a program of struggle with the automobile manufacturers.[12]

While Mortimer and other Communists worked within the AFL federal labor unions to build the rank and file movement for an international, industrial union, Phil Raymond and others had continued to operate within the Auto Workers Union. Both groups, however, struck the same note. On June 30, 1934, for example, at an AWU conference in Detroit attended by 161 delegates from Ford, Briggs, Hudson, Hayes and other plants, Raymond had stressed the need to work for one industrial union in the industry. While operating in both arenas, the Communists gradually shifted their emphasis to the AFL. The reasons were clear. For all of the limitations of AFL policy, the federal labor unions had a greater capacity than the AWU to attract auto workers and provide a framework for a real organizational drive. Moreover, within the federal labor unions Communists like Mortimer found it possible to do effective organizing without facing explusion for their political or dissident ideas. Reflecting the shift in Communist emphasis toward the AFL, as early as April 1934 a writer for the *Nation* observed that the AWU had "practically vanished from the scene, with most of the Communists functioning as opposition groups in the AFL or the MESA." In December 1934, the AWU dissolved. At that time the union had only 21 locals and 450 members; most of the 630 Communist party members in the industry were already functioning in the AFL and MESA unions. The Communist shift of tactics in the auto industry foreshadowed the Popular Front policy adopted by the Communist International at its Seventh Congress in 1935. With the Popular Front came the abolition of the TUUL and all of its affiliated unions.[13]

After the 1934 convention, contradictions within the AFL Executive Council on the question of an auto international made Green and others increasingly disturbed over Communist influence in the federal labor unions. On the one hand, certain craft unions opposed any move toward an international that would infringe on their jurisdictional claims. In November the machinists declared that they would "not stand idly by and without protest, permit the Federation, or any other organization, to trespass upon its jurisdiction except in the most limited way." On the other hand, John L. Lewis pressed the Executive Council to grant an international charter to the automobile workers "at once" and to make "every effort" to organize the automobile industry "at the earliest possible date." Faced with this volatile situation, Green and AFL organizers became especially resentful of Communist agitation for an international charter. In December, AFL organizer, T. N. Taylor, reported to Dillon that at a recent meeting of the Seaman local in Milwaukee "a communist was nominated for every office in the Local Union." After the Seaman local decided to send delegates to the next conference of Mortimer's rank and file movement scheduled in Detroit on January 26, 1935, AFL organizer Paul Smith informed Green that radicals had taken over the local; he asked Green to "notify all automobile organizations" that the rank and file conference "is for no other purpose than to set up a dual organization . . . and is openly sponsored by the Communists."[14]

Because of their initiation of the rank and file movement, Mortimer's Cleveland group particularly disturbed Green and Dillon. Just before the rank and file conference scheduled for January 26, the federation president and auto organizer tried to undermine the Left's influence in Cleveland. In December, Green informed Dillon that if Mortimer was a Communist, he should be removed from office. Early in January, the AFL called a meeting of the White Motor local. Tom N. Taylor, Harry McLaughlin, James McWheeney, and George McKinnon, all AFL officials, attended the meeting. As soon as Mortimer opened the meeting for business, Ed Gockel, an AFL loyalist, took the floor and moved that the local rescind its previous action sending delegates to the Detroit conference. In the discussion that followed, each AFL official spoke in favor of the motion. McKinnon charged that the rank and file movement "not only does not have the approval of the A.F. of L., but it has its utter condemnation." Pointing accusingly, McKinnon said: "And you, Mortimer, are a com-MUNE-ist and I will lift your charter." Mortimer later recalled that the federation stalwarts put on "one of the fanciest Red-baiting tirades I have ever heard, and I have heard plenty." The tirade, however, intimidated neither the local nor its leader. One local member said: "This rule from the top is fascism. We want everything controlled by all of us workers." Taking the floor on his own behalf, Mortimer said that red-baiting was one of the employers' oldest weapons against industrial unionism. He attacked the lackluster achievements of those who were attempting to dictate to the local union. So what if he were a Communist, Mortimer asked. Was being a Communist a crime? Referring to McKinnon's threats to lift the local's charter, Mortimer answered that a union without a charter had more importance than a charter without a union. After Mortimer's speech, the White Motor local reaffirmed its decision to send delegates to the Detroit rank and file conference.[15]

Despite federation efforts, 37 unionists from 18 locals attended the Detroit Conference. Mortimer delivered the keynote report. The White Motor leader described the worsening conditions in the industry and the deteriorating position of the union. He heaped blame on the federation for this situation and pointed out that his own local was "able to improve the workers' conditions and maintain a strong organization because we did not allow these top [AFL] officials to halt our local's activities." Mortimer argued for a renewed organizational drive and preparation for strike action against the auto companies. To apply pressure for an international union, the conference decided to initiate a petition drive in every local and to send a delegation to the February 23 meeting of the National Council.[16]

During the first six months of 1935, union sentiment swung decisively behind the rank and file demand for an international charter. Besides the agitation of the rank and file movement itself, new evidence of the AFL's glaring ineptitude motivated the swing. In January 1935, the NIRA's Henderson Report revealed the continued existence of deplorable conditions in the auto industry. Annual earnings remained so low and employment so sporadic that most auto workers had to depend on relief for at least four or five months each year. Company spy systems flourished. Speedup continued. Moreover, the AFL had yet to produce effective government assistance for the union drive. In spite of Green's protests, in January 1935, as in November 1934, President Roosevelt again renewed the loathsome NRA auto code. By the spring, the AFL had yet to recruit large numbers of auto workers. The federal labor unions contained only 22,000 paid-up members, a bare 5.4 percent of the auto work force. Detroit's AFL had only 2,197 paid-up members, and a mere 1,413 additional members in Michigan.

The federal labor unions had only sixteen signed contracts; eight of these belonged to the militant Toledo Local 18384, and another belonged to the White Motor local. No signed contracts existed in Michigan. Furthermore, the AFL had failed to unite the unionized auto workers. Not only did the MESA and the AAWA continue to operate as independents, but in April a new independent union, the Automotive Industrial Workers Association (AIWA) formed in the Dodge plants.[17]

The turning point in the movement for an international occurred in the spring of 1935, when the possibility of a general strike again arose. The Communists had repeatedly argued that only a strike could build the union. The rank and file conference in Detroit on January 26 had called on the National Council to convene a national conference in preparation for a "united general strike." The strong left-wing locals in Cleveland had likewise argued such steps for some time, and on March 10 the Cleveland Auto Council recommended holding a conference of federal labor unions to plan a walkout. Outside the Communist sphere of influence, Musteites in Toledo, Carl Shipley, head of the Bendix local, and Ed Hall, a member of the National Council demanded action. When William Green toured the major auto centers in February 1935, he found little sympathy among auto workers and leaders of the National Council for his own reluctance to call a strike. At his last stop in Detroit on February 23, Green told reporters: "We are not talking of pulling a strike. We haven't made any such plans." When the AFL president addressed a meeting of Detroit auto workers in the Light Guard Armory, Communists distributed leaflets calling for strike preparations, and when Green implied that he would not oppose a strike under certain conditions, the workers applauded lustily. Several days after Green's speech, the National Council defiantly authorized a strike vote in all 176 federal labor unions; two months later Francis Dillon revealed that all but a few locals had authorized Green to call a strike when the time was propitious.[18]

In spite of overwhelming sentiment in favor of a strike, Green failed to move. On the contrary, he boasted to the Executive Council that the auto workers "wanted to engage in a general strike, but I stopped that." Green may have stopped a general strike, but it cost him what remained of his respect among auto workers. This became clear during an unauthorized strike by the

Toledo Chevrolet workers. The walkout of 2,100 workers began on April 22. The union sought certain changes in hours, wages, seniority, and job-timing, as well as exclusive bargaining rights. Conflicts between the nine-man Chevrolet strike committee (which was dominated by radicals including Musteite James Roland and Communist Robert Travis) and AFL officials, including Green, Dillon, as well as Green's personal representative, James Wilson, and the local's business agent, Fred Schwake, dominated the walkout from beginning to end. Schwake, for instance, stopped the radicals from playing the role they had played in the Auto Lite strike the year before, by prohibiting Musteites, Communists, and members of their affiliated organizations from joining the picket lines. Also, a major dispute between the strike committee and the AFL officials occurred over a question of spreading the strike. Since the Toledo Chevrolet plant produced all transmissions for Chevrolets and Pontiacs, the shutdown soon idled 32,000 workers in GM plants throughout the country. The strike committee tried to use this strategic advantage to stimulate a general strike of GM plants. The committee's call for a general strike resulted in walkouts in Norwood and Cleveland and evoked a favorable response from unionists in Atlanta, Flint, and elsewhere. Green and Dillon, however, thwarted all attempts to turn the Toledo strike into a general strike against GM.[19]

Another conflict between the radicals and AFL officials occurred when Dillon forced a settlement on the union. The settlement, which Dillon, Schwake, and Wilson had negotiated with GM representatives, gave the workers an 8 percent wage increase and some slight gains with regard to seniority and the timing of jobs. The settlement pleased few local members, however, since GM refused to grant exclusive bargaining rights and refused to sign a formal agreement. On the evening of May 13, 1,500 strikers met in Toledo's Civic Auditorium to consider the settlement. Communists and Musteites distributed literature opposed to the settlement. A motion approved by the body confined the speakers to members of the strike committee and specifically denied Dillon the floor. Dillon responded by stalking out of the meeting and declaring that the union was no longer in the AFL. Thereupon, the meeting reversed itself and invited Dillon back. Dillon returned and spoke. For 30 minutes he urged the union to accept the settlement. After Dillon spoke, Roland, the head of the strike committee, urged the meeting to reject the settlement. Dillon then told Roland if the meeting rejected the agreement, he (Roland) was "out." After Schwake gave a sympathetic summary of the agreement gains, the meeting voted 732 to 385 for acceptance. Two weeks later the local approved and sent to Green a resolution condemning Dillon for preventing the Flint workers from joining the strike, for putting on "a childish exhibition of bad temper" at the settlement meeting, and for using "intimidation and terrorization" to achieve approval of the strike settlement.[20]

For AFL officials, the Toledo settlement represented the best that could be achieved under the circumstances. In their minds, the opposition simply represented Communist machinations. Wilson, for instance, described Roland as a "Red" and said "so are a couple more on the [strike] committee." Dillon told Green: "We were confronted in Toledo by a hostile employer upon one side and Communists on the other." Green himself felt "that the Communist influence was exercised among the workers on strike and that some of them were influenced by Communist propaganda." Green rejected the local's censure of Dillon because he was "fully convinced that it was inspired by those who are properly classified as real enemies of the American Federation of Labor." For many auto workers, however, the Toledo settlement represented another example of the AFL's caution and incompetence and another reason for demanding an international union under their own control. In June 1935, a survey of 28 locals revealed that 93.3 percent of the membership favored an international union. Moreover, the obsessive fear of Communist manipulation had less currency in local union halls than in the AFL headquarters. In spite of a special trip that Dillon made to Cleveland in April to warn the Fisher Body local against associating with groups unsympathetic to the AFL, the union had walked out in sympathy with the Toledo strikers and had accepted an offer of support from the Communist Hungarian-language newspaper, *Uj Elore*. During the walkout, the union and the paper sponsored joint strike support meetings. At the same time, the Communists in the Cleveland plant reported that the "red scare" feelings among workers had vanished and that "the auto workers almost unanimously agree with the Party's proposals and especially endorse the demand for immediate action during the present production season."[21]

After the Toledo strike, as the June survey indicated, sentiment for an international became irresistible. Following a meeting with William Green on June 17, Dillon announced the federation's decision to call an auto union convention on August 26 to establish an international. Within two weeks the rank and file movement, now calling itself the Progressives in the United Automobile Workers' Union, held a two-day conference in Cleveland to prepare for the convention. With the fight for an international all but won, the 41 delegates from 18 unions focused their attention on the kind of international they wanted. They demanded a union with complete jurisdiction over all auto workers and an organization controlled by the rank and file. Since they believed "the one sure path to winning the demand for the auto workers" was "the path of organization and militant strike action," the Progressives raised the strategy of "a national strike to win a national agreement." In line with Communist thinking and the universal distaste with government boards under the NIRA, the Progressives condemned the Wagner Labor Disputes Bill then before Congress.[22]

Even though AFL officials at Seaman Body in Milwaukee, and possibly elsewhere, conspired with the AFL national office to prevent "nominees sponsored by the Communist Party" from becoming delegates to the first auto convention, the Progressives, including Communists, brought a strong and determined contingent to the assembly that opened in Detroit's Fort Shelby Hotel on Monday morning, August 25, 1935. William Weinstone, who had replaced John Schmies as head of the Michigan CP in 1934, attended the convention as an observer. Also present were such Communists as Wyndham Mortimer and Henry Kraus of Cleveland White Motor, Bob Travis of Toledo Chevrolet, John North of Grand Rapids Hayes, Bill McKie of Detroit Ford, and such Progressive delegates as Richard Reisinger, Ed Stubbe, John Soltis and William Kics of Cleveland, Tom Johnson of Detroit and George Addes of Toledo. Progressives or those sympathetic with Progressive views on the jurisdictional question controlled all of the major delegations except that of the Seaman Body union. The delegations of White Motor and the eight other Cleveland locals, the consolidated Toledo local, the Kenosha Nash local, the Norwood Chevrolet and Fisher Body local, and the two South Bend locals lined up with the Progressive cause.[23]

The Progressives outlined their position in a printed statement distributed to the delegates the first day of the convention. The format was familiar: a condemnation of the AFL's avoidance of struggle and futile dependence on the NRA and ALB; a call for an industrial, democratic and autonomous international union; and advocacy of an aggressive organizing campaign and preparation for strike action aimed at winning a national union agreement. Along with their customary appeals, the Progressives added a bitter indictment of the manner in which Dillon hamstrung the Toledo Chevrolet strike in the spring of 1935 and a preemptory defense against the anticipated red-baiting of their cause by Green and Dillon. The Progressives warned of a possible attempt to stampede the delegates with a red scare and argued that there was "no truth in Dillon's contention that the Progressives are a 'bunch of reds.'" The Progressives described themselves as "loyal union men and women," who were at the convention not "to advocate communism" but "to help build a powerful union able to protect the interests of the auto workers."[24]

During the first session of the convention, differences between the Progressives and AFL leaders became clear. In the convention's keynote address, William Green presented the auto workers with an international charter containing two controversial provisions: a limitation of the union's jurisdiction to those workers involved "directly" in the manufacture and assembly of automobiles and a provision for the appointment of the union's officers by the federation president. Green ended his address with an attack on the Communists. Because of Communist party opposition to the Wagner Bill (which the last Progressive conference had likewise condemned), Green called the CP "a traitor to labor." In an indirect slap at the Progressives, the federation president charged the Communists with "trying to poison the workers against the American Federation of Labor." He urged auto workers to adhere to the federation's "American philosophy," its faith in American institutions and disinterest in overthrowing the government. "Don't be misled," Green admonished, "by those who call upon you to follow some visionary program."[25]

In his report, Dillon defended his controversial handling of the Toledo Chevrolet strike, extolled the performance of AFL organizers, and derided Communists and other radicals. The chief auto organizer described the Toledo strike as a success and said the Communists, Musteites, and GM were the main forces militating against an "equitable and honorable adjustment." Dillon claimed that AFL organizers had "made a reality" of the auto workers union, despite "the poison and slime which emanated against them from the foul lips of self-appointed Messiahs, would-be progressives, deserters, Musteites and Communists."[26]

On Tuesday morning the convention considered an official resolution asking Green to appoint Dillon as first president of the auto union and requesting the federation to finance the salaries of the union officers and expenses of the union headquarters. Carl Shipley immediately countered with a motion mandating the convention to elect its own president. Assuming the chair, Green heaped praise on his chief organizer, the "faithful whole-hearted, sincere, honest Frank Dillon." After a floor debate in which Mortimer and the other Progressives supported Shipley's motion, Green ruled the motion out of order and called the question on the official resolution. By a vote of 164.2 to 112.8 the Progressives defeated this resolution. The Cleveland, Toledo, South Bend, and Kenosha locals accounted for 142.2 of the opposition votes. The result threw the convention into an uproar. The AFL leaders, according to Mortimer, "looked as though they had been hit by a pile-driver." They adjourned the convention, called off the afternoon session, and did not resume serious business for two days.[27]

Thursday's session opened explosively. The delegates ordered all federation organizers to leave the convention floor. Divisive debate on the jurisdictional question followed. Speaking as leader of the Progressives, Mortimer declared: "The craft form of organization fits into the automobile industry like a square peg in a round hole. My union is on record for an industrial union and I won't support anything else." After Dillon ruled a resolution calling for an "industrial union with full jurisdiction" out of order, the meeting approved a motion accepting the charter as granted but protesting its limited jurisdiction.[28]

Thursday afternoon Green returned to the podium. He had spent the two preceding days consulting the AFL loyalists on how to deal with the convention's rejection of the resolution empowering him to select Dillon as the union's chief officer. Green's solution was simple. He merely announced that the AFL had mandated him to select the union's officers, and that was what he would do. Dillon would be president, Homer Martin vice-president, and Ed Hall, secretary-treasurer. To serve on the union's Executive Board,

Green appointed the same nine AFL loyalists who, with Martin and Hall, had made up the former National Council. Mortimer later recalled the effect of Green's edict on the delegates: "Pandemonium broke loose! A large number of delegates from Toledo started to walk out in revolt against such high-handed action. Bob Travis, Henry Kraus, and I rushed to the door. We stopped them. We told them to go back to their seats. I said, 'You damned fools, don't you see this is exactly what they want us to do?' Travis and Kraus also urged them to remain in the convention, as the fight had just begun. After much confusion and argument the Toledo delegation returned to their seats." The Progressives had won an international charter, but they had yet to win self-government, total jurisdiction, and a policy geared to strike action. Therefore, before the convention adjourned, the Progressives laid the basis for continuing their struggle. On a motion by Progressive Tom Johnson, the convention selected seven delegates to attend the next AFL Executive Council meeting and protest Green's autocratic selection of the union's officers. The protest committee contained such well-known Progressives as Johnson of Detroit Ford, John North of Grand Rapids Hayes Body, George Addes of Toledo Willys-Overland, and Carl Shipley of South Bend Bendix. Selected to head the Committee of Seven was Wyndham Mortimer.[29]

The Committee of Seven carried the protest of the auto convention to the AFL Executive Council that met in Atlantic City before the October 1935 AFL convention. Speaking for the delegation, Mortimer told the Executive Council: "We are here to register a protest against the undemocratic actions of President Green in arbitrarily appointing the officers of our newly chartered international union. We maintain that we are as capable of electing our own officers as are the members of any other affiliate of the American Federation of Labor." The crusty craft unionists of the Executive Council bristled. William Hutcheson of the Carpenters Union said that the council might well retract the auto charter altogether. David Dubinsky of the International Ladies Garment Workers questioned Mortimer about how many members of the committee were Communists. In the end, the Executive Council merely accepted the committee's protest without acting on it.[30]

At the AFL convention the Progressive auto workers found a vigorous ally in the president of the United Mine Workers (UMW). John L. Lewis emerged as the leading spokesman for the interests of the incipient industrial unions in auto, rubber, steel and other mass production industries. Throughout the 20s, the UMW president had been as cautious and conventional as any of his stalwart colleagues on the AFL Executive Council. Even more than some, Lewis had railed against the "Communist menace," and his organization had barred from membership any person belonging to the Communist party. With the coming of the New Deal, however, Lewis underwent a transformation. The opportunity to organize the mass production industries captured Lewis's imagination; in the inner councils of the federation, he became a vigorous proponent of the organization of the unorganized into industrial unions. After having his vision repeatedly obstructed by the federation's old guard, he was, by late 1935, prepared to precipitate a break with the AFL, to throw in his lot with the young rebels in auto, rubber and steel, and even to work side by side with Communists and other radicals. Lewis welcomed the industrial unionists to his headquarters in the President Hotel, listened to their problems, gave advice, and promised support. Moreover, Lewis made it clear, as one leftist later recalled, that he was indifferent as to whether "they were right or left, or red or pink, or whatsoever color." Within the convention, Lewis operated in a way calculated to win the respect of the insurgents. At one point during a floor debate, when Mortimer was trying in vain to secure recognition from the chair, Lewis summoned the leading auto Communist to his side and advised him to go to the platform and, following the present speaker, to step to the microphone. "Green does not have enough courage to stop you. I know Bill Green." Mortimer did as Lewis suggested and gained the floor.[31]

More important than the friendly gestures was Lewis's support for a resolution that called for the organization of the unorganized workers in the mass production industries into industrial unions. Though the craft union majority easily beat back this proposal, it provoked the convention's most serious debate and provided Lewis with an opportunity to make a stirring plea for industrial unionism. He described the history of craft union organization of the mass production industries as "a record of twenty-five years of constant, unbroken failure." Lewis claimed that he was "seduced" by the purported intentions of the craft unionists, who at the previous convention had promised industrial unionism but had failed to administer this policy. "Now, of course, having learned that I was seduced, I am enraged and I am ready to rend my seducers limb from limb." He warned the craft unions, which now stood as "mighty oaks," that they might not always be able "to withstand the lightning and the gale" and advised them to prepare for this eventuality "by making a contribution to your less fortunate brethren, heed this cry from Macedonia that comes from the hearts of men. Organize the unorganized. . . ."[32]

Lewis's fighting words greatly impressed Mortimer and the other Communist and Progressive delegates, but even more catalytic was a confrontation the following day between Lewis and the Carpenter's head, William Hutcheson. A young delegate from the Rubber Workers was speaking on the need for industrial unionism in his industry, when Hutcheson interrupted with a point of order. Leaping to the younger delegate's defense, Lewis declared: "This thing of raising points of order all the time on minor delegates is rather small potatoes." The towering and hefty leader of the Carpenters bellowed, "I was raised on small potatoes, that is why I am so small." Before Hutcheson finished, Lewis unleashed a punch that sent the federation's tenth vice-president sprawling over a table onto the floor. Mortimer who was standing nearby, had to restrain Arthur Wharton, head of the Machinists, from striking the Mine Worker president with a folding chair. Len DeCaux, a Communist sympathizer, who attended the convention as a reporter for the Federated Press, captured the punch's impact on the Communist and Progressive delegates when he later recalled, "With this blow, Lewis hammered home one of the main points he had come to the AFL convention to make—that AFL fakers were blocking a real union drive, and that he was ready to lead the workers in shoving them aside and getting down to the job."[33]

Lewis met immediately after the convention with union heads sympathetic to industrial unionism—Charles P. Howard of the Typographical Union, Max Zaritsky of the Hat, Cap and Millinery Workers, Thomas McMahon of the Textile Workers, David Dubinsky of the International Ladies Garment Workers Union and Sidney Hillman of the Amalgamated Clothing Workers of America. On November 9, the same group along with Harvey Fremming of the Oil Field, Gas Well and Refinery Workers of America and Thomas Brown of the Mine, Mill and Smelter Workers Union met in Washington and set up the Committee for Industrial Organization (CIO). The Committee elected Lewis as chairman and declared its purpose was "to encourage and promote organization of the workers in the mass production and unorganized industries." On November 23, Lewis sent a one sentence letter to Green foreshadowing the CIO's later split with the parent organization: "Effective this date, I resign as Vice-President of the American Federation of Labor."[34]

For the Communists, the formation of the CIO signified not only that Lewis had thrown his prestige and resources behind precisely the same purpose that the Communists had been advocating, but also that Lewis showed a willingness to work closely with Communists at all levels. Lewis soon brought such Communists or avowed Communist sympathizers as Len DeCaux and Lee Pressman into the inner circle of the CIO. He hired other Communists and left-wing Socialists as organizers. Shortly after the formation of the CIO, Lewis met in his Washington office with Mortimer and Kraus and agreed to their request that, early in February 1936, he make his first address to the nation's auto workers at a meeting sponsored by the Cleveland District Auto Council. Such behavior gave substance to Earl Browder's later remark that Lewis, "the nemesis of the Communists in the twenties, was transformed into their patron saint in the thirties."[35]

Lewis never provided a very satisfactory explanation of his changed attitude toward the Communists. When challenged about their participation in the CIO, he would at times profess unconcern: "I do not turn my organizers or CIO members upside down and shake them to see what kind of literature falls out of their pockets." At other times, he reacted with indignation. "Industry should not complain if we allow Communists in our organization," he once remarked. "Industry employs them." On yet other occasions he would plead practicality: "It's a pretty good rule to work with anyone who will work with you," and "In a battle I make arrows from any wood." When Dubinsky protested against the CIO's reliance on known radicals, Lewis with cold calculation could entone: "Who gets the bird, the hunter or the dog?" For whatever reasons Lewis changed his attitude, his alliance with the Left greatly served the drive to organize the mass production industries.[36]

Along with the formation of the CIO, developments within the UAW in late 1935 also aided the Communists' union objectives.

Most importantly, a growing rift developed between Francis Dillon, the UAW President, and the other union officers, particularly Vice-President Homer Martin, and Secretary-Treasurer Ed Hall. Dillon antagonized his fellow officers by a series of insensitive actions. The most important of these occurred during a strike at the Motor Products plant in Detroit. Richard Frankensteen's Automotive Industrial Workers Association (AIWA) called the strike in November 1935. MESA members in the plant joined the walkout. Dillon denounced the walkout as "the most ill-advised and unpopular strike ever called in Detroit" and induced UAW workers in the plant to cross the picket lines of the other unions. The Communists accused Dillon of "following a dangerous and despicable course," and the Communist Automotive Workers Faction said: "Dillon is trying to ruin the A.F. of L. in auto. Our policy has to be to build and strengthen the A.F. of L. in auto. This requires a unity policy in the Motor Products strike." Similarly, Progressives at Motor Products denounced Dillon's "reactionary role" in "stampeding" workers through the picket lines. Many feared that Dillon's actions would make it impossible to induce the independent unions in the industry to join the UAW. In addition to his actions during the Motor Products strike, Dillon also neglected to call meetings of the Executive Board, to assign responsibilities to other officers, or to consult them on decisions. He layed off Executive Board members who had served as organizers. He refused to issue a charter to the left-wing Toledo local, and he tried to avoid paying the expenses incurred by the Committe of Seven.[37]

As disillusionment with Dillon and the AFL increased, UAW officers, Homer Martin and Ed Hall, became amenable to cooperation with the union's Communists and Progressives. Late in 1935, Martin and Hall went to Cleveland to talk to Mortimer about their displeasure with Dillon. Mortimer later said: "They were looking for allies and they knew that I was the recognized leader of one of the largest segments of the newly chartered union." A short time after this meeting, Hall expressed regret over his previous opposition to Mortimer's group and confided to the Cleveland radical that "from here on in I am in your camp."[38]

In February, at a Toledo meeting to prepare for the second UAW convention scheduled for April, the Progressives assigned a committee of 12 headed by Mortimer to draft a program. A subsequent caucus of 150 Progressives in South Bend on March 14 and 15 approved of the committee's resolutions calling for industrial unionism in mass production industries, expanded jurisdiction for the UAW, a massive organizing drive in auto, an invitation to other auto unions to affiliate with the UAW, an expansion of the number of union vice-presidents from one to three, a reduction of the power of union officers, and the investment of local unions with the authority to decide on strikes. In addition to incorporating the basic union objectives long advocated by the Progressives, the program also included a call for the Popular Front's major political goal, the creation of national and local farmer-labor parties.[39]

The UAW convention that opened in South Bend, Indiana, on April 27, 1936, represented the triumph of the Communist-initiated Progressive movement for an international, industrial union that was controlled by the rank and file and was geared to militant organizing and strike action. The Progressive Caucus, which had the support of three of the largest locals (Toledo Local 12, White Motor and Seaman), dominated the proceedings. Communists who attended the convention, either as delegates or guests, included Wyndham Mortimer, the leader of the left forces, William Weinstone, Robert Travis, Henry Kraus, William McKie, and John Anderson. Other Progressives included George Addes, a metal finisher at the Willys-Overland plant and financial secretary of Toledo Local 12; John Soltis, first vice-president of the Cleveland Auto Council; Lloyd Jones, an activist in the Briggs and Murray strikes of 1933 and the Motor Products strike of 1935; and Walter Reuther, a Ternstedt worker of only a few weeks, who gained credentials after Mortimer spoke on his behalf to the Credentials Committee. An array of left-wing observers such as Norman Thomas, Tucker Smith, Carl Haessler, Rose Pesotta, and Leo Krzycki also helped lend a radical tenor to the proceedings. Even Homer Martin, Ed Hall and other officers, whom Green had appointed to serve under Dillon the year before, now sided with the Progressives on such key questions as jurisdiction, rank and file control, and strike policy. AFL loyalists and diehards consisted of only a couple of organizers from Detroit and a few delegates from South Bend, Kenosha, and elsewhere. Haessler recalled that "the delegates' prime purpose was to run Frank Dillon out of the convention . . . and this was done with a great deal of relish." After addressing the delegates Dillon left "being hooted and catcalled all the way out." Two years later, when Communists in the UAW were under attack from factional opponents, Joe Brown, a non-Communist, reminded others that the union had to give credit "to the Communists for leading the fight on Green and Dillon. It is mainly through their efforts that the AFL was forced to relinquish control of the UAWA." By "their efforts," Brown explained that he meant the rank and file movement that was "organized, led and extended by the Communists."[40]

The Progressive Caucus dominated the election of officers and carried its entire program. Though the Progressives originally backed Mortimer for president, he withdrew. For president, the convention elected Homer Martin, a former Baptist minister from Leeds, Missouri, who possessed indisputable oratorical skills but an erratic and unstable personality. Mortimer became first vice-president. Ed Hall, whom Green had appointed secretary-treasurer but who had turned against Dillon and aligned himself with the Progressives, became second vice-president. Walter Wells, a master mechanic from Detroit with no particular political bent, became third vice-president. George Addes, a leader of the Progressive movement in the strong Toledo Local 12, became secretary-treasurer. The Progressives or leftists also gained dominance on the eleven-member Executive Board. Observers considered five Executive Board members—Lloyd Jones, Walter Reuther, Lester Washburn, Frank Tucci, and John Soltis—as strong left-wingers and three others—Delmond Garst, J.J. Kennedy, and Willis Marrer—as left-leaning.[41]

Progressive influence also manifested itself in the convention's resolutions. Most importantly, the convention adopted positions on jurisdiction, unity, and strikes that the Communists and Progressives had advocated for two years. The convention called for the UAW's "full jurisdiction" in the auto industry and favored "the Industrial form of organization in all mass production industries." In line with these sentiments, the convention invited representatives of the major independent unions in the industry to address the convention. John Anderson, a Communist, who represented the Detroit District Committee of MESA, told the convention that it was impossible to organize the auto industry "without a strong, united, progressive organization." After the convention, Anderson brought the three largest Detroit MESA locals into the UAW. The AAWA and AIWA soon followed suit. The convention also declared itself in favor of a general strike in 1937, if the employers failed to negotiate. It endorsed a resolution on behalf of freedom for the Scottsboro Boys, nine Alabama blacks whose unjust conviction for allegedly raping two white girls in 1931 was made a national and international issue by the Communist party and the Communist-led International Labor Defense. The convention also endorsed the creation of a farmer-labor party, an idea strongly backed by the Communist party. Shortly after the convention, Joe Brown said, "The Communists are riding high, wide and handsome in the United Automobile Workers. One of their crowd is first vice-president. All of their resolutions were passed by the convention."[42]

Even though the Communists exercised considerable influence in the drive to obtain an international, industrial union and on the shape and character of the union that emerged at the 1936 convention, the actual number of Communists and active Communist supporters in the union remained small. Moreover, neither Mortimer, Travis, Kraus, McKie nor any other Communist in the union openly proclaimed his political allegiances. Such political reticence was common among all leftists at this time. It did not imply that politics was irrelevant, but rather that leftist influence depended on the way in which the Communists and others translated their political ideas and experiences into practical activity. In this respect, the Communists fared well. Several had gotten in on the ground floor and helped to build some of the strongest UAW locals. Also, well before others in the union, they had advanced ideas that conformed to the objective needs of the auto workers— an industrial union, rank and file control, unity of all union forces, militant strike action, a repudiation of AFL leaders and policies, and support for the CIO. Through the rank and file movement, they had actively persuaded others of these ideas and had united in a nonsectarian way with all who agreed with these ideas. Commenting on the unity of the "left-wing elements" who were "pretty well in control of the convention" a non-Communist observer said: "I am including those who are quite definitely Communist in character, Socialists, and the general run of the more militant 'rank and file' members of the union. The influence of the CIO was, of course, also quite definitely to the left."[43]

The united front between Communists and non-Communists at the UAW convention dovetailed with the party's general Popular

Front line. The Popular Front had been developing for some time. In 1934 the eighth convention of the Communist party placed a major emphasis on work within the AFL. The next year the Seventh Congress of the Communist International gave full expression to the Popular Front. The Seventh Congress saw the rise of fascism as the chief danger to the working class. According to Georgi Dimitroff, who gave the main report to the Congress, the rise of fascism meant that the main choice for the working class was "not between proletarian democracy and bourgeois democracy, but between bourgeois democracy and fascism." Resistance to fascism, according to Dimitroff, required a strong united front of workers on the basis of an anti-fascist and democratic program. It also required a popular front of workers and other progressive sections of the population, including the petit bourgeoisie, farmers, and intellectuals. Two months after the 1936 UAW convention, the Communists held their ninth party convention and adopted a popular front program. Its aims included raising the living standards of the workers, extending trade unions to basic industry through "militant industrial unionism," extending social and labor legislation, and defending democratic rights and civil liberties. The Communists also declared their desire to encourage the formation of a national farmer-labor party and to cooperate with the Socialist party. Though the Communists criticized President Roosevelt and said they could not support him in the forthcoming election, they also expressed their desire to cooperate with supporters of Roosevelt and promised to direct their "main fire" in the election campaign against the Republican Alf Landon, who was the "chief enemy." The Communists also condemned William Green of the AFL for having aligned himself with conservative interests and praised the CIO as "the head" of a "renaissance movement in the trade unions."[44]

Given the leftist tenor of the 1936 UAW convention, one might well have asked why the Communists did not achieve more than they did? Or why, at least, did they avoid an attempt to achieve more? Why did Mortimer settle for the office of first vice-president rather than seeking the office of president? Why did the Communists fail to go further in openly proclaiming support for the Communist party, socialism, and independent political action? References to the alleged revisionism of the Communist party or to the alleged over-cautiousness of Communist policy under the

Popular Front provide little insight into these questions. Rather, the actual, objective situation that the Communists faced alone gives a sufficient explanation. An attempt by Mortimer to secure the presidency, for instance, would have endangered the young and fragile organization. The attempt would have created a dangerous split between his followers and Martin's. Even had Mortimer won, his close connections with the CP might have alarmed AFL leaders, alienated CIO representatives, and repelled the industry's southern-born and conservative-minded workers. According to Carl Haessler, who regarded Mortimer as the only successful organizer in the union and the person whose experience and integrity best qualified him for the union's highest office, such considerations motivated Mortimer's decision to withdraw. Similar considerations accounted for the Communists' public reticence about their political views and allegiances. After all, the longest and most vituperative debate during the entire convention occurred over a resolution that all locals "immediately expel from membership all known Communists," and a substitute resolution that "no known Communists be permitted to hold office" in the union. The convention avoided a devisive showdown on these issues by referring the matter back to the Constitution Committee. Later, the convention approved, without debate, an innocuous committee resolution that expressed "unalterable opposition to Fascism, Nazism and Communism and all other movements intended to distract the attention of the membership of the Labor Movement from the primary objectives of unionism." The existence of what Communist Nat Ganley called "a strong opposition to communism" by "many forces from the Indiana area," as well as by scattered delegates from Flint, Kenosha, Cleveland, Detroit, and elsewhere indicated the limits on political advocacy beyond which the Communists would have been foolish to tread.[45]

Other limits existed. After voting to give "the strongest and widest support to the setting up of National, State, and Local Farmer-Labor Parties," the convention rejected a resolution endorsing the reelection of President Roosevelt. Apparently, the Socialists, at least one of whom spoke, favored the rejection more strongly than the Communists, who remained silent. However, the rejection caused Adolph Germer, who represented Lewis at the convention, to declare: "Communists and Socialists have taken over the convention and are voting not as auto workers but according to their political views." Lewis let it be known that he would withhold a promised contribution of $100,000 for organizing, unless the union backed Roosevelt. Consequently, the Communists and Socialists could have maintained this extreme commitment to independent political action only at the risk of losing CIO support. Just before the convention adjourned, Martin prevailed upon the delegates to reverse themselves. In short, the prevalence of anti-Communism and the strong commitment of the CIO to the reelection of President Roosevelt placed objective limits on what the Communists could have achieved. If Mortimer and his comrades had pushed any harder than they did for power, socialism, or independent political action, they would only have jeopardized their own influence and positions and would have endangered the immediate future of the union.[46]

For the Communists and Progressives, the 1936 convention represented only a victorious battle not a victorious war. They had achieved an international charter and rank and file control. They had established the principle of industrial unionism. They had won a commitment to an aggressive organizing drive and to a general strike. The most difficult struggles, however, remained ahead. Now they had to put into action the ideas they had won in debate.

# VII

### • • •

# THE SIT-DOWN STRIKES

The 1936 UAW convention laid the basis for a confrontation with GM. The convention not only declared its support for full jurisdiction but also decided that if the employers failed to negotiate, the Executive Board should plan to call a general strike in 1937. The Communists had a great deal to do with this orientation. For three years, between June 1933 and June 1936, the Communists fought against the craft union and antistrike ("class collaboration") policies of the AFL leadership. The Communists also differed with the leaders of the newly formed CIO, who shared the same aversion to strikes as the AFL stalwarts. When CIO spokesman, Charles P. Howard, told the auto convention that the CIO was "not even considering the possibility of a strike in the auto industry, as we preach industrial peace," Communists criticized the CIO for "failing to see that the fight for industrial unionism is clearly connected with the need for class struggle." The Communists advocated a more aggressive course for the UAW than that advocated by either Green or Lewis. The "class struggle" program of the Communist-led Progressive Caucus prevailed at the convention and characterized the outlook of the majority of officers and Executive Board members elected to lead the union.[1]

The union's General Executive Board selected the leading spokesman of "class struggle," Wyndham Mortimer, to lead the campaign against GM. Both background and temperament made Mortimer better qualified for the position than President Homer

Martin. Martin, the son of a school teacher, had almost no union or shop experience. He had graduated from William Jewell College in Liberty, Missouri, served as a pastor of a Baptist church in Leeds, Missouri, and had worked for a few months in a Chevrolet plant in Kansas City. By contrast, the fifty-three year old Mortimer had spent his entire life as a wage worker, including two decades as an auto worker at White Motor. Whereas Martin had no consistent political beliefs, Mortimer was a Communist. Some sources alleged that Mortimer joined the party in 1933 and served thereafter (under the name George Baker) on the party's Central Committee. While Martin had risen to the top of the union largely by dint of his oratorical abilities, Mortimer had gained his prestige by patient organizing in Cleveland. In 1937, Mortimer became the union's leading organizer and bargainer, while Martin proved an inept administrator, gullible negotiator, and inconsistent policymaker. Mortimer was reliable; those who worked with Martin "did not know from one minute to the next what he was going to do." CIO representative, John Brophy, called the union president "a drunken butterfly," and CIO attorney, Lee Pressman, declared that Martin "was absolutely as queer as a human being could possibly be."[2]

In meetings after the 1936 convention, Mortimer and other union leaders learned from tool and die maker, John Anderson, that the key automobile dies for the entire GM operation were located in two plants—Cleveland Fisher Body and Flint Fisher Body No. 1. Since a shutdown at these two shops would cripple all GM production, Mortimer decided to make them his primary targets. In June, Mortimer moved to Flint to begin strike preparations.[3]

According to the local superintendent of the Methodist Episcopal Church, the city Mortimer entered was "decidedly a Company Town." General Motors employed 47,000 persons—over two thirds of Flint's working population. Most local officials owned GM stock. City manager, John M. Barringer, ran a factory that supplied metal castings to Buick. Mayor Harold Bradshaw was a former Buick paymaster; Chief of Police, James V. Wills, was a former Buick detective. The city's radio station and daily newspaper, the *Flint Journal*, openly sympathized with their key advertiser—GM. "Both outfits [the radio and press]," Bob Travis later informed Adolph Germer, "shiver in their boots when an attempt is made to obtain publicity for the automobile workers." To insure GM's dominance company spies pervaded the city. The La Follette Committee revealed that from 1934 to 1937 GM had paid $836,764.41 to detective agencies and had established "a far flung industrial Cheka" that included 52 Pinkerton detectives who reported on union activity in GM plants.[4]

No sooner had Mortimer arrived in Flint than an anonymous phone call advised him to "get the hell back where you came from if you don't want to be carried out in a wooden box!" Unidentified persons tailed Mortimer's movements. Spies occupied rooms adjoining Mortimer's in the Dresden Hotel, and the desk clerk eavesdropped on his phone conversations. This kind of intimidation typified Flint. "A cloud of fear hung over the city," Mortimer recalled, "and it was impossible to find anyone who would even discuss the question of unionism." "Sports, women, dirty stories, and the weather" constituted the only "safe" topics.[5]

Mortimer first undertook the rebuilding of the Flint locals that had declined disastrously following Roosevelt's auto settlement of March 1934. When Mortimer undertook this project, the five Flint locals had a combined membership of 122 persons, a treasury of $24.41, and debts of $700. Most of the active members were unreliable. Many were spies. Some belonged to the Black Legion, a Klan-type group concentrated in Michigan. Still others supported the discredited Dillon leadership. "The vast majority of GM workers," Mortimer recalled, "regarded these 122 men as paid agents of General Motors and would have nothing to do with them." To revitalize the union and eliminate unreliable people from the existing leadership, Mortimer revoked the charters of the five existing locals, created the amalgamated Local 156, and postponed the election of local officers until the union had grown. Homer Martin, however, undermined Mortimer's plan by ordering immediate elections. As Mortimer feared, some of the old untrustworthy officers achieved reelection. The La Follette Committee investigations of Local 156's thirteen officers later revealed that three worked as spies for the Corporation Auxiliary, and at least two served as Pinkerton agents.[6]

In the early organizing Mortimer and later Bob Travis relied heavily on local Communists, because they were people who could be trusted. In 1936 the Communist party in Flint had between sixty and a hundred members. Many of the party members were foreign-born. They included Finns, Bulgarian-Macedonians, Slovaks, Russians, and Czechs. Some of these groups had their own organizations and halls which served as centers for leftwing cultural and political activity. The Bulgarian-Macedonian Workers' Educational Club, for example, had a hall in the St. John's area of Flint near the Buick plant that served as a regular meeting place for speakers, films and dances. Travis made some early contacts through the party-related International Workers Order (IWO). "A lot of IWO workers worked in Buick," Travis said. "They were militantly trade unionists, you could always depend on them." Mortimer and Travis also relied on members of CP units in the plants. According to Bud Simons, the Communists "had units in damn near every plant." These included units in the important Fisher No. 1, Buick, and Chevrolet plants. In Fisher Body No. 1 Bud Simons, Walter Moore, and Joe Devitt became the key organizers for Mortimer and Travis. Travis later said that the three "were Communists [who] saw eye to eye on every kind of thing," and that Simons was "one of the best organizers . . . I have ever seen." After Mortimer and Travis brought Henry Kraus to Flint to put out the *Flint Auto Worker,* they relied on an unemployed Communist, Charles Killinger and his ten children, to distribute the paper. The *Party Organizer* said that "during the whole organizational campaign preceding the strike all efforts were centered on helping the organization of the auto workers."[7]

Since Flint officials refused to grant the union a permit to distribute leaflets at plant gates and the prevalence of spies made it too dangerous to hold open meetings, Mortimer had to devise other methods of reaching Flint's auto workers. Using old union membership lists and the Flint city directory, the head of the Flint drive compiled a list of 5,000 GM workers to whom he mailed a series of ten open letters. In these letters, Mortimer stressed that the UAW now acted as an autonomous organization quite different from the old federal labor unions dominated by William Green and Francis Dillon. The union had a new leadership responsive to the rank and file. Mortimer urged auto workers to adopt "the doctrine of class consciousness as against craft consciousness," and to strive for the "unity of all workers as against the disunity of the Red Baiting days." To combat the widespread fear, Mortimer promised to meet workers privately and to use a "secret system of joining the organization" under which only Mortimer would know of a worker's membership. The veteran organizer argued that the workers should not fear the union but speedup and poverty. Without a union they would continue to live in "shacks and hovels" with insufficient food and clothing for their children, and they could only look forward to premature retirement as burned-out assembly line slaves, a burden to their friends and family. Building a labor movement represented "a class problem" according to Mortimer. "Don't be misled . . . the fight is between the robber and the robbed, between the exploiter and exploited. . . . On which side are you?"

Mortimer made a special effort to combat the redbaiting that Dillon had encouraged. In his open letters Mortimer claimed that the union's new leadership had no concern with a worker's "creed, color, race, nationality, or political and economic opinions." In the new UAW a member could "hold an opinion originating since the Civil War, without being called a "Red or a Communist." When Delmar Minzey, the union leader at AC Sparkplug, suggested that holding communist ideas serve as a basis for excluding a worker from the union, Mortimer insisted that the only criterion of membership was employment in an auto plant. "We're conducting an organizing campaign," the union vice-president said, "not a witch-hunt."[8]

To facilitate recruitment Mortimer set up small, clandestine meetings in workers' homes. Some meetings occurred in darkened basements with the windows covered and a single candle illuminating the room. Mortimer usually supplied the union pitch as well as ice cream and cookies or doughnuts and cider. Mortimer and his assistants took special pains to reach ethnic and black workers. Late one night, Mortimer attended a meeting in a spiritualist church arranged by a black worker named Henry Clark. A preacher introduced the UAW representative as "an emissary of God," and Mortimer explained how the union would improve living conditions and fight Jim Crow. Afterwards 18 black foundry workers mainly in Buick paid their initiation fees and joined the union.[9]

Under Mortimer's direction, the campaign in Flint progressed steadily during the summer. The officers of Local 156, however, resented Mortimer's secret methods and his reliance on radicals. The officers informed Homer Martin that Mortimer intended to build a "Red empire in Flint." The UAW president had already become wary of his talented vice-president. Even though Martin once assured Mortimer that "nothing could be farther from my intention or purpose than to raise a red scare about anybody . . . let alone you," by the summer the UAW president feared a Communist plot to "capture" the union. In response to the local's charges, Martin sent Fred Peiper to investigate the Flint situation. Later, Martin called a special meeting of the International Executive Board on the Flint situation. He neglected to invite Mortimer to this meeting. When Mortimer learned of the meeting, he drove quickly from Flint to Detroit, where he gave an impassioned defense of his actions and assailed the uselessness of the local officials. Second vice-president, Ed Hall, and secretary-treasurer, George Addes, strongly praised Mortimer's work. Nevertheless, "to keep peace in the family" Mortimer decided to leave his Flint post providing that Martin appoint Bob Travis as a replacement. Martin agreed.[10]

The thirty-year old Travis was an auto worker with 12 years experience in various Toledo shops. At Toledo Overland, his interest in unions was first stirred by having to work "ten, twelve, even fourteen hours a day—all at high speed." After building up "a terrific antagonism year after year to the general conditions of life," Travis began to organize a small union at Toledo Overland. In 1934, he aided the Toledo Auto Lite strikers and the next year, helped form a federal labor union in Toledo Chevrolet. During the 1935 Chevrolet walkout, Travis served on the strike committee, and a short time later he became president of the Toledo local. The struggle against Dillon brought Travis and Mortimer together, and the two dissidents formed an alliance between their two important locals. This alliance produced a long and devoted friendship. Years later, Mortimer referred to Travis as "a worker I knew well and trusted," and Travis declared that Mortimer provided "the main influence in my life, in raising things that I'd never heard about before in a way that seemed logical to me." Left-wing politics naturally provided a strong basis for both their personal friendship and union cooperation. "They were Communists," William Weinstone later remarked, "and therefore they had a common ideological outlook and a common aim."[11]

Reflecting Communist thinking on strikes in the mass production industries, Mortimer and Travis believed, along with William Z. Foster that unlike most trade union conflicts, the forthcoming ones "should be thoroughly prepared, organizationally and ideologically." Foster stressed the importance of thorough publicity to familiarize the workers and the public with "the meaning of the struggle" and urged the early involvement of black and ethnic workers in the strike preparations. Such thinking informed Travis's work as it had Mortimer's before him. Travis organized a "great number of meetings . . . in the homes, small townhalls outside the union hall and little house parties" and set up committees of "foreign speaking people." In his work, Travis generally followed the precedents that Mortimer had established, including the practice of relying on local Communists and other leftists.[12]

A Communist who proved particularly helpful to Travis was Charles Kramer. Previously a member of a Communist unit within the Agricultural Adjustment Administration, Kramer headed a group of Senate investigators that Senator La Follette's Civil Liberties Committee sent to Detroit in September 1936. Like Kramer, his associates, Ben Allen, Harold Cranefield, and H. D. Cullen, sympathized with the union. Soon after the investigators began their work, Travis asked them to obtain "all information that is possible on the General Motors Corporation in Flint." Kramer and his associates supplied the union with the names of several GM spies. Using this information, Kraus printed explosive exposés of GM espionage, and Bob Travis and Roy Reuther startled a meeting of Chevrolet unionists with the revelation that their welfare committee chairman worked for Corporation's Auxiliary. By such disclosures, Travis discouraged stoolpigeon activity, boosted the union's prestige, and bolstered the workers' morale.[13]

In Fisher No. 1, Travis built a disciplined cadre around the Communists Bud Simons, Walt Moore, Joe Devitt and Jay Green. This group had the main responsibility for recruitment in the plant. When Roosevelt's reelection encouraged spontaneous "quickie" work stoppages in early November, the Fisher cadre promoted the union openly for the first time. One November night, employees on the "bow line" stopped work to protest the suspension of three workers who had questioned the speed of the assembly line. Though the union did not instigate the work stoppage, the union cadre started yelling, "Bring them [the dismissed workers] back or we do not go to work." Bud Simons jumped on a table and spoke about the union. "From now on," Simons declared, "I think that we need the corporation to understand that they are dealing with the union, and they are not dealing with individuals." Work did not resume that night until the Flint police located the dismissed men (who had already left for home), and the company returned them to their jobs. News of this small victory spread quickly through the city. "We have cracked her open at last," Mortimer said. Within weeks Travis reported that the Flint membership, which stood at only 1,500 before the Fisher No. 1 success, was increasing at the rate of 500 a day.[14]

The quickie strikes at Fisher in November were really minature sit-down strikes, since the workers stopped working but did not leave the plant. This raises the question of the origin of the sit-down tactic and the role, if any, played by Communists in introducing the tactic to auto workers. The tactic had indeterminate origins. Its first use by American workers in the twentieth century occurred when IWW members sat down in the General Electric Company in Schenectady in 1906. In 1907 engineering workers in Coventry, England used a sit-down. After World War I, Italian workers, often led by Communists, seized many factories for a time and continued to run production. In the early 1930s, coal miners in Yugoslavia, Hungary, Poland, England, Wales, and France used the sit-down or stay-down tactic. In 1933, 1934, and 1935 auto workers in body shops conducted a few quickie sit-downs. The tactic, however, did not achieve widespread attention until 1936, when Goodyear, Firestone, and Goodrich rubber workers in Akron, Ohio, conducted brief sit-downs in February, and a wave of mass sit-down strikes occurred in France in May and June. The first major sit-down strike in the auto industry occurred at the Bendix Products Corporation in South Bend, Indiana. Beginning on November 17 and lasting a week (before reverting to a conventional walkout) this strike won the local recognition as the bargaining agent for its members. UAW and CIO leaders followed these events in Akron, South Bend, and France. During the Goodyear strike, for instance, Mortimer led a delegation from the Cleveland Auto Council to Akron to offer assistance to the strikers, and Homer Martin and Walter Reuther led a delegation of UAW leaders to a post-strike celebration. Thus, by the end of 1936, the sit-down idea was in the air and was the property of no particular group in the union.

Though the Communists did not originate the sit-down, they

apparently introduced it to the key rank and file leaders in Flint and Cleveland with whom they had contact. Rudy Miller, a worker in the Cleveland Fisher Body plant, later recalled that he had heard about the sit-down strikes in Italy, France and Akron from the Communist workers, Jerry Strauss and Lester and John Downy, "guys in the plant who were pretty well read up on all those things." Similarly, Bud Simons later recalled that as early as September 1936 he had "kicked this idea around" with Mortimer, Travis, Walt Moore and Joe Devitt. "They," Simons said, "followed the one in France, and the one in Midland Steel [in November]. They got a hold of those people, interviewed them, found out what tactics they used and everything. . . . We had it all worked out in our heads of what to do . . . when we had the sit-down."[15]

The Midland Steel Products Company strike (as Simons suggested) and a strike at Kelsey-Hayes in Detroit provided both Communists and non-Communists with practical experience with the sit-down before its use against General Motors. On November 27 about 1,200 workers on the day shift sat down in the Midland Steel plant, halting the production of body frames for Ford and Chrysler. Communists played a small but significant role in the week-long strike that followed. John Anderson, the head of UAW Local 155, helped direct the strike. Nat Ganley, a former TUUL organizer in New York and New England and a former punch press operator in Detroit, who helped Anderson organize Local 155, edited the strike paper, the *Midland Flash*. The paper's lay-out and style resembled earlier CP shop papers. Dorothy Kraus, the wife of the editor of the Flint *Auto Worker*, Henry Kraus, organized the women workers, who were not permitted to remain in the plant, into committees to visit and reassure the wives of strikers in the plant. She also supervised the strike kitchen, a role she later performed in the GM strike. Michigan Communist party secretary, William Weinstone, called upon Communists to support the strike on the outside, and according to one observer, "every Communist on the east side" must have come "bringing food and assisting in the strike, so many that I could not name them all." The strikers showed little concern over the Communist presence, and when an anonymous leaflet advised the workers to "get rid of" the reds the workers denounced it as a stoolpigeon attempt "to break our ranks." Mortimer helped negotiate the agreement ending the strike. The agreement provided for a wage increase, the abolition of piece rates, and access for the union to the workers. The *Daily Worker* hailed the outcome of the strike and predicted that the sit-down would "take the automobile industry by storm."[16]

A series of three brief sit-down strikes at the Kelsey-Hayes Wheel Company in December provided not only lessons in sit-down tactics but also an exercise in cooperation between Communists and Socialists such as would later occur in Flint. Though these strikes won few concrete concessions from management, except for an increase in overtime pay, they built the union's membership and represented the first gain for Walter Reuther's large West Side Local 174. The three Socialists who led the strike, Walter and Victor Reuther and Merlin D. Bishop, were later active in the GM strike. During the Kelsey-Hayes strike they worked closely with the Communists and their supporters, including Stanley Nowak and William McKie. Walter Reuther symbolized the blending of allegiances that occurred among some Socialists and Communists at this time. Reuther's father, Valentine, had been a Socialist member of the Brewery Workers Union in Wheeling, West Virginia, and after migrating to Detroit in the late 1920s, Walter had joined the Socialist party while working at Ford and attending Wayne State University. Between 1933 and 1935, Walter and his brother Victor worked 15 months in the Gorky Ford plant in the Soviet Union and developed an admiration for the "genuine proletarian democracy" they found there. After returning to the United States, Walter lectured under the auspices of the Friends of the Soviet Union and worked with Communists in the auto union. The Communists aided Reuther in securing credentials at the UAW South Bend convention and backed his successful bid for a seat on the Executive Board. At the time of the Kelsey-Hayes and General Motors strikes Reuther belonged to the Socialist party, but he also met frequently with William Weinstone and other Communists and, according to several associates, paid dues for a time to the CP.[17]

As the strike movement gathered momentum, one of the Communists' concerns was to guard against "untimely local strikes." The UAW Communists were particularly fearful of precipitous moves against GM. In November, Travis stated that he needed at least a month more of preparation. Mortimer had three reasons for not wanting a strike until after January 1. It was "very bad psychology" to have the strike occur over the Christmas holidays. If a strike occurred before December 18, the workers would lose a fifty dollar bonus that GM had promised. Finally, on January 1, the Democrat Frank Murphy would replace the Republican Frank Fitzgerald as governor of Michigan, and Murphy had a much better labor record than the incumbent. The question of timing became a major source of division between the Communists and Martin.[18]

In the middle of November, Fred Peiper, a Martin follower, ordered his Fisher Body local in Atlanta, Georgia to wear union buttons in violation of company rules. The Fisher management fired several employees, thereby provoking a sit-down strike. Anxious for strike action, the inexperienced UAW president immediately authorized the Atlanta strike and wired other UAW locals to "stand by for notification from the international union concerning action to be taken." According to Kraus, this news came as "a thunderbolt to the other general officers." "All of us at Detroit headquarters," Kraus recalled, "ran around bordering on insanity." No one knew where to reach Martin. Finally, Ed Hall contacted Martin by phone in Kansas City. "You dumb son-of-a-bitch," Hall yelled, "you get your ass back here by tonight or that'll be the last trip you'll ever take." After Martin's return to Detroit, Mortimer, Travis, Hall, and Addes convinced the Executive Board to reject an immediate strike. In mid-December strikes erupted at Libby-Owens-Ford and at Martin's home local in Kansas City, but Mortimer and Travis successfully contained the key Fisher Body plants in Cleveland and Flint.[19]

During the latter part of 1936, Mortimer kept in touch with the unionists in the Cleveland Fisher Body plant and indicated the desirability of having a strike at the end of the year. The organizing of Cleveland Fisher Body was done by the workers in the plant. The president of the local was Louis Spisak. He was not a very effective leader but he was popular with the Slovenians, the largest ethnic group in the plant. The main support for the union came from radical Hungarians and Slovenians, who were mainly production workers, and from skilled tradesmen, who had previously belonged to MESA. Several leftists such as Charles Beckman, John DeVito and Paul Miley, and a small group of Communists were the main leaders in the plant. A Fisher Body worker said, "Later on I was surprised [by] all the people I knew that were members of the Communist Party. . . . I believe if it hadn't been for the Communist Party there wouldn't have been a strike. . . . Let me tell you the truth, the Communist Party members were our teachers." Though the Fisher Body unionists had recruited only a minority of the workers by December, they prepared for a strike. After Christmas, according to Paul Miley, who became the leader of the strike committee, talk of a strike "was going back and forth like wildfire." Miley said, "We knew that we were going out at the first opportunity." The opportunity came on December 28, when workers in the plant spontaneously sat down after the company had postponed a bargaining meeting with Spisak.

Within minutes after the Cleveland workers had ceased work, Spisak notified Mortimer in Flint. Mortimer needed to keep the Cleveland plant shut down until the union could close Fisher No. 1 in Flint and negotiate a national agreement. After instructing Spisak to avoid negotiations under any circumstances, Mortimer left immediately for Cleveland. Two hours after the strike began, Cleveland Mayor Harold Burton proposed to Spisak that the strikers resume work pending negotiations. Spisak told the men in the plant about the proposal. Miley, Beckman, DeVito, and the dozen or so members of the Communist nucleus in the plant recognized the danger and rejected the idea. A short time later, Mortimer arrived in the city and informed waiting news people that the strike rested in the hands of the international union. He said the union rejected the Burton plan, and the settlement of the Cleveland dispute would have to be part of a national agreement. Mortimer then rushed to the Fisher Body plant, where he encouraged the strikers to keep up the strike. Their fight, he said, had become "an issue for the entire working class." Afterwards, Mortimer called Travis and advised him to close Fisher No. 1 as soon as possible.[20]

The day after the Cleveland sit-down began, William Weinstone met with Flint CP section head, Walt Moore, on Moore's lunch break. When Moore informed the head of the Michigan Communists of imminent strikes in Fisher No. 1 and No. 2, Weinstone looked aghast. "You're not prepared for a sit-down strike," Weinstone admonished. "You only have 2,500 members. You haven't got Flint organized. What are you talking about?" After further discussion, Moore said, "Well, Bill, we can't stop it. The sentiment's too great." Weinstone said, "Well, all right. If you can't stop it, you can't stop it. But organize yourselves so you don't go home on January 1." Moore assured him, "We're already organizing."[21]

At 7:00 a.m. on December 30, three plant guards came into the body line section of Fisher Body No. 2 to escort three inspectors out of the plant. The three inspectors had ignored a management order either to quit the union or to return to their former jobs as metal finishers. A number of workers surrounded the patrolmen and warned them not to touch the inspectors or "there would be some trouble." The patrolmen left, but the incident prompted an immediate sit-down that idled 1,000 workers and halted the production of Chevrolet bodies. Later the same day, Travis, who awaited an opportunity to move, received word from unionist "Chink" Ananich that GM was transferring the dies out of Fisher No. 1. By turning on a 200 watt, red lightbulb outside of the union headquarters across from the plant, Travis summoned unionists to a hurried lunch meeting, where he explained that the transfer of dies might well threaten their jobs. The workers' resentment swelled as one. Workers shouted, "Shut her down! Shut the goddamn plant!" As the workers raced back toward the sprawling plant, Kraus and Travis waited expectantly on the sidewalk across the street. Kraus recalled: "The starting whistle blew. We listened intently. There was no responsive throb. . . . Then suddenly, a third-floor window was flung open and there was 'Chink' Ananich waving his arms, shouting 'Hooray, Bob! She's ours!'"[22]

Communists inside and outside the UAW had one overriding objective during the sit-down—to win the strike. The Communist party "heartily supports the CIO organizing campaigns" noted Foster during the GM conflict, "for the same reason that it supports every forward movement of the workers wherever it may originate or whatever form it may take, whether it be a strike, an organization campaign, the carrying on of independent working class political activity, or what not. The Communist Party has no interests apart from those of the working class, and every victory of the workers is a victory for the Communist Party."[23]

Stimulated by the collective action around them, the Communists worked tirelessly on behalf of the strike. According to the *Party Organizer*, Communist sections in Cleveland and Flint placed "themselves at the disposal of the union" and did "everything possible towards winning the strike." Weinstone, party secretary of Michigan, and John Williamson, party secretary of Ohio, both acted as advisors to the strike leaders. According to Carl Haessler, who handled the union's press relations in Flint, Weinstone played "a very considerable role" as "one of Travis's braintrusters." In Cleveland, Williamson met daily with members of the Fisher strike committee to discuss "ideas on how to make the strike more effective." Other Communists collected food and money for the strikers and joined picket lines outside the plants.

A similar activism prevailed among Communists within the struck plants where party members tried to "show by example that the Communists are among the most active workers," in the strike. "A Party member," the *Party Organizer* reported, "who does not stand in the forefront of the struggle, does not fulfill the very first requirement of a Communist." Before the strike began, the Cleveland Fisher Body shop nucleus had only a dozen or so members and reportedly "branch life was barren," but the excitement of struggle brought the plant's Communists to life. The Communist nucleus grew to 50. The Fisher Body nucleus met daily and discussed the needs of the strike, sold the *Daily Worker*, and prepared special editions of the unit paper, *Sparkplug*. In an unnamed auto plant, a Communist unit reportedly grew from five to fifteen members, six of whom were former party members who desired to work with the nucleus "as soon as they saw that Party members were active in the strike." Communists in Fisher No. 1 reacted with similar energy. Joe Devitt later declared that "those that were called left-wingers . . . played a most active part in the organizing and conduct of the sit-down strike. They played a major role." So active was Devitt's comrade, Walter Moore, that the Fisher No. 1 strike committee had to command "that Walt Moore be put to bed."[24]

The Communists knew that in "a big strike the capitalists will frantically howl that the whole movement is an insurrection, a revolution." Indeed, attempts to blame the strike on Communists came from all quarters. The *IMA News*, the paper of the Industrial Mutual Association (a welfare capitalist creation that provided recreation for GM employees), asserted that the strike resulted from Russian Communism and amounted to "a vast conspiracy to destroy all for which life is worth living." Father Charles Coughlin saw an attempt "of union labor to Sovietize industry." Catholic Bishop Michael S. Gallagher called the sit-downs "illegal and Communistic" and said he feared "that it's Soviet planning behind them." City Manager John Barringer blamed the strike on Communists and persuaded the municipal government to hire between 30 and 50 guards for the city's water works, sewage disposal plant, pumping station and dams, which he contended, the Communists planned to destroy.[25]

To undercut the effect of such charges, the Communists deliberately played down their political ideas. Haessler recalled that even though the "people at the center of things were largely Communists," there was very little "politicing" [sic] during the Flint sit-down. No national CP functionaries spoke in Flint or visited the union headquarters. Weinstone declared later: "I didn't speak at any strike meeting and wouldn't." When local party members spoke at rallies, they did so as union members and not party members. Likewise, the party told its members in the union to propose "Party policies" in the various strike committees of which they were members but warned: "This does not mean that Party comrades in such committees make these proposals in the name of the Party. They make these proposals as union men." In one plant, a party nucleus met everyday during the sit-down, but it broke into small groups and acted inconspicuously so as not to afford "stool-pigeons" the opportunity "to say that cliques are forming." So politically covert were the Communists, that Roy Reuther, who worked closely with Travis, believed that the sit-down leader simply acted as "a good trade union guy" who had no politics until later.[26]

The Communists avoided revolutionary or socialist sloganeering. They believed that even though the sit-down represented "a more advanced form" of encroachment on property rights than most strikes, it still aimed at traditional union goals. Weinstone observed shortly after the conflict that "the workers were not motivated by revolutionary aims in occupying the plants but were limiting themselves to a form of pressure to achieve their immediate ends." Under these circumstances, raising revolutionary slogans would only have divided the strikers, confused public opinion, and played into the hands of those who were imputing revolutionary objectives to the strikers. Instead, the Communists stressed the workers' "reasonable and modest demands"—a contract, better wages, hours and working conditions. In a radio broadcast during the strike, Mortimer said: "Those sit-down workers are staying at their work-places; no one else has a better right to be there than have these men themselves. . . . The sit-down strikers have performed valuable services in those factories; General Motors and the public alike have profited by those services. To call them trespassers now . . . is logically unsound and is manifestly unjust." In a public statement Weinstone said: "There is nothing against the law or against the right of private property in striking in the plants. The workers are not invading the rights of private property, because they are peaceful and orderly and have not disturbed a single piece of machinery or injured a single piece of property. They are there solely to protect their jobs against lawless action of the companies in importing scabs and strikebreakers."[27]

Though the Communists focused their main attention on "the day-to-day activities" necessary to winning the strike, they also accomplished "some political tasks." Communist strikers brought pamphlets on Spain, Hearst, and other political topics into the plants and also distributed the *Daily Worker*. When someone in Fisher No. 1 objected to the circulation of the *Daily Worker*, the issue came before the strike committee. By a unanimous vote, the strike committee decided that the Communist paper was "the best paper that comes into the plant." Explaining the decision, Bud Simons told a meeting of strikers, "We are only here to better our conditions at home, and men who can make a decision as to this are able to make their own decision as to reading material." A *Daily Worker* reporter said that the paper attracted "regular readers" among both strikers and picketers and that the arrival of the *Daily Worker* distributor at the plants signaled "a daily rush" to get the paper. After the sit-down, Weinstone claimed the party had distributed 150,000 copies of the *Daily Worker* in Flint. He noted that "quite generally the workers welcomed the paper."

In the *Daily Worker's* "Auto Strike Section," Weinstone made a low key appeal to the auto strikers "to see the truth about us Communists," to realize that Communists betokened neither "dreamers with far-fetched plans" nor "Russians who sneaked over in the dark of the moon," but "practical" people "whose main aim is to convince the workers that they must stand up for their every day rights and fight to improve their living standards." Since Communists tried to "master the lessons of all previous experiences", Weinstone argued, "if more militants were Communists then there would be that many more live wires who would strengthen the battle line in all directions." Within the plants, Communists did some recruiting. The number of Communists in Cleveland Fisher body doubled from 24 to 50 during the strike, and in another auto plant the party nucleus recruited 6 members during the shutdown and 21 immediately afterwards. Such party work, however, occupied only a small portion of Communists' time, so much so that Weinstone later lamented that during the strike in Michigan "there was no Party building carried on by the Party Units or Party members." After the euphoria of the strike had dimmed, a party member acknowledged that "individual comrades had become so immersed in the practical tasks of winning the strike that the political tasks of the Party were sorely neglected."[28]

Though Socialists played important parts in the sit-down, they had considerably less importance than the Communists. Six months after the sit-down, when the SP had only 67 members in Michigan auto branches, Flint Socialist, Hy Fish, said: "The party entered auto late. We entered during [the] strike, having no previous base in the union. True, we had some Socialists working in auto plants and members of the union. . . . Those few who did have influence and somewhat of a mass base, had these without the aid of the party. . . . The party was nowhere to be felt." In contrast, Ben Fischer, a Michigan Socialist functionary, said: "The CP had a real base in auto long before we did. They did not have the problem of developing among their people discipline in mass organization work. During the GM strike and for a while after that their people played a leading role in the local unions." Nevertheless, soon after the strike began Norman Thomas wished Martin "all possible success," promised that the SP "will do what it can," and asked "every Socialist to do all in his power to aid the unions in their struggles." Subsequently, Powers Hapgood, Roy and Victor Reuther, and Kermit and Genora Johnson assumed prominent strike roles. This led Frank Trager to claim in the *Socialist Call* that outside of Bob Travis, "all of the rank-and-file leaders are well-known Socialists." At variance with the reality and with the Communists' self-imposed modesty, such claims prompted Weinstone to accuse the Socialists of "unjustified boasting" and "harmful sectarianism." Even the moderate Socialist, James Oneal, remarked that Trager's boast showed that "these crackpot followers of Thomas are obsessed with one thing—the limelight."[29]

The Socialists also tended to read more revolutionary implications into the sit-down than the Communists. *Socialist Call* editors proclaimed that the "stay-in strike" offered "a direct challenge to the capitalist concept of private property" and "must bring the workers into conflict with the capitalist state. . . . Factory after factory will become the battleground for miniature civil wars." Likewise, Norman Thomas argued that the sit-down represented "a weapon, which by its nature challenges some of the basic premises of the capitalist system." He acclaimed the Flint strikers as "Harbingers of a new society." Diverging from the Communists' caution about using the strike for purposes of socialist propaganda, Leo Krzycki, former national chairman of the SP and a CIO organizer in Flint, talked to a meeting of strikers about the necessity of building a society in which workers would own the means of production. Addressing a meeting in Pengelly Hall in Flint immediately after the strike, Thomas said: "Our battle is not only against General Motors; it is against the whole system of private ownership." The Communists viewed such talk as "radical phrase-mongering" that imperiled workers' struggles by playing "directly into the hands of the William Randolph Hearsts, who seek to scare wavering elements by picturing every fight of the workers for civil rights or wage improvements as a threatening revolution."[30]

The Communists also had subtle but important differences with Socialists over the proper attitude towards the government. In 1936 the Socialist party had merged with the small band of American Trotskyists, and by the time of the Flint strikes, both the Socialists and Trotskyists strongly opposed "capitalist politicians." Consequently, during the sit-down the Socialists repeatedly stressed their concern over "the dangerous faith that the workers still have in Murphy-Roosevelt." Throughout the strike the Socialist press tried to correct the auto workers' "illusions" by relentless criticism of the government and repeated warnings to labor not to "expect that the President, class representative of the capitalist state, will fight its battles." The Communists also warned against the folly of relying on the Roosevelt administration, "a capitalist government." The Communists recognized, however, that both Roosevelt and Murphy had committed themselves to collective bargaining and had depended on labor support for their elections. The Communists tried to use these circumstances to pressure Roosevelt and Murphy into aiding the strike. Communists announced that "the people" expected the President and Governor to fulfill their pro-labor election utterances and urged workers to bring "mass pressure upon the government" to "force a strike settlement favorable to the workers." Instead of denouncing the government, the *Daily Worker* either commended or chastized Roosevelt and Murphy, depending upon whether their given actions aided or impeded the victory of the strikers.[31]

In spite of their differences with the Socialists and their even more profound differences with many non-Socialist union members, the Communists believed in a strong united front as a prerequisite for victory. "A unified command," Foster stated, "is a fundamental principle of strategy in all strikes." The Communists promoted unity between themselves, the Socialists, the non-political UAW leaders, and the CIO representatives. Although Mortimer, Travis, Kraus and the Communists in Fisher No. 1 prepared the sit-down and occupied the key positions, they cooperated fully with the Socialists in all levels of strike activity. The Socialist CIO organizer, Adolph Germer, worked with Travis in planning and executing strike strategy. Larry Davidow served as one of the UAW's lawyers. Roy and Victor Reuther manned the sound truck. The CIO organizers, Powers Hapgood and Leo Krzycki, the rubber workers, B. J. Widick and William Carney, and Local 174 leaders, Walter Reuther and Merlin Bishop, helped out in various ways. All were Socialists. The Socialist Kermit Johnson became the strike leader in Chevrolet No. 4, and the Socialists Phil Wise and Pete Kennedy played leading roles in Fisher No. 1. Genora Johnson organized an arm of the Women's Auxiliary called the Women's Emergency Brigade. The brigade eventually consisted of 400 women, who dressed in red berets and armed themselves with rolling pins, broom handles and two-by-fours. Throughout the conflict the *Daily Worker* editors gave favorable coverage to the activities of such Socialists as Walter Reuther and Genora Johnson. Afterwards, Weinstone commended the Socialists for their "worthwhile activity in the strike."[32]

Though the Socialist party had a score or so of members active in Flint during the strike, few actually had employment in the shops. By contrast, the Communist party had a hundred members in Flint, a good portion of whom were rank and file workers. The Communists had particular importance in the sit-down at the crucial Fisher No. 1 plant. William Weinstone later claimed that strike committee members, Walter Moore, Joe Devitt and Jay Green, belonged to the CP, as did Bud Simons, a 33 year old torch solderer, who served as strike committee chairman. The slim, dark-eyed, energetic Simons was born in southern Indiana. After an argument with a teacher, he quit junior high school and became an itinerant, working at various farm and industrial jobs. In the early 20s he participated once in an IWW strike in Des Moines. In 1925, Simons settled in South Bend, Indiana, and worked for three years in the city's Studebaker plant. Moving to Grand Rapids, Michigan, in the early 30s Simons found work at the Hayes Body Co., where he met Walter Moore, a native of rural Michigan, and Joe Devitt of South Dakota. Moore and Devitt shared Simon's radical political outlook, and the three men became strong personal friends. Simons, Moore and Devitt joined the AWU and led a short sit-down at Hayes in 1933. A short time later the three men moved their families to Flint and found work together in the Fisher No. 1 plant, where they became involved in the union movement. Shortly after the sit-down, Adolph Germer praised Simons as "the man who actually had the courage to go to the front in Fisher No. 1 when courage was needed and to him belongs much of the credit for building the organization in that plant."[33]

Simons, Devitt, Moore, Green, and the other Communists tried to implement the strategic imperatives that the Communist party had developed through years of class struggle. The Communists believed that success depended on involving strikers in democratic decision-making and building a disciplined organization in the plant. "The broad strike committee," Foster had written, "gives the workers the realization that the strike is really their affair. It awakens in them an intelligent discipline and not merely a blind obedience to orders; it raises their morale, avoids the usual mass passivity and brings about the maximum mass activity. Above all, it provides the means for the strikers to contribute their intelligence to the shaping of strike policy." According to their own accounts, the Communists pursued this strategy in the auto sit-down. At Cleveland Fisher Body, Williamson claimed that the Communists in the plant joined with other unionists to create an "effective and democratic strike leadership" and in an unspecified GM plant "the first task" of the Communists reportedly "was to see that democratic elections were initiated to set up strike machinery inside."

Both democracy and discipline prevailed in the Fisher No. 1 plant during the strike. To head the sit-down Simons established a 17 person strike committee with an executive committee consisting of Simons and four other strikers. Final authority, however, rested in the strikers themselves, who reviewed the decisions of the strike committee in daily mass meetings. The plant organization reminded Professor Robert Morss Lovett of "a soviet." Henry Kraus described it as "townhall gatherings of a basic democratic society." The strikers drew up their own rules to insure the protection and safety of company property, the cleanliness and order of their improvised living quarters, and the health and sobriety of the strike participants. A "special patrol" of 65 trusted workers policed the plant, and a kangaroo court meted out punishments such as assigning extra clean-up duty to those who failed to observe sanitation rules. Much of the court's procedure occurred tongue-in-cheek; reporter, Edward Levinson, noted that there was "more substantial and original humor in a single session of the Fisher strikers' kangaroo courts than in a season of Broadway musical comedies." All of the strikers participated on committees that handled food, information, safety, postal services, education, entertainment, sanitation and athletics. Many visitors to the plants commented on the "military control and discipline that prevail among the strikers." A striker explained, "Every guy is assigned to some duty. We take turns in the kitchen, on the clean-up squad, doing guard duty, and the other things that have to be done around here." Enthralled by this "new and special kind of community" a *Daily Worker* reporter observed, "The whole set-up in the Fisher Body Plant No. 1 is splendid evidence of the powers of the workers to do things in common efficiency and in a disciplined manner."[34]

Both discipline and morale were stronger among the sit-down strikers in the Fisher No. 1 plant than in either the Fisher No. 2 or Chevrolet No. 4 plants. In Chevrolet No. 4, where a sit-down did not occur until early February, strike leader Kermit Johnson warned Travis about "growing dissention [sic] among the boys in here. These boys don't need democracy they need a king." According to the National Guard, the married men in the Fisher No. 2 plant became "decidedly worried" about their situation. At one point during the 44-day seige, when the number of persons occupying the Fisher No. 2 plant fell to only 20, striker leader, Red

Mundale, had to seek outside assistance to bolster his ranks: "God damn, let's have some action out there. I haven't enough men in here to hold." No similar morale problems occurred in Fisher No. 1. The prevalence of Communists in the Fisher No. 1 plant and the democratic, disciplined organization they created contributed greatly to this difference. Weinstone accurately observed that "the Communists sought to imbue the strikers and the workers with the greatest discipline, organization and perseverance" and where "the Communists were active, particularly in the most decisive points of the struggle . . . the strike was the strongest, and this made for the success of the whole battle."[35]

Believing that "a general participation of the whole strike bound population" would contribute to "the maximum striking power of the workers," the Communists naturally encouraged the active participation of women in the strike. Communists scoffed at the notion that "women's place is in the home" and commended the "wives and daughters of the strikers" for their "indispensible" work in the strike kitchen and on the picket lines. Nevertheless, both Communist and non-Communist union leaders thought it inappropriate for women workers to remain in the plants with the men. Except for a January strike at Bohn Aluminum, in which the women workers refused to leave the plant, the union limited the contribution of women to strike support efforts.[36]

Communist women played a leading role in Flint. Dorothy Kraus, of the food committee during the Midland strike, set up a "chiseling committee" to obtain food from sympathetic grocers and supervised the strike kitchen that operated in a restaurant across the street from Fisher No. 1. To cook for the strikers, Kraus imported Max Gazan, a former chef at the swank Detroit Athletic Club. Aided by scores of women, including Hazel Simons and Donna Devitt, Kraus and Gazan fed as many as 5,000 persons a day throughout the strike. During the first days of the strike Dorothy Kraus and Margaret Anderson, wife of John Anderson, formed the Women's Auxiliary of the UAW. The Women's Auxiliary established a speaker's bureau, publicity committee, nursery and first aid station. It also engaged in picketing, collected food and money, and visited strikers' homes to reassure their families and distribute relief. Drawing on her previous experience as founder of the People's Theater of Cleveland, a theater devoted to proletarian drama, Dorothy Kraus also arranged the performance of dramatic skits for the entertainment of the strikers. Kraus later collaborated with Mary Heaton Vorse and Josephine Herbst to write *Strike Marches On*, a play based on the Flint strike and performed by strike participants.[37]

The Communists emphasized the necessity of "well-organized strike publicity." Such publicity should "dissipate the charges of revolution" leveled at strikers, "expose the vast riches and profits of the employers," and keep participants abreast of strike developments. Besides including a weekly four-page supplement on the auto sit-down, the *Daily Worker* contained thorough, front page coverage of strike events. *Daily Worker* reporters augmented their news reports with features that contrasted the workers' ruinous lives and "reasonable" demands to GM's huge profits, salaries and dividends. The *Flint Auto Worker*, that Henry Kraus continued to publish during the strike, represented another important source of news and publicity.[38]

Kraus's publicity work was supplemented by that of Len DeCaux. The son of an affluent English family, DeCaux left Oxford University in 1921, and with the "dream of becoming a worker," he immigrated to America. Here DeCaux rode the rails, worked as a harvest hand, day laborer and meat packer. In the late 20s, DeCaux attended Brookwood Labor College and then became a reporter of the Federated Press, a labor news service. During the GM sit-down, DeCaux acted as an advisor to John Brophy and handled publicity for the CIO. While not a member of the CP, DeCaux later acknowledged that he "had close sympathies with the Communists, had many friends among them, and associated myself with them in a number of ways." Like party members, DeCaux refrained from flaunting his political ideas, and Brophy later claimed he "had no idea then that DeCaux worked closely with the Communists."[39]

Carl Haessler worked closely with Kraus and DeCaux. Haessler's parents were Milwaukee Socialists, and Haessler worked on Victor Berger's *Milwaukee Leader* before serving a prison sentence for his refusal to participate in World War I. On his release from prison in 1920, Haessler worked for the Federated Press and acted as the news service's managing editor from 1922 until 1956. Like DeCaux, Haessler was not a member of the Communist party. In a 1971 interview, however, Haessler claimed the Communists always "trusted" him, and he helped them in many ways. When Adolph Germer once suggested that Haessler sue Homer Martin for having called Haessler a Communist, Haessler replied that he did not regard the charge as an insult. While in Flint reporting on the strike for the Federated Press, Haessler accepted an invitation from Germer to handle press relations for the union. Haessler composed press releases, dispensed news favors to sympathetic reporters, and reprimanded reporters who put out false or misleading stories. He also wrote two favorable articles on the strike for the *New Masses* and helped Kraus edit the *Flint Auto Worker*.[40]

One of the union's three lawyers, Lee Pressman, had close connections with the Communist party. A bright, aggressive, and ambitious Harvard law school graduate, Pressman was the chief legal counsel of the CIO and an influential advisor of John L. Lewis. He was also a radical. Between 1933 and 1935, Pressman belonged to the Communist group in the Agricultural Adjustment Administration. Though Pressman later claimed that he quit the party on leaving the government in 1936, he admittedly retained his ideological ties and personal contacts with the party until he resigned from the CIO in 1948. John Brophy described Pressman as "the principal advocate of the Communists in the CIO." Brophy, however, "never saw any evidence of his [Pressman's] proselytizing for Communism." Pressman became involved in defending the union from a court injunction early in the strike and later became one of the union's three principal negotiators with GM.[41]

Another UAW attorney during sit-down was Maurice Sugar, a Detroit lawyer with a well-deserved reputation for tireless devotion to civil rights, radical, and labor causes. Though not a Communist, Sugar never engaged in red-baiting and consistently defended and worked with Communists in such groups as the AWU, International Labor Defense, Friends of the Soviet Union, John Reed Club, and Michigan Farmer-Labor Party. Like Pressman, Sugar's strike activities ranged far beyond legal defense. Sugar aided Travis with strike strategy and frequently represented the union in contacts with Governor Frank Murphy, a former classmate of Sugar. Sugar also contributed his skills as an amateur song writer, and soon sit-down strikers everywhere were singing the lyrics of his song, "Sit-down":

> When they tie the can to a union man,
>  Sit down! Sit down!
> When they give him the sack, they'll take him back,
>  Sit down! Sit down!

When the speed-up comes, just twiddle your thumbs,
　　Sit down! Sit down!
When the boss won't talk, don't take a walk,
　　Sit down! Sit down![42]

The importance of such politically radical attorneys became apparent the first week of the strike. At that time GM went to Judge Edward D. Black of the Genesee County Court and obtained an injunction that ordered the union to cease picketing and to evacuate the plants. Both Homer Martin and UAW attorney Larry Davidow wanted to abide by the law. Davidow informed Travis: "There's nothing you can do. You'll have to obey the order. Otherwise the sheriff can deputize an army of a thousand men if necessary to take the plants over." The Communists thought differently. They believed that strikers should "follow the traditional American trade union policy of ignoring such court orders." Reflecting this view, Pressman, Sugar and Germer came up with a plan by which the union might safely defy the injunction. If the union could demonstrate that Judge Black had violated Michigan state law by adjudicating a case in which he had a vested interest, then the injunction would be void. By having his law partner in New York check the list of GM stockholders, Pressman discovered that Judge Black owned 3,365 shares of GM stock valued at $219,000. The union released this information to the press and announced it would seek the impeachment of Judge Black. The judge responded: "[I]t sounds like Communist talk to me." He was partly correct, but under the circumstances no one took time to notice. The injunction quickly became a dead letter. "If G.M. was calling us 'red,'" Pressman later observed, "it was nothing compared to the red face General Motors had after we broke this. It was a real break for us."[43]

As leaders of the strike, Mortimer, Travis and Simons did not attempt to impose an uncompromising position on the union, and Communist-supported strategies exuded no more militance than those acceptable to such other strike leaders as John Brophy, Roy and Victor Reuther. As with the Judge Black injunction, however, the Communists often supported more militant measures than the moderates in the union leadership. The willingness of Mortimer and Travis to resist the blandishments of Governor Murphy, defy the compromises and threats of GM, and resort to violence if necessary to defend the struck plants, occasionally brought the Communists into conflict with more timorous union officials.

Violence was an ever-present danger. In the first week of the strike an aggressive back-to-work organization called the Flint Alliance formed. The union feared that the Alliance might use violence against the strikers. Also, early in the strike, GM supervisors attacked a union sound truck outside the Chevrolet plant. In the face of these threats, the Communists argued that the workers must prepare to defend themselves in case either police, plant guards or vigilantes tried to force the strikers from the plants. When Flint Alliance leader, George Boysen, threatened to use force against the strikers, Travis declared, "The only way to get us out of these plants is to pull us out." Such notations, in Bud Simons's "order-book" as "Prepare hoses on second and third floors" and "Establish pickets in stairways" indicated the close supervision the head of the strike committee gave to plant security. Over the plant windows of Fisher No. 1, strikers placed metal sheets with holes in which to place fire hoses. Though the strike committee forbade the presence of firearms, the strikers made ammunition piles of door hinges and constructed blackjacks out of rubber hoses, braided leather, and lead. Once, when forceful eviction by the police appeared imminent, Simons wrote his wife that "if it comes I will be here to do my duty as a warrior of the working class. If anything happens it will be for the best cause on earth."[44]

During the second week of the strike, an attempt by GM guards to evict the men in Fisher No. 2 led to a furious street fight that became known as the Battle of Bulls Run. Fisher No. 2 was particularly vulnerable because the strikers occupied only the second floor, while plant guards controlled the ground floor. In the afternoon of January 11, the guards locked the plant gates, turned off the heat and prevented the delivery of food to the strikers. Apprised of this situation, Travis rushed to the scene. Over the union's sound car, he ordered the men to seize the gates. The small band of guards phoned the police and then locked themselves in a nearby ladies room. Under the pretext that the strikers had kidnapped the guards, the Flint police attacked the plant with teargas. Workers from Fisher No. 1, men from Travis's local in Toledo, and a group of unemployed workers organized by Communist Charles Killinger fought the police with bottles and rocks. From inside their fortress, sit-down strikers pelted the police with door hinges and soaked them with fire hoses. Victor and Roy Reuther yelled encouragement and directions over the sound car loudspeaker, and Travis directed operations in the front lines. In the course of several hours fighting, the workers successfully repelled several police assaults and demolished the sheriff's squad car. Seven workers received gunshot wounds, and Travis required brief hospitalization for gas burns.[45]

Three days after the conflict at Fisher No. 2, Governor Murphy arranged the first conference between GM and the UAW. After 13 hours of negotiations between GM's William Knudsen, John T. Smith, and Donaldson Brown and the union's Homer Martin, Wyndham Mortimer and John Brophy, the governor announced that the two parties had "arrived at a peace." The peace was short-lived. At this time the union had strikes in progress at 17 GM plants. Some were traditional walkouts, and some were sit-downs. As part of the "peace" agreement, the union agreed to withdraw its people from the occupied plants within three days, and the company agreed to engage in negotiations with the UAW for 15 days, during which period the company would not resume operations or remove dies, tools, machinery or material. Brophy, Travis and other local leaders in Flint disliked the agreement. "You can't win by quitting," Travis told Addes and Germer. Nevertheless, the union proclaimed the settlement a "partial victory" and, on January 16, abandoned the sit-down strikes in three minor plants, Cadillac, Fleetwood and Guide Lamp. Before the planned evacuation of the Flint shops, however, Travis learned from reporter William Lawrence that Knudsen had agreed to negotiate with the Flint Alliance.

The Flint Alliance for the Security of Our Jobs, Our Homes, and Our Community, better known as the Flint Alliance, had proclaimed itself an organization of "loyal" GM employees. Its leader, George B. Boysen, a former Buick paymaster and vice-president of a GM supplier, little resembled a wage worker. Moreover, Flint professional and business people openly supported and financed the Alliance activities. The organization welcomed all citizens, including GM supervisors and foremen. According to a state police investigator, the Alliance was "a product of General Motor's brains." The Communist party and the union viewed the Alliance as "a company controlled vigilante outfit" that represented a potential threat of violence and an immediate threat to the union's claim to represent the workers.

Naturally, Lawrence's information that GM planned to meet

with the Flint Alliance alarmed Travis. He immediately called Martin in Detroit. GM's plans did not worry for the UAW president. He told Travis to proceed with the evacuation. "Like hell I will," Travis replied. The Flint leader then contacted Brophy, who agreed with the seriousness of this new development and persuaded Martin to call off plans to abandon the Flint plants. Mortimer, who was to have directed the evacuation of the Flint plants, called a hurried meeting of Fisher No. 1 strikers and explained the GM "doublecross" and the decision to cancel the evacuation. The sit-down strikers cheered the news. Mortimer then informed 5,000 strike supporters outside Fisher No. 1 that the workers would stay in the plants until GM agreed to exclude the Flint Alliance from negotiations.[46]

After the failure of the January 14 truce, the conflict entered a prolonged stalemate. Following the Fisher No. 2 disturbance, Governor Murphy had sent over 1,200 National Guard troops to Flint to assist local authorities in maintaining the peace. He gave strict orders, however, to the troops to remain off the streets and avoid taking sides. Murphy also pressured the Genesee County prosecutor, Joseph R. Joseph, to hold in abeyance the 300 John Doe warrants issued against strikers connected with the Fisher No. 2 riot and to release on bail Victor and Roy Reuther, Travis and Kraus, who were arrested for their part in the Fisher No. 2 battle. Throughout January, the strike of 37,000 GM employees continued to idle about 130,000 employees in 17 plants in Flint, Cleveland, St. Louis, Kansas City, Atlanta, Detroit, Norwood, Janesville, and Anderson. Though GM was losing approximately $2 million a day in sales, the corporation tenaciously refused to recognize the UAW as an exclusive bargaining agent. GM also refused to negotiate until the union vacated the plants. During the last two weeks of January, repeated efforts by Secretary of Labor, Frances Perkins, failed to induce GM representatives to meet with union negotiators.[47]

With the failure of Washington's efforts to start bargaining, GM signalled a renewed back-to-work movement, and the prospect of violence again loomed in the strike areas. On January 22, Knudsen announced GM's intention to reopen its strike-free plants; on January 27, 40,000 Chevrolet workers in Flint and elsewhere returned to work. The next day GM supplemented efforts to break the strike by seeking another injunction against the union, this time from

Judge Paul V. Gadola, who had no ostensible financial interest in the corporation. At the same time, George Boysen, head of the Flint Alliance, hinted at the use of force. "Now that the Washington negotiations have collapsed," Boysen declared, "we feel our duty is to take once more an active part in efforts to reopen the plants." On January 26, the Alliance held a meeting of more than 8,000 supporters. Though Boysen argued for doing things in "a legal way," other speakers advised the crowd to "go to the plants . . . and get those boys out."

At the end of January, violence erupted against unionists in Anderson, Indiana, Detroit, and Saginaw. In Anderson on the evening of January 26, a mob led by members of the Citizens League for Employment Security, a loyalty group similar to the Flint Alliance, attacked a meeting of Guide Lamp strikers, beat up union members, ransacked the union headquarters, and drove local UAW leaders out of town. The next day police in riot gear assaulted picketers in front of the Cadillac plant in Detroit. On January 27, to stimulate support for a UAW meeting scheduled for January 31, Joe Ditzel and three organizers from the United Mine Workers in Saginaw had to seek police protection after a group of 20 thugs, including several GM foremen, threatened them with clubs in the lobby of their hotel. Later, the four union men attempted to return to Flint in a Yellow Cab escorted by Saginaw police. Carloads of vigilantes followed the caravan, and unidentified assailants in a gray sedan forced the Yellow Cab off the road and into a telephone pole. The accident seriously injured Ditzel and his companions.[48]

The reopening of plants, the impending injunction, the increasing boldness of the Flint Alliance and vigilantes created a serious crisis for Travis and other strike leaders. "We felt," Kraus recalled "the strike was inevitably weakening," that an impression was developing "that the union had long since demonstrated its major strength." Travis became convinced that the union must take the offensive." Together with Kermit Johnson, Roy Reuther, Powers Hapgood, Henry Kraus and Wyndham Mortimer, Travis developed a plan to "shatter this impression of union weakness," reveal the continuing "vulnerability" of the corporation, and refocus public attention from the "partisan courts" to the "immediate arena of struggle." The brilliant and daring scheme called for the union to seize the Flint Chevrolet No. 4 plant.

The Chevy No. 4 plant, the largest single unit in the GM empire, employed 7,000 workers and produced a million Chevrolet motors a year. Chevy No. 4 was located across Chevrolet Avenue from Fisher No. 2, and 300 yards from both Chevrolet No. 9 and Chevrolet No. 6. The three Chevrolet plants formed an equilateral triangle bisected by the Flint river. The plan called for the fabrication of a disturbance in Chevy No. 9 that would draw the plant guards away from the other plants, thus enabling the union members to initiate a sit-down in Chevy No. 4. The plan was very risky, since a "veritable army" guarded Chevy No. 4, and the union lacked strength in all three of the Chevrolet plants. Both Brophy and Germer expressed skepticism over the plan.

Travis carefully set the stage for the action. To prepare the Chevrolet workers for a strike, Travis complained that, after resuming operation on January 27, Chevrolet discriminated against union members. Travis demanded a conference with plant manager, Arnold Lenz, and called a protest meeting in Pengelly Hall. The meeting of Chevy No. 4 workers approved a resolution that "the time had come for action." Afterwards, Travis asked everyone to leave the hall except for the 150 Chevrolet stewards. Travis then had these men file through a darkened room where he, Kraus and Roy Reuther handed slips of paper to 30 stewards inviting them to a secret meeting later that night in Fisher No. 1. The other stewards received cryptic messages such as "follow the man who takes the lead" or "watch for the American flag." At midnight, Travis told the 30 select stewards that the union strategists had decided to seize Chevy No. 9. He stressed the importance of taking this plant and urged the workers in the other two plants to wait in their places and "watch for developments." After the meeting, Travis confidentially told Ted La Duke and Tom Klasey of Chevy No. 9 that they needed only to create a disturbance for 30 minutes in Chevy No. 9, since their plant would serve only as a distraction for a sit-down that would occur in Chevy No. 6. All of this was a ruse to protect the union's real plans. Travis had intentionally included several suspected stoolpigeons among the 30 stewards and had elaborately staged the secret meeting to insure the relay of false information to the company. No more than seven people knew the real plot to capture Chevy No. 4.

In the afternoon of February 1, a large group of union sympathizers, including women of the Emergency Brigade, gathered in Pengelly Hall in response to a union call for a demonstration at the court house where hearings on the injunction were in session. At 3:20, according to previous design, Dorothy Kraus rushed up to Travis, then addressing the group, and handed him a blank piece of paper. After pretending to read a message, Travis announced that trouble existed at Chevy No. 9, and everyone should go there at once. Travis and Kraus remained at the union headquarters to coordinate the operations over two phones. At that very moment, minutes before the shift change, day shift workers in Chevy No. 9 started running through the plant proclaiming a strike. Tipped off to the coming trouble, Arnold Lenz had concentrated his plant guards in the personnel building near Chevy No. 9. At the first sign of disturbance, Lenz led his guards into Chevy No. 9, and a battle ensued between guards and strikers. Alarmed by the sights and sounds of the conflict inside, members of the Emergency Brigade began smashing the plant windows with clubs, in order to allow the tear gas inside to escape. Within 30 minutes the fight terminated, and the bested unionists left the plant.

Meanwhile, at 3:35 Ed Cronk, a union steward, sounded a loud siren in Chevy No. 6. Putting a small American flag in one hand and a lead pipe in the other he began parading around the plant, calling his fellow workers to follow him. Merlin Bishop and John Monarch sat in a union sound car on a bluff overlooking the plant. As Cronk emerged from Chevy No. 6 leading a small band of workers, Bishop and Monarch directed them to Chevy No. 4. Inside Chevy 4, Kermit Johnson waited nervously, his "previous confidence . . . rapidly giving way to fear," when suddenly Cronk burst through the door "his chest bare to his belly" leading "the most ferocious band of twenty men" that Johnson had ever seen. Since this hardly constituted a sufficient number to close the huge, sprawling Chevrolet No. 4, Cronk and Johnson "huddled together" and made a quick decision to go back to Chevy No. 6 for help. When they next returned to Chevy No. 4, nearly 200 workers armed with hammers, pipes and chunks of sheet metal returned with them. Together with another 200 union members already in the shop, they marched down the aisles shutting off machines and "asking, pleading, and finally threatening the men who wouldn't get in line." Though the foremen and supervisors actively resisted the strikers, and many fearful workers left the plant rather than join the sit-down, the union men gained complete control by 5:30.

A *Daily Worker* reporter called the successful stratagem "a dramatic counter-offensive" that "the American workers will long remember."[49]

The union's capture of Chevy No. 4 broke the strike's stalemate, and two days later negotiations between the UAW and GM resumed. Before the conclusion of a settlement, strike strategists Roy Reuther, Travis, and Mortimer faced several additional crises. Several hours after the union seized Chevrolet No. 4, Governor Murphy ordered the deployment of National Guard troops around the Fisher No. 2 and Chevrolet No. 4 plants. Suspecting the presence of outsiders in the Chevrolet shop, Murphy instructed the guard to prevent delivery of food and supplies to the Chevrolet strikers. Only after Travis, Kraus, Brophy, and Roy Reuther toured the plant and assured the Governor that no outsiders remained except Walter Reuther and Powers Hapgood (whom Travis asked to leave) did the Governor relent and permit the union to feed the plant's occupants. Another crisis developed when Arnold Lenz tried to freeze-out the strikers by turning off the plant's heat and lights. Travis quickly secured a reversal of this decision by threatening to have the strikers keep the windows of the shop open, thus freezing the factory's sprinkler system and invalidating the firm's insurance policy.[50]

More serious than the shortage of food and heat, was the threat of a new injunction. The union's radical lawyers, Sugar, Davidow, and Pressman, tried to delay a decision by Judge Gadola as long as possible. At the same time the lawyers, union, and Communist party defended the legality of the strike in broad political terms aimed at winning popular support. "'Rights,'" Maurice Sugar argued, "do not exist in a political or economic vacuum." Sugar and other spokesmen contended that the sit-down strike protected the workers' jobs, and that the strikers' "right to work" has as much legitimacy as the employers' "property rights." The union also held that the corporation had broken the law. The attorneys argued that GM's use of labor espionage, the blacklist and company unions, as well as its refusal to bargain with the UAW, contravened the National Labor Relations Act. GM's violations of the law invalidated its plea for an injunction, since an appellant must be "free from any blame for illegality." Pressman argued, "The issue is whether the company can make use of a court of equity to deny National and State laws and government officials."

Judge Gadola failed to see things that way. On February 2, Gadola decided that the protection of GM property rights justified issuing an injunction.

Gadola's injunction menaced the strike more than Black's. It set a deadline for evacuation at 3:00 p.m. on February 3 and stipulated a fine against the union of $15,000,000 in case of noncompliance. The union had good reason to fear the enforcement of this injunction, for notwithstanding Murphy's sympathies for labor and his repeated desire to avoid bloodshed, the governor was coming under increasing pressure from various Michigan officeholders and citizen groups to enforce the state's laws against the strikers. Moreover, Flint officials shared little of the governor's flexibility and showed a readiness to enforce the injunction.[51]

The Gadola injunction again posed the question of how the union should respond to official force. At a meeting on the night of February 2, strike strategists considered three options: passive resistance, active resistance, and an intermediate position calling for a brief resistance, as a protest, and then surrender. For Communists, the choice between passive resistance or violence involved less a matter of principle than a question of tactics. In this crisis, as in previous ones, the Communists took a more determined position than others in the leadership. According to Kraus, Travis argued against the intermediate plan. "You're not going to tell workers to fight five minutes by the clock and then stop," Travis advised. "Either they won't fight at all, or if they once get started, nothing you've agreed to beforehand will mean a damn thing." Travis also opposed passive resistance, for it would mean that the men would "march out of those plants like whipped dogs. Not all the talk in the world afterwards would change that. By taking the plants away from those boys now it would mean tearing the heart right out of them." The strike leader concluded, "We've got to tell them to be prepared to fight." The others at the meeting eventually concurred.[52]

After the meeting, Travis, Sugar, and Pressman composed drafts of two telegrams expressing the strikers' determination to hold the plants at all costs. The sit-down strikers in Fisher No. 1 and Fisher No. 2 approved the wires and sent them to Governor Murphy. One telegram read: "[W]e have decided to stay in the plants. We have no illusions about the sacrifices which this decision will entail. We fully expect that if a violent effort is made to oust us, many of us will be killed, and we take this means of making it known to our wives, to our children, to the people of the state of Michigan and the country, that if this result follows from the attempt to eject us, you are the one who must be held responsible for our deaths." To give further evidence of the union's determination, Mortimer and Travis called auto locals "all over the country practically" and asked them to send supporters to Flint before the 3:00 deadline. The union also proclaimed February 3, Women's Day and invited members of the Women's Auxiliary from throughout the state to come to the city.[53]

The next day over 10,000 people demonstrated in front of the struck plants. They were determined to resist forceful eviction. Half the demonstrators were women, many of whom wore the red berets and red armbands of the Emergency Brigade and carried stove pokers, staves, crow bars and lead pipes. Children carried such signs as "My Daddy is a Union Man" and "My Daddy Strikes for Us Little Tykes." About 3:00 p.m., the crowd and strikers received official word that neither the sheriff nor National Guard would seek to enforce the injunction until GM obtained a writ of attachment. Tension melted into joy. Brophy called it "a gala day."[54]

The fear of violence persisted until the end. On February 5, GM returned to court and obtained a writ of attachment. In the meantime, however, GM and the UAW began negotiating. Therefore, Murphy refused to enforce the injunction. Except for the sheriff, local officials lacked the governor's patience. City Manager Barringer and Chief of Police Wills raised a "Citizen's Army" of 1,000 persons, and Wills announced, "We are going down there [to the plants] shooting." The threat of trouble from this quarter abated, however, after a midnight conference at the office of Guard Commander Joseph Lewis, at which Roy Reuther and Travis agreed to disarm the picketers, while Barringer and Mayor Bradshaw promised to demobilize Barringer's private army. On February 10, Arnold Lenz posed another threat to the strikers when he prepared 350 plant guards to assault Chevrolet No. 4. Fearing bloodshed, William Knudsen, executive vice-president of GM, overruled Lenz's plan. The determination of Travis and the workers to meet physical eviction with forceful resistance probably did much to deter Murphy, Bradshaw and Knudsen from following the aggressive schemes developed by their subordinates.[55]

After the capture of Chevy No. 4, Murphy arranged the renewal of negotiations. For eight days, following February 8, Murphy's skill and persistence kept the two sides bargaining. William Knudsen, Donaldson Brown and John T. Smith represented the corporation. Pressman and Travis summoned John L. Lewis to Detroit to head the union's bargaining team. Pressman and Mortimer assisted Lewis throughout most of the talks. Originally, Homer Martin also participated in the talks, but the UAW president "seemed to blow his top" under the strain. After Martin began disappearing into all-night theaters and weeping hysterically on Detroit street corners, Mortimer, Addes, and Hall convinced their slightly unhinged leader to make a speaking tour. Thereafter, Mortimer took Martin's place at the bargaining table.

During the talks Mortimer and Travis insisted on two demands, first that the duration of the contract be at least one year, and second, that the contract apply at least to the 17 struck plants. At one point, when Roosevelt urged a 30-day contract on the union, Mortimer and Travis talked the matter over with the men in the plants, and all agreed that "we must not under any circumstances agree to less than six months." That length of time was necessary to build a "real union" in the plants. When GM demurred at including all 17 plants in the agreement, Travis told Lewis, "We've got 'em by the 'balls,' squeeze a little." On both of these crucial matters Lewis deferred to the judgment of Mortimer and Travis. In the final settlement reached on February 11, the corporation recognized the UAW as the collective bargaining agency for all GM employees who were members of the union. It agreed not to restrain or coerce employees who were members of the union. It promised to begin collective bargaining with the union on February 16. It agreed to resume production rapidly and to rehire workers without discrimination for union or strike activity. And it agreed to dropping all injunctions and contempt proceedings against the union. The corporation also sent a supplementary letter to Governor Murphy in which it promised not to bargain with any other union or group for six months without the approval of Murphy. On the day the agreement was signed, GM unilaterally granted a 5 percent wage increase to all employees, and two days later Knudsen, at the union's request, sent a letter to Martin stating that GM did not object to the employees wearing union insignia. As part of the settlement, the union agreed to end

the strike, evacuate the plants, and refrain from coercing employees. It also agreed to refrain from workstoppages during the
negotiations beginning on February 16 and during the life of any
agreement coming out of those negotiations until all opportunities
for settling a grievance were exhausted. Though the final settlement was modest, it was still a breakthrough. "The settlement,"
Martin said, "is the greatest advance of any single event in the
history of the labor movement."⁵⁶

On the evening of February 11, Mortimer and Travis took the
agreement into the Fisher No. 1 plant for discussion. After their
long hardships, many strikers expressed disappointment with the
terms of the settlement and raised "a lot of complaints." Eventually, however, the strikers approved the agreement unanimously.
Under a banner proclaiming "Victory is Ours," 400 sit-down strikers, clutching personal belongings under their arms, marched out
of the plant singing "Solidarity Forever." Thousands of wives,
children and well-wishers cheered and showered them with bal-
loons, streamers, confetti, and flowers. Led by a flag bearer, two
drummers, and a drum major, the throng marched to Fisher No. 2
and Chevrolet No. 4, where repeated scenes of jubilation occurred. After a procession through downtown Flint, the strikers,
their families, and supporters gathered at Pengelly Hall for victory
speeches and songs. "These people sang and joked and laughed
and cried deliriously joyful," Rose Pesotta noted. "Never had anything like this been seen in Flint."⁵⁷

The favorable outcome of the GM strike resulted from innum-
erable factors, including the impartial mediation and humanitarian
restraint of Governor Murphy, the assistance of such experienced
unionists as Adolph Germer, John Brophy, and John L. Lewis, and
the courage and dedication of the strikers and their families. Also,
of major importance in determining the outcome was the influence
of the Communists. "The major fact to keep in mind," Larry
Davidow observed in 1960, "is that the whole strategy of the sit-
down strike was communist inspired, communist directed and
communist controlled." Though the strike certainly did not result
from a Communist plot, the Communists supplied a core of experienced and selfless people who participated in every aspect of
strike activity—from the organization in the shops, to publicity,
relief, entertainment, negotiations, and legal work. The Communists also had much to do with the entire strategy of the sit-

down, from the preparation and timing of the original work stoppage to the capture of Chevy No. 4 and the decision to hold the plants by force, if necessary. Years later, Mortimer said that while many non-Communists played prominent roles, "the main strategy of the sit-down strike itself was conducted by the Communists. . . . I think the Communists had a lot to do with winning the strike." No person involved in that momentous affair was in a better position to know.[58]

The UAW's victory over GM represented the most significant triumph ever for the UAW, the CIO, and mass production workers generally. In the first CIO executive board meeting following the strike, John L. Lewis declared that in the GM strike the "CIO faced a united financial front—[the] GM settlement broke it." The GM victory stimulated a massive wave of sit-down strikes. One day, shortly after the GM settlement, Detroit experienced 18 sit-down strikes, and Detroit Superintendent of Police, Fred M. Frahm, claimed that Communists were active in "practically all" of them. With or without Communists, sit-downs, conventional strikes, and strike threats soon produced UAW contracts with Chrysler, Hudson, Packard, Studebaker, Briggs, Murray Body, Motor Products, Timken Detroit Axle, L.A. Young Spring and Wire, Bohn Aluminum, and most other major auto firms except Ford. UAW membership jumped from 88,000 in February to 400,000 in October. The impact of the GM strike spread well beyond auto. In 1937, some 477 sit-downs occurred, affecting 400,000 workers. According to Thomas W. Lamont, of the House of Morgan and United States Steel, "the disastrous strike in the General Motors plants" frightened Myron C. Taylor with the specter of a strike against U.S. Steel that might cause millions of dollars in losses for the workers and stockholders and that "might prove such a major crisis as to constitute almost a social revolution." Such fears, according to Lamont, prompted the U.S. Steel president to settle with the CIO before a strike occurred. In this way, the GM strike led to major CIO breakthroughs outside of auto and established the CIO as a permanent trade union center in the mass production industries.[59]

The sit-down strikes and ancillary organizational struggles of the UAW also produced immeasurable political and organizational benefits for the Communist party. By their immersion in these popular struggles, the Communists brought socialist consciousness to more auto workers than did other radicals of previous years in any mass production industry. The struggles themselves brought thousands of workers into practical class conflict and into close relations with class conscious leaders. The union victories brought an end to company-town conditions and unbridled shop authoritarianism, where fear of repression or firing had stifled even elementary political discussion or simple literature distribution. A Flint Communist, for example, reported that before the union was established "the comrades were afraid" to hold meetings, but afterwards the party held public forums and openly distributed the *Daily Worker* and shop papers at plant gates. Both the union and the shop became a political forum, where Communists and other leftists debated ideas and sold popular socialist literature and cheap editions of the Marxist classics. Under these conditions, Communists greatly increased their membership and influence. Communist membership among auto workers jumped from 630 in 1935 to 1,100 in 1939. More importantly, the Communists won a wide circle of sympathizers, and an even wider circle of toleration. In Detroit the CP had 28 shop nuclei operating in 1937, and their members were active in nearly every major UAW local in the city. A considerable portion of Communists, as well as others popularly identified as party members, won positions as local presidents, business agents, educational directors, financial secretaries, and organizers. Also, in the late 1930s the Communists expanded their influence among Detroit's ethnic working class. The social clubs and halls of Polish, Russian, Slovakian, Ukranian, Finnish, Lithuanian, Hungarian, Armenian, and a dozen other ethnic groups became centers of Communist social and political life. In short, the union struggles of 1937 served as a paradigm for what the Communists accomplished under the Popular Front.[60]

# VIII

$\bullet\ \bullet\ \bullet$

# FACTIONALISM

Between 1937 and early 1939, the UAW experienced a protracted factional struggle that eventually led to the overthrow of President Homer Martin and the division of the union. In assessing the causes of this factionalism, historians have generally laid much responsibility at the doorstep of the Communists. According to a commonly held view, the Communists raised havoc in the union in order to discredit the leadership and gain control. Max Kampelman asserted that the Communists "fomented" wildcat strikes, "broke-up union meetings and created so much discord that the union lost more than a third of its original strength." Similarly, David Saposs claimed Communists used "belligerent and disruptive" tactics "to embarrass and destroy" President Homer Martin and his associates. Though Irving Howe and B. J. Widick made a more balanced assessment of the factional struggle than Kampelman and Saposs, they likewise assumed that the Communists aimed to "control" and "capture" the organization and resorted to "power maneuvers" and "Machiavellian methods."[1]

The truth of the factional struggle was more complex than these historians suggest. Indeed, on most points, the above passages completely misrepresented Communist aims and behavior in the UAW. In general, the factional strife fell into two periods. In the first, from April 1937 until January 1938, Homer Martin attempted to consolidate his control over the union by strengthening his administrative position and reducing the authority of locals in

186

general and Communists and Socialists in particular. During this period, the Communists refused to engage Martin in open battle and instead pleaded for unity. In the second period, from January 1938 to March 1939, the Communists and other dissidents waged a struggle against Martin and his policies. By this time Martin's erratic and intemperate actions had so alienated the rank and file and secondary leadership, that the Communist opposition lacked singularity.[2]

When Martin first attacked the CP in March 1937, the party exercised considerable but hardly overwhelming influence in the union. Party membership among auto workers ranged from between 630 in 1935 to 1,100 in 1939. In Detroit, where the Communists were active in all major locals of the UAW, the party contained 28 "shop nuclei," most of them in auto plants. The party had noticeable strength among the city's ethnic auto workers, particularly the Poles, Russians, Slovakians, Ukranians, Finns, Lithuanians, Hungarians, and Armenians. Only a few CP members, such as John Anderson and Nat Ganley of Local 155 and Bill McKie of Local 600, functioned openly as Communists, but many UAW members and local officers gained wide reputations as leftists who associated themselves with the party. Such unionists included UAW Vice-President Wyndham Mortimer; Flint sit-down leader, Bob Travis; and *United Automobile Worker* editor, Henry Kraus.[3]

Under the Popular Front program adopted in 1936, the Communist party pressed for a broad coalition, a popular front against "reaction, fascism and war." Within the trade union movement, the Communists took a cooperative and conciliatory approach toward the Socialists as well as such moderate union leaders as Homer Martin. In the words of William Z. Foster, the party neither aimed "to 'capture' the mass organizations" nor assumed that "all competent and honest leadership is contained in its own ranks." The party instructed its member not to "scramble for official posts" and argued that Communists were entitled to union posts only if they showed "superior work in the class struggle." In *The Underground Stream,* a novel by Albert Maltz about Detroit Communists, a party functionary named Turner explained the party's attitude toward work in the trade unions: "No substituting advice or kibitzing for work. If there's messy work or office work, or anything to be done and nobody to do it, our comrades have got to take it as their own responsibility to see that it's done. 'Build the union' must be the central slogan."[4]

Immediately after the GM sit-down strike, Martin became obsessed with the idea of ridding the union of Communists, whose evil hand he saw everywhere. On the advice of David Dubinsky, president of the International Ladies Garment Workers Union (ILGWU), Martin sought the assistance of Jay Lovestone, whom Dubinsky regarded as an expert on combatting Communism. For two years Lovestone had served as executive secretary of the Communist party. In 1929, however, the party had expelled him and a couple of hundred of his followers for failing to carry out the program of the Communist International. After the expulsion, Lovestone headed a series of sects in the 1930s, the Communist party (Majority Group), Communist party (Opposition), Independent Communist League, and the Independent Labor League, each more opposed to the Communist party and the Soviet Union than the last. Lovestone provided Martin with about a dozen followers to fill posts in the international and with a stream of advice on running the union and undermining Communist influence. (According to Lee Pressman, the Communists were quite aware of Lovestone's machinations, because one of their number managed to tap Lovestone's phone conversations with Martin.)[5]

In March, Martin attacked the CP for the first time. Martin accused the Communists of fomenting opposition to the way he handled the sit-down strike which began on March 8 at Chrysler. After two weeks a settlement was reached, under which John L. Lewis and Martin agreed to evacuate the plants, and Chrysler agreed not to remove machinery or resume production while bargaining continued. On April 6, the union and company reached an agreement that was virtually identical to the GM agreement in February. On March 25, many workers refused to leave the plants, and after April 6 many workers opposed the final agreement for failing to provide sole collective bargaining rights to the union. Martin promptly blamed the delayed evacuation and dissatisfaction on the Communists and threatened to "purge" them from the union.[6]

Though some rank and file Communists at Chrysler expressed dissatisfaction with the settlement, party leaders publicly chastized them. Earl Browder, party secretary, declared that "some comrades were entirely in error in thinking they saw intolerable compromises and wrong methods in the settlement of the Chrysler strike." William Z. Foster added that some Detroit party members had "too sharply and also incorrectly criticized progressive elements [Lewis]." Michigan District Organizer, William Weinstone, praised the Chrysler settlement as "Another step forward."[7]

Shortly after the Chrsyler settlement, Martin began blaming the Communists for wildcat strikes in the industry. In the two months following the GM settlement, GM workers engaged in 30 wildcat strikes. By June, the number rose to 170. Wildcats soon spread to other recently organized plants. In the two years following June 1937, GM reported 270 work stoppages or slowdowns, Chrysler 109, Hudson over 50, and Packard 31. In a series of editorials in the UAW paper, Lovestoneite William Munger accused "a small 'left wing' group" of advocating the "helter-skelter use of strike action" in order "to prevent the growth of the whole organization rather than risk loss of [their] control." The *New York Times* also carried Martin's side of the story. Relying on unidentified union sources, *Times* writer, Russell Porter, claimed that William Weinstone was stirring up wildcat strikes in Flint.[8]

Martin's innuendos lacked foundation. The wildcat strikes resulted from the workers' newly discovered power, as well as the union's and employers' inexperience with the handling of grievances. "We had quickies in nearly every department," a union official at Hudson recalled. "My time was filled completely with attempting to keep the plants running. The people were so exuberant over [their] freedom . . . from the yoke of the boss . . . that in many instances they even took the boss and threw him right out of the plant." *Federated Press* reporter, Joe Brown, asserted that Martin gave the Communists "entirely too much credit" for the work-stoppages. Brown wrote that because the "plain facts of the matter" showed that GM "openly violated" the contract, the workers "took matters in their own hands."[9]

Beginning in April 1937 and repeatedly thereafter, Communists denied that they encouraged or favored wildcat strikes. Weinstone called the *New York Times'* stories "misrepresentations and slanders." The Michigan district leader said, "The Communist Party rejects as ridiculous the charges leveled against it in certain circles of fomenting strikes or inciting revolutionary actions. . . . The CP has always counselled against indiscriminant or helter-skelter use of the sit-down strike." Without referring to Martin by name, a May editorial in the *Communist* branded his accusations of Communist responsibility for wildcats as "Ridiculous! Rubbish!" At the same time the editorial indicated that the Communist party opposed Martin's condemnation of all wildcats and his call for the punishment of wildcat leaders.[10]

Communists in the union echoed the party's position. On April 1, Mortimer issued a statement saying: "Sit-down strikes should be resorted to only when absolutely necessary." In the *Flint Auto Worker*, Henry Kraus wrote several editorials calling for union discipline. "The problem," Kraus declared, "is not to foster strikes and labor trouble. The union can only grow on the basis of established procedure and collective bargaining." Travis likewise introduced resolutions in Flint Local 156 pleading for restraint in the use of sit-down strikes. At the same time, Kraus and Travis refused to blame the workers for wildcats. Instead, Travis placed the blame on GM contract violations, the provocations of company agents, and the workers' new-found freedom. "We must never forget," Travis said, "the terrible conditions under which our members have worked before the union came: oppression, fear, the whip-lash of the foreman. It is entirely understandable that they should blow off some steam when they had attained their freedom. To recognize this unquestionable fact does not mean that one sanctions or has sanctioned these actions. It merely means that one is realistic and places the original blame where it belongs." In answer to Martin's continued insinuations against the Communists, Mortimer issued a statement in July explaining that when wildcats had occurred he "acted quickly to bring them to a close." Bert Cochran, a Cleveland UAW organizer in 1937, recalled that Mortimer came to the city on numerous occasions that year to settle wildcat strikes.[11]

Between April and July 1937, Martin used the issue of wildcat strikes to justify curbing leftists in the union. First, he demoted Kraus from editor to assistant editor of the *United Automobile Worker* and a little later dismissed Kraus altogether from his editorial position. The UAW president tried to exile Mortimer to St. Louis and Victor Reuther to Adrian, Michigan. Martin next began "tagging" Travis "a communist from one end of the International to another." The UAW president then removed Travis's three assistants, Roy Reuther, Ralph Dale, and William Cody, from Flint, assigned four of his own men to the city, and demoted Travis from general organizer to organizer. Adolph Germer, Lewis's representative in Michigan, expressed amazement over the demotion of Travis, "who more than any other individual is responsible for the growth of the Flint movement." While pointing out that he held "no brief for the Communists," reporter Joe Brown nevertheless thought the dismissal of "the fighting, militant leaders who led the fight against General Motors," showed that "Martin and his crowd were ruthless."[12]

The Communists refused to satisfy what they saw as Martin's desire "to provoke a fight." They believed that preserving union solidarity had primary importance. While denying responsibility for the wildcat strikes, the Communists carefully avoided any reference to Martin's contrary claims. When Martin dismissed leftists in Flint, Kraus and Travis protested to the Executive Board but did not force a confrontation with Martin over the issue. Walter Moore, a party member in Flint, "complained" that the party refused to let Flint Communists "fight against the political moves of Martin." Socialist Hy Fish noted that Travis showed "no willingness to fight" Martin, even though Travis was "losing his influence" as a result of Martin's moves. Fish scoffed at the CP's "cautious game of not antagonizing anybody." Joe Brown credited the UAW Communists with an "almost Christ-like" attitude in their desire for "unity at almost any cost."[13]

Before the August 1937 convention, Martin organized the Progressive caucus. Martin excluded the Left from his caucus and formulated a program stressing the centralization of union power and the elimination of unauthorized strikes. In a not too subtle reference to the Communists, the Progressive program warned the membership against "a group outside of the union with members in the union" that inspired wildcat strikes and sought to impose its policies on the international. For the two vice-president positions then held by Wyndham Mortimer and Ed Hall the Progressives nominated two caucus members—Richard Frankensteen and R. J. Thomas.[14]

In response to Martin's formation of the Progressive caucus, the Communists, Socialists, and rank and file dissidents formed the Unity caucus. The Unity program echoed the Progressive call for union discipline and an end to wildcat strikes. The Unity caucus also stressed the need for unity, local democracy, local autonomy, and a determined organizing campaign among Ford workers. B. K. Gebert, a party functionary in Detroit said: "To release all the strength of the union it was necessary to establish, not only the unity of all the forces, but to have inner union democracy, as there can be no progressive militant policy toward the employers with bureaucratic suppression of the will of the membership within the organization." At the suggestion of the Communists, the Unity caucus nominated a slate of officers that contained both Progressive and Unity members. The Unity caucus endorsed Martin for reelection and supported an expansion of the number of vice-presidents from two to four, for which the Unity group backed Frankensteen, Thomas, Mortimer, and Hall.[15]

At the August convention in Milwaukee, the Unity caucus carried its program, though Martin retained control of the Executive Board. The delegates condemned unauthorized strikes, endorsed a Ford drive, and beat back Martin's attempts to centralize his authority. The convention refused to give Martin power to dismiss organizers, opposed the elimination of local papers, and quashed an effort to complicate the calling of special conventions. After John L. Lewis told the body he favored the retention of the current officers, Martin accepted a compromise that retained Mortimer and Hall and created three more vice-presidents for three of Martin's followers—Frankensteen, Thomas, and Walter Wells. On the last day of the convention, Unity leaders, Mortimer and Walter Reuther, averted a potentially disruptive floor fight by urging the delegates to accept, for the sake of unity, Martin's controversial ruling against accreditation of Unity delegates from Flint Local 156.[16]

Martin's setback at the convention impelled him to take drastic measures to consolidate his position and undermine the Left. In the fall of 1937, Martin and the Executive Board, which his supporters dominated, prohibited communications between locals, prevented rank and file conferences to ratify agreements, and disallowed public discussion of Executive Board affairs. Martin established a secret intelligence system to supply him with information on Communist activity, and the Executive Board granted him the power to suspend union members without trial. Martin also denied important assignments to Wyndham Mortimer, Ed Hall, Leo La Motte, Walter Reuther, Paul Miley, and Tracy Doll, the six members of the Unity caucus on the Executive Board. Moreover, Martin abolished local papers, a move aimed directly against the

Left, which controlled the *Flint Auto Worker, West Side Conveyor* and *Allis-Chalmers Workers' Union News*, the three largest local papers in the international.[17]

Martin directed his strongest fire at the Communists connected with the Flint local. He accused Travis and Mortimer of having "badly managed" Flint affairs and of squandering a "great deal of money," some of which, he implied, found its way into the coffers of the Communist party. Mortimer and Travis denied the accusations. Though Martin refrained from bringing formal charges against the men and even admitted finding "no dishonesty," he used the shadow of suspicion to justify removing Travis from Flint and placing the local under receivership. Simultaneously, Martin removed Eugene C. Fay, the educational director of Local 156, who had CP connections, and assigned Mortimer to organize farm implement workers. The Communists did not fight these assignments, but they did complain. Travis told a Flint gathering at a testimonial dinner on his behalf: "Today we have in the high places in the Flint local, men who were on the sidelines during the big battle last winter," but with resignation he added, "that is neither here nor there." (Travis temporarily found employment with United Mine Workers District 50.) Adolph Germer, the official CIO representative in the UAW and the unofficial eyes and ears of John L. Lewis in Detroit, saw no justification for Martin's attacks. "The people who really built the organization [in Flint]," Adolph Germer told Lewis, "are pushed out of the picture and mere dummies put in their places."[18]

As Martin's purges intensified, rank and file opposition to them grew. At this stage, however, Socialists rather than Communists spearheaded the opposition. In September, Martin dismissed 17 Detroit area organizers, most of whom belonged to the Unity caucus. Among them was Stanley Nowak, a very popular Polish-speaking organizer closely associated with the Communist party. Nowak's dismissal particularly upset Ternstedt workers, who credited him with having "organized Ternstedt practically single-handed." To protest Martin's firing of Nowak, Ternstedt workers set up a picket line outside UAW headquarters. When a delegation from the picket line went to Martin's hotel room, the union president pulled a gun and punched one of the group in the face. This incident gained wide publicity and infuriated many. The Socialists "more or less openly fomented discontent," and Carl

Haessler, an assistant of Reuther's, publicly described Martin's actions as "hysterical" and declared "the union chief is in need of a long rest." The Communists, however, went no further than to label the dismissal of the organizers as "unfortunate" and "unwise."[19]

Through 1937 the trouble in the union stemmed largely from Martin's drive for personal power. Some of the issues Martin raised, such as Communist responsibility for wildcat strikes and general disruption, contained no substance and served merely as pretexts for his maneuvers. Other issues, however, represented real differences between Martin and the opposition. Questions of centralism versus localism and consolidation versus expansion, which had figured in the original formation of the contending caucuses, became increasingly salient after the convention. In August, Lovestone advised Martin that the goal of the UAW "should be . . . to help insure stability, and equilibrium, a balanced approach, throughout the entire CIO." Embodying this view, the Progressives stressed consolidation. They advocated moderation in the calling of strikes, strict adherence to contracts, tight administrative control of locals, and severe penalties for those engaged in unauthorized strikes. As early as April 1937, the Communists detected a cooling of strike ardour among some CIO leaders and privately considered this tendency "a great danger." In October, B. K. Gebert declared that the UAW "has every opportunity for further expansion." Reflecting this view, the Unity caucus believed that the union remained in an organizing phase should continue to follow an aggressive course and press for the organization of Ford and other industries under UAW jurisdiction.[20]

The conflict between Martin and the Left sharpened when the rank and file indicated that it favored the aggressive path advocated by the Unity caucus over the cautious one followed by the Progressive caucus. An economic slump in the fall of 1937 caused a drastic cutback in auto production, threw 320,000 auto workers out of work, and reduced the membership of the UAW by three fourths. At Lovestone's advice, Martin responded to the crisis by pursuing a conciliatory attitude in the negotiations then in progress with GM and Chrysler. This furthered disillusionment with Martin's leadership. On September 16, Martin sent GM a "letter of responsibility" granting the company the right to fire any employee whom the company claimed was guilty of provoking an unauthorized strike. In November, a conference of union delegates from GM plants unanimously repudiated the letter. In January, Martin's problems multiplied. The union made no headway in organizing Ford, and Martin accepted contracts with GM and Chrysler that contained no gains over the initial contracts of the preceding year. When William Munger justified Martin's policies to a union conference by comparing them to the Russians' strategic retreat at Brest-Litovsk, Socialist George Edwards replied: "If we had no ammunition, and no men and no arms, I'd be willing to give GM Poland too!" John Anderson, the head of Local 155, told Munger that the union needed "backbones" instead of "wishbones."[21]

In January 1938, the factional disagreements entered a new stage. For the first time the Communists openly condemned Martin. At a meeting of the Executive Board on January 13, Martin's supporters and the Socialists joined to endorse Congressman Louis Ludlow's proposal for a constitutional amendment requiring a national referendum before Congress could declare war (except in cases of invasion). Since the Communists believed that only a collective security alliance among non-fascist nations could guarantee peace, they naturally found much "discomfort" in the Executive Board's action and expressed regret that "the confusion sowed in progressive ranks throughout the country by the Ludlow war referendum amendment has also penetrated the auto union." In a press conference on February 3, Martin claimed the Communists wanted to drag America into war to defend Stalin, and declared that "Communists are Fascists in every sense of the word." Until this time the Communists avoided direct, public criticism of Martin. But now, with the union declining and dissension over Martin's leadership ascending, the Communists counterattacked. They called Martin's press conference remarks "irresponsible ravings" and compared his position on collective security to the ideas of the Hearst press and Liberty League. Moreover, the Communists accused Martin of repeatedly spreading "union-splitting falsehoods" about Communist activity. Mortimer denounced Martin's "slanderous remarks" and "hysterical behavior" and admitted to looking forward to "a good house cleaning" at the next convention. This incident ended the Communist attempt to co-exist with the union president.[22]

Differences over policies for dealing with the impending war also ended the united front between the Communists and Socialists. Declaring their opposition to all capitalist wars, the Socialists opposed the idea of collective security because it took "a step toward war" and favored the Ludlow Amendment as "a protest against being stampeded into war." The Socialists believed that foreign policy constituted "the main bone of contention in the union" and had initiated the UAW's endorsement of the Ludlow Amendment. Afterwards the Socialist party quickly moved from a rejection of the CP's stand on collective security to a rejection of all Communist trade union policies. By April, the Socialists regarded the Communists as "confused," "opportunist," "reactionary," and "disruptive." Leading Communists concluded, "We cannot depend on the Socialist Party to continue as a constructive force." The final break came at the Michigan CIO convention in April. At the last moment, Communist delegates withdrew their support from Victor Reuther who was a candidate for vice-president of the Michigan CIO. This gave the election to Martin's nominee, Richard T. Leonard. After this, Walter and Victor Reuther and other Socialists began to build their own faction in the UAW.[23]

Meanwhile, the Communists constructed a new Left-Center coalition between themselves, George Addes and Richard Frankensteen. At the 1937 convention, Addes had sided with neither caucus, and both had nominated him for reelection as secretary-treasurer. Shortly thereafter, however, Martin's dictatorial and incompetent behavior drove the union's honest and competent secretary-treasurer into the Unity caucus. Frankensteen supported Martin until the spring of 1938. Martin pushed Frankensteen for vice-president and made Frankensteen his presidential assistant. Nevertheless, the UAW local elections in March convinced the handsome and ambitious vice-president that his association with Martin no longer benefited either himself or the union. In these elections, Unity candidates defeated Progressives in all major locals except Flint, and Unity candidates defeated six of eight Progressives whom Frankensteen had backed for office in his own Dodge local. Subsequently, Frankensteen talked with Mortimer, William Z. Foster, and William Weinstone, who helped Frankensteen formulate a 16-point program to end union factionalism. (Years later Weinstone failed to recall such meetings, but Frankensteen later recalled them, and in July 1938 Adolph Germer reported to John L. Lewis that Mortimer admitted the role of the three Communist leaders in Frankensteen's break with Martin.) On April 25, the *Daily Worker* approvingly reported Frankensteen as saying, "I recently have taken a position to end factionalism in the UAW, and I am going to stand on it, win, lose or draw."[24]

Frankensteen's defection made Martin furious. The Lovestoneites charged that Frankensteen was an "agent of the Communist Party," and Martin stripped the vice-president of his rank as assistant to the president. Martin was especially outraged because Frankensteen's desertion gave Martin's opponents the majority on the Executive Board. When the next meeting of the Executive Board rejected an insurance scheme that Martin had arranged for the union, Martin suspended five officers—Mortimer, Hall, Frankensteen, Addes, and Walter Wells. Martin said he had acted to combat the Communist party, whose "record for union-wrecking is a matter of history" and whose "guilty hand" had created the "confusion and division that for months has brought reproach upon our union." Later, Martin linked the suspended officers to a "vicious conspiracy" designed "to turn over the rule of the International Union to the Communist Party."[25]

In July and August, the Executive Board tried the five officers. Martin charged the men with a long list of offenses including involvement in a Communist conspiracy "to seize power by a coup d'etat." Maurice Sugar, attorney for the suspended officers, argued that the only conspiracy in the union was that "between Homer Martin and an irresponsible, disruptive political adventurer and intermeddler, Jay Lovestone." As proof of his contention, Sugar introduced Lovestone's correspondence with Martin and Lovestone's followers, who worked for Martin. The letters revealed a concerted effort on the part of Martin and the Lovestoneites to remove Henry and Dorothy Kraus, Bob Travis, Eugene Fay, and others from union posts and to prevent local elections in the Flint local. Less than an hour and a half after Sugar revealed the letters at the trial, Munger phoned Lovestone in Quebec to say, "They really got the dope on us." Lovestone said, "Well you know we can repudiate it." Munger replied, "They've got too many original letters." Lovestone then said, "Well we can say they stole them and minipulated [sic] them." Two days later, in New York, Lovestone announced to the press that "special experts of the Russian G.P.U." had stolen the letters from his home. This lame defense did little to relieve Martin's embarrassment. However explosive as evidence, the Lovestone correspondence had no effect on the trial's outcome. The suspensions had restored Martin's majority on the Executive Board, and he had no difficulty finding the votes necessary for conviction. In due course, the Executive Board extended the suspension of Wells and expelled Mortimer, Hall, Frankensteen, and Addes.[26]

Martin's actions alienated both the UAW rank and file and the leaders of the CIO. In June, the Detroit District Council, representing 200,000 UAW members, demanded the reinstatement of the suspended officers, and by July 15, 43 local unions made similar demands. In September, John L. Lewis intervened on behalf of the expelled officers and forced Martin to restore the five men to their official positions and to submit any outstanding disagreements to a panel headed by Phil Murray and Sidney Hillman. The CIO's intervention swung the balance of power on the Executive Board back to the opposition.[27]

The Executive Board soon limited Martin's authority. It removed the union newspaper from Martin's control and insisted on approving all his public statements. The Executive Board also forced Martin to remove the Lovestoneites from his personal staff, the paper, the research and educational department, and the women's auxiliary. The board blocked an attempt by Martin to put the left-wing Plymouth Local 51 under receivership and criticized Martin's private meetings with representatives of the Ford Motor Company. By January 1939, only three members of the Executive Board continued to support the president. In desperation, Martin denounced Lewis for having intervened in the union's affairs, resigned his position as CIO vice-president, and suspended 15 of the 25 Executive Board members, including Mortimer, Hall, Addes, Frankensteen, and Walter Reuther.[28]

Several weeks of turbulence punctuated by instances of physical violence followed Martin's move. Martin's men seized the UAW headquarters and barred members of the opposition. The suspended officers obtained the union's addressograph plates from a friendly printer (thus retaining contact with the membership), declared themselves the real leaders of the UAW, and suspended Martin. On several occasions when representatives of the opposing groups tried to address locals, fist fights occurred. Within weeks, the suspended officers won the allegiance of the UAW's largest locals and the vast majority of the union's secondary leadership. The CIO leadership gave the suspended officers its "complete support and recognition." On March 1, the Martin group held a small convention in Detroit, and in June his organization affiliated with the AFL. The bulk of the auto workers, however, remained loyal to the UAW-CIO.[29]

On March 27, 1939, a special convention of the UAW-CIO opened in Cleveland. Because of the prestige it had acquired in the successful struggle against Martin, the Left-Center coalition led by Mortimer, Addes, and Frankensteen had more support than any group at the convention. The Communists had about 50 delegates. Because of the great popularity of the Left-Center group, the convention would have readily elected either Mortimer, Frankensteen, or Addes as president. Mortimer recalled that the sentiment among the delegates made the choice "a toss up" between George Addes and himself. Yet, if the Communists had campaigned against Martin in order to gain control of the union, their behavior at the convention showed no evidence of it.[30]

Behind the scenes, Sidney Hillman and Philip Murray worked to prevent the election of Addes or anyone else from the Left-Center group. Murray and Hillman believed that the recreation of organizational unity out of the chaos left by Martin required a leadership more moderate than the Left-Center coalition could provide. In private meetings with the Communists and union leaders, the two men argued that Addes stood too far to the left, too close to the Communists, and too identified with the anti-Martin fight to enable him to win over wavering Martin supporters and unite the organization. For the UAW presidency, Murray and Hillman favored R. J. Thomas, a steady, apolitical union leader who had recently defected from Martin's camp. The two CIO representatives would permit Addes to stay as the secretary-treasurer but urged the abolition of the vice-presidential posts since that would eliminate Mortimer, Frankensteen, and Hall from the leadership.[31]

The intervention of the CIO created a dilemma for the Communists. If they took the advice of Murray and Hillman, they would lose the opportunity to place the Left-Center in charge of the union and would even lose Mortimer's influence at the top. If they defied Murray and Hillman, the Communists would endanger the cooperation between the Left and Center in the CIO.

Believing that defiance of the CIO leadership would endanger the very Left-Center cooperation that had produced such great strides in industrial organization during the preceding two years, Communist leaders Earl Browder, Louis Budenz, Bill Gebert, and Roy Hudson told the Communist fraction at the convention to support the Hillman-Murray proposal. The Communist fraction followed this advice but not without misgivings. When Hillman told Mortimer that Browder favored Thomas, Mortimer said that "he did not care who Browder was for." John Anderson said he was voting for Thomas only because Thomas was the CIO's choice. Thomas himself later said that Anderson's remark "pretty well" expressed the Communist desire "to avoid every place they possibly could of going against the policy of the CIO." With Communist support Thomas was elected president.[32]

Though the elimination of vice-presidential posts removed Mortimer from the Executive Board, the Communists refrained from pushing any of their people on to the new board. Both Mortimer and Nat Ganley declined nominations to the Executive Board. Thus, for the first time since the founding of the UAW, no officer or Executive Board member was a Communist. Several of the new board members, however, supported Communist positions. Reflecting the sentiments of Reuther's caucus, the *Socialist Call* reported that "CP influence on the executive board does exist," but it "is not dominant." The Communists, nevertheless, expressed satisfaction that the convention had reestablished unity in the UAW. The *Daily Worker* said that the new Executive Board represented the best in the union's brief history, and Gebert praised the "decisive role" played by the "seasoned veterans," Hillman and Murray, and rejoiced that the convention had struck a "death blow against all factional groups."[33]

The decision of Communist leaders to back Thomas reflected the general drift toward the right of the CP under the Popular Front. In 1939 the party made two important moves to ease cooperation between Communists and non-Communists in the unions. It abolished the shop papers that had served as a major vehicle for Communists in the plants to project their own identity. It also abolished the Communist fractions within the unions. The fractions had served as caucuses in which the Communists developed their own positions on union issues, bound themselves to discipline and recruited union members to the party. The party decided, however, that the fractions created suspicions among other workers and eliminating them would make "it easier to unify all constructive forces in the union." By 1939 the Communists had dropped most of their criticism of President Roosevelt and the New Deal. Though the Communists continued to advocate the longterm goal of socialism, in their immediate union activity, they acted as the leftwing of a broad New Deal coalition. In a report on the UAW convention in 1939, Gebert did not criticize any aspect of the union's policies, and he praised the convention for supporting "all of the progressive features of the New Deal," and he praised the new union president as "a New Deal Democrat."

So moderate and conciliatory was the CP at the 1939 UAW convention, that many Communists later criticized its role. For Al Richmond the party's "self-abnegation" at the convention symbolized the "fatal flaw" of the Left's policy under the Popular Front—namely, that the policy became "all alliance and no struggle." Similarly, William Weinstone later declared that the party "should not have interfered" on behalf of Thomas and "should have permitted the union to elect leftwing elements and should not have yielded to Murray and Hillman." Many years after 1939, Bob Travis said that backing Thomas "sure was a mistake," and Mortimer said, "I think . . . we made a tremendous mistake in not just overriding Hillman and Murray." Mortimer added, "Were it not for the interference of Murray and Hillman at the Cleveland convention a far different CIO would probably exist today [1971]. George Addes or I would have unquestionably become President of the UAW, and the union would have played a more militant and decisive role in the years that followed." However dubious such predictions, they suggested how doggedly the Communists pursued unity in both the UAW and CIO in 1939.[34]

Communist behavior in the UAW failed to provide any substance for the right-wing criticism that the Communists purposefully provoked factionalism and disruption in the union to aggrandize their own power. Communist behavior, however, also incurred left-wing criticism. Particularly in 1937, the Socialists argued that, under the influence of the Popular Front, the Communists were too conciliatory, self-effacing, and accommodating toward conservatives in the UAW and CIO and that the Communists, thus, abandoned the opportunity to mold a socialist-minded, militant union. While initially cooperating with the

Communists, the Socialists considered themselves more left-wing than the Communists because the Socialists advocated a fight against Martin and other "reactionaries" in the union, they opposed support for Democratic candidates, they remained critical of John L. Lewis, and they wanted to keep America out of war. Michigan Socialist, Tucker Smith, wrote to Norman Thomas in October 1937:

> There is no Communist plot to capture the union, has been none, will be none. I have disagreed with the Communist line here, but it was because they supported Martin, not because they opposed him. Quite properly they have not taken the lead in attacks upon him. But I have felt that they should support attacks lead [sic] by others. . . . Mortimer is without question the stabliest [sic] and ablest trade unionist in the whole international staff. But he is too god-damned pacifistic, and just won't take any active leadership in an anti-Martin movement. He has no political ambitions and is too self-negating and retiring to be effective. The myth that he is trying to capture the union is just plain lying nonsense.

Similarly, the Socialist Gus Tyler wrote:

> The base of the CP is composed of essentially militant workers, emotionally of revolutionary caliber, who were attracted to the CP because Communism still sounds like revolution to the American masses. These workers properly belong in the SP. In the long run, the Popular Front line of the CP . . . must disillusion and disgust these worker militants.[35]

Such left-wing criticism, however, had no more plausibility than the right-wing criticism. In 1937–38, the UAW still wore swaddling clothes; it represented only a minority of workers in the industry and lacked even a firm basis in GM, Chrysler, and other newly organized plants. While prominent among the union's leaders and organizers, Communists and other left-wingers represented only a tiny minority; many workers, recent migrants from the South or members of ethnic enclaves, remained under such conservative influences as the Ku Klux Klan or the Catholic church. Under these circumstances, if the Communists had refused to cooperate at first with Martin and later with Frankensteen, if they had openly defied Lewis and other CIO leaders, and if they had pressed more aggressively than they did against Martin, for strikes, or for independent political action, they would have isolated themselves or provoked a split in the union. The history of the Socialists provided strong evidence of the unfeasibility of a more left-wing policy than the Communists pursued. The so-called left-wing course of the Socialists simply led them into incomprehensible vacillations and irrelevance.

In 1937 the Socialists were Martin's most outspoken critics in the union. In 1938, however, many Socialists supported him. While Martin grew ever more erratic and irresponsible, the Socialists became impressed with his "left-wing" opposition to war and John L. Lewis as well as his willingness to cooperate with the Socialists against the Communists. Michigan Socialist, Ben Fischer, who, in March 1938, had criticized Martin's refusal "to break with the reactionaries," in June delcared that "Martin's attitude is extremely friendly now," and he "consults with us." Fischer continued: "The anti-war congress in Washington has had a very good effect on our work. . . . Martin has promised considerable support to the labor division of the congress [Committee to Keep America Out of War Congress]." When Martin undertook his expulsions in June 1938, the Socialists refused to join the Martin opposition and tried to remain above the fight. The Socialists criticized Martin's suspensions but also criticized the Communists for engaging in a "power drive" to "capture" the union. In the fall of 1938, when opposition to Martin was growing, the UAW's most prominent Socialist, Walter Reuther, expressed a willingness to support Martin's reelection. As late as February 1939, after Martin had lost nearly all support in the union and in the CIO, Norman Thomas declared that "Martin is, to a very considerable extent, the victim of the Communists and that it is a great weakness for us to desert the only labor leader who ever came near to indorsing [sic] our anti war stand." By this time, what support the Socialists had not lost by their cooperation with Martin, they lost by their refusal to support Frank Murphy, whom the UAW had endorsed for reelection as governor of Michigan. After Murphy's defeat in November 1938, Ben Fischer, admitted that a "considerable resentment against us" Socialists existed in the UAW. In short, the Socialists' attempts to chart a course to the left of the Popular Front simply led them to anti-Communism, opportunism, and isolation.[36]

The years between the GM sit-down strike and the 1939 convention represented a perilous time for the union. Composed of inexperienced members, saddled with an irresponsible leader, consumed with internal factionalism, and faced with hostile employers and a severe economic downturn, the union might easily have divided and collapsed or evolved into an authoritarian and complacent business union. Instead, the Communists, Frankensteen, and Addes managed to form a broad coalition in the union that succeeded in deposing Martin, maintaining a strong, viable organization, and renewing the union's efforts to organize the Ford Motor Company and the aircraft industry in the years ahead.

# IX

# THE NATIONAL DEFENSE
# STRIKES

The 1939 convention marked a high point of Communist strength and influence in the UAW. Some Communists functioned effectively as local leaders, while openly admitting their party membership. Such was the case of John Anderson and Nat Ganley, officers of Local 155, and William McKie, a founder of Local 600. Wyndham Mortimer and Bob Travis enjoyed a great deal of popular support, and their association with the CP was an open secret. Moreover, in trade union work and on political issues, a large circle of local officers and a couple of Executive Board members consistently associated themselves with the policies of the CP. Some of these unionists were CP members; some were not, but as a practical matter the difference was unimportant. Also, the Communists were part of the dominant union caucus that claimed a thirteen to five edge on the Executive Board. The leaders of the dominant caucus, Richard Frankensteen and George Addes, eschewed redbaiting and cooperated fully with the Communists.

The removal of Martin unified and revitalized the UAW. Factionalism did not end, but at least Reuther's minority group agreed with the majority on the need to renew the vigorous organizing that had slackened under Martin. Unanimity on this point contributed greatly to the union's consolidation and expansion. In a series of strikes and National Labor Relations Board elections at Chrysler, General Motors, and other plants, the UAW-CIO easily defeated Martin's rival AFL organization and reestablished the UAW's legitimacy. Also, the union soon launched organizing drives at Ford and in the California aircraft industry. As in the initial union upsurge of 1936–37, Communists would play an active part in the new drives.[1]

Though the outlook for the UAW and the UAW's Communists was bright, the clouds of factional discord already gathered around Walter Reuther. The leader of the large Local 174 on Detroit's westside was unusually capable and ambitious. While opponents regarded his ambition as personal and ruthless, friends believed it was selfless and high-minded. No one, however, denied its existence. Len DeCaux summed up Reuther as a person who "worked hard . . . fought well . . . deserved much credit . . . [and] saw that he got it."[2]

Using Local 174 as a base, Reuther built his caucus around two groups—Socialists such as his brothers, Victor and Roy, George Edwards, Leonard Woodcock, and members of the Association of Catholic Trade Unionists (ACTU). By this time, however, the politics of such Socialists meant very little, since, as Frank Marquart noted, they "became so involved in union activity that they completely forgot about their socialism." Indeed, Walter Reuther quietly resigned from the Socialist party in 1939, and in the next three years Victor Reuther, Leonard Woodcock, and other members of the caucus did likewise. Uniting these Socialist, ex-Socialist, and Catholic trade unionists was their common hostility toward the Communist party. Marquart recalled that "the ACTU and the socialists very often worked together on issues . . . trying to offset the machinations of the communists." The "right-wing group, the Reuther group," recalled Woodcock, "was really a grouping of those who had been socialists, independents, or ACTU people . . . who were just repelled by certain communist tactics." Tracy Doll, chairman of the Reuther caucus in 1939, declared: "We thought . . . that we were the only force that was keeping the Communist Party from taking us [the union] over." Thus, like Martin before him, Reuther made anti-Communism the *raison d'être* of his factional struggle. Reuther, however, drew on reserves unavailable to Martin. The Hitler-Stalin pact and the shadow of approaching war produced a great deal of government and media reinforcement for Reuther's anti-Soviet and anti-Communist thrusts. Reuther would thus have greater success than had Martin in exploiting the Communist issue for factional gain.[3]

The anti-Communism of the Reuther caucus might have fallen flat had not the Communists contributed to their own undoing by adopting several unpopular political positions. In response to the Soviet-German Pact of August 1939 and the German invasion of the Soviet Union in June 1941, the American Communist party twice changed its policy on the questions of war and peace. Each time the change occurred abruptly and lacked adequate explanation, and the party took positions that had little support among American trade unionists. Each time the governing rationale was the need to protect the Soviet Union from the threat and then the actuality of German invasion. For those who believed in the necessity of defending the world's only socialist nation from outside attack, the CP's policy changes had eminent justification. Unfortunately for the Communists, few Americans shared this assumption. At best, Communists found themselves without much support on foreign policy; at worst, their opponents called them fools, traitors, and puppets of Moscow.

The chain of events that would eventually cause trouble for Communists in the UAW began in Moscow on August 24, 1939. In the early hours of that day, representatives of the Soviet Union and Germany told a startled world that their governments had concluded a mutual nonaggression pact. In the event of war, each party agreed not to aid the enemies of the other. For Stalin, the pact answered his overriding desire to keep the Soviet Union out of war as long as possible. It also reflected his distrust of the ability and resolve of Britain and France to oppose German expansion. Moreover, in a secret protocol that accompanied the pact, Germany recognized Soviet spheres of influence in Finland, Estonia, Latvia, Bessarabia, and eastern Poland. The Soviet Union eventually seized eastern Poland, invaded Finland, and annexed the Baltic states. For Hitler, the pact guaranteed Soviet neutrality in case of war with France and Britain and, thus, cleared the way for a German invasion of Poland. A week later, German troops marched into western Poland, and Great Britain and France declared war on Germany. The European war impelled the United States to begin national defense preparations. On September 8, Roosevelt proclaimed a limited national emergency, and on November 4, a special session of Congress passed a revised Neutrality Act that repealed an earlier arms embargo and permitted "cash and carry" exports of arms and munitions.[4]

For American Communists, the news of the nonaggression pact came as a "megaton shock, stunning, sudden, wrenching." The pact reversed four years of Popular Front policy, in which Communists had made fascism the *bête noire* of their agitation and had echoed the Soviet Union's appeal for collective security. The country to which American Communists looked for leadership had finally despaired over consummating an alliance with Britain and France and had turned for self-protection to an agreement with Nazi Germany. The leader of the socialist world dined with fascist diplomats and made a toast to the Fuehrer's health. However shocking, the reversal of Soviet policy had compelling justification, at least for American Communists. Like Stalin, American Communists believed that Chamberlain and Hitler differed only in degree. Chamberlain's hostility to the Soviet Union was as well known as Hitler's. Also, Soviet spokesmen implied that British and French reluctance to form an alliance with the Soviet Union prompted the Soviet Union to seek the pact with Germany. Soviet foreign minister, V. M. Molotov, claimed that "the decision to conclude a non-aggression pact . . . was adopted after military negotiations with France and Great Britain had reached an impasse," and the Soviet Union had to "explore other possibilities for insuring peace." Accordingly, American Communists accepted the agreement as a tactical maneuver for both parties and argued that a nonaggression pact hardly signified a friendly alliance. In the months ahead, Stalin gave numerous indications of his continuing distrust of German intentions. After the nonaggression pact, the American CP dropped the idea of collective security and raised a new slogan, "Keep America Out of Imperialist War."[5]

Abandonment of the Popular Front meant that opposition to war replaced opposition to fascism as the main basis for party alliances. Accordingly, the party adopted a critical stance toward Roosevelt, who was edging a reluctant Congress into increased war preparations. In late 1939 and early 1940, as Roosevelt advocated increases in the defense budget and aid to Britain and France, Communists accused him of leading the nation into war. They argued that the "old division" between Democrats and Republicans, between New Deal and anti-New Deal forces, was "losing its former significance." Both parties promoted "the predatory interests of American imperialism." Communists warned that Roosevelt favored "a war and hunger budget," and they vowed to fight for the protection and improvement of "living standards, democratic liberties, and the right to organize and strike."[6]

The Roosevelt administration answered the new Communist position with prosecution. In the fall of 1939 the FBI arrested Earl Browder, William Weiner, and Harry Gannes for old passport violations. A federal court found Browder guilty and sent him to prison. To discourage photographers, federal officials insisted on taking the Communist leader to jail ignominiously clad with a bag over his head. The government also revoked the citizenship of William Schneiderman, secretary of the California party. In 1940, Roosevelt signed the Smith Act, which required the registration of aliens and prohibited the advocacy of force and violence to overthrow the government. At the same time, Congress passed the Voorhis Act, requiring that political organizations subject to foreign control register with the Department of Justice. Rather than register, the Communist party disaffiliated with the Communist International. The Communists argued that defense preparation against the German fascists provided a field day for fascist repression at home. "Mr. Roosevelt," Browder charged, "has studied well the Hitlerian art and bids fair to outdo the record of his teacher."[7]

The CP's opposition to American involvement in the war did not in itself harm the party's standing among trade unionists. Labor, as well as the vast majority of Americans, opposed U.S. intervention. In October 1939, William Green declared, "Labor firmly believes that we should have no part in the European War." Similarly, John L. Lewis told the 1939 convention of the CIO that labor fundamentally opposed participation in the war. With some justification Browder later claimed that the reversal of policy following the pact barely hurt the party's standing among trade unionists, who were "basically isolationists themselves." This, however, represented only part of the story. The Communists, after all, linked their opposition to the war with attacks on Roosevelt and with support for the Soviet Union's "defensive" invasions of Poland and Finland. Communist criticism of Roosevelt hardly appealed to most rank and file auto workers who admired the President. Moreover, the very sentiments that inclined auto workers against war in general made them unsympathetic to Soviet military actions. After the fall of France and Roosevelt's subsequent decision to aid Britain, the main drift of labor opinion became favorable to Roosevelt's war preparations. In June, the CIO reiterated its desire to keep the United States out of war but pledged its cooperation in the defense effort. William Green went even further than the CIO. He promised that the AFL would do its part in the national defense program because "the fate of our free labor movement is bound up with the fate of democracy."[8]

The extent of the Communists' alienation from the mainstream of union opinion became apparent at the 1940 UAW convention in St. Louis. On the general issue of avoiding American involvement in the war, Communists and non-Communists found agreement. In his keynote address, John L. Lewis warned the auto workers to avoid beguilement "into war hysteria." The convention approved Bob Travis's condemnation of the Burke conscription bill then before Congress and went on record as unanimously opposing a peacetime draft. The convention also declared its opposition to "any involvement of the United States in any war on foreign soil." The Communists applauded these stands, but they had little else about which to cheer.[9]

In the major foreign policy debate, the Communists could muster only feeble resistance to a Reuther-backed resolution condemning the Axis powers and the Soviet Union for their "brutal dictatorships and wars of aggression." Even Thomas, Frankensteen, and Addes, ostensible factional allies of the Communists, deserted them on this issue. Frankensteen and Addes minimized the importance of their vote by explaining that they favored the resolution because, whatever the truth of the foreign situation, most UAW members failed to perceive a difference between the German and Soviet military actions. Frankensteen and Addes also differentiated themselves from the passionate Reuther supporters, who taunted the resolution's opponents about "boats leaving every day for Russia." Frankensteen and Addes expressed the hope that passage of the resolution would not produce a "purge." Reservations aside, the break of the two men with the Communists remained. Boos and jeers greeted John Anderson and Nat Ganley, when they spoke against the resolution. Defying the hecklers, Anderson said he was "not afraid to be put on the spot." Speaking in "the interest of truth," he reminded delegates of the Soviet Union's peace efforts through the League of Nations and its material aid to the Spanish and Chinese in their fight against fascism. For these reasons, he argued that "it is rather ill-advised and very unfair to classify the Soviet Union in the same category as Germany or Italy." Ganley accused the Reuther caucus of introducing the resolution in order to stir up factionalism and "make political capital." When the vote came, several Executive Board members with Communist sympathies "were conveniently in the washroom." Less than 30 delegates voted against the resolution.[10]

The Communists also fought a lonely battle against the convention's endorsement of President Roosevelt. In this fight, the Communists had the implicit support of John L. Lewis, who had strongly hinted that he opposed Roosevelt's race for a third term. In the debate, Mortimer argued that backing Roosevelt would imply "a direct kick in the face to the greatest labor leader that America or any other country had produced." Mortimer added, "I would not give one hair of John L. Lewis' bushy eyebrows for all the politicians in both the Democratic and Republican parties." Other Communists maintained that an uncritical endorsement of the President would ignore his failure to end unemployment, his support of military conscription, and his grants of defense contracts to "violators of labor laws." Reuther blasted the Communists for trying to "hide behind" Lewis and for changing their views on Roosevelt because of "a deal between Stalin and Hitler." Reuther concluded, "Let Lewis lead the C.I.O. and let Roosevelt lead the nation." Addes, who was chairing the session, failed to speak on the question. Frankensteen again broke with the Communists. Summing up the feelings of many delegates, he contended that an endorsement of Roosevelt simply meant support for "a man whose record has been good as far as labor is concerned." By a vote of about 550 to 40 the convention endorsed Roosevelt.[11]

The 1940 convention marked the first serious setback for the Communists in the UAW. Not only had they lost badly in the resolutions relating to the Soviet Union and Roosevelt, but they found themselves isolated from the rest of the Addes-Frankensteen caucus on these issues. Moreover, just before adjournment, the convention approved by a close vote a resolution barring from union office any member of an organization declared illegal by the government. This was an indirect rebuke to the Communists. Even though Leo LaMotte of Local 51 was reelected to the Executive Board, several other Communist sympathizers were not. Nat Ganley later acknowledged that the Communists at the convention represented "a small group trying to defend their [*sic*] views on foreign policy." Similarly, the *Socialist Call* reported that "the CP influence is on the wane."[12]

Between the 1940 and 1941 UAW conventions, the union engaged in four major strikes—at Vultee, Allis-Chalmers, North American, and Ford. Communists participated in all of them in much the same way that they had played a major role in the strike wave of 1937. Unlike the earlier strikes, however, the disputes of 1940–41 occurred in a period of national defense preparations, and three of the walkouts occurred in sensitive defense-related industries. Consequently, Communist involvement became a point of controversy, and the idea quickly spread that, in line with their opposition to the war, the Communists had inspired the strikes in defense industries in order to disrupt the defense effort. In the *American Mercury* of August 1941, the inveterate critic of Communists in the labor movement, Benjamin Stolberg, said simply, "They [the defense strikes] were genuine Fifth Column efforts inspired by the Kremlin to show Hitler what it could do for him in these United States." Several years later the House of Representatives Committee on Labor and Education concluded that the union leader at Allis-Chalmers called the 1941 walkout "for the purpose of carrying out its [the Communist Party's] program." Louis Budenz, onetime *Daily Worker* editor, who became a government informer, declared, while in his latter role, that the Communists called the UAW defense strikes "for one purpose only—that of embarrassing the Roosevelt administration and keeping arms from Britain." Little solid documentation, however, existed for the charges. All four strikes had legitimate grievances, unrelated to Communism. The Communists supported these walkouts, but they always supported clearly legitimate strikes. While their aversion to war in this period made the Communists scornful of no-strike appeals, the Communists never suggested that they desired any disruption of defense industries.[13]

The first major defense strike occurred in November 1940 at the Vultee Aircraft Co. near Los Angeles. The strike followed a year-long organizing campaign conducted by International Representative Wyndham Mortimer, Region 6 Director, Lew Michener, and Henry Kraus, all of whom had close associations with the CP. Following the UAW's 1939 decision to concentrate on the aircraft industry, Mortimer and Kraus moved to California. With the help of Kraus, that summer Mortimer initiated a weekly paper, the *Air-*

*craft Organizer.* After winning an NLRB election against the rival International Association of Machinists, the UAW demanded that management increase wages that then averaged a meager fifty cents an hour. When the Vultee management refused to negotiate, a walkout began on November 15, 1940. The company, press, and federal government put terrific pressure on the 4,000 strikers to end the work stoppage so as not to slow down defense work. Attorney General Robert H. Jackson charged that Communists were deliberately prolonging the strike. In the union, however, no one questioned the legitimacy of either the workers' grievances or the Communists' participation. When the strike ended after 12 days with an agreement providing for a pay increase of twelve and a half cents an hour, the *United Automobile Worker* noted: "President Thomas paid warm compliments to the Vultee workers and *their leaders* [emphasis added] for the fine victory which, he said, will pave the way for UAW advances in aircraft all along the line." Still, the avalanche of redbaiting created tensions in the union. When R. J. Thomas coyly answered reporters' questions about Communist influence in the strike by saying that "nobody is calling *me* a Communist," Mortimer told the union head that his remark was "the worst chicken shit statement I ever heard!"[14]

The second defense strike occurred at the Allis-Chalmers plant, a Milwaukee supplier of parts for navy ships. It began on January 21, 1941 and lasted 76 days. A strong group of militant left-wing unionists led the Allis-Chalmers Local and the strike. Local 248's president was Harold Christoffel, a 28 year old unionist, who sympathized politically with the CP but who throughout his career repeatedly denied that he was a member of the Communist party. During the strike, Representatives Martin Dies and Clare Hoffman held the local's alleged Communist leadership responsible for the trouble, and later the House committee on Naval Affairs blamed the strike solely on "the willful deception" of "a small group of leaders." The actual circumstances of the strike, however, strongly suggested that the company deserved whatever censure was in order. The local demanded a wage increase, a grievance procedure, and some kind of closed shop. The Allis-Chalmers management could easily have granted the wage increase since it had just received $20 million worth of government contracts. Early in March, when the Office of Production Management (OPM) proposed a settlement, the union accepted it, but the company did not. Meanwhile the company tried to discredit the strike by an appeal to the Wisconsin Employment Relations Board. In support of the company's charges of vote fraud, a handwriting expert told the Board that 2,200 of the strike ballots were forgeries. Even though 2,200 fraudulent ballots would not have changed the outcome of the strike vote, which favored a walkout by a ballot of 5,958 to 788, Secretary of the Navy Frank Knox and Office of Production Management Director William Knudsen used this testimony as a basis for instructing the Allis-Chalmers president, Max Babb, to reopen his plant and for ordering the strikers to return to work.[15]

On March 29, a mass meeting of strikers voted overwhelmingly to remain off the job. When Babb attempted to resume production on April 1 and 2, violent clashes between strikers and police occurred outside the plant, forcing Governor Julius Heil to order the closing of the factory. Eventually, the National Mediation Board arranged a settlement that granted the union a five cents an hour increase in wages, as well as a grievance procedure, and exclusive organizing rights within the plant.[16]

As in the Vultee strike, only the people connected with the company, press, or government questioned the legitimacy of the Allis-Chalmers walkout. During the conflict, the UAW Executive Board gave unanimous support to Local 248 and declared that the "sole responsibility for continuation of the strike rests on the shoulders of the corporation." R. J. Thomas asserted that the union should not accede to the order of Knox and Knudsen to return to work. In spite of the charge of fraudulent votes, George Addes said the struggle represented "a bona fide strike." Even Walter Reuther, whose hostility for Harold Christoffel knew no bounds, granted that the "Allis-Chalmers workers . . . fought a glorious battle against one of the most vicious reactionary employers in this country." Thus, with a great deal of justification, the *Daily Worker* commented after the strike: "This settlement gives the lie to all accusations that the strike was for any purpose other than improvement of the conditions of the workers who called it. The settlement shows that there is nothing to which the company could not have agreed 75 days ago, and thus avoided the strike."[17]

The unity that characterized the Vultee and Allis-Chalmers strikes fell apart during the North American strike of June 1941. The reasons for this disintegration were apparent. As a result of the first two strikes, officials in the Roosevelt administration and Congressional leaders spoke openly of the need for extreme measures to prevent strikes in defense industries. Assistant Attorney General Thurman W. Arnold, for example, raised the possibility of outlawing strikes. In March, the administration took the first modest step in this direction by establishing the National Defense Mediation Board. Consequently, many moderate labor leaders grew wary of pursuing aggressive struggles with employers for fear of inviting further repressive measures. In short, moderate labor leaders—rather than the Communists—began "changing their line" on strikes. The Communists, however, remained firm in the belief that the labor movement should not retreat in the face of reaction. They argued that the trade unions should resist erosions of the right to strike, civil liberties, and living standards. Such differing attitudes brought Thomas, Frankensteen, and the Communists into conflict during the North American situation. For the first time in the union, Frankensteen raised the charge that a Communist desire "to sabotage the defense program" caused the strike. As in the previous strikes, the circumstances failed to support the charge.[18]

The strike at the North American Aviation Co. in Inglewood, California, resulted from the UAW's continuing drive to organize the aircraft industry. Michener, Mortimer, and Kraus spearheaded a recruitment effort and, duplicating their success at Vultee, they again bested the rival IAM in a NLRB election. During the warfare of leaflets that preceded the election, the UAW made a major issue of the low wages of North American workers, and in the negotiations with the company that followed, the union made an increase of the fifty cent an hour wage the central demand. Though North American had recently received $200 million in defense contracts, it stubbornly resisted a wage boost.[19]

After the strike ended, Richard Frankensteen charged that it resulted from Communists' "advocating action, and immediate action." This was a dubious assessment. Since an FBI clearance was necessary for employment in defense industries, few if any Communists actually worked at North American. During the negotiations that preceded the strike, Mortimer, who had led the organizational campaign, was in Seattle, Washington. Elmer Freitag, head of the negotiating committee, was registered in the California CP for voting purposes but was not an active party member. In any case, the Communists did no more to foment the strike than Frankensteen himself. Frankensteen handled the union's negotiations throughout May, and not only did he fail to question the legitimacy of the workers' grievances, but also he later confessed to having "rabble-roused and told these people to get militant and stand behind their union." Freitag credited Frankensteen with having "a basic responsibility . . . in working up the strike sentiment." Indeed, the UAW leader declared late in the month that "we are not going to surrender our demand for the 75¢ minimum and a 10¢ blanket raise."[20]

When negotiations deadlocked in late May, the National Defense Mediation Board (NDMB) summoned the parties to Washington. Few unionists had any confidence in the NDMB. Phil Murray had said in March that the board would only serve "to maintain the status quo." The Communists felt the board served "to break strikes and keep wage levels down." At the time the North American case came before the board, O. M. Orton, president of the International Woodworkers Union, denounced the way the board had handled a recent case involving his organization. Naturally, the North American local leadership expressed "misgivings" about the NDMB, and even while its case was under consideration the local approved strike action by a vote of 5,829 to 210. At a local meeting early in June, however, both Michener and Mortimer urged patience and succeeded in having the local postpone a scheduled strike. As the mediation process dragged on for several days, local leaders grew impatient. Even though the board promised to make any wage agreement it achieved retroactive to May 1, the local negotiating committee unanimously decided to strike. Freitag explained that the decision resulted from the belief "that further delay would be perilous to the continued strength of the union, since many men were quitting the organization and others were beginning to heed the call for wild-cat action." On Thursday, June 5, a massive picket line of several thousand workers closed the plant.[21]

The strikers faced a solid wall of hostility. The *Los Angeles Times* reported that "the picket lines formed at the nine gates put the plant out of action as effectively as if it had been bombed by saboteurs." On Friday, President Roosevelt's cabinet meeting asserted that "communistic influences" were at work at North American "because it has large orders for aircraft." According to Harold

Ickes, the cabinet meeting even considered authorizing the construction of "concentration camps" for "labor agitators," and the
President suggested "that we might load some of the worst of
them on a ship and put them off on some foreign beach with just
enough supplies to carry them for awhile."[22]

The press and government had reacted similarly to previous
defense strikes. Unlike the previous strikes, however, this one
provoked opposition within the union itself. On learning of the
walkout while in Detroit, Frankensteen became furious. He was
afraid that "repressive labor legislation would be the result of this
action." On Saturday, Frankensteen flew to Los Angeles and
summoned the negotiating committee and International Representatives to his hotel room. He told them to end the strike immediately, or otherwise "Washington would give us the kind of
legislation that would not only affect the workers in North American, but the workers of the entire labor movement of this country."
Frankensteen then turned to Mortimer, the most influential person
present, and asked if he agreed. Mortimer replied that he had
spent the last two years telling the aircraft workers that the UAW
would raise their living standards and that he would not betray
them now. "I am with the rank and file," he said. "You want to
stand with the rank and file," Frankensteen shot back. "You are
now a rank and filer, because you are fired." The negotiating
committee and the other four International Representatives at the
meeting sided with Mortimer, and Frankensteen fired them too.[23]

That night Frankensteen made a radio broadcast, in which he
called the walkout a wildcat that resulted from the "irresponsible,
inexperienced and impulsive action of local leaders." He added
that "the infamous agitation and vicious underhanded manuever-
ing of the Communist Party is apparent." The Communists denied
having underhanded motives, and the *Daily Worker* noted simply
that members of the CP "are now and always have been in the
forefront of every fight" of the workers for economic gains. On
Sunday, Frankensteen came to a meeting of the strikers in a
beanfield across from the plant and tried to read telegrams from
Phil Murray and R. J. Thomas opposing the walkout. Angry at
Frankensteen's radio remarks, the strikers prevented him from
finishing his statement. They booed and hooted him off the stage,
and a strike patrol escorted him from the field. "We felt," Freitag
explained, "that he had already stated his case to the whole world,

and we could see no reason why he should be given an additional hearing by us."[24]

Unable to count on the backing of either the International or the CIO, the strikers faced certain defeat. With the approval of Sidney Hillman, President Roosevelt ordered the army to reopen the plant. On Monday, June 10, over 2,500 troops with fixed bayonets dispersed the picket lines and arrested scores of strikers. This action shocked even those UAW and CIO leaders who had opposed the strike. In what John L. Lewis called the "blackest week in American labor history," the army broke the strike. After the troops intervened, Mortimer urged a meeting of the local to end the work stoppage, and the demoralized strikers decided to return to their jobs.[25]

Communists achieved even greater prominence in the organization of the Ford workers and in the Ford strike of 1941 than they had at North American. Since Ford was doing little defense work, the Ford strike did not evoke the touchy prospect of government intervention, provoke division in the union, or make Communism an issue. Communist activity at Ford dated back to the old AWU of 1928, when Communists had formed nuclei in the plant and issued shop papers. John Barron, once an AWU activist, was fired seven times in twelve years for his union activity at Ford. During the early years of the depression, Communists organized Ford workers into Unemployed Councils and led the Ford Hunger March of March 6, 1932. Communist Bill McKie was one of the founders and first president of the union at Ford. By 1938, 200 Communists worked in the Ford River Rouge plant, and Ford CP members issued a shop paper called the *Ford-Dearborn Worker*. John W. Anderson, an auto worker with no sympathy for Communist politics, noted that by 1941 the "Communist Party had a large membership in the Rouge plant, particularly among the Negroes, but also among the foreign born workers, especially the Italians, but also among the Polish." CP members, Anderson declared, were "scattered throughout practically every section of that huge plant. And they had a decisive influence on the development of Local 600."[26]

The dictatorial operations of the Ford Service Department and the omnipresence of company spies and informers made open union recruitment impossible at Ford. When the union attempted to distribute leaflets at the Ford plant in the spring of 1937, Ford servicemen severely beat Walter Reuther, Richard Frankensteen and several left-wing union organizers. Until the Supreme Court invalidated a municipal antileaflet ordinance, the union lacked the freedom to distribute literature anywhere in Dearborn. So repressive were conditions within the plant that Ford fired a Communist worker named John Gallo in November 1940 for laughing and smiling during working hours. The union did not even attempt to hold open recruitment meetings for Ford workers. Consequently, most recruitment was done secretly by intrepid and dedicated rank and file workers who were usually left-wing militants. William Allen, Detroit reporter for the *Daily Worker,* said: "The actual Jimmy Higgins work of signing the [Ford] guy up, getting his card, and collecting dues was done by the rank and file workers in the shop themselves, most of whom learned their organizational experience from the left wing auto workers union [AWU] and from the Communists. . . . And around these left wing forces arose the whole net work [*sic*]. It was like a net work [*sic*] of scores of little groups that met in homes, basements, and even in autos." The "union didn't organize Ford," Allen observed, "Ford was organized by the communists and the left wingers."[27]

Communists outside of the Ford plant also played a great part in recruiting Ford workers to the union. Because of the difficulty of organizing in the plant, Mike Widman, director of the Ford campaign, called for stewards in other plants to become volunteer Ford organizers. In answer to this call, Leo La Motte, Detroit East Side Regional Director, called a conference of several hundred UAW stewards; State Senator Stanley Nowak conducted a meeting for Polish-American auto workers in Detroit; and E. J. "Pop" Edelen, president of Plymouth Local 51, devoted the local's annual educational convention to the Ford drive. La Motte, Nowak, and Edelen had close associations with the Communist party. Three left-wing Detroit locals—51, 155, and 208—formed a joint Ford organizing committee, and by the end of the month they led the city in Ford recruitment. The National Negro Congress, an organization sparked by the CP, played an important role in the black community by repudiating Ford's paternalism toward Negroes, combatting the anti-union preachments of the National Association for the Advancement of Colored People (NAACP), and recruiting black Ford workers to the UAW. Most active in this effort were Le Bron Simmons, Rev. Charles Hill, Paul Kirk, Coleman Young, and Shelton Tappes.[28]

In February, after the Supreme Court refused to review a

lower court decision upholding an NLRB order against Ford, the union turned the corner in its Ford drive. In March the UAW petitioned the NLRB for a representation election. On April 1, 1941, Ford summarily dismissed eight union committeemen, and within hours Ford workers began spontaneous sit-downs in various Ford departments. The next day workers surrounded the immense industrial complex at River Rouge with a mass picket line 10,000 strong. While Harry Bennett, head of the Ford Service Department, railed that the strike was "a gigantic Communist plot threatening national defense," William Allen adorned the staid pages of the *Daily Worker* with some uncommonly lyrical reporting. "The Rouge plant is a city," Allen wrote. "Today its streets are bare of vehicles, its 100 miles of railroad tracks clogged and still. The fires in the mammoth factory were out or banked. The ships in its river were laying quiet at their docks. They said in America it could never happen. But the great organized strength of the Ford workers was mightier than all of Ford's millions and his tons of propaganda and thousands of Gestapo-like servicemen and stoolpigeons."[29]

After ten days the strike ended with Ford's agreement to reinstate five of the discharged committeemen, arbitrate the cases of the other three, establish a grievance procedure, and expedite an NLRB election. Several weeks later the UAW-CIO won the election with 52,000 votes to the UAW-AFL's 20,000. In June, the Ford workers approved a contract that granted a union shop, a check-off system, the reinstatement of discharged workers, and other union demands. The UAW paper called the agreement "the best contract ever won from a large manufacturer," and the *Sunday Worker* said the agreement marked "a red letter day in the annals of American labor."[30]

The Communists played an indispensible role as rank and file organizers in the Ford drive, but unlike the GM struggle, the Communists occupied few official positions in the local and the international at the time of the strike. Consequently, the Communists gained strength in Local 600 but not elsewhere. In the eyes of most UAW members, the credit for the Ford victory went to the international union officers and Michael Widman, head of the Ford drive.

The Ford strike and contract only briefly distracted the union from the European war. On June 23, newspaper headlines conveyed the news of Germany's invasion of the Soviet Union. The Communist party reacted with another reversal of policy. Abandoning its noninterventionist stance, the CP called for "full support and cooperation with the Soviet Union in its struggle against Hitlerism!" Five days later, the Executive Committee of the Communist party approved a report by Foster that argued that the German attack "changes the character of the world war." The war was no longer a struggle between "rival imperialist power groupings," but a threat to both "the life of the first socialist country" and "the democracy and national independence of every people." The CP called for American military aid to all nations fighting Hitler and promised to support Roosevelt in this effort. At the same time, the party maintained a vigilant stance within the labor movement. In August, communist leader, Roy Hudson, stressed that "national unity in the struggle against Hitlerism, calls for continued and intensified efforts to strengthen labor and defend its economic interests."[31]

With rhetoric reminiscent of the Popular Front, the party called on "labor to become united, to unify all of the anti-fascist forces under its leadership." Workers, however, lacked unity on the war; few shared the Communist desire for American intervention. The CIO supported aid to the Soviet Union, but John L. Lewis maintained a position of nonintervention. Also, the anti-Communism that had developed in the nation and the unions over the past several years remained resilient. In June and July, Communist leaders of UAW locals endorsed aid to the Soviet Union, but most other UAW leaders kept silent. Of the international officers, only Addes made a shift on foreign policy similar to the Communists.[32]

At the 1941 UAW convention in Buffalo, the antifascist unity that the Communists anticipated remained illusive. Rather, the Reuther caucus turned the proceedings into the most divisive and anti-Communist of any to that time. The question of seating the Allis-Chalmers delegation, disciplining those responsible for the North American strike, and barring Communists from union office provoked the most intense debates of the convention. The Reuther caucus used each of these issues as an occasion to attack Communists in the union.

In the case of the Allis-Chalmers delegates, the Credentials Committee submitted a divided report. The majority opposed seating the delegation because of constitutional violations involved in the election of delegates. The minority favored seating the delegation because the irregularities involved only minor and common infractions. The alleged Communist, Harold Christoffel, led the Allis-Chalmers delegation, which consisted largely of anti-Reuther leftists. Capitalizing on the government's recent attacks on Christoffel's politics, the Reuther group couched the majority report in strong anti-Communist language. The Allis-Chalmers delegates had won election, the report concluded, "in the same manner as Hitler and Stalin hold their elections." Walter Reuther gave the main speech on behalf of the majority report. In the debate that followed, both Thomas and Frankensteen sided with the majority report, while Addes opposed it. The convention voted to bar the delegation and ordered another election. Thomas appointed a committee of three to go to Milwaukee and supervise a new election of delegates. In a couple of days the committee returned to the convention, and two of the three committee members reported that no election occurred because Christoffel refused to cooperate. The third member of the committee disagreed and said the local president had cooperated. During the heated floor debate, Richard Leonard, a member of the Reuther caucus, threatened Christoffel with physical violence, and Christoffel gave an impassioned defense of his actions and his administration of the local. Eventually, Thomas appointed a new committee and ordered it to try to hold an election. This time the balloting occurred, and the Allis-Chalmers workers reelected the original delegation led by Christoffel. Reuther's indictment failed to discredit Christoffel in the eyes of his local.[33]

On the question of punishing leaders of the North American strike, the Grievance Committee at first submitted a unanimous report calling on the convention to place the California region under an administratorship. The Reuther group attacked this recommendation as too lenient for those leaders who had supported an unauthorized strike and "encouraged the Communist Party." Walter and Victor Reuther demanded the suspension of Michener. President Thomas admitted that the "abnormal influence" of the CP in the California union appalled him and that Michener had made a "grave mistake" in supporting the strike, but he regarded the recommended punishment as just. Frankensteen agreed. The convention, however, voted to send the report back to the committee for reconsideration.

The committee next submitted three reports. The minority report, the harshest, called for an administratorship, the expulsion of Michener, and five year suspensions for Mortimer and the other international representatives involved in the strike. The majority report, backed by the Reuther group, asked the convention to ban Michener from union office for a year. The most lenient recommendation came in the form of a super-minority report that asked the convention to deprive Michener of his seat on the Executive Board for a year. Frankensteen backed this measure because he thought the other reports meant "crucifying a young fellow by the name of Michener who was thrown in with the like [*sic*] of Mortimer and the Communist Party." Leo LaMotte, the only member of the Executive Board closely identified with the Communists, also backed the super-minority report. Michener and Mortimer supported none of the reports. Michener confined himself to criticism of Sidney Hillman and "his red-headed stooge in this convention, Walter Reuther," whose defense policies, Michener argued, caused the North American tragedy. Mortimer denied that Communists represented an important factor in the strike, castigated Frankensteen's role in the affair, and passionately defended his own decision to side with the rank and file. Mortimer said that he told Frankensteen in Inglewood that if "the strike was authorized, the Army would not come in." Mortimer added, "I still believe that was true." After a lengthy debate, the convention approved the lenient punishment recommended by super-minority report.[34]

The third issue of controversy involved the majority recommendation of the Constitution Committee, headed by Victor Reuther, to disallow from union office any "member or supporter" of an organization which had "loyalty to a foreign government" or approved of "totalitarian forms of government." Some supporters of the Reuther faction endorsed a super-minority report that was almost identical to the majority report. It called for barring from office anyone who was "a member or subservient to any political organization, such as the Communist, Fascist or Nazi organization." Though this report differed only in phrasing from the majority report, it gave the Reuther group a parliamentary advantage, since the super-minority report would come under consideration before the minority report. The minority report, submitted by delegates close to Addes, would have excluded Communists from office, but it made the definition of a Communist narrower than the other reports. Only someone "subject to the discipline" of a Communist, Fascist, or Nazi organization was ineligible to hold union office. The minority report also barred from office any "member or agent" of the Socialist party. James Lindahl, who introduced the minority report, said that the real issue concerned not the Communist party but "whether or not the Socialist Party in the person and voice of Walter Reuther and Victor Reuther and the rest of the Reuther family is going to have a privileged minority position in this union."

Though the minority report was slightly more favorable to the Communists than the others, the Communists supported none of the three resolutions. John Anderson argued that all three reports undermined the very democracy that "demagogues profess to protect." He defended the Communists in the union against the attacks implicit in all three reports. "You never saw a Communist walk through a picket line in your life," Anderson said. "I make no apologies for my honest beliefs. . . . And if those Red baiters want to see this Scotchman crawl, their whiskers will trip them before that day comes." Several other delegates, including one who described himself as "just a half-baked liberal," likewise rejected all three reports. Nevertheless, the super-minority report carried. Unlike the previous year when the convention had condemned the Soviet Union, neither Frankensteen nor Addes expressed the hope of avoiding a purge.[35]

In attacking the Communists, Reuther discovered a lever for important factional gains. This assault disrupted the Left-Center coalition in the UAW by forcing Thomas and Frankensteen to declare themselves against the Communists. At the 1941 convention, no major differences existed between the Reuther group and Frankensteen and Thomas on the main issues. Thomas and Frankensteen agreed with Reuther on opposition to the Allis-Chalmers delegation, on the need to punish the North American strike leaders, and on the exclusion of Communists from union office. Moreover, the Reuther group gained control of half of the Executive Board. Addes, the only officer who had leaned toward the Communists on the questions of seating the Allis-Chalmers delegates and barring subversives from office, nearly lost the election for Secretary-Treasurer to Reuther supporter, Richard Leonard.[36]

The defense period represented a difficult time for the UAW's

Communists. On the one hand, by their aggressive organizing and determined defense of workers' interests in the Allis-Chalmers and Ford strikes, the Communists and their left-wing allies won increased prestige and strength at the local level. On the other hand, by their abrupt changes of line on foreign policy and by their refusal to follow the UAW leadership's changes in line on the advisability of strikes in the aircraft and other defense industries, the Communists and their allies made themselves vulnerable to the attacks of the government and professional anti-Communists outside the union and to the Reuther-ACTU forces inside the union. Consequently, at the national conventions of 1940 and 1941 the Communists found themselves isolated, particularly on questions pertaining to foreign policy, the North American strike, and the barring of Communists from office. Moreover, because of the anti-Communist atmosphere generated by the Reuther-ACTU forces, several Communists and Communist-supporters were forced from positions of influence. At the 1941 convention, Leo LaMotte resigned from the Executive Board rather than face an uncertain election, and Michener incurred a suspension. Two of the union's most prominent Communists departed. Bob Travis, who had rejoined the UAW after Martin's departure, left the union to work for the CIO in Illinois. Mortimer remained fired as a result of Frankensteen's suspension. After the 1941 convention, the veteran organizer asked Thomas to lift his suspension, but Thomas merely added insult to injury by replying, "I am a very busy man and it is practically impossible for me to set any date for a meeting." With this remark Mortimer's UAW career came to an end, and he took a position with the CIO in Utah. Pearl Harbor buried the foreign policy differences in the union and ended the difficulties and isolation that Communists had experienced during the defense period. The war, however, provided even greater challenges to Communists than had the years of war preparations.[37]

# X

# EVERYTHING FOR VICTORY

During the 30 years since World War II, a conventional view of the wartime experience of Communists in the auto industry has developed largely through the work of such historians as Joel Seidman, Irving Howe, B. J. Widick, Art Preis, and most recently Bert Cochran, all of whom have written from a Trotskyist or Social-Democratic perspective. The conventional view holds that the left-wing caucus in the UAW, the caucus of the Communists and Secretary-Treasurer George Addes, lost influence during the war because the Communists and their allies sacrificed the immediate interests of the workers for the cause of victory over fascism. In this view the Communists made themselves unpopular by their ardent advocacy of incentive pay and the no-strike pledge. The conventional view also holds that the main reason the Communists were so willing to sacrifice the immediate interests of workers was because the "prime allegiance" of the Communists was not to the workers but to the "needs of the U.S.S.R." Consequently, the right-wing caucus led by Walter Reuther, who opposed incentive pay and vacillated on the no-strike pledge, gained sufficient influence during the war to elect Reuther president of the UAW at the union's first postwar convention in 1946.[1]

The conventional view simplifies a complex and contradictory history in two major respects. The first simplification involves the reasons for the decline of Communist and left-wing influence. To point to the Communist neglect of the workers' immediate inter-

ests through the advocacy of incentive pay and the no-strike
pledge provides at best only some of the pieces to the puzzle of
why left-wing influence declined. The decline of Communist
influence in the UAW was also closely related to two important
developments outside the union: the decline of labor and left-
wing influence generally in the country during the war, and the
internal crisis in the Communist party over Browder's policies.
Even if the Communists in the UAW had acted differently, these
developments outside the union would have eroded Communist
influence. Moreover, to argue that the Communists supported incentive pay and the no-strike pledge because of Communist sub-
servience to the needs of the Soviet Union merely adds simplification to simplification. As allies, the Soviet and American
people arguably possessed the same wartime goal—victory over
the Axis. Both Communists and non-Communists recognized that
sacrifices were necessary to achieve this goal, and both Communists and non-Communists supported incentive pay and the
no-strike pledge. In short, the Communist wartime experience in
the UAW cannot be easily separated from the developments outside the labor movement and from the behavior of many non-
Communists in the labor movement.

The second oversimplification of the conventional view involves the extent of the decline of Communist and left-wing
influence during the war. Though the Communists experienced a
decline of influence at the expense of the right-wing Reuther
caucus, the decline was marginal rather than decisive. After 1941,
the right-wing and left-wing groups had nearly equivalent
influence. When Reuther defeated R. J. Thomas for president in
1946, his margin of victory consisted of only 124 votes of over
8,700 votes cast. Moreover, the left-wing caucus retained control
of the Executive Board in 1946, and for several years after 1946
the Communists remained an influential force in such locals as 51,
155, 190, 248, and 600. Hence, the nature and effect of Communist
activity in the auto industry during the war was more complex
than the conventional view suggests. Whereas the Communist
policies with regard to incentive pay and the no-strike policy dam-
aged left-wing influence, other Communist activity in support of
workers' immediate interests compensated for the loss. The entire
pattern of events must be understood to appreciate the Communist
experience in auto during the war.

From Pearl Harbor until the end of the war, Communist labor policy coincided with the policy of the UAW and CIO leadership. The day after Pearl Harbor, the *Daily Worker* coined the CP's wartime slogan, "Everything for Victory." The party pledged its loyalty to the war effort and supported national unity, increased production, and a no-strike pledge. Party leader, Earl Browder, said that labor must make sacrifices for the war because "hope for the existence of free labor" depended on "destroying Hitler and his Axis." Similarly, after meeting with President Roosevelt on December 17, 1941, CIO leaders agreed to a no-strike pledge and promised "to promote and plan for ever-increasing production." Phil Murray said that Hitler and the Axis threatened "all our civil liberties," and that labor must counter this threat with the slogan: "Work, Work, Work, Produce, Produce, Produce!" The same coincidence of purpose developed in the UAW. At the union's War Emergency Conference in April 1942, Communists Nat Ganley and John Anderson strongly supported the program of "Victory through Equality of Sacrifice" prepared by George Addes and Walter Reuther, the leaders of the two contending union factions. Unity on the wartime program between the Communists and UAW leadership also prevailed at the UAW's 1942 convention. At this convention, the Communist-backed Addes nominated the anti-Communist Reuther for vice-president, while Reuther nominated Addes for secretary-treasurer. Also, Victor Reuther introduced a resolution supported by Communists calling on President Roosevelt to begin preparations for a second front in Europe "at once." During the war, the Communists remained faithful to the CIO and UAW wartime program.[2]

Naturally, a tension existed between labor's traditional commitment to improve wages and working conditions and its new commitment to avoid strikes and provide increased production for the war effort. The Communists recognized this tension. They hoped to minimize the tension, however, by urging workers to build national unity, strengthen the war effort, protect their living standards, and safeguard their trade unions. After the war, party leader William Z. Foster acknowledged that the party had often failed to pursue both objectives adequately and that the commitment to wartime exigencies had crippled party militancy. Yet, the picture was not onesided. In spite of the war, the Communists engaged in a remarkable amount of traditional union activity and

struggle. Commenting on Communist efforts in a UAW wartime organizing drive in Baltimore, a non-Communist organizer declared:
"As far as I'm concerned, you can't win a drive without them [the
Communists]. They do all the work, distribute the leaflets, sweep
the hall, make the sandwiches. You know—they're the only ones
who always turn up and can be depended upon."[3]

One area in which the Communists actually increased their
activity and influence during the war was in the UAW's educational
and political programs. In 1941, the union removed the head of
the Education Department, Richard Deverall, a leader of ACTU
because of his alleged fascist and anti-Semitic sympathies.
Thomas replaced Deverall with a leftist, William Levitt. Levitt
removed many of Deverall's appointees and hired Communists
and other leftists. Of the dozen or so people in the department,
Francis Downing, David Erdman, Elizabeth Hawes, Tony
Marinovitch, and Levitt himself were close to, if not in, the Communist Party.[4]

Levitt and his staff expanded the operations of the Education
Department greatly. The number of local educational committees
grew from 75 in 1940 to 240 in 1943. The number and size of UAW
summer schools grew from one school and 97 participants in 1941,
to five schools and 300 participants in 1944, and to eight schools
and 1,231 participants in 1945. The length of the summer sessions
expanded from one week to two. Levitt also ran an extensive
series of weekend educational conferences; by 1943 sixteen such
conferences in nearly every UAW region had trained over 5,000
local officers. He developed new publications including initiation
kits, correspondence courses, posters, union calendars, educational curriculums for locals, monthly news reviews, and an educational column in the *Auto Worker*, the UAW paper. He sent
copies of the union magazine, *Ammunition*, to UAW members in
the armed services. The department greatly enlarged the variety
and distribution of pamphlets and leaflets. In the first six months
of 1943, the department distributed 817,115 publications compared with 52,194 in the entire year of 1940. Other innovations
that occurred under Levitt included the establishment of a co-op
store, the development of radio programs, and the development
and distribution of educational films.[5]

The Communists also did much to increase the political
awareness of UAW members. Since, through boards like the Na-

tional War Labor Board (NWLB), the government assumed control over all aspects of labor policy during the war, the Communists argued that labor must intensify its political action. Under Levitt, the Education Department directed most of its efforts toward this end. While the general emphasis of the Education Department stressed the union's role in the war effort and the benefits of the Roosevelt administration, the educational conferences and summer schools also ran programs on particular wartime problems such as housing, breaking the government's Little Steel formula (which limited wage increases to 15 percent above 1941 wages), and discrimination. *Ammunition* began printing the voting records of Congressmen and analyses of bills before Congress. Educational pamphlets carried such titles as *Let the Solders Vote, Labor's Stake in Abolishing the Poll Tax, Every Worker a Voter, A Woman's Guide to Political Activity, The People's Program of 1944, Jobs for All After the War, The Negro in 1944.* After the formation of the Political Action Committee in 1944, the Communists redoubled their efforts on Roosevelt's behalf, and the Education Department printed such pamphlets as *Back to the Bread Line With Dewey* and *Who Is Behind Dewey,* that attacked the Republican candidate and supported Roosevelt.[6]

The Communists and their allies became particularly active in the pursuit of better conditions for women, over 300,000 of whom became members of the UAW during the war. "It is a pressing necessity," Browder declared in 1942, "to abolish all existing remnants of inequality between men and women." Communists castigated ACTU for maintaining that nature designed women to keep the home and criticized the UAW for failing to do more about the "scandalous situation that prevails in the handling of the special problems of the women workers." Within the union, the Communists supported the successful effort of the UAW to obtain a government ruling on equal pay for women. Elizabeth Hawes, the UAW's first woman international representative in the Education Department, visited UAW locals from coast to coast "to help the women start to help themselves" in struggling for seats, equal pay, seniority rights, improved cafeteria food, and other issues. Among other things, Hawes helped women organize petition drives demanding seats for women in work areas. "Where a real effort was made," Hawes reported, "seats were obtained—for men as well as women." Hawes observed: "To say we could accomplish nothing except by striking was a lie. We got things all the time by sheer mass pressure."[7]

The failure of the Communists in the UAW and elsewhere to support A. Philip Randolph's March on Washington Movement on behalf of demands to end racial discrimination in defense employment and the military led some observers then and later to charge that the Communists had sacrificed the struggle for black rights to the war effort. This was untrue. The Communists opposed Randolph's tactics, not his objectives. They believed that Randolph's attacks on Roosevelt undermined the war effort and his exclusion of whites from the movement "would lead to the isolation of the Negro people from their most important allies." Whether or not the Communists correctly assessed the impact of Randolph's tactics, their criticisms revealed no slackening of interest in equal rights. Rather, party spokesmen repeatedly stated that, although the war required some compromise of the class struggle, it demanded an intensification of the struggle for democratic rights. Browder, for example, said: "Here it would be disastrously destructive of national unity to try to make our peace with the status quo, which is a status of shameful heritage from chattel slavery based on Hitler-like racial conceptions." Moreover, a poll by the *Negro Digest* in 1944 found that a majority of blacks (67 percent in the South, 68 percent in the North, and 73 percent in the West) believed that the Communists had remained loyal to the fight for Negro rights. The *Digest* noted: "The majority opinion was that the Communists in their all-out support of the war are supporting a cause which is synonymous with the fight for racial equality." Such opinions were certainly consistent with the activity in the UAW, where the Communists actually increased their struggle for minority rights during the war.[8]

The racial situation in Detroit during the war posed a serious challenge to both the Communists and the UAW. In search of war work, 440,000 whites and 60,000 blacks migrated to Detroit between 1940 and 1943. This influx produced an acute housing shortage. Most blacks had to live in a miserable, overcrowded ghetto called Paradise Valley. There some 3,500 houses had toilets that consisted of shacks over holes in the city sewer mains. Over 50 percent of the blacks in Detroit lived in "substandard" housing, compared to 14 percent of the white population. In spite of the efforts of the Fair Employment Practices Commission and the protests of the NAACP and the CIO, employer discrimination kept many blacks out of war plants and consigned others to poor jobs. In 1943, blacks constituted 10 percent of Detroit's population, but only 8.4 percent of the work force in 185 major war plants; 55 plants employed less than 1 percent blacks. Moreover, racial prejudice prevailed among many auto workers, particularly among recent southern migrants, many of whom were followers either of the Ku Klux Klan or of Detroit's racist demagogues—Father Charles Coughlin, Reverend Gerald L. K. Smith, and Pastor J. Frank Norris. Often encouraged by employers, many white workers actively resisted integrated housing and the hiring and upgrading of black workers. Commenting on the widespread prejudice, a Detroit auto worker declared: "About forty percent of the workers here are Polish—there are also a lot of southern whites. Both of them are very prejudiced. The rumor got out not long ago that Negroes were going to start to work in the trim department where I work. Most of the men there are southern whites. They said I'll be goddamned if I am going to work with a goddamned Black Nigger."[9]

Wartime conditions and prejudiced attitudes led to racially motivated wildcat strikes, to organized attacks on blacks, to many minor racial confrontations, and to a major race riot in June 1943. When white workers in protest over black hiring and upgrading engaged in wildcat strikes at Curtis Wright aircraft and Packard in 1941, at Hudson in 1942, and at Packard again in 1943, R. J. Thomas and other UAW leaders acted to reduce racial tensions and defend black rights. Thomas removed wildcat leaders and ordered white workers either to work with blacks or to leave the plants. Opposing both the segregated housing policies of the city administration and the demonstrations and physical assaults of white mobs, the UAW successfully supported the right of blacks to occupy a federal housing project called Sojourner Truth. During the race riot of June 20–23, 1943, in which 34 people died, Thomas mercilessly criticized the conduct of the mayor and police, joined black leaders in calling for martial law, and mobilized union stewards to end the violence. Though no one in the union could claim sole credit for the UAW's racial policies, certainly the prevalence of Communists and their left-wing allies in the leadership of local unions, on the staffs of R. J. Thomas and George Addes, and among the Executive Board members contributed to the forthright positions.[10]

At the 1943 UAW convention in Buffalo, the Communists and their allies led a fight to have a black elected to the International Executive Board (IEB). The issue emerged in the debate over establishing a Minorities Department. The majority resolution merely called for the president, with the approval of the IEB, to appoint the head of the Minorities Department. The Communist-backed minority resolution, however, called for the convention to elect the head of a Minorities Department and called for this person to serve as a member of the IEB. In introducing the minority report, Communist Nat Ganley said:

Although the minority report does not make it mandatory that a Negro be a director of the Minority Department, I feel confident that this great International Convention would want to demonstrate to the entire nation our policy of racial solidarity by electing a Negro to this post. . . . Such a sound American position can easily be distorted by smoke screen arguments that it represents Jim Crowism,—that women, Italians, and welders would want special representation to the Board. None of these problems have anything in common with the Negro problem. Women and welders are not lynched in America just because they are women and welders, but Negroes are lynched because they are Negroes.

Ganley's argument for the special condition of blacks naturally had a certain force because of the race riot in Detroit earlier in the year and because of the persistence of lynching in the South. In the South three persons were lynched in 1943, five in 1942, four in 1941, and five in 1940.[11]

The whole issue of minority rights was extremely controversial at the 1943 convention. Both the debate over the Minority Department resolution and a later debate over a Minority Rights resolution were tumultuous. Boos and shouts of "Time!" and "Sit-down!" repeatedly interrupted speakers. The debate over the Minority Rights resolution, which Communist ally, Shelton Tappes, had introduced, and which among other things called for the protection of the "rights of all minority groups to fully participate in our social, political and industrial life," revealed strong racist attitudes among some members. A delegate from Reuther's Local 174, for instance, declared: "I do not believe this convention should go on record as endorsing their [blacks'] participation in social life. . . . There is a natural difference between the two races which cannot be overstepped. . . . I would never go to any union function and take my wife and daughter when they were supposed to mingle socially with the negro race." Even the UAW leadership split over the question of electing a Negro to the IEB. R. J. Thomas, Victor and Walter Reuther opposed it; George Addes and Richard Frankensteen supported it. Victor Reuther said: "We should not establish the practice of giving special privileges to special groups, because that is a Jim Crow privilege." Though the convention eventually passed the Minority Rights resolution, it defeated both the majority and minority resolution on a Minority Department. Clearly, if the Communists had been reluctant to jeopardize the wartime unity, they would have avoided taking the advanced positions that they took on the question of minority rights at the convention.[12]

The Communists and other left-wingers in the Education Department devoted special attention to minority group problems. The University of Michigan UAW summer school offered a class on minority group problems; the 1945 education conference, which brought together educators from all levels of the union for a week of study, devoted a session to discrimination in the plants and community. The department also issued such pamphlets as *To Unite—Regardless* (a discussion of black contributions to American history), *To Stamp Out Discrimination, There Are No Master Races, What Do the People of Africa Want* by Mrs. Paul Robeson, and a condensed version of Gunnar Myrdal's *American Dilemma.* Films like *The Negro Soldier,* a movie stressing the commonalities of black and white soldiers, were distributed by the department. Elizabeth Hawes recalled that black and white staff members and organizers also engaged in direct action, known as "knocking over" an establishment, to force the integration of bars and restaurants. Hawes said: "Discrimination against Negroes was rampant at the beginning of the war, both among union members and management. UAW did a swell educational job on that."[13]

The intense activity of Communists in support of black rights during the war naturally resulted in increased party membership and influence among black auto workers. In the early months of 1943, the Michigan CP recruited some 120 black members. They represented 40 percent of the party's entire recruitment in the state. The Communists achieved an especially noteworthy influence among the 20,000 black workers at Ford. Communist influence among black workers at Ford dated back to the 1930s, when Clarence Oliver had organized an Unemployed Council in Ecorse. Communists and such members of the National Negro

Congress as the Reverend Charles Hill had played an important part in recruiting black workers to the UAW. During the war, Ford Communists favored public protest to force the upgrading of black workers, most of whom were concentrated in the foundary. At this time, the two most open Communists in the Ford plant were black workers, Nelson Davis and Joe Billups. Another black Communist at Ford's, Art McPhaul, who was elected UAW district committeeman at Ford's in 1943, openly sold the *Daily Worker* and other Communist literature in the plant. McPhaul later recalled that one year during the war he sold 400 subscriptions to the *Daily Worker* in the plant and that of the 785 workers in his department, 450 read the Communist paper regularly.[14]

Even though the Communists support for both the war and certain interests of workers won them support particularly early in the war, on the whole Communist influence suffered. To understand this, one must first understand the overall consequences of the war for labor. Three major developments of the war years undermined labor's power. The first wartime development was the growth of unprecedented government interference and regulation of labor relations. This government regulation occurred through the tripartite NWLB established in January 1942. The NWLB served as an agency of mediation and arbitration designed to stop industrial conflict. It also occurred through imposition from above, as in the notable case of the government wage policy known as the Little Steel formula. Imposed by an executive order in July 1942 and sanctioned by Congress in October 1942, the formula limited wage increases to 15 percent above their 1941 levels. Government regulation also occurred through such Congressional legislation as the War Labor Disputes Act (Smith-Connally) passed in June 1943, which set up barriers to strikes and prohibited labor's financial contributions to candidates for federal office. Though the government sanctioned "maintenance of membership" helped increase union membership from ten and a half million at the time of Pearl Harbor to fourteen and three-quarters million by V-J Day, the overall effect of government regulation was to erode labor power. Labor had effective representation in government only on the NWLB. Though at times extremely critical of government policy, labor, with the exception of John L. Lewis, had committed itself to national unity and the no-strike pledge and had no effective recourse to the policies imposed on it.[15]

The second wartime development that undermined labor's

power was the intensification of class conflict. With the help of cost-plus contracts and government-enforced wage controls, the corporations reaped gigantic profits. Profits before taxes soared from $9.3 billion in 1940 to $24.3 billion in 1944. Workers' wages failed to keep pace with either the soaring profits or the rising cost of living. Because of full employment, a shift in employment from low to high paying industries, and increases in benefits and over-time pay, real wages increased during the war. These increases, however, failed to match the soaring inflation. According to the official figures of the NWLB, between January 1941 and October 1944, basic wage rates increased by 20 percent, while the cost of living increased 30 percent. The CIO maintained that the actual gap between wages and cost of living was greater than the official figures revealed since the actual cost of living had increased by 45 percent. The figures on strikes for the period indicated the extent of worker discontent. The number of strikes increased in the three full years of war from 2,968 in 1942, to 3,752 in 1943, to 4,956 in 1944. The number of strikers also increased from 840,000 in 1942, to 1,981,000 in 1943, to 2,116,000 in 1944. The number of strikes and strikers, which in 1944 surpassed the comparable figures for the strike wave of 1937, indicated the intensification of class ten-sion during the war. Since the overwhelming majority of these strikes were wildcats, which the AFL and CIO leaders refused to support or finance, their incidence represented a serious deterio-ration of the leadership's authority over the ranks. As the NWLB tersely observed of the UAW leadership's attempts to quell strikes: "Such action has not increased the popularity of these representatives."[16]

The third wartime development that undermined labor's power was the growing political strength of conservative, antilabor forces. In spite of the CIO's political activism in forming the Politi-cal Action Committee in 1944, conservative, antilabor forces ad-vanced. Among other things, they secured the passage of the Smith-Connally Act and other antilabor acts at the state level. In part, this growth of conservative political forces resulted from the return of economic stability brought on by war production. The reemergence of economic stability raised the prestige of American corporate leaders from its nadir during the depression. Con-versely, during the war, the popular protest movements of the 1930s collapsed; no new program of social reform emerged. The removal of Henry Wallace from the Democratic ticket in 1944 symbolized the defensive political posture that old New Dealers and labor assumed during the war.[17]

In the face of increased government regulation, the intensification of class conflict, and the growing shift to the right of national politics, the Communists clung unflinchingly to the CIO policy of national unity, increased production, and the no-strike pledge. Whatever justification this policy had at the war's outset, the need for it became less evident as the United States avoided involvement in the war's major European theater until 1944 and then opened a second front against the Germans only after the Soviet Union had already turned the tide. The dogmatic adherence to a policy of labor sacrifice at a time when neither domestic nor international conditions clearly warranted it, inevitably eroded the influence of the Communists and CIO leaders as well. In the UAW this became evident in the controversies around both incentive pay and the no-strike pledge.

The idea of incorporating an incentive pay scheme into the automobile industry originated outside the CP when, in the fall of 1942, GM proposed the idea for the automobile industry, and the NWLB encouraged the idea by exempting wage increases due to incentive plans from the restrictions of the Little Steel Formula. Though they did not originate the idea, the Communists embraced it. Late in 1942, over the objections of William Z. Foster and others, Browder proposed incentive pay, and the Party endorsed it. Early in 1943, the CP issued two pamphlets by Browder— *Production for Victory* and *Wage Policy in War Production*—that set forth a case for incentive pay. Browder stressed two points. First, incentive pay provided a way to encourage the increased production essential for victory in the war. Second, it enabled workers to circumvent wage stabilization restrictions and profit economically from increased production. As the largest union in the nation representing over one million workers, and as a union representing workers engaged in between 22 and 28 percent of all wartime production, the UAW naturally became an important target for Communist agitation on behalf of incentive pay. In the spring of 1943, Browder defended incentive pay in a letter to the president of UAW Local 600 and in a half-page ad in the *Detroit News*. Nat Ganley wrote a letter to the *News* praising Local 155's experience with incentive pay. Communist ally, C. G. "Pop" Edelen, president of Plymouth Local 51, issued a pamphlet entitled *Production with Incentive Pay*, in which he reiterated Browder's basic arguments on behalf of the system.[18]

Though the Communists became prominently identified with the issue of incentive pay, others backed the idea as well. Locals that already operated with some kind of piecework system supported incentive pay. Also, on the IEB the issue had the backing of Frankensteen and Addes. Frankensteen, who was in charge of aircraft organizing, argued that incentive pay provided a way to circumvent the government's wage restrictions and believed that it would greatly facilitate recruitment of aircraft workers. Addes agreed with Frankensteen's position and also supported incentive pay as a war measure geared to increase military production.[19]

In spite of such backing, the issue of incentive pay failed to win significant support in the UAW. When in March 1943 Frankensteen introduced a proposal for incentive pay, the Executive Board by a thirteen to seven vote affirmed its "traditional opposition" to incentive payment plans. In April, Emil Mazey of Local 212, the most militant opponent of the union's whole war program, led a delegation of eleven Detroit local presidents to the Executive Board meeting in Cleveland to argue against incentive pay, and the Board tabled a motion on its behalf. In May, delegates to two UAW War Problems Conferences in New York and Detroit overwhelmingly repudiated incentive pay proposals. At the Michigan CIO convention from June 28-July 1, 1943, where over 80 percent of the 1,800 delegates were from UAW locals, a large majority also rejected incentive pay. So widespread was the opposition at the Michigan CIO meeting that no Communist even bothered to speak on behalf of incentive pay. When the 1943 UAW convention soundly defeated incentive pay, the issue finally died.[20]

There were a number of reasons for the defeat of incentive pay. First, piecework as well as speedup and the confusing wage schemes associated with it had been a major grievance of auto workers in the preunion days. In the plants of the major auto companies, the UAW had largely eliminated piecework in the 1930s. Though incentive pay differed from piecework by being based on group rather than individual productivity, sufficient similarity between the two plans existed to evoke strong resistance among the rank and file. A Flint auto worker probably summed up the

sentiments of many when he said, "Outside of some of those pa-
triots and commies, nobody ever wanted to go back to piecework."
Second, incentive pay became a symbol for the whole panoply of
wartime sacrifices. Although most auto workers undoubtedly supported the war and realized that some sacrifices were necessary to
defeat fascism, many also resented much about their wartime
situation: the wage freeze, the overtime, the relinquishment of
premium pay, the growing unresolved grievances, the inability to
strike, and the delays and partiality of government boards. Such
resentment surfaced at the UAW convention in 1942. Thereafter, it
grew. At the 1943 Michigan CIO convention, for example, the delegates not only defeated incentive pay but also passed resolutions
opposing the Little Steel Formula and the no-strike pledge, and
applauding John L. Lewis and the mine workers for defying the
wartime no-strike pledge.[21]

A third and perhaps the most important reason for the defeat
of incentive pay was Reuther's success in turning incentive pay
into a factional issue. The two leading factions in the union had
united behind the Equality of Sacrifice wartime program and, over
considerable opposition, had secured its passage at the 1942 convention. Afterwards, Reuther broke ranks. Reuther began criticizing aspects of the wartime sacrifices. This was a dangerous course,
for while trying to appeal to the many workers who resented wartime sacrifices, he had to avoid appearing disloyal to the CIO,
which strongly backed the war effort. Since Murray took no position on incentive pay, and since incentive pay was not an original
part of the UAW's wartime program, Reuther could reap the benefits of attacking another proposed wartime sacrifice without appearing disloyal to the CIO's and the UAW's commitment to winning the war. Reuther became the leading opponent of incentive
pay on the IEB. There Reuther's attempts to link the idea of incentive pay with piecework and the Communist party carried the
day.[22]

The 1943 UAW convention in Buffalo became a factional circus
with Reuther's attack on incentive pay in the center ring. In the
convention's halls and caucuses, Reuther's people charged that, by
supporting incentive pay, Addes, Frankensteen, and the Communists were selling out the union for Russia. Reuther supporters
sang an original song to the tune of "Reuben and Rachel," that
included the lines: "Who are the boys who take their orders/

Straight from the office of Joe Sta-leen?/ No one else but the grue-some twosome,/ George F. Addes and Frankensteen." The Addes forces countered with their own lyrics: "You have fought a dirty battle,/ You've yelled RED, you've lied and schemed./ We know you by this time Reuther/ So we'll take Addes and Frankensteen." The Communists tried to counter the factionalism by withdrawing from the Addes caucus and appealing for unity for the sake of the war. Their efforts were quixotic. In spite of continuing to support such major elements of the wartime program as the no-strike pledge, Reuther's group turned a number of issues into factional causes. Reversing its stand at the previous convention, the Reuther group defeated a Communist-backed proposal calling for the opening of a second front. The Reuther group also obtained a qualified, rather than unqualified, endorsement of President Roosevelt. And by tapping the convention's resentment against wartime sacrifices and by playing on anti-Communism, the Reuther group also soundly defeated incentive pay.[23]

Unquestionably, the Communists and the Addes caucus suf-fered because of their support for incentive pay. The *Detroit News* observed: "Reuther is the fair-haired boy of the rank and file . . . principally for his stand against the introduction of the incentive pay system in the automobile industry." Communist spokesman, Nat Ganley, similarly acknowledged that Reuther's "most effec-tive slogan was: 'Down with Earl Browder's piecework in the UAW.'" Incentive pay, according to Ganley, was the "one advan-tage" Reuther had in winning "strong rank and file support within the UAW." In the local elections of 1943, the incentive pay issue figured in the defeat of Communist-backed candidates for pres-ident of Chrysler Local 7 and Packard Local 190. In Ford Local 600, where a left-wing slate headed by Percy Llewellyn and Shelton Tappes defeated the incumbents headed by ACTU vice-president Paul Ste. Marie, the left-wing publicly repudiated in-centive pay. At the Michigan CIO convention in 1943, for the first time no candidate associated with the Communists won a place on the CIO executive board. At the 1943 UAW convention, Addes's identification with the incentive pay issue almost defeated his bid for reelection as secretary-treasurer of the union.[24]

Even more than the controversy over incentive pay, the grow-ing violations of the no-strike pledge posed a challenge to the Communists and UAW leaders as a whole. In the first full year of

American involvement in the war, the union's pledge to refrain from strikes had a compelling logic. The outcome of the war was uncertain, and the need for total mobilization was apparent. As conversion of Detroit's auto industry to military production got under way, the work force in the city's auto and auto equipment manufacturing fell from 270,000 in 1940 to 59,000 in 1943, while simultaneously the work force in aircraft, ordinance, and tanks expanded from 3,000 to 432,000. Also, in the war's first year, the belief was widespread that capital and labor would sacrifice equally for the war. Consequently, the uncertainties of the war's outcome, the exigencies of mobilization, and the belief in equality of sacrifice produced a popular loyalty to the no-strike pledge. In 1942, only fifty strikes occurred in auto, and the average strike lasted only one and a half days.[25]

Between 1943 and the war's end, however, much of the basis for the no-strike pledge disappeared. The United States launched the South Pacific and African campaigns but remained on the periphery of the major fighting in Europe until June 1944. By the time the U. S. engaged the German forces in Europe, the Red Army had already determined the war's outcome on the eastern front. Because of the delayed opening of the second front, the war never assumed for Americans the character of a life and death struggle with fascism that it had for their allies. At home the war failed to produce an equality of sacrifice; disparities in class conditions soon became apparent. Corporate profits and executive salaries soared. General Motor's net profits rose from $47 million during the first six months of 1942 to $69 million in the same period one year later. Meanwhile, the auto workers lived and labored under extreme, wartime hardships. At the same time that the Little Steel formula imposed limits on wage increases, the cost of living in Detroit rose higher than the average for the nation's 34 largest cities, and "food costs rose most sharply." The rapid influx of people to Detroit put tremendous strains on the city's housing and other public facilities. The Department of Labor discovered that workers at Ford's Willow Run bomber plant "found it necessary to live in make-shift substandard dwellings, such as shacks, trailers, basement apartments, and tents, with sanitary facilities so inadequate as to present a serious health hazard to the entire Detroit area." Detroit's schools, hospitals, and other public facilities were "overtaxed far beyond their capacity." Wartime production also aggravated conditions in the plants. A UAW staff member observed: "At times during the war the workers were so tired from long hours and no vacations, and provoked by endless petty management malpractices, that they wanted to walk out just to get a rest."[26]

In response to such conditions, the auto workers began transgressing the no-strike pledge. In 1943 the auto workers engaged in 153 wildcat strikes. These strikes accounted for 0.20 percent of the available working time. While the median average strike involved 340 workers, 43 of the strikes involved over 1,000 workers, and 2 strikes involved more than 10,000 workers. In 1944, the strikes increased in number, size, and duration. In 1944, 224 strikes occurred. These strikes accounted for 0.58 percent of the available working time, making auto the most disrupted industry that year. The median number of workers involved rose to 399, and 68 strikes involved more than 1,000 workers; 5 strikes involved over 10,000 workers. Considering only strikes involving more than six workers and lasting over eight hours, more than half of all the workers in the industry participated in strikes in 1944. Counting strikes involving less than six workers and less than eight hours, 800 of which occurred in the first 11 months of 1944, well *over* half of all auto workers participated in strikes. That year, George Romney, managing director of the Automotive Council for War Production, told a Congressional committee: "There have been more strikes and work stoppages and more employees directly involved during the first 11 months of 1944 than in any other period of the industry's history." UAW President R. J. Thomas said that "the UAW-CIO today faces one of the greatest crises in its history" and that "strikes are destroying the UAW."[27]

The epidemic of strikes in auto had several important characteristics. Though the strikes increased in duration throughout the war, they remained short, averaging only 3.5 days in the peak year of 1944. Hence, although the strikes manifested widespread worker dissatisfaction, they did not pose a real threat to war production. Few of the strikes occurred over the issue of wages. Of 118 strikes in December 1944 and January 1945, only 4 involved wage disputes, and none involved questions of organization. Most of the strikes represented protests over discipline, discharge, and other company policies. Some firms were more strike prone than others. Two of the most strike prone firms were Briggs and Ford.

Briggs had 28 strikes in 1943 and 114 in 1944. From the time it signed a UAW contract in 1941 until the end of the war, Ford had 773 strikes. This amounted to one strike almost every other day. Naturally firms like Ford and Briggs that had authoritarian and oppressive managements and locals like Ford 600, Willow Run 50, and Briggs 212 that contained leading opponents of the no-strike pledge were more strike-prone than others.[28]

In the face of widespread strikes by auto workers, the Communists held inflexibly to the no-strike pledge. In June 1944, the *Daily Worker* called a walkout by Chicago Dodge workers a "disgraceful spectacle." The paper added: "The real strike is on the war fronts. To call any other kind of strike is to scab, and scabs should be treated as scabs." Early in 1945, the *Daily Worker* decried a walkout by Detroit Dodge workers as "nothing less than a stab in the back of our armed services." Many reasons existed for the Communists' continued support of the pledge. Mainly, the UAW leadership itself continued to support the no-strike pledge, and in February 1944 it even announced a new policy for disciplining those responsible for unauthorized strikes. Also, the Communists supported the pledge because they believed that to do otherwise might disrupt national war production, one fourth of which the auto workers produced, or of provoking repressive government action against the union. Still, both the Communists and UAW leaders held more dogmatically to the no-strike pledge than international and domestic conditions after 1943 justified. After the war, William Z. Foster and others admitted that the Communists had tried to enforce the pledge "too rigidly."[29]

Vocal opponents of the no-strike pledge existed from the beginning of the war and grew in number as the war progressed. The most extreme opposition came from the Trotskyists. Both the orthodox Socialist Workers party (SWP) and Max Shachtman's recusant Workers party (WP) linked their opposition to the pledge to a general opposition to the war. For this reason, among others, neither party gained much of a following among auto workers. The SWP had only 110 members in the UAW; the WP had even less. A WP member later acknowledged that the party drew most of its membership from the middleclass people and worker-intellectuals who found industrial jobs during the expanded war production. Besides the Trotskyists, several local leaders including Emil Mazey of Briggs Local 212, Tom De Lorenzo of Brewster Local

365, Bill Jenkins of Chrysler Local 490, and Brendon Sexton of Willow Run Local 50 opposed the pledge. Mazey argued for revocation of the pledge in order "to regain our collective bargaining" and "to force decent wages from industry and government." By 1944, Briggs Local 212, Willow Run Local 50, Brewster Local 365, GM Local 599, and Chrysler Local 7 had taken stands against the pledge. Also, though Reuther formally backed the pledge, he and some of his close supporters expressed open sympathy for certain strikes.[30]

Controversy over the no-strike pledge peaked at the 1944 UAW convention in Grand Rapids, Michigan. For two days debate raged over the union's strike policy. The Communist-Addes group supported the majority resolution calling for a reaffirmation of the no-strike pledge. The Reuther group backed the minority resolution calling for a reaffirmation of the pledge until the defeat of Germany and then the revocation of the pledge in plants engaged exclusively in civilian production. A rank and file caucus, composed of 25 or 30 people led by Larry Yost of Local 600, Art Hughes of Local 140, and backed by the WP, supported a "super-duper" minority resolution calling for the immediate revocation of the pledge. Tempers flared. Insults flew. Fist fights erupted. Members of Local 212 mocked patriotic arguments on behalf of the pledge by waving small American flags and wiping away imaginary tears. While supporters warned of reactionary legislation and the defeat of Roosevelt if the pledge was revoked, opponents warned of the union's deterioration if the pledge was reaffirmed. The delegates, who were about equally divided on the three resolutions, voted down each in turn. Only then did the convention reach a compromise, that reaffirmed the pledge until a referendum of the entire membership could decide the issue.[31]

The Communists and the rank and file caucus played active roles on opposite sides of the referendum campaign. W. G. Grant, president of Local 600 and a close Communist ally, headed the UAW Committee to Uphold the No-Strike Pledge. The committee contained three union officers—R. J. Thomas, George Addes, and Richard Leonard—eleven of eighteen regionl directors, and such Communists and their close allies as John Anderson, Nat Ganley, and Shelton Tappes. Also, the CIO News supported the committee by devoting an issue to the pledge. The Communists and other pledge supporters issued leaflets, held meetings, and used sound trucks at plant gates to generate enthusiasm for the pledge. A typical Communist leaflet declared that "advocates of strike threats or strike actions in America in 1945 are SCABS in the war against Hitlerism, they are SCABS against our Armed Forces, they are SCABS against the labor movement." The rank and file caucus headed by Larry Yost and backed by the Workers party spearheaded the opposition campaign. The rank and file's steering committee located in Detroit printed and distributed a four-page newspaper, *Rank and Filer*. The paper argued that under the pledge the corporations had sacrificed nothing and gained everything — government-financed factories and machinery, cost-plus contracts, and huge profits — while the workers had sacrificed everything and gained nothing. In order "to defend our threatened interest," the union had to repeal "the straight-jacket of the No-Strike Pledge." During the referendum campaign Reuther equivocated. He ostensibly supported the pledge but refused to work with either group. In spite of the intense campaign waged by both sides, only 320,000 of the 1,250,000 auto workers voted in the referendum, which upheld the pledge by a two to one margin.[32]

Even though the referendum upheld the pledge, the Communists' campaign for the pledge hurt their influence. Saul Wellman, head of the party's Auto Commission after the war, claimed that Communist activity on behalf of the pledge "didn't help" the party, "and it didn't hurt it." Even this modest assessment was overly sanguine. Considering the substantial minority of auto workers who voted against the pledge, the large number who abstained from voting, and the vast number of auto workers who participated in workstoppages in the year preceding the vote, it was easy to see that few auto workers shared the Communists' enthusiasm for the pledge. Opponents of the pledge made the most of this disparity. Even though the Communists shared the same position on the pledge as the CIO and UAW leaders, both Mazey and the rank and file committee attacked the Communists more vigorously than they attacked Murray or Thomas. Reuther, too, tried to make political capital of the Communist position. He accused the Communists of organizing and dominating the Committee to Uphold the No-Strike Pledge and gave this as his reason for refusing to join the committee. Evidence that support for the pledge eroded Communist influence appeared in local elections during the referendum campaign. In Locals 490 and 50,

Communist-backed incumbents suffered defeats, and in W. G. Grant's Local 600, the Communists lost control of the General Council and Executive Board.[33]

Related to the damage to Communist influence caused by the incentive pay and no-strike pledge controversies was the damage caused by the structural changes and postwar outlook adopted by the party in 1944. After the Teheran conference at the end of 1943, at which Roosevelt, Churchill, and Stalin pledged to work for an enduring peace after the war, the Communist party carried its wartime policy of national unity to astonishing extremes. Browder, who regarded Teheran as the "most important turning point in all history," drew from it the implication that the wartime national unity should be extended for "an indefinite term of years." Browder even announced that Communists would oppose "an explosion of class conflict in our country when the war is over" and would defend "capitalism as it exists in our country." (However extreme this position, it shared with the bulk of Communist wartime policy, the dubious virtue of consistency with the viewpoint of the AFL and CIO leadership, which in March 1945 had joined with the Chamber of Commerce in a joint pledge of post-war cooperation.) As a demonstration of its commitment to national unity, the party, which in June 1943 had already abolished shop branches, in May 1944 abolished itself and created the educational Communist Political Association (CPA).[34]

The idea of extending national unity and, by implication, the no-strike pledge, after the war had no basis in reality. The war had increased rather than decreased class antagonism; the strike wave of 1944–45 and the explosion of postwar strikes made this abundantly clear. Within a year, the Communists recognized the absurdity of the Teheran perspective. After a debilitating factional fight in 1945, which eventually resulted in the expulsion of Browder, the party repudiated the Teheran perspective and reestablished the party and shop branches. Before then, however, the Teheran perspective wrecked havoc on Communist influence in auto. The abolition of the party structure and the idea of postwar class cooperation disoriented and alienated many rank and file Communists and their allies as well as auto workers in general. Recalling that "a large number of Communists were at one time in favor of pledging not to strike after the war was over," Elizabeth Hawes said that "the idea seemed idiotic to many, if not all" good auto unionists. Similarly, Nat Ganley acknowledged that the idea put a "stigma" on the entire Left-Center (Communist-Addes) coalition in the UAW. Art McPhaul, a black Communist in Local 600, said that both the abolition of the party and the idea of postwar cooperation "permanently disillusioned" many Communist auto workers, who left the party and "did not return to the party even after Browder was removed." Moreover, the factional struggle in the party in 1945 further weakened party influence by distracting Communists from mass work and recruitment.[35]

Looking at Communist activity in the auto industry over the entire war period reveals a varied and contradictory pattern. Immediately after Pearl Harbor, the Communists' avid support for the war aims of the nation and the union and their vigorous work on behalf of organizing, education, political action, and the rights of blacks and women greatly increased Communist influence. In 1942 the party's recruitment in Michigan averaged 39 members a month, more than double the monthly average of 19 in 1941. In the first months of 1943, the party recruited 300 new members in Michigan, 225 of whom were auto workers. This represented a "tempo that far exceeded the rate of growth ever achieved in any other recent period." According to organizational secretary, John Williamson, the party "nearly doubled" its membership in auto and aircraft, which meant that membership went from 629 in April 1942 to around 1200 in 1943. Sales of the *Daily Worker* at this time greatly exceeded the pace of membership gains. Also, early in the war, the Communists secured many important positions in local unions and on the International staff. Elizabeth Hawes recalled, "There were a large number of officials, high and low, who did not regard the Communists as the Enemy but rather as a vital and energetic group of people." Besides those in the Education Department, the Communists counted among their members and close supporters General Counsel, Maurice Sugar; Research Director, James Wishart; and such clerical workers in the International office as Eleanor Bush.[36]

As the war continued, and the Communists rigidly supported incentive pay, the no-strike pledge, the Teheran perspective, and the abolition of shop branches and the party itself, their influence eroded. Even if the party's membership in the UAW increased after 1943 (something which was not clear), it did not keep pace with the growth of union membership that more than doubled during the war. By the end of the war both the circulation of the *Daily Worker* and the sale of theoretical literature declined. In 1944 membership fluctuation greatly increased. In January 1945, Williamson reported that two-thirds of the CPA membership in Detroit had joined within the previous year and that not even 10 percent of the members had been in the organization several years. Consequently, the political development of Communists in auto fell to a new low. "The average [Detroit] member," Williamson noted, "differs but little in political development from a progressive trade unionist." Also, with the abolition of the party and the shop branches, organizational discipline deteriorated. Williamson noted: "Tasks handed down to the [Detroit] clubs are either not tackled at all or are inadequately fulfilled." Yet another indication of the party's declining influence in auto was that the recruitment of nonworkers in Detroit began to exceed the recruitment of workers. During 1944, the Michigan district, which traditionally had the highest industrial concentration of any in the party, suffered a decline in the proportion of workers from 66 percent to 58 percent. The decline of the party's influence was particularly evident in Reuther's GM bailiwick. Williamson concluded that, because of the party's wartime policies, UAW Communists had "forfeited leadership to the Reuthers and other radical phrasemongers."[37]

Years later in an interview, Nat Ganley echoed Williamson's conclusion: "Reuther had the advantage of going into the post-war period with the belief that he was the champion of the economic interest of the auto workers during the wartime period as against the Addes-left coalition which was so bent on winning the war that they were ignoring the grievances of the workers." Why did this occur? Was Reuther concerned with the economic interests of the workers whereas the Communists were only concerned with the interests of the Soviet Union? This was too pat. If Reuther was more successful than the Left in balancing the needs of war with the interests of auto workers, his success derived from a combination of his political sagacity and personal ambition. In the pursuit of the UAW presidency, Reuther was willing to vacillate on such aspects of the CIO's war policy as the no-strike pledge. As for the Communists, their rigid and overly enthusiastic pursuit of the CIO's war policy derived less from an abstract adherence to the interests of the Soviet Union than from their overestimation of the degree of sacrifices by American workers needed to win the war, from their desire to maintain a Left-Center alliance with Murray by loyally supporting the CIO's war policies, and from the mistaken ideas of Browder with regard to the possibilities of postwar class cooperation.[38]

Although the Communist and Left forces lost some influence in the UAW during the war, this conclusion demanded several qualifications. First, the decline resulted from more than the Communists' policy on incentive pay and the no-strike pledge. It also resulted from the whole wartime context, in which the Communists and the CIO as a whole pursued a policy of sacrifice, cooperation, and increased production while the government increased its repressive regulation of labor relations, class conflict increased, and the political spectrum shifted dramatically to the right. The decline also resulted from the ideological and organizational confusion experienced by the Communist party as a whole because of Browder's policies and the struggles against those policies. Second, the conclusion must be qualified by the recognition that while the Left's decline was sufficient to help insure the election of Reuther in 1946, the decline was still marginal. The decline was only marginal because in spite of their mistakes the Communists did much that won rank and file respect. The Communists' enthusiasm for the war effort certainly appealed to workers who were for the most part patriotic. Moreover, in spite of the wartime restraint, the Communists vigorously pursued the union's objectives in organizing, educational, and political work. The Communists also engaged in important struggles on behalf of black and women workers. All of this contributed to the Communist-Addes group maintaining an important influence in the union after the war. Consequently, the Cold War, rather than the Second World War, would provide the setting for the decisive defeat of the Communists in the auto industry.

# XI

**• • •**

## REUTHER AND REACTION,
## 1946–1949

The decisive decline of Communist influence in the UAW occurred
not during World War II but during the Cold War. Certainly, the
least remarkable feature of this decline was that it occurred. During the period of the Cold War and McCarthyism, Communist and
left-wing influence declined in all unions and aspects of American
life. Nothing in the UAW made the Communists there an exception
to the pattern. Given the general pattern of the decline of left-
wing influence in America in the postwar period and given the
relatively small number of Communists in the UAW, what was remarkable was that it took a major effort on the part of Walter
Reuther and his supporters to discredit and mitigate Communist
influence. The history of the anti-Communist drive in the UAW had
three stages: first, Reuther's election as president of the union at
the UAW's 1946 convention; second, the ascendency of the
Reuther-right-wing group over the Addes-left-wing group in the
inter-convention period, 1946–47; and third, Reuther's assault
against the leftists on the staff and in local unions in 1947–49.

Reuther's election to the presidency of the UAW in 1946 set
the stage for the drive against the Communists in the union. Because of this, it is tempting to see Reuther's election itself as a sign
of rising anti-Communism among auto workers. Moreover, since
Reuther was elected before the Cold War was well under way, it is
tempting to interpret Reuther's victory as a repudiation of the
Communist-left-wing policies in the union during World War II.

Here the argument might run that, during the war, Reuther established himself as a militant fighter for the interests of the rank and file by opposing the Communist-Addes forces who strongly backed incentive pay and the no-strike pledge. Reuther further consolidated this militant posture against the Left by leading the first major postwar strike—the 113 day walkout against GM that ended just days before the 1946 convention. The rank and file then rewarded Reuther's militancy and repudiated the Left by electing Reuther president. However plausible, this view will not withstand close inspection.

Throughout the war the two major caucuses—the Reuther-right-wing group and the Addes-left-wing group—held about equal strength. The President, R.J. Thomas, assumed a centrist, mediating role between them. The 1946 convention failed to represent a major shift of allegiances. Thomas, who by then had aligned himself with Addes, was defeated by Reuther for the highest office by a slim majority of 124 votes of the 8,765 votes cast. After removing Thomas from the highest office, the convention then elected him vice-president and also elected representatives of the Addes-Communist group to a majority of the Executive Board. With the convention so closely divided between the two major caucuses, it was impossible to say what factor or group of factors made Reuther's narrow victory possible. Moreover, a close examination of the events leading up to the 1946 convention reveals that however much Reuther tried to reap political advantage by portraying himself as a militant leader and an anti-Communist, he succeeded only marginally in the effort.

As early as September 1945, *Daily Worker* columnist George Morris charged that Reuther was planning a GM strike to advance his own political position in the union, and later the Communists charged that Reuther had "jumped the gun" in calling the GM strike ahead of a strike in steel, in order to capture favorable publicity for himself. Whether the Communists were right about Reuther's motives remains uncertain. Yet the circumstances surrounding the strike lent credence to the charge. Reuther initiated the strike without prior approval of the UAW Executive Board. Calling the strike on November 21 made little tactical sense. GM's huge reserves, the promise of tax rebates under the tax law, and the carryback provisions of the excess profits tax repeal all served to cushion the economic pressure of a strike in 1945. Because GM's major competitors, Ford and Chrysler, had not yet converted to full peacetime production, the strike placed GM under little competitive pressure. The steel industry, not auto, was the natural pacesetter for collective bargaining in the industrial sector, and Reuther eventually had to settle for exactly the wage gain that the steel workers would secure in February. The strike, however, did have an important political rationale. By launching the first major postwar strike Reuther could capture the national limelight before the upcoming UAW convention.[1]

Initially, Reuther gained from the strike. The strike tapped the pent up frustration of 180,000 GM workers who were tired of four years under the no-strike pledge and the wage freeze, and who voted enthusiastically for the strike by a five to one margin. The strike also vaulted Reuther into the national headlines. *Time* ran a cover story on "the U.A.W.'s tack-sharp Vice President," and *Fortune* and *Life* devoted major articles to the "model union leader" and "smart young strategist." Important in drawing public attention to the GM strike leader were Reuther's demands that GM grant a 30 percent wage increase, that GM provide a "wage increase with no price increase," and that GM "open the books" to federal investigators to prove that the company could afford such a wage hike without raising prices.[2]

In the end, however, the strike bestowed little lasting grandeur on Reuther. The walkout dragged on for 113 days. During this time it consumed $125 million in workers' wages and depleted the union's treasury. Reuther's highly publicized slogans of "a wage increase with no price increase" and "open the books" played no part in the settlement. Moreover, Reuther settled the GM strike in March for an eighteen and a half cents an hour raise, no more than acheived in other settlements in auto and steel. On January 26, without a strike, the UAW signed agreements with Ford for eighteen cents (15.1 percent) and with Chrysler for eighteen and a half cents (16.2 percent). Early in February, following short strikes, the United Steel Workers (USWA) settled with U.S. Steel for eighteen and a half cents, and the United Electrical Workers (UE) settled with GM for eighteen and a half cents. Even though Reuther's supporters argued that the GM strike "spearheaded" the other settlements, GM had offered no more than thirteen and a half cents until the steel settlement. The conduct, length, and unexceptional outcome of the GM strike attracted much criticism. The

Communists attacked Reuther for "jumping the gun," for his "one at a time" strategy, and for prolonging the strike unnecessarily. Though UAW officers kept a discrete unanimity during the strike, afterwards President Thomas declared that the walkout had started six weeks too early and lasted six weeks longer than necessary. As early as December, *Time* reported that Reuther's one-at-a-time strategy "appears to have failed." At the end of February, *Business Week* opined that Reuther's hopes for the presidency "appear to have washed out in the length of the GM strike."[3]

Reuther apparently sensed that the strike's length and settlement made him vulnerable to criticism, so he counterattacked and placed the blame on the Communists. At an Executive Board meeting in February, Reuther charged that the UE, a union under Communist influence, had undermined the union bargaining position by settling secretly with GM for a penny less than recommended by a Presidential fact finding committee in January. According to Reuther, the UE had "stabbed" GM strikers in the back. Reuther implied that the Communist leadership of UE had settled for a penny less than Reuther sought in order to undermine the GM strike and undercut Reuther's appeal in the UAW. Thus, Reuther's charge was in the same category as the Communist charge of Reuther's "jumping the gun." Both rested on implied motivations that were impossible to prove. Again, however, the circumstances failed to weigh in Reuther's favor. First, in a letter to the UAW, UE officials denied that they had engaged in secret negotiations and claimed that three times between October and January they had offered to enter joint negotiations only to have Reuther's GM department decline. Second, the Communists gave unstinting support to the GM strike. The Communist-Left leadership of Local 600 donated more to the GM strike than any other local; Communist-led Local 155 donated $45,000; and Ben Gold's Fur and Leather Workers gave $25,000 to the GM strikers.[4]

If the GM strike provided little basis for a swing of auto worker sentiment from the Left to Reuther, any of a myriad of other circumstances may have contributed to Reuther's victory. In large measure, Reuther's victory rested on the support he received from the Association of Catholic Trade Unionists (ACTU). Backed by Francis Cardinal Spellman, a couple of New York utility workers formed ACTU in 1937. Its purpose was to spread Catholic teachings and fight Communism in American trade unions. The following year with the support of Detroit's Bishop Edward Mooney, an ACTU chapter in Detroit was organized. Under the leadership of Paul Weber, an assistant editor of the *Detroit Times* and vice-president of the Michigan CIO, Detroit ACTU soon became the largest chapter in the nation. By 1946, Detroit ACTU had 1,000 members, published a weekly paper, the *Wage Earner,* and ran over a score of labor schools that trained hundreds of workers in trade union techniques mixed with hefty doses of anti-Communism. Detroit ACTU had a strong influence and following among auto workers, particularly in Ford Local 600 and Chrysler Local 7.[5]

ACTU leaders, Paul Ste. Marie and Pat Hamilton of Local 600 and Tom Doherty of Local 7, as well as the ACTU paper backed Reuther in the union. As early as 1939, ACTU and Walter Reuther found an affinity in their mutal opposition to the UAW's Communists, and in subsequent years ACTU played a crucial role in Reuther's rise to power. In a situation where factions of equal size were maneuvering for power, organizational ability weighed heavily in the balance. Through its newspaper, schools, and local caucuses, ACTU was able to play the same organizational and ideological role for the Reuther-right-wing faction as the Communist party played for the Addes-left-wing faction. In local unions, ACTU served as a political machine, recruiting candidates, and providing them with a program and support. Al Leggat, an activist in Ford Local 600 said: "[ACTU's] main course in life was to strengthen the Catholics to move into positions of leadership to fight the 'commies' . . . . They got Catholics who would normally just be members [to] suddenly become leaders. . . . [M]ost of the Catholics at Ford in a position of responsibility in the union did belong to ACTU." ACTU strength in Ford Local 600 alone represented sufficient votes to give Reuther the election in 1946. During the war, the ACTU-right-wing and Communist-left-wing groups engaged in a seesaw battle for control of Local 600. ACTU vice-president, Paul Ste. Marie, won the leadership of the local in 1941; the Communist-left-wing won in 1944; Joe McCusker (who had two brothers in ACTU) led the ACTU-right-wing group to victory in 1945; and the Communist-left-wing came back to win the chairmanship in all 16 plant committees in 1946. At the time of the 1946 election the Communist-left-wing controlled 43 delegates, and the ACTU-right-wing controlled 33 delegates, but the 33 ACTU delegates represented 227 convention votes, more than a 100 votes over Reuther's margin of victory. In other locals, notably Chrysler Local 7, where Tom Doherty was active, ACTU forces helped deliver votes to the Reuther column. After the election, *Fortune* declared: "Indeed, ACTU's support of Walter Reuther against the Thomas-Addes-Leonard slate was a major factor in the outcome of the recent UAW elections." Carl Haessler only slightly exaggerated when he later declared: "The history of the UAW after Reuther made his alliance with the Catholics early in '39 is therefore a history of the Reuther-Catholic power caucus' march to power."[6]

Reuther had other assets as well. For instance, the small band of Trotskyists in the UAW backed Reuther in 1946. This occurred not only because the Trotskyists shared Reuther's anti-Communism, but also because they shared similar positions on labor policy during the war and because Reuther's "open the books" demand had originally been part of the Trotskyist program. Additionally, Reuther had a more favorable public image than his opponent, Thomas. Major stories in Henry Luce's *Fortune, Life,* and *Time* before the 1946 election cleverly combined fact and fantasy in egregious rewrites of UAW history. These stories portrayed Reuther as founder of the union, strategist of the sit-down strikes, savior of the union from Martin, organizer of Ford, and innovator of wartime production and postwar reconversion programs. Such articles invariably portrayed Reuther as bright, bold, energetic, eloquent, and anti-Communist and Thomas as bumbling, cigar-smoking, poker-playing, and liquor-drinking. Even Reuther's opponents conceded that these divergent public images contained enough truth to make them stick. The left-wing leader of Local 248, Harold Christoffel, later conceded that Thomas was "no match" for Reuther. "You didn't find Reuther going around playing cards," Christoffel said. "He was busy all the time."[7]

Alongside Reuther's assets, the Addes-Left forces suffered from many liabilities. A serious defect in the Addes-Left forces was its lack of a unified front and a common program. In the weeks preceding the convention, Addes allowed rumors to circulate that he might run for the presidency, and Addes failed to endorse Thomas until several days before the convention opened. Even at that late date, Thomas and Addes forwarded no common program. Moreover, Thomas made no serious effort to counter Reuther's red-baiting. Indeed, Thomas tried to outdo Reuther in making groundless attacks against the UE for its alleged betrayal of the GM strike. While Reuther filled press pages with accusations that Thomas was a Communist "tool" and "stooge," Thomas merely responded with the accusation that Reuther was a stooge of ILGWU president David Dubinsky. The Addes-Left group also suffered from the defection of the union's once popular vice-president, Richard Frankensteen, who left the union to become the head of a Detroit manufacturing company. Widespread booing greeted Frankensteen's appearance before the convention. Browder's liquidation of Communist shop units during the war also weakened the Addes-Left group. The *Daily Worker* acknowledged that because of Browder's policy the party had "no organization in auto plants in certain districts" and failed to deliver the votes of such traditional left-wing locals as White Motor and Plymouth Local 51. The Addes-Left group made certain tactical errors. Most importantly, they failed to challenge the delegates from Willow Run Local 50, a paper local that the convention eventually abolished, which delivered 132 votes to Reuther's column. Consequently, even apart from Reuther's assets, any one of these liabilities of the Addes-Left forces might have provided Reuther's slim margin of victory.[8]

Reuther's victory in 1946 resulted from a complex interweaving of Reuther's personal, organizational, and tactical assets and the Addes-Left's programmatic, organizational, and tactical weaknesses. Though Reuther's anti-Communism played a part in his campaign for office and contributed to his ACTU and Trotskyist support as well as to his favorable press image, it was not a wave of anti-Communism among auto workers that swept Reuther into office. However, if anti-Communism played only a minor role in propelling Reuther to the UAW presidency, it was destined to play the major role in Reuther's consolidation of power and in the erosion of Communist-left-wing influence in the auto workers union. In his first press conference after assuming office, Reuther announced that he intended to unite 90 percent of the union against the 10 percent with "outside loyalties," by which, he said, he meant the Communists. The new president established the basis for a fight that would absorb the union until the next convention eighteen months away.[9]

Between the March 1946 convention and the November 1947 convention, the factional conflict between Reuther, who controlled the presidency and the Addes-Thomas-Communist group, which controlled a majority of the Executive Board, dominated the life of the union. Clancy Sigal, a UAW staff member during this period, noted that "factional disputes took precedence over all other issues." This factionalism "was conducted like a war, the terms of which were often squalid." In a certain sense the conflict simply occurred over the question of power and the spoils of office, in which differences of personality, ideology, and trade union policies played only a subordinate role. Though Reuther, Addes, and Thomas were more opportunists than ideologists, the presence of ACTU, Socialists and ex-Socialists in the Reuther group and the presence of Communists in the Addes-Thomas group gave both factions a definite political coloration. Moreover, some real questions of orientation and policy divided the factions. They differed on the desirability of linking wages with productivity, the acceptability of Communists in the union, the importance of racial discrimination, the propriety of Truman's foreign policy, and the necessity of complying with the Taft-Hartley Act. As Sigal noted, these differences really boiled down to the questions of varying attitudes toward the Soviet Union and the durability of capitalism, and "most often, this took the form of forcing a stance vis-à-vis the American Communist Party, whose existence counted for far less than its symbolic value."[10]

The Cold War and its accompanying anti-Communist hysteria acted as the unseen hand shaping the factional conflict in the UAW and undermining Communist and left-wing influence in the union. Though anti-Communism had been a persistent feature of UAW politics since the days of Homer Martin and the advent of the ACTU, the Cold War, and anti-Communist hysteria that developed rapidly in 1946–47 gave Reuther's anti-Communism a potency unknown in earlier years. Beginning with Winston Churchill's "iron curtain" speech delivered two weeks before the UAW's 1946 convention, President Truman enunciated the major features of his anti-Soviet and anti-Communist foreign policy during the next eighteen months. This included the Truman Doctrine, the Marshall Plan and George Kennan's "containment theory." In April 1947, Bernard Baruch coined the term that would become synonymous with U. S. foreign relations, when he declared: "Let us not be deceived—today we are in the midst of a cold war." Truman's foreign policies gave a great impetus to domestic anti-

Communism by their implication that the United States was locked in an international struggle with a perfidious, expansionist, and totalitarian Communist power and that consequently American Communists were agents of a hostile foreign power and, hence, actual or potential Fifth Columnists, spies, and saboteurs. Between 1945 and 1948 several small incidents, sensationalized by the press, fed these fears. Early in 1945 government agents discovered stolen State Department documents in the office of the magazine *Amerasia*. In 1946 the Canadian government announced the discovery of a Soviet spy network. In 1947 and 1948 Elizabeth Bentley and Whittaker Chambers, former Communists, told a federal grand jury and a Congressional committee that Soviet espionage rings operated within the U. S. government. Domestic anti-Communism also gained an impetus from a postwar growth of Republican and business reaction that blamed New Deal liberals, statists, and Communists for wartime economic controls, favorable labor legislation, and the 1946 strike wave.[11]

The anti-Communist hysteria in 1946–47 was fed by the actions of the Truman administration and Congress. In March 1947, Truman issued an executive order establishing loyalty oaths for government employees and the Attorney General's list of so-called subversive organizations. The same month, Secretary of Labor Lewis B. Schwellenbach advocated outlawing the Communist party. The Eightieth Congress initiated 22 Communist investigations, including the House Committee on Un-American Activities' (HUAC) investigations of Gerhard Eisler and the Hollywood Ten. The anti-Communist hysteria was also fed by the actions of the Republican party and leading business groups. Republican National Committee chairman, B. Carroll Reece, billed the 1946 election a choice between "Communism and Republicanism," and the November balloting sent Joseph McCarthy, Richard Nixon, and other extreme anti-Communists to Washington and gave the Republican party control of both houses of Congress for the first time since 1928. In 1946 the Chamber of Commerce published 400,000 copies of a 40-page pamphlet entitled, *Communist Infiltration in the United States*. Two more pamphlets followed the next year—*Communists Within the Government* and *Communists Within the Labor Movement*. Francis Cardinal Spellman and Bishop Fulton Sheen became militant spokesmen of Catholic anti-Communism. *Life, Look, Colliers, Saturday Evening Post,* and daily newspapers headed by the Hearst press provided a steady diet of anti-Communist articles and exposés in 1946–47. the *Readers' Guide to Periodical Literature,* which listed only 17 articles under Communism and the Communist party in the United States for 1945, listed 114 articles for 1946–47. The Cold War and anti-Communist hysteria provided the essential backdrop for the UAW conflicts in 1946–47, for, as Frank Marquart noted, "The Reuther forces could never have achieved their solid control over the UAW without the handy weapon of Cold War anti-communism."[12]

No reliable information exists on the size and nature of Communist party membership in the automobile industry in the 1946–47 period. Saul Wellman, who served as secretary of the party's Auto Commission in 1946, later estimated that in 1946–47 3,000 auto workers belonged to the CP and that 1,500 of these resided in Michigan. Though these figures may have exaggerated the actual membership by as much as a third, they provide an approximate gauge to the number of party members and close supporters. They also indicate that the party reached as great a strength in auto in the immediate postwar period as at any time in its history. In lieu of more reliable sources, the testimony of government agents and ex-Communists before Congressional committees provide at least the rough contours of the Party organization among Michigan auto workers. According to this testimony, when the party reorganized its shop branches in 1945, two Detroit auto sections came into existence—the East Side Council and the West Side Council. The East Side Council contained 17 or 18 shop branches, including Bohn Aluminum, UAW Local 205, UAW Local 155, Plymouth Motors, Packard Motors, Briggs Body, and Dodge. The West Side Council included the large party branch at Ford, plus branches at Cadillac, Timken, Ternstedt, Kelsey-Hayes, DeSoto, and other small shops. The party also had shop branches in the outlying cities of Flint, Pontiac, Saginaw, Bay City, and Midland that were organized into the Saginaw Valley section of the party. In Flint the party had branches in Fisher Body, AC Sparkplug, Chevrolet, and Buick. Most of the shop branches in Detroit and the outlying cities embraced only a handful of people; the Flint AC-Fisher branch, for example, had seven or eight members and the Detroit Cadillac branch had eleven. By far the largest shop branch existed at Ford. It contained about 450 members organized into groups in about nine of the seventeen major Ford departments.[13]

In spite of their modest numbers, Communists enjoyed a great deal of respect, influence, and an even greater degree of toleration in local unions and on the international staff. Some functioned in their shops and locals more or less as open Communists. These included: Chris Alston, a Packard worker and chairman of the East Side Council; Paul Brooks, a Murray worker and secretary of the East Side Council; Fred Williams of Bohn Aluminum, John Anderson, Nat Ganley, and John Nowak of Local 155; James Walter of Local 205; and Merrill Work of Local 835. Many more or less open Communists belonged to Ford Local 600, including William McKie, a trustee; John Gallo, a guide; Ed Lock in the motor plant; Dave Moore in the axle plant; Paul Boatin in the motor plant; and Nelson Davis in the foundry. These workers and many others linked to the CP held important positions in their locals, and by forming Left-Center coalitions like the Progressive caucus in Local 600, often became part of the dominant factions in local unions. Though international staff members had to act more circumspectly about political matters than workers in the shop, Communist and close Communist allies, many of whom had come into the union during the war, permeated the international staff in 1946–47. Prominent among this group were Maurice Sugar, James Wishart, William Levitt, Allen Sayler, Irving Richter, and David Erdman. One member of this group later wrote:

> To be asked to join the party in those days in Detroit was commonplace. Communists were everywhere, down in the shops, up at staff, on the sidelines. It was an open secret that the [Thomas] forces conferred with party liason men. Wherein derived the power of the party? The answers to this question, contrary to the mysterioso music played by the popular press, were fairly simple. The Communists had a philosophy based squarely on what they hoped were the interests of the workers; they were tough (but by no means *that* tough); they were disciplined (and *that* disciplined); they had proved their loyalty to the union many times over . . . they were articulate, and selfless and *ready*; above all, they were needed.[14]

Between the 1946 and 1947 conventions, Communists and the issue of Communism figured prominently in four major conflicts that engulfed the union. These conflicts consisted of: 1. the question of the politics of staff and local officers, 2. the Allis-Chalmers strike, 3. a proposed merger of the UAW with the Farm Equipment Workers Union (FE), and 4. the question of compliance with the Taft-Hartley Act. Each of these conflicts pitted the Reuther forces against those of the Addes-Thomas-Communists and contributed to Reuther's consolidation of power. Over each conflict loomed the ever-lengthening shadow of Cold War anti-Communism.

Reuther raised the question of the political affiliations of international staff members immediately after his election in March 1946. Following his post-election announcement that he intended to unite 90 percent of the union against the 10 percent "with outside loyalties," Reuther told a meeting of the Executive Board in April that he intended to enforce Article 10, Section 8 of the UAW Constitution that banned from all elective and appointive positions anyone who was "a member of or subservient to any political organization, such as the Communist, Fascist or Nazi Organization which owes its allegiance to any government other than the United States or Canada." Addes and Thomas countered with a program, subsequently approved by the Executive Board, that called on the union to avoid redbaiting and to grant equal rights to all members irrespective of their political affiliations. Lacking a majority on the Executive Board, Reuther was unable to effect the purge he desired. Still, by clever maneuvering, Reuther managed to eliminate a couple of the leftists on the staff, to transfer others, and to put all of them on the defensive. By giving generous assignments to Leonard and other vacillating opponents, Reuther got the board to approve the appointment of his brother, Victor, as head of the Education department in place of the leftist William Levitt, who was transferred to veteran affairs. Reuther transferred Allen Sayler and Noble Combs out of the Education Department and fired David Erdman, editor of *Ammunition*. Reuther also temporally withheld the reappointment of Al Glenn, a member of Joseph Mattson's regional staff, and Irving Richter, the union's Washington legislative representative, because the two men allegedly had Communist sympathies.[15]

The Richter case had particular importance for what it revealed about Reuther's brand of liberal, anti-Communism. Since 1943, after leaving a position as a Labor Department economist, Richter had served as the union's legislative representative in Washington and as a regular columnist on legislative affairs for *Ammunition, Flint Weekly Review, Ford Facts,* and other local papers. Richter later described his political orientation as similar to that of Levitt, Sayler, and "many other UAW"staff who "cooperated with the CP and other leftist parties and leftist individuals." Reuther first raised the matter of Richter's politics before the Executive Board in June 1946, when the new president refused to approve Richard Leonard's reappointment of Richter to Leonard's staff on the Political Action Committee. Reuther charged that in 1945 Richter had supported the Communist-backed May-Bailey national service bill, which the UAW and CIO had opposed. When Leonard countered that Richter had "led an effective legislative fight against the bill and may be given substantial credit for its defeat," Reuther retreated and agreed to approve Richter's appointment until he had ascertained the facts.[16]

Between Reuther's introduction of the Richter case in June 1946 and its reappearance before the Executive Board in March 1947, the anti-Communist storm in the labor movement and in the nation gathered considerable force. As anti-Communism became the reigning orthodoxy, debates between conservatives and liberals, Republicans and Democrats, increasingly occurred within the boundaries of the orthodoxy. The debates between conservatives and liberals assumed the character of an unquestioning acceptance of the irrational premises of anti-Communism and of unremitting competition over the sincerity and effectiveness of those opposing Communism. By serving to legitimate the premises, this debate actually increased the national fears over heterodoxy of any kind. Until 1947 conservatives, led by the Chamber of Commerce and the House Un-American Activities Committee, dominated the anti-Communist field, but with the formation of the Americans for Democratic Action (ADA) in January 1947, liberal anti-Communism made its appearance. As one of the ADA's organizing committee of 25 along with David Dubinsky, Leon Henderson, Reinhold Niebuhr, and Walter White, Reuther became one of the national leaders of the new, liberal anti-Communism.[17]

At the time of ADA's founding, Reuther had already established himself as one of the most powerful anti-Communists in the CIO. At the CIO's convention in November 1946, Reuther had served on the six man committee that wrote the "resent and reject" resolution directed against Communist "interference" in the CIO. Thereafter, Reuther became the main exponent of ADA's liberal anti-Communism in the labor movement. Reuther first elaborated his views in March 1947 after Kim Sigler, Republican Governor of Michigan, had testified before HUAC that "upwards of 15,000 Communists" had "absolute control of certain unions" in his state and that R. J. Thomas, George Addes, and Richard Leonard were "captives of the Communist Party." In response to Sigler, the UAW leader reiterated his own active opposition to "Communist interference in our unions" and attacked Sigler for launching "a Red hunt whose ultimate victims are intended to be, *not* Communists, but all effective labor leaders and labor unions." Reuther also charged that by smearing "innocent people," Sigler actually "performed a valuable service to the Communists." A year later in a *Colliers* article entitled "How to Beat the Communists," Reuther elaborated on these themes. He attacked the Communists for a variety of alleged sins committed in their "fanatical preoccupation with conquest of organized labor." He also assailed "the stupid and indiscriminate Dies-Rankin-Thomas brand of Red-baiting" for actually aiding the Communists. And he appealed to "decent unionists and honest liberals" to fight the Communists by "making democracy work," by defeating it in "the market place of ideas," and by using "exposure" rather than "repression." In short, Reuther's liberal anti-Communism accepted without question the premise that the Communists represented a relentless, diabolical, and totalitarian force that had to be opposed; it opposed the conservative methods because they aided Communism by being too indiscriminate, and it proposed as effective weapons against Communism the traditional liberal tools of exposure, free debate, and social reform.[18]

The Richter case illustrated how Reuther's liberal anti-Communism worked in practice. At an Executive Board meeting in Louisville in March 1947, Reuther again raised the question of Richter's employment. Reuther made the same charge as before: "I have not charged Richter with being a Communist, in my opinion, I think he is a Communist; I have said I only believe Richter . . . subordinated the interest of his union to the interest of the Communist Party." To support this charge, Reuther, who claimed to have left his documentation in Detroit, could offer only the unsubstantiated allegation that Richter had supported the May-Bailey bill. The union president, however, now added embellishments to his original charge. The *Detroit News*, the *Wage Earner*, and other papers had given prominent coverage to Reuther's earlier charges of Richter's pro-Communism. Subsequently, conservative Congressmen Louis C. Rabaut and George Dondero used these articles to attack Richter and the UAW. On the basis of such attacks, Reuther then argued for Richter's removal on the grounds that the presence of someone on the staff closely associated with the CP undermined the "effectiveness of our Washington work" and made the union "vulnerable" in the face of "growing witch-hunts." Here were witch-hunting techniques to rival anything developed by HUAC. Reuther used guilt by association to lend credence to the unsubstantiated charge of Richter's insubordination and disloyalty on May-Bailey, and he then used the Congressional fury generated by his own original charges to question Richter's effectiveness. Moreover, instead of arguing for the union to close ranks and resist the Congressional red-hunt, Reuther used the existence of a national hysteria over Communism, that he had helped create, to argue for a preemptive witch-hunt in the union.[19]

In spite of his shabby case, Reuther nearly succeeded in having Richter removed. By 1947, Dick Leonard, Richter's superior and a reluctant and vacillating member of the anti-Reuther caucus, was willing to accede to Richter's dismissal. During the Louisville board meeting, Leonard called Richter to say: "Walter really seems to have a strong case against you. He says you employed an atomic spy's wife [Edith Marzani] and that Congress won't work with you because of the political reputation you've gotten." Only after Richter told Leonard that Donald Montgomery, a Reuther man, had originally hired Marzani and convinced Leonard that Reuther was really directing this attack against the entire Addes-Thomas caucus, did Leonard agree to allow Richter to meet with the entire left-wing caucus of the board. The Left caucus then agreed to sponsor Richter's appearance before the board in his own defense. Despite his belief in "the free market place of ideas," Reuther opposed Richter's appearance before the Executive Board. The Left majority on the board, however, overruled the president. In his presentation, Richter denied membership in the CP, denied having supported May-Bailey, and submitted numerous letters and telegrams from Senators, Congressmen, and unionists testifying to his opposition to the bill and to his general effectiveness as a legislative representative. Confronted with hard evidence and a hostile majority on the board, Reuther and his supporters again retreated. The board unanimously averred that "no cause for action" existed in the Richter case; Richter remained at his post until Reuther won the majority of the Executive Board in the fall of 1947 and then fired Richter as part of his general purge of leftists.[20]

Undaunted by his loss on the Richter case, Reuther continued to raise the issue of Communism in the union because it kept his factional opponents on the defensive and provided an easy avenue to favorable publicity and public support. In the spring of 1946, Reuther had originally raised the matter of Section 8, Article 10 of the UAW Constitution banning Communists from elective or appointive office. With the CIO's passage of the Reuther coauthored "resent and reject" resolution and other developments creating a favorable anti-Communist climate, Reuther again raised the matter. In April 1947, Reuther asked the Executive Board to approve three interpretations of Section 8: (1) that Section 8 applied to members of the Communist party, (2) that where a union member had admitted his membership in the party or where no question of fact existed, "such member shall automatically [i.e. without a trial] be disqualified from holding any elective or appointive office," and (3) where a question of fact pertaining to party membership existed, the matter should be handled through a trial procedure as provided by the Constitution. Reuther's initiative revealed that, in spite of his well-publicized belief in defeating the Communists by "making democracy work," this liberal anti-Communist was willing to enforce political criteria on office-holding and to deprive alleged Communists of a trial. The opposition's response to Reuther's initiative revealed how far the anti-Communist orthodoxy had spread since April 1946. Even though in April 1946 Addes and Thomas had supported the right to hold office regardless of political affiliation, a year later they joined in the unanimous approval of Reuther's first interpretation, including members of the American CP in the Constitutional ban. Moreover, though Addes, Thomas, and other leftists on the board managed to defeat Reuther's second and third interpretation by a vote of fourteen to eight, Addes then felt compelled to offer his own interpretation that called for a trial for any office holder accused of being a Communist. As approved, the Addes interpretation posed little threat to alleged Communist officers since the local that conducted any trial would also have elected the officers being tried. Yet, the whole debate forced the Left into a defensive position.[21]

Stymied on the Executive Board by the Left majority, Reuther nevertheless managed to score certain triumphs at the local level. Relying on the pervasive anti-Communist atmosphere and the slogan "Let's clean up Schiller Hall," Reuther and ACTU forces made a determined effort to unseat the Anderson-Ganley administration of Local 155. In the local election in February 1947, Anderson retained his post as president, but a Reutherite, Ernest Marion, defeated Ganley for the post of business agent. Ganley, the most well-known Communist in the UAW, declared that his defeat was accomplished by the "anti-labor forces outside of the labor movement headed by the reactionary Republican Governor Sigler," who just before the election had announced that his drive against Communists would "help the union membership to clean its own house." In the spring vote at Local 600, the Reuther and ACTU forces conducted a redbaiting campaign that, according to one observer, reached "a height never before seen" in a UAW election. *Life, Time, Colliers, Look,* and other national magazines contributed to this campaign. During the campaign, for instance, *Life* carried a story that publicized Secretary of Labor Schwellenbach's recent urging that unions should bar Communists from office. The story featured a three-quarter page picture of a supporter of Mike Magee, the Reutherite candidate for president, campaigning outside the Ford gates dressed as Stalin and surrounded with signs reading "I'm for Tommy and the Commies/Vote for Magee" and "The Strings that Control Local 600 Lead to Moscow/Cut us Free/Vote for Magee." While the Reutherites won several posts at Local 600, Tommy Thompson, the Communist-backed centrist, defeated Magee, and two well-known Communists, William McKie and Johnny Gallo, were elected trustee and guide. More important for the fortunes of Reuther and the Left than these local elections was a strike then in progress at the Allis-Chalmers Company.[22]

All of the pressures against labor and the Left generated by the Cold War and domestic reaction in 1946–47 became dramatically telescoped on the UAW strike against Allis-Chalmers, the most important postwar labor conflict. The strike pitted Local 248, one of the most militant and left-wing UAW locals, against Allis-Chalmers, one of the most conservative and hardbitten foes of labor, in a conflict lasting eleven months. The significance of the strike far transcended the village of West Allis. The uncompromising bargaining stance of the company, whose president Walter

Geist was honored by a cover story in *Business Week* during the walkout, became a symbol of corporate resistance to the 1946 strike wave. The strike also became a focus of business and conservative demands for restrictive labor legislation and for the elimination of Communist influences in the labor movement. Relatedly, Local 248 and its left-wing leaders became the target of the swelling national hysteria over Communism. Inevitably, the strike also became embroiled in the factional conflict within the UAW, and Reuther and his allies undercut the local's leadership and undermined the strike. The glue uniting all of these forces and assuring the strike's defeat was anti-Communism. *Daily Worker* reporter, William Allan, accurately reported that the Allis-Chalmers strikers became the object of "the most vicious nationwide red-baiting campaign this country has ever seen." After 327 days, the walkout ended in the utter defeat of the workers and in the nearly total collapse of the union. The defeat served as the turning point in the fight between Reuther and the Thomas-Addes-Communist group.[23]

Local 248 traced its origins back to 1933, when Harold Christoffel, a young Socialist, had started an AFL federal labor union in the plant. With the help of Communists and other militant workers, Christoffel solidly organized the plant, took the union into the CIO in 1936, won a contract in 1937, and achieved sole collective bargaining rights in 1938. With its well-organized flying squadron, the union successfully resisted attempts by Homer Martin to place the local under the right-wing administratorship of George Kiebler in 1938 and also successfully resisted repeated attempts by the Allis-Chalmers management to undercut the union's authority. Under Christoffel's leadership, the local established a strong educational program and an aggressive committeeman system. The local and its officers consistently supported Communist political positions, Communist-related united front organizations, and Communist rallies, demonstrations, and petitions. Using the strong base of Local 248 which was the strongest CIO local in Wisconsin, Christoffel, Emil Costello, and their Communist supporters also achieved control of the Milwaukee County Industrial Union Council and the Wisconsin Industrial Union Council. In 1939, the union conducted a 23 day strike over wages and union security, and in 1941 the union conducted a controversial 76 day strike over wages, union security, and a grievance system. At the time of the 1946 strike, Robert Buse was president of Local 248, replacing Christoffel, who had been drafted in 1941. Christoffel returned to Milwaukee in October 1946 and joined the bargaining team.[24]

Allis-Chalmers consisted of eight different plants spread around the country. With 11,500 production workers and about 5,000 office and supervisory personnel, the West Allis plant represented the largest Allis-Chalmers unit. Allis-Chalmers was the third largest manufacturer of agricultural implements and the country's eighty-seventh largest manufacturing enterprise. Besides farm equipment, the company also manufactured machinery for warships, powder and power plants, mining, flour and saw mills, cement making, and building. During the war Allis-Chalmers had reaped windfall profits, earning over $36 million in after-taxes profits and paying out over $14 million in dividends in the period 1941–45. The company had a long history of anti-union activity that dated back to its defeat of an iron molders strike in 1905 and a machinists strike in 1916. During the New Deal period, the company had tried to thwart unionism by setting up a company union in 1933—the Allis-Chalmers Works Council—and by subscribing to the anti-union services of the Metal Trades Association and the Pinkerton Detective Agency. The Allis-Chalmers management represented the extreme right-wing of the political spectrum. During the 1941 strike, when the company raised the cry that the union was sabotaging defense work, Max Babb, Allis-Chalmers president, served as chairman of the Milwaukee Chapter of the America First Committee, and Babb's successor as Allis-Chalmers president, Walter Geist, served as head of the Wisconsin America First Committee. This Committee opposed American involvement in the war, and one of its national leaders, Charles Lindberg, expressed openly anti-Semitic and pro-Nazi sympathies. Harold Story, vice-president of Allis-Chalmers and head of the company's negotiating team during the 1946 strike, was an anti-Communist of the Martin Dies variety. Both the company's windfall profits during the war and the carry-back provisions of the Revenue Act, which guaranteed government rebates for losses sustained during 1946, placed Allis-Chalmers in a strong position to resist a postwar strike.[25]

The Allis-Chalmers strike began on April 30, 1946. From the start, no CIO or UAW official questioned the walkout's legitimacy.

Local 248 merely followed the pattern of other CIO unions in seeking to catch up with wartime inflation and to retain certain wartime gains. Allis-Chalmers, however, resisted these demands more stubbornly than had GM, Ford, or Chrysler earlier in the year. The local's contract with Allis-Chalmers had expired on April 15, 1944; two years of futile negotiations had followed. In September 1945, the War Labor Board (WLB) had issued an order with respect to vacation pay with which Allis-Chalmers had only partially complied. In December 1945, shortly after losing its wartime powers, the WLB issued a final report on Allis-Chalmers with recommendations on wages and conditions which the union adopted as its bargaining position, but which the company rejected. Three issues assumed primary importance: (1) maintenance of membership, (2) grievance procedure, and (3) wages. The union demanded retention of maintenance of membership, which the WLB had granted in 1943, and also sought a wage increase of eighteen and a half cents, corresponding to the postwar pattern. Allis-Chalmers refused these demands and offered a wage increase of thirteen and a half cents. The company insisted on revisions in the grievance procedure that would have restricted the authority of committeemen and would have made the first step consist of a meeting between a grievant and a foreman. In March, Allis-Chalmers had refused a request of Secretary of Labor Lewis B. Schwellenbach to meet with union representatives in Washington. Before and during the walkout, Local 248's leaders offered to submit differences to arbitration or to Presidential fact finding; the company rejected both ideas. In April, government conciliators failed to produce an agreement. Consequently, on April 29 in a secret ballot supervised by UAW international representatives, Local 248 voted 8,091 to 251 in favor of a strike, and the next day mass picketing began.[26]

In October of 1946, the sixth month of the strike, Allis-Chalmers launched a back-to-work movement coupled with a massive redbaiting attack on the leadership of Local 248. In this drive Allis-Chalmers found eager allies in the Milwaukee *Journal* and Milwaukee *Sentinel*. On September 22, 23, 24, and October 6, 1946, the *Journal* ran a series of four articles charging that Buse, Christoffel, and Joseph Dombek, vice-president of Local 248, were Communists. Beginning September 23 and proceeding for 59 consecutive days, the Milwaukee *Sentinel*, a Hearst paper, ran a

sensational series of articles by "John Sentinel." The John
Sentinel articles claimed that Communists dominated Local 248
and that the following were either Communists or consistent
party-liners: Christoffel; Buse; Dombek; Linus Lindberg, financial
secretary; Fred McStroul, recording secretary; and eight members
of Local 248's bargaining team. Four years later, Hugh Swofford,
the labor editor of the *Sentinel* at the time of the strike, admitted
that *Sentinel* publisher, Frank L. Taylor, and *Sentinel* managing
editor, James J. Packman, had arranged for this series of articles at
a meeting with Lee Baker, a public relations officer of the Allis-
Chalmers Co. Ellis Jensen, a research consultant for Allis-
Chalmers, had secretly written the articles. Naturally, the articles
dovetailed with the position of Allis-Chalmers that the strike involved no legitimate trade union issues and that the Communist
leaders of the local were unnecessarily prolonging the walkout for
purely disruptive, political ends. On October 11, 1946 the company sent a letter to all its employees with photostats of Communist party nominating petitions for the governor of Wisconsin in
1946 containing the signatures of many of the local's officers,
committeemen, and stewards. The national press and news magazines picked up the anti-Communist theme from Allis-Chalmers
and the Milwaukee press. On November 11, *Newsweek* described
the CP nominating petition. The story claimed that the CP had
"stranglehold over the CIO in all Wisconsin," that the Communists
had prolonged the strike at the West Allis plant while other Allis-
Chalmers locals in Wisconsin, Illinois, Indiana, Ohio, and Pennsylvania had returned to work, and that the Communists "had
strung out . . . a strike which has hamstrung American reconversion at a time when Soviet-American relations are strained." On
November 26, the *New York Times* reported on the back-to-work
movement and quoted an anonymous spokesman, who delcared:
"We have returned to work after being taken to the cleaners by a
bunch of Communist revolutionists."[27]

The union made valiant efforts to resist the redbaiting and
back-to-work movement. The union argued that the company was
attempting to hide the real strike issues behind a smokescreen of
anti-Communism. "If there are as many 'reds' among Allis-
Chalmers workers as corporation publicity would have you believe," a union spokesman declared over a local radio station, "I
challenge the Allis-Chalmers Corporation to reveal just what con-

ditions are in their plant that manufactures so many 'reds.'" Beginning in October the union attempted to resist the back-to-work movement by setting up mass picket lines at plant gates. Augmented by supporters from other CIO unions in Wisconsin and from UAW locals as far away as Local 600 in Detroit, the picket lines at times numbered as many as 15,000. On October 28–31, November 25, and December 4 and 9, violent clashes occurred between the strikers, scabs, and police. Responding to a company complaint of illegal picketing in December, the Wisconsin Employment Relations Board (WERB) limited the number of pickets to two at each gate. By January, the continuous assaults on the local's leadership and the back-to-work movement resulted in the return to work of about 4,000 employees. The same month a new threat to the strike emerged. Led by Walter Peterson, a group of workers who had returned to work announced the formation of a rival union, the Independent Workers of Allis-Chalmers. The Independent petitioned the WERB for a representation election. In the balloting at the end of the month, Local 248 won a bare plurality. Local 248 obtained 4,182 votes, the Independent 4,010, and no union 117, with 50 challenged ballots. Since Local 248 failed to win a majority, the WERB moved to set up a runoff election.[28]

Meanwhile, to the strike's detriment, Local 248 became embroiled in the political tug-of-war going on in the International. While the Executive Board gave unstinting support and financial aid to Local 248, Reuther and his supporters subtly undercut the local leadership. The *Wage Earner* lent credence to the company's anti-Communist attack by referring to the "avowed Communist leadership" of the local and by repeatedly calling Buse a member of the auto commission of the Communist party. The *Wage Earner* also condoned the strikebreakers who had formed the Independent union by describing them as "former UAW members who have soured on the union's leaders." Moreover, for over seven months a group of seven right-wing UAW locals in Wisconsin headed by Walter Cappel, a Reuther man, refused to support the strike and attacked the leadership of Local 248. Cappel reversed himself only after, R. J. Thomas, whom the International had placed in charge of the strike in November, complained to the International of Cappel's "sabotaging," and after Reuther personally urged Cappel to lend full support to the Allis-Chalmers workers. What Reuther gave with one hand, however, he took back with the other. At the December Executive Board meeting, Reuther said that because of the "attack being made by the Corporation respecting the political character of the leadership," the officers of 248 should resign. The board rejected this idea. Nevertheless, at the very time the union faced the election challenge from the independent, reports of Reuther's suggestion and of the same suggestion from Herman Steffes, a right-winger who had recently defeated Buse for the presidency of the Wisconsin CIO, appeared in Milwaukee papers. Also in January 1947, Reuther further undercut the local leadership by meeting secretly with representatives of the company in a futile attempt to arrange a strike settlement. Thomas charged that Reuther had been duped by the company's "divide-and-conquer" strategy and that the secret negotiations had "only served to confuse the workers and provide the company propaganda machinery with the opportunity of misleading the workers."[29]

The final blow against Local 248's strike landed at the end of February and early March when both HUAC and the House Committee on Education and Labor conducted hearings on the Allis-Chalmers situation. Congressman J. Parnell Thomas opened the HUAC hearings on February 27, with the declaration that the committee was taking "the first step" in its effort "to spotlight the sorry spectacle of having outright Communists controlling and dominating some of the most vital unions in American labor." HUAC heard testimony from Walter Peterson, Leon Venne, and Floyd D. Lucia, three leaders of the independent union, who had returned to work. Though Lucia said that "not over 25 Communists and not over 25 fellow travelers" existed in the union, he agreed with Congressman Martin Dies and Committee investigator Robert Stripling that the union was "Communist-dominated" and the strike was "Communist-inspired." Lucia testified: "I believe that it was their [the Communists'] intention to retard reconversion and that the Allis-Chalmers plant was a strategic place to accomplish that." Indicative of both the character of these witnesses and the temper of the hearings was Venne's unchallenged statement: "If Local 248 is broken the laboring man at Allis-Chalmers can get a gun and go out and get the Communists who are the cause of breaking the union at Allis-Chalmers."[30]

In February and March 1947, the House Committee on Education and Labor, under the chairmanship of Congressman Fred A. Hartley of New Jersey, made an investigation of the Allis-Chalmers strike the centerpiece of its hearings on revisions of the National Labor Relations Act. These hearings led to the passage of the Taft-Hartley Act in June 1947. As with HUAC, the labor committee hearings focused almost exclusively on the alleged Communist leadership of Local 248. On February 24, five officers of the Allis-Chalmers Company led by Harold Story testified before the committee and presented committee members with an elaborate brief bound in a leatherette cover with gold imprint. The brief contained multi-colored photostats and photographs and took up over 70 pages of the committee record. The officers' brief and testimony claimed that the Communists hoped to use the labor movement "to overthrow American democracy," that Communists and party-liners dominated Local 248, that Local 248 "has not operated as a bona fide labor union" but as an "adjunct of the party," that the local had avoided serious collective bargaining and had called and prolonged the strike "to interfere with reconversion," that the union had relied on illegal mass picketing and violence to make the strike effective, and that the Communist leadership of the local had relied on undemocratic measures and physical intimidation to preserve its control. In the entire testimony and brief, the officers barely mentioned the actual contract issues — wages, grievance procedure, and maintenance of membership.[31]

Two days later, on March 1, 1947, the committee heard testimony from union representatives. In spite of the importance of this hearing, Reuther failed to request an appearance to defend the local. Thomas, however, did appear. Thomas stated: "The whole purpose of my desire to testify before this committee . . . is to try to explain that the issue which has caused the strike at Allis-Chalmers is not communism—as Mr. Story would have you believe—but the failure of the company to sit down and bargain collectively. . . . It is a straight labor-management dispute." Thomas said that communism was a "phony issue," that the issues of wages and a grievance procedure had nothing to do with communism, that these were "the same demands which every union in the CIO" made of industry. As proof of the sincerity of the union's desire to settle rather than prolong the strike, Thomas said that he had offered to submit the issues to arbitration and that this was the "first time" in his experience in the labor movement that he had offered arbitration over wages. Thomas charged that in his entire experience he had "never met a man who is worse at labor relations than Mr. Story." Thomas also denied that the picketers at Allis-Chalmers had engaged in violence and described instances where police had pulled pickets into the plant and beat them up.[32]

On March 1 and again on March 3, the committee heard the testimony of Buse and Christoffel. Both men tried to explain the real issues behind the strike and the union's repeated offers to submit the unresolved questions to arbitration or fact finding. The committee, however, showed no interest in the strike issues. Instead, using the Allis-Chalmers brief and recently published statements by ex-Communist Louis Budenz, the committee members subjected the two unionists to hours of grilling about Communist influence in Local 248. Buse and Christoffel denied that they were Communists, denied substantial Communist influence in the local, and charged the company with using the Communist issue as a "smokescreen" to hide the real issues of the dispute. Christoffel denied knowing Louis Budenz and Wisconsin Communists and called Budenz's claim that the Communist party had ordered the Allis-Chalmers strike of 1941 "a tissue of lies." Ten days later, Budenz testified. One-time editor of the *Daily Worker,* who had resigned from the CP in 1945, Budenz became a professional informer in the post-war period. Between 1946 and 1957, he testified before Congressional investigations 33 times. Budenz claimed that he knew Christoffel "quite well," that both Buse and Christoffel were members of the Communist party, and that the CP had ordered the 1941 strike. Budenz's contradiction of Christoffel's testimony served as the basis for a subsequent perjury indictment against Christoffel.[33]

Amidst such conflicting testimony where did the truth lie? Whether Buse, Christoffel, and others actually were members of the Communist party was as unknowable as it was irrelevant. Clearly, the weight of evidence showed that a substantial sympathy and an even greater toleration existed for the Communist party and Communist policies in Local 248. Open Communists existed in the plant. The local had given financial and other support to Communist-related groups. Communists had spoken at local meetings and had taught courses for local members. The local had followed the party line on such issues as the Hitler-Stalin pact, and officers of the union had attended and spoken at

CP meetings and had signed Communist petitions. Equally clear, however, the sympathy for Communists and Communist ideas reflected a general left-wing orientation of the membership and not just the machinations of a few leaders. The company's brief showed that 40 percent of the stewards, and many members of the union's committees, and several of the union's attorneys and officers had signed the petition of the Communist candidate for governor of Wisconsin. The pervasiveness of left-wing sympathies in the local resulted from many causes: the company's militant anti-unionism, the socialist background of Milwaukee, and the socialist background of those who built the union and worked in the plant. Christoffel later said: "Remember Milwaukee was a socialist town. . . . West Allis had a lot of Croatians, and the Croatians had a very militant background. There was much leftwing activity . . . and this philosophy permeated the entire organization." By attempting in their testimony to minimize the left-wing influence of themselves and their union, Buse and Christoffel doubtlessly had been somewhat less than candid.[34]

The real question was not whether Communist influence existed in Local 248, but whether it had the nefarious effect imputed by the committee and the company. The Communist-orientation of Local 248 did have an effect on the operation of the local, but not the effect alleged by Allis-Chalmers. For instance, the political complexion of the local contributed to its strong educational and grievance systems. The local put a strong emphasis on political education, and at one time the educational director was the local's only full-time officer. "In the long run," Christoffel later said, "we knew we needed . . . some political education, education toward socialism in the broad sense." The union also possessed an extremely strong steward system and had a policy of encouraging workers to pursue their gripes however trivial. Christoffel later said: "We did have many, many grievances compared to other unions. . . . I think it was the heart of the union." The left-wing complexion of the union also contributed to its willingness to use militant tactics—flying squadrons and mass picketing—in strike situations. But did Communist influence in the local also mean that the Communists ordered and prolonged the strike for political reasons, or that the leadership represented a barrier to a settlement? This implied a logical leap that neither facts nor logic bridged. No evidence existed that the CP desired to disrupt reconversion. Nor did any reason exist to doubt Buse's assertion that "there never has been any interference with our union by the Communist Party." Nor did any rejoinder exist to the argument of Thomas, Buse, and Christoffel that the union's offer to arbitrate the differences refuted the idea of desiring to prolong the strike. Moroever, 25 miles from West Allis in Racine, a UAW local under Reutherite leadership was waging a 14 month old strike against the J. I. Case Company, the nation's fourth largest agricultural implement producer. The Case strike involved issues similar to those of Allis-Chalmers and had lasted even longer than that in West Allis. Yet, no one accused the Case local of running a political strike or having officers that were an obstacle to settlement. No reason existed to assume that the two strikes would have developed any differently had the political complexion of the two locals been reversed.[35]

Did Communist influence in the local result in the use of violence on the picket lines? Violence certainly accompanied the strike. Writer Clancy Sigal, who worked for the UAW at the time, later described the strike in his novel, *Going Away:* "It was like a blazing scene from the thirties, goons dragging pickets inside the plant gates and beating them up for 'trespassing,' trucks full of scabs ramming the massed union lines, mounted cops charging full tilt at strikers and being met with a barrage of ball bearings." By trying to force deliveries through picket lines and by encouraging the back-to-work movement, the company certainly bore as much responsibility for the violence as the union. Moreover, though the Communists undoubtedly favored flying squadrons and mass picketing, neither these weapons nor picket line violence had ever been confined to Communist-led unions.[36]

Did Communist influence in the local result, as the company charged, in an undemocratic administration in which the leadership squelched free speech and used parliamentary maneuvers, intimidation and violence to stay in power? A certain rough-and-tumble democracy did prevail in the union. The leadership used the local paper for self-promotion, kept a tight control of union meetings, and showed intolerance for dissidents even to the point of expelling them from the union or having the company fire them. Such intolerance toward opposition, however, characterized many unions regardless of political orientation. Such limitations on democracy reflected less the politics of the leaders than a siege mentality of a union whose existence had been threatened for ten years by a truculent company, by four independent unions, and by three raids of the AFL. The dissidents themselves often lacked a clean record. For instance, during the 1946 strike, the local expelled Leon Venne and Walter Peterson, two leaders of the Independent, after the two men, in violation of all union ethics, had returned to work and had placed an ad in local newspapers decrying the union leadership. Though Venne told HUAC of two instances before 1946 where the local's flying squadron had roughed-up dissidents, such practices were rare. Another leader of the Independent told Congressman Richard Nixon that he knew of no instances of violence against opponents of the leadership. Moreover, Venne admitted that even after he had released a statement to the press attacking the officers of Local 248, the union had invited him to air his grievances at a local meeting. The most telling evidence that Local 248 leaders retained office by popular support rather than by undemocratic maneuvers occurred in elections held during and after the strike. In January, Local 248 won a plurality in the WERB election; early in 1947 the local reelected Buse president, and, in July 1947, Local 248 again won a plurality against the Independent and the UAW-AFL in an NLRB representation election. These electoral endorsements occurred during or immediately after a protracted and unsuccessful strike and an unprecedented attack on the local's leadership by the company, press, Congress, and the right-wing of the International union.[37]

On March 23, three weeks after the House Education and Labor Committee investigation, Local 248 called off the eleven month strike and returned to work without a contract. The end of the strike, however, did not bring an end to Local 248's troubles. After having fired Robert Buse and Joseph Dombek in December 1946 and Christoffel in March 1947, Allis-Chalmers discharged 91 of the strikers. Meanwhile, the House Education and Labor Committee sent a subcommittee to Milwaukee to gather evidence of perjury against Buse and Christoffel. In July, a federal grand jury indicted Christoffel on six counts of perjury for denying before Congress that he was a Communist. In a 1948 trial, and again in a 1950 retrial, Christoffel was convicted on the perjury charge and sentenced to a prison term of two to six years. Meanwhile, with the passage of the Taft-Hartley Act, Local 248 failed to gain NLRB certification because Buse and other local leaders refused to sign the non-Communist affidavits. By November of 1947 Local 248's membership, that once numbered over 8,000 dropped to 184 dues paying members. After Reuther won reelection and complete control of the Executive Board in November, he immediately removed the local's leaders and placed the local under the administratorship of Pat Greathouse. In October 1948 the local, then under Reutherite leadership, tried and expelled Christoffel, Buse, and seven other former leaders on a charge of misusing local funds. Such sustained attacks by the company, the government, and the International finally smashed the popular, left-wing leadership of Local 248 and in the process irreparably crippled what had been the strongest union in Wisconsin. Years later Christoffel reflected: "When we were only fighting the government and the company that wasn't bad you see, as long as the union supported you. But then when . . . Reuther starts moving in, then the workers knew that this was it. There was no chance. Then we were fighting all three."[38]

Throughout the period between the 1946 and 1947 conventions both Reuther and his opponents engaged in ceaseless political intrigue and maneuvers to strengthen their respective positions. Just as Reuther had used staff appointments and the Allis-Chalmers strike to undermine the Left in the union, so the Addes-Thomas-Communist group tried to use a proposed merger of the Farm Equipment Workers Union (FE) with the UAW to outflank Reuther. Headed by Grant Oakes, the FE represented one of the most left-wing of the CIO unions. By 1947, the FE had organized International Harvester, John Deere, and Caterpillar and contained about 43,000 members, a majority of unionized workers in the farm equipment industry. Almost from FE's inception in 1938, it had fought bitter, expensive, and often violent jurisdictional battles with the UAW and had engaged in sporadic and futile merger negotiations. In 1945, the CIO urged the two organizations to merge, and in 1946 Reuther appointed a merger committee. Though strong and legitimate reasons existed for a merger, the Addes-Thomas-Communist group also had factional interests in the move. If the merger occurred before the 1947 convention, the FE could bring at least 430 votes into the Addes-Thomas column. At the June 1947 meeting of the Executive Board, the merger committee, composed of three members in the Addes-Thomas-Communist camp, unveiled a merger proposal. Over objections of the Reuther group, the opposition majority of the board approved the proposal and authorized a membership referendum on the proposal to be conducted by July 15, 1947.[39]

The entire maneuver boomeranged on the Left. Part of the reason for this was that the merger proposal granted so many favorable concessions to the FE—its own division, an elected representative on the Executive Board, the retention of all its staff—that Reuther effectively attacked it for setting up an "autonomous" unit that endangered the industrial structure of the UAW. Moreover, the haste with which the Left pushed for a referendum vote allowed Reuther to charge that the Left was using its "mechanical majority" on the Executive Board to usurp the constitutional prerogatives of the convention. Also, the left-wing character of the FE opened the proposal to redbaiting attacks by Reuther's supporters. In the weeks during which the referendum vote occurred, the *Wage Earner* repeatedly pointed out that FE was "strongly Communist-dominated." According to unionist, John W. Anderson, the debates within locals preceding the election "gave Reuther and his followers and his international representatives an opportunity to do a tremendous red-baiting campaign throughout the union." The referendum defeated the merger proposal by over a two to one majority. Clancy Sigal, who had been involved in the negotiations with FE, later observed: "It was the wrong move. Wrong and fatal. It gave [Reuther] just the issue he needed to push him over the top."[40]

Between the FE vote and the 1947 convention, the main issue before the UAW concerned the question of compliance with the non-Communist affidavit clause of the Taft-Hartley law, which Congress had passed over Truman's veto in June 1947. Congressman Fred Hartley later explained that the reason Congress had included the anti-Communist clause in the act was because the "Communist dominated" Local 248 had conducted strikes "ordered by Moscow" in 1941 and 1946 that had disrupted war production, "seriously hampered our nation's reconversion effort, and conversely aided Russian foreign policy." As proof of the Communist domination of Local 248, Hartley referred to Harold Story's testimony before the Congress and to a Reuther statement that the Allis-Chalmers local was "dominated by political racketeers of Communist stripe." After contributing to the inclusion of the anti-Communist clause in the Act, Reuther used the clause to force his opponents into an awkward and defensive position. At a time when John L. Lewis, Phil Murray, and other labor leaders were denouncing the law and refusing to sign the non-Communist affidavits, Reuther became the first CIO opponent of the law to advocate compliance. At the UAW Executive Board meeting in August, Reuther argued for compliance, "so that we can meet the practical problems of the situation," which was to say, so the union could continue to pursue its cases and elections with the National Labor Relations Board. Thomas and Addes opposed compliance, because it would "weaken the fight" and "reconcile the CIO to the slave law." The entire debate put Addes and Thomas in the awkward position of seeming to put a defense of Communists in the labor movement ahead of the practical welfare of the UAW. So effective was Reuther's maneuver that he actually won the approval of the Executive Board. Eleven members opted for compliance; six abstained, and R.J. Thomas, George Addes, William Stevenson, Percy Llewellyn, and Kenneth Forbes voted against. The Addes-Thomas-Communist group had fractured over what would be the key issue at the upcoming convention. Once again, Reuther's dogged anti-Communist attacks and the spreading anti-Communist orthodoxy had taken its toll on the Left.[41]

In preparation for the November convention, both Reuther and the Left turned out reams of reports, letters, leaflets, and press releases filled with programs, charges, countercharges, insults, and smears. On such central trade union issues as opposition to Taft-Hartley and the need for increased wages, pensions, vacations, and organizing, little differentiated Reuther and Thomas-Addes. Yet, differences did exist. For Reuther the main enemy was Communism and the Soviet Union; for Thomas-Addes it remained the large corporations. Reuther supported the Cold War and the Marshall Plan and eventually opposed participation in the World Federation of Trade Unions (WFTU); Thomas retained a certain cordiality toward the Soviet Union and sympathy for the WFTU. Reuther believed that no Communists should hold union office and that open Communists should be automatically removed from office; Thomas and Addes still argued, however weakly, for no discrimination because of political beliefs and for the use of a trial procedure before removing anyone from office. Reuther favored compliance with Taft-Hartley's non-Communist affidavits; Thomas and Addes opposed compliance. Reuther favored linking wages with productivity; Thomas and Addes opposed it. In the past, Reuther had opposed, and Addes had supported, special minority representation on the Executive Board. Such real policy differences, however, were generally obscured by the slander and red-baiting that characterized the preconvention campaigning.[42]

In a "Report to the Membership," which was distributed to over 900,000 UAW members, Reuther made the issue of Communism central to his entire program. Reuther blamed his opponents for the union's factionalism. He accused them of wasting a half a million dollars trying to organize Thompson Products in Cleveland, and scored them for sponsoring the ill-conceived FE merger. Reuther also attacked his opponents for blocking the enforcement of the Constitutional ban on Communist office-holding. In defense against the charge that he supported speedup, Reuther said that those making the accusation—the Communists and their allies—had supported speedup during the war. In a section of the report, entitled "For Democracy—Against Totalitarianism," the UAW president said: "The American Communist Party is not a political party in the legitimate sense. Communist Party members in America and in our union are governed by the foreign policy needs of the Soviet Union, and not by the needs of our union, our membership or our country." In October, after Local 45's *Eye Opener*, Local 51's *Plymouth Beacon*, Local 600's *Ford Facts*, and Local 155's *Common Sense* had accused the union president of favoring increased production through speedup, Reuther replied with a letter to all union members, in which he referred to the Communist party 24 times in eight pages to make a case that those "who are responsible for the current smear campaign have blown hot and cold with the Communist Party on every basic question." Such attacks led a *New Republic* writer to observe that Reuther "has been happy to ride along with the Communist hysteria sweeping the country."[43]

The Thomas-Addes forces presented their case to the membership in a 24-page pamphlet entitled *The Bosses' Boy* and in a little periodical entitled *FDR*. Sigmund Diamond, Irving Richter, and other left-wing staff members wrote *The Bosses' Boy*, and Carl Haessler edited the first issues of *FDR*, whose acronym insiders jokingly interpreted to mean "F**k Dirty Reuther." While scoring Reuther's desire to link wages and productivity, the low wages in Reuther's GM division, the president's neglect of minority representation, and his constant redbaiting, these publications also made exaggerated claims of Reuther's support of speedup, which the union president easily refuted. Less refutable was the voluminous documentation in *The Bosses' Boy* that the greatest praise for Reuther's anti-Communism came from the most anti-labor forces in the country—the Hearst press, the Chamber of Commerce, the National Association of Manufacturers, Gerald L.K. Smith, and Harold Story. In the process of redbaiting Local 248 into submission, for instance, Story had declared: "There is no question about the Americanism of Mr. Reuther." Yet, so potent had the anti-Communist orthodoxy become, that the editors of *FDR* paid it obeisance even while they attacked Reuther's redbaiting and defended "the democratic rights of all individuals." The editors proclaimed "no sympathy with the Communist Party and its policies" and disingenuously averred that "R.J. Thomas and his associates have no connection or sympathy with the Communist Party or any of its affiliates or its program or methods." Such statements reflected the earlier actions of the Addes-Thomas group in forcing the Communists out of open participation in the caucus, while continuing to accept Communist support. Such disavowals and duplicity provided sure evidence of the efficacy of Reuther's redbaiting.[44]

The 1947 convention witnessed Reuther's complete triumph over Addes-Thomas-Communist forces. A *Newsweek* reporter noted that "the left-wingers sat glum and silent, while Reuther's anti-Communist steamroller clanked over them." Reuther's opening address set the convention's tone. "The answer [to labor's problems]," Reuther declared, "will not be found in any of the so-called magic totalitarian formulas where you trade freedom for bread. The answer will be found in making democracy work." Reuther called upon the convention to reaffirm "in clear and unmistakable language" the policy of the CIO in resenting and rejecting Communist interference. The president also called upon the union to affirm "beyond question" its loyalty to the United States and Canada. In the convention's first test vote, the Reuther forces won approval by a three to one majority of a resolution to set the election of officers to the third, rather than the fifth day. In the only major substantive debate, the Reuther forces again won by a three to one majority the convention's approval of compliance with the Taft-Hartley Act. The "redheaded, apple-cheeked" president then swept the elections for officers. For president, the Addes-Thomas group offered only the token candidacy of John DeVito of Cleveland Local 45. Reuther supporters drowned in boos DeVito's statement that Reuther had done "the best job of Red-baiting and fear psychology that I have ever seen in my life." Reuther obtained 5,593 votes to DeVito's 303, with 1,218 abstentions. Emil Mazey, a member of the Socialist party and a leader of the fight for Taft-Hartley compliance, defeated George Addes, the secretary-treasurer of the union since 1936. John Livingston and Richard Gosser beat R.J. Thomas and Richard Leonard for the vice-presidential posts. Reuther forces won all but four of the twenty-two seats on the Executive Board. The new Reuther leadership represented a combination of such Socialists and social-democrats as Mazey, Leonard Woodcock and Martin Gerber, such ACTU supporters as Joe McCusker and Pat Greathouse, and "old-line union machine politicians," like Gosser.[45]

Outside the UAW, nearly universal approbation greeted Reuther's triumph. Approving of Reuther's plans to rid Communists from the union payroll, Henry Ford, Jr., said: "We are as much opposed to Communists as Walter Reuther." *Newsweek* predicted that under Reuther labor-management relations "probably will be more peaceful." The weekly expressed confidence that the "Socialist coloration" of the new leadership meant little since "the history of all Socialist-run unions, almost without exception, is that while their leaders continue to employ the slogans and verbiage of Socialism they disregard them in their work." *Business Week* observed that the convention gave "the nation's most articulate anti-Communist labor leader unchallenged control of the nation's largest union." It predicted that Reuther would become "Hillmanized"—as a trade unionist he will be like his "more conservative brethren," but as a sloganeer he will be "as radical as ever." In the symphony of praise, only the *New Republic* carried an untoward note. Its editors expressed "worry in the anti-Communist overtones" of Reuther's victory, because the real threat to the country was posed not by Communists but by "native American fascism whooping up anti-Communist emotion, and Reuther did not mention this genuine danger."[46]

The Reuther victory meant not just the defeat of the Addes-Thomas-Communist faction, but its complete disintegration. Some leaders of the Left-Center group left the union voluntarily; others faced dismissal, expulsion, or defeat in local elections; still others reconciled themselves to Reuther's regime and in many cases became fanatical anti-Communists. Following the convention, R.J. Thomas took a job with the CIO. George Addes became a tavern owner. The defeated board members, Joseph Mattson and William Stevenson, made their peace with Reuther and accepted staff positions. Of the four Addes men elected to the board in 1947, Charles Kerrigan and George Burt soon aligned themselves with Reuther, while Richard Reisinger and Paul Miley, Ohio Regional Directors, declined to run for office in 1949 and accepted staff appointments. Richard Leonard returned to his job as a welder at De Soto. For awhile Leonard worked with Tracy Doll, a former Executive Board member from Hudson Local 154 and onetime president of the Wayne County CIO, and Samuel Sage, former president of Briggs Aircraft Local 742 and onetime secretary-treasurer of the Wayne County CIO. They attempted to build an opposition group called the Progressive Unity Caucus. The high point of this small caucus's efforts was its publication of a four page report on racketeering in the UAW that had been authorized by Thomas in 1946. The report conveyed its attitude toward Reuther in a cartoon of a kneeling worker lapping the shoes of a cigar-smoking magnate. The caption read, "So that's what the boy means by licking the boss!" After the 1949 convention, at which Reuther beat the Progressive Unity candidate for president by a twelve to one margin and expelled Doll and Sage from the union, the caucus disappeared. Leonard eventually took a job on the CIO staff and when Reuther succeeded Murray as CIO president, Leonard became his administrative assistant.[47]

Immediately after his sweep of the 1947 convention, Reuther purged all Communists, Communist sympathizers, and other leftists from the international staff. Within two weeks he fired 77 staff members including: Maurice Sugar, the union's legal counsel since 1936; James Wishart, head of the Research Department; Allen Sayler and Sigmund Diamond, members of the Research Department; and Irving Richter, legislative representative. Some of the departing staff went into business for themselves; others found jobs with progressive unions; still others went into university teaching. Sugar formed a Detroit law firm with Ernest Goodman and George Crockett, Jr., which gained prominence in the 1950s for its defense of victims of the Smith Act, HUAC, and

McCarthyite deportations. Wishart eventually became Research Director of the Packinghouse Workers Union, and Sayler eventually went to work with the National Education Association. Richter took a job in an unorganized GM plant in Elyria, Ohio. After GM fired him for union activity and Emil Mazey refused to process his case before the NLRB, Richter worked under Bob Travis as Assistant Labor Director of the Henry Wallace campaign in Michigan and subsequently established his own business in Detroit. David Erdman, Sigmund Diamond, and Richter later became professors.[48]

Using the power of a sympathetic Executive Board and a subservient staff, Reuther moved quickly and ruthlessly against left-wing leaders of local unions. On December 1, Reuther removed the officers of Allis-Chalmers Local 248, three of whom had refused to sign the Taft-Hartley affidavits, and placed an administrator, Pat Greathouse in charge. Subsequently, a new Reutherite leadership of the local expelled Christoffel, Buse, and seven other officers. The convention of 1949 upheld the expulsions. In 1948, Reuther used his international representatives and financial resources to beat leftist incumbents in local unions. He allegedly gave "thousands of dollars" to help Russell Leach beat John Anderson, the organizer and original president of Local 155. Anderson, one of the most prominent Communists in the union, later said his defeat was largely due to "events that were beyond our control"—namely, "the Cold War and all the Cold War meant." Anderson soon left the union and the party and became a successful labor relations specialist for the employers' tool and die makers association. After the local elections in the spring of 1949, an observer noted: "What remains of leftist opposition is concentrated in Flint and in a bare handful of the 101 locals in Detroit. And even in these few, the opposition is dwindling."[49]

Ford Local 600, the last bastion of Communist and left-wing influence in the UAW, remained a thorn in Reuther's side for many years. Here several hundred Communists had strong support among the 65,000 Ford workers. The Communists had played a crucial role in organizing the local and leading the 1941 strike; they had strong backing among ethnic and black workers in such divisions as the glass plant, pressed steel, foundary, and spring and set-up; and they formed an integral part of the Progressive caucus. Still, Reuther's victory in 1947 and the growing anti-

Communist hysteria fortified the ACTU and other right-wingers and weakened the Left. Tommy Thompson, president of Local 600, whom the Communists had helped elect in 1947, moved into the Reuther camp in 1948. Others such as Lee Romano and Archie Acciacca, who had been members of the CP, and Shelton Tappes, who had worked closely with the CP, likewise became Reutherites. After leaving the Communist party in 1946, Romano helped lead a split in the Progressive caucus in late 1947 and early 1948. Acciacca, an officer in pressed steel, left the party about 1947 and became "bitterly opposed" to the Communists. Both Romano and Tappes eventually accepted jobs on the international staff. When HUAC came to Detroit in 1952, all three men testified against Communists in Ford Local 600. In 1948, after Local 600 voted 7,654 to 4,740 to comply with the Taft-Hartley Act, Johnny Gallo and Bill McKie, who had been elected guide and trustee as open Communists, resigned their positions rather than sign the non-Communist affidavits. McKie, an active unionist at Ford since 1932 and the first president of the local before it had bargaining rights, wrote in his letter of resignation: "It is certainly well-known by most members of this local that I cannot abide by any such order since I am, and intend to remain, a member of the Communist Party."[50]

Following the 1947 UAW convention, the Communists discussed and analyzed the reasons for the debacle. On November 26 and 27, 1947, the *Daily Worker* published a two-part article by John Williamson entitled, "Why Reuther Won in Auto." On December 13 and 14, the Michigan State Committee of the Communist party discussed the auto situation, and Saul Wellman summarized its conclusions in the internal party bulletin, *Emphasis*. Discussions in the Michigan district eventually led to a draft report entitled "A Critical Review of Party's Work in Auto," that appeared in the *Worker* on June 27, 1948. Except for Williamson, who mentioned in passing that Reuther's victory "cannot be separated from the intensive drive of reaction everywhere," the Communist analysis focused on the weaknesses and failures of the party and the Addes-Thomas-Leonard coalition. "Since 1939," the Michigan Communists noted, "our main line has been to weld a progressive coalition of Communist and non-Communist auto workers to isolate and defeat the Reuther policy and leaders which plays the role of Social Democratic lackey to the imperialist course of Wall Street." While this policy was and remained "correct," serious weaknesses marred its execution. Under the pressure of growing reaction, the non-Communist leaders of the Addes-Thomas-Leonard coalition "drifted away from a fighting progressive program" such as that passed by the EB in April 1946. Consequently, the coalition lost popular support and increasingly resorted to "factional maneuvering." This factional maneuvering manifested itself in the Farm Equipment merger, in support for an "unsound" pension plan at Ford, in "catering to white-chauvinist, anti-Negro groups" in some locals, and in partial capitulation to anti-Communism (agreeing with Reuther that Section 8 of the Constitution applied to the CP and expelling Communists from the caucus). As the non-Communists in the Addes-Thomas-Leonard coalition drifted to the right, the Communists not only failed to stop the drift but often found themselves "a prisoner of our allies in the coalition."[51]

The party analysts recognized that weaknesses in the party contributed to the debacle in the UAW. The "main contributing factor" was the failure of the party to establish a "clear independent Communist leadership based on a mass Communist Party securely rooted in the shops." "Fearful of breaking the coalition, self-conscious over our numerical weakness," and tainted by factional maneuvering, the Communists "tended to measure Party trade union strength by top relations and neglected work down below with [the] rank and file." Moreover, when the party separated itself from the position of the coalition, as on the issue of the fight for a Negro vice-president, "workers did not know it." Even if Communist policy required greater independence and more attention to the rank and file than the party showed in the recent past, the Communists recognized the futility of trying to "'go it alone.'" The Addes-Thomas-Leonard coalition may have "evaporated beyond recovery," but effective mass action still required alliances between Communists and non-Communists. Consequently, Communist analysts projected a struggle for a "realignment of forces" in the union by trying to develop "a united front from below" on the basis of such issues as wage increases, speedup, a guaranteed workweek, and Taft-Hartley.[52]

By projecting the strategy of a united front from below, the Communists were returning full circle to the strategy they had pursued in the auto industry in the 1920s. In many respects, as far as the Communists were concerned, the late 1920s and late 1940s had much in common. In both periods, the American capitalists had recently emerged from a war stronger than any other capitalists in the world. They enjoyed high profits and public prestige, while the workers enjoyed a freedom from unemployment and gradually rising real incomes. In both periods political reaction and anti-Communism were on the rise, and the possibilities for Communist cooperation with the current labor leaders had nearly disappeared. In both periods, the Communists found themselves a tiny, isolated minority in the shops. In the late 1940s as in the 1920s, Communists began publishing shop papers. Under these circumstances, the Communist return to an emphasis on building a united front from below and working for a realignment of forces in the UAW remained the only realistic strategy open to them.[53]

In many ways, of course, the Communists faced a much different situation in 1948 than in 1928. In some ways these differences posed even greater obstacles to Communist strategy than those faced in the 1920s. The most important difference was that the auto workers had won the battle for industrial unionism. As Wyndham Mortimer noted in a letter to Nat Ganley on the twentieth anniversary of the UAW's 1936 South Bend convention: "A mighty tree has really grown from the seed we planted, and many thousands have lived under its protection and shade." Through this battle the Communists acquired an immense amount of practical experience in class struggle, including the lessons of their own mistakes. Victory in this battle meant that the auto workers no longer worked under the most extreme conditions of speedup, deprivation, authoritarianism, insecurity, and racial segregation. While the victory of industrial unionism meant that future class conflicts would be fought on a different and higher plane than before, it also meant that auto workers had come under an anti-Communist hegemony that embraced their own union leaders as well as the employers, the government, and the press. Another important difference from the 1920s was that the government in 1948 was a more active participant in labor relations than ever before. After Taft-Hartley, the government not only ostensibly guaranteed the rights of workers to organize, but also interpreted and restricted those rights, intervened actively in industrial disputes, and regulated internal union affairs.[54]

Other important differences unfolded in the years ahead. The post-World War II prosperity lasted longer than that of the 1920s. Between 1948 and 1965, unemployment remained low and the real take-home pay for factory workers rose by about 2.1 percent a year. Also, the Cold War anti-Communism possessed a greater virulence and persistence than reaction in the predepression decade. In 1948, Communists and other progressives still would have to endure another decade of repression. Ahead lay the Smith Act trials and imprisonments of Communist leaders, the CIO expulsions of the so-called Communist internationals, the McCarthy investigations, the party's underground existence in the period 1950–55, and three major Congressional investigations in 1952, 1954, and 1957 of Communists in the auto industry. All of this meant that after the defeat of 1947 the Communists in auto lacked the opportunity to rebuild. Consequently, Communist hopes of building a new united front that would lead the auto workers in a renewed fight for better conditions and for socialism faced an indefinite postponement.[55]

# NOTES

(*Archives of Labor History and Urban Affairs,*
*Wayne State University, is abbreviated to WSU throughout.*)

## I. INTRODUCTION

1. Benjamin Stolberg, *The Story of the CIO* (New York: Viking Press, 1938), pp. 136, 142, 150; Max Kampelman, *The Communist Party vs. the C.I.O.: A Study in Power Politics* (New York: Frederick A. Praeger, 1957), p. 255; Irving Howe and B.J. Widick, *The UAW and Walter Reuther* (New York: Random House, 1949), p. ix; Jack Barbash, *The Practice of Unionism* (New York: Harper & Brothers, 1956), pp. 324–325; Statement of Philip Taft in U.S., Congress, Senate, Committee on Labor and Public Welfare, *Communist Domination of Unions and National Security, Hearings before a Subcommittee of the Senate Committee on Labor and Public Welfare.* 82d Cong., 2d sess., 1952, p. 170; Irving Bernstein, *The Lean Years: A History of the American Worker, 1920–1933* (Baltimore: Penguin Books, 1966), pp. 136–141; Walter Galenson, "Communists and Trade Union Democracy," *Industrial Relations* (October 1974), 236.

2. On the dual character of Communist parties, see E.J. Hobsbawm, *Revolutionaries: Contemporary Essays* (New York: Random House, 1973), pp. 3–7; on the origins of the American Communist party, see Theodore Draper, *The Roots of American Communism* (New York: Viking Press, 1957) and William Z. Foster, *History of the Communist Party of the United States* (New York: Greenwood Press, 1968), pp. 157–195.

3. Earl Browder, "The American Communist Party in the Thirties," in Rita Simon, ed., *As We Saw the Thirties* (Urbana, Chicago, and London: University of Illinois Press, 1969), pp. 233–234, 240; "Notes from Interview with Earl Browder on February 1, 1956" in the Daniel Bell Collection (Tamiment); Philip J. Jaffe, "The Rise and Fall of Earl Browder," *Survey* (Spring 1972), 25; William Z. Foster, *From Bryan to Stalin* (New York: International Publishers, 1937), pp. 268–274; for the history of the Communist International, see Franz Borkenau, *World Communism: A History of the Communist International* (Ann Arbor: University of Michigan Press, 1963); Jane Degras, ed., *The Communist International,*

291

*1919–1943: Documents* (London, New York, and Toronto: Oxford University Press, 1960); Institute of Marxism-Leninism, Central Committee of the Communist Party of the Soviet Union, *Outline History of the Communist International* (Moscow: Progress Publishers, 1971), and William Z. Foster, *History of the Three Internationals: The World Socialist and Communist Movements from 1848 to the Present* (New York: International Publishers, 1955).

4. William Weinstone to Roger Keeran (July 27, 1979); on factionalism among Socialists and Trotskyists see Daniel Bell, *Marxian Socialism in the United States* (Princeton: Princeton University Press, 1962), pp. 153–182.

5. Robert Alperin, "Organization in the Communist Party, U.S.A., 1931–1938" (Ph.D. dissertation, Northwestern University, 1959), pp. 121–128; J. Peters, *The Communist Party: A Manual on Organization* (Workers Library Publishers, 1935; reprint ed., San Francisco: Proletarian Publishers, 1975), pp. 44–62, 99–102; "Notes from an interview Tuesday, January 10, 1956 with Dan Bell, Bill Goldsmith, Earl Browder," in Daniel Bell Collection (Tamiment).

6. Roy Hudson, "The Path of Labor's United Action," *Communist* (October 1939), 935–936.

7. For the general development of the Communist party line see Irving Howe and Lewis Coser, *The American Communist Party: A Critical History* (New York: Frederick A. Praeger, 1962) and Foster, *History of the Communist Party of the United States*; for the party line in the 1920s see Theodore Draper, *American Communism and Soviet Russia* (New York: Viking Press, 1963); for the party line in the 1940s see David A. Shannon, *The Decline of American Communism: A History of the Communist Party of the United States since 1945* (London: Stevens & Sons, 1959), pp. 3–51 and Joseph R. Starobin, *American Communism in Crisis, 1943–1957* (Cambridge: Harvard University Press, 1972).

8. For typical views on the Communists during the pact period and war, see Howe and Widick, pp. 79, 115; Kampelman, p. 26; Walter Galenson, *The CIO Challenge to the AFL: A History of the American Labor Movement, 1935–1941* (Cambridge: Harvard University Press, 1960), pp. 185–188. For a different view, see Prickett, "The Communists and the Communist Issue in the American Labor Movement, 1920–1950" (Ph.D. dissertation, University of California, Los Angeles, 1975), pp. 247–261; Bert Cochran, *Labor and Communism: The Conflict that Shaped American Unions* (Princeton: Princeton University Press, 1977), pp. 157–195.

9. James R. Prickett, "Some Aspects of the Communist Controversy in the CIO," *Science and Society* (Summer-Fall 1969), 299–321; Victor Reuther, *The Brothers Reuther and the Story of the UAW* (Boston: Houghton Mifflin, 1976), pp. 418, 423; Center for the Study of Democratic Institutions, *Labor Looks at Labor* (Santa Barbara: Fund for the Republic, 1963), pp. 13–14. For discussions of the negative consequences of the expulsion of Communists, see Frank Emspak, "The Break-up of the Congress of Industrial Organizations (CIO), 1945–1950" (Ph.D. dissertation, University of Wisconsin, 1972), pp. 328–402; Prickett, "Communists and the Communist Issue," pp. 293–304; Frank Marquart, *An Auto Worker's Journal: The UAW from Crusade to One-Party Union* (University Park and London: Pennsylvania University Press, 1975), pp. 109–148.

10. Kampelman, pp. 251–252; James Prickett, "Anti-Communism and Labor History," *Industrial Relations* (October 1974), 220.

11. Alfred Hirsch, "They Broke His Back . . . but Not his Spirit," *March of Labor* (September 1951), 7–8; *New York Times* (August 6 and October 30, 1950; February 29, March 1, 12, 13, 15, 1952; May 2, 15, 1954; June 20, 1954); *Labor Action* quoted by B.J. Widick, *Detroit: City of Race and Class Violence* (Chicago: Quadrangle Books, 1972), pp. 127–134; U.S., Congress, House, Committee on Un-American Activities, *Communism in the Detroit Area.* 82d Cong., 2d sess., 1952; U.S., Congress, House, Committee on Un-American Activities, *Investigation of Communist Activities in the State of Michigan.* 83rd Cong., 2d sess., 1954.

12. Oral History Interview of Wyndham Mortimer (Wayne State University), p. 1; Wyndham Mortimer, *Organize! My Life as a Union Man* (Boston: Beacon Press, 1972), pp. 8–68; Oral History Interview of Bob Travis (University of Michigan—Flint); Oral History Interview of Nat Ganley (Wayne State University), pp. 1–10; Oral History Interview of Bud and Hazel Simons (University of Michigan—Flint); Phillip Bonosky, *Brother Bill McKie: Building the Union at Ford* (New York: International Publishers, 1953), pp. 11–17, 107, 125–127.

13. David Saposs, *Communism in American Unions* (New York, Toronto, London: McGraw-Hill, 1959), pp. 119–121; Sidney Fine, *Sit-down: The General Motors Strike of 1936–1937* (Ann Arbor: University of Michigan Press, 1970), p. 65.

14. Saposs, p. vii.

15. Edward Levinson, *Labor on the March* (New York and London: Harper & Brothers, 1938), p. 282; Irving Bernstein, *Turbulent Years: A History of the American Worker, 1933–1941* (Boston: Houghton Mifflin, 1971), pp. 782–783.

16. Fine, pp. 217–224.

17. Figures for 1930–1938 from Alperin, p. 49; figures for 1942–1949 from Nathan Glazer, *The Social Basis of American Communism* (New York: Harcourt, Brace & World, 1961), pp. 92–93.

18. Glazer, p. 115; Alperin, p. 53; John Williamson, "The Organizational and Educational Tasks of Our Party," *Communist* (October 1943), 932.

19. Hadley Cantril, ed., *Public Opinion 1935–46* (Princeton: Princeton University Press, 1951), pp. 130–132, 244; Robert and Helen Lynd, *Middletown in Transition: A Study in Cultural Conflicts* (New York: Harcourt, Brace & World, 1965), pp. 266, 356–357, 413–414, 575.

20. Morris L. Ernst and David Loth, *Report on the American Communist* (New York: Henry Holt and Company, 1952), p. 14; Prickett, "Communists and the Communist Issue," p. 35; Cochran, p. 124.

21. Alperin, pp. 194–207; Prickett, "Communists and the Communist Issue," pp. 36–46.

22. Cochran, pp. 115–120; John Brophy to Adolph Germer (December 19, 1936) in Adolph Germer Papers (State Historical Society of Wisconsin).

23. James Weinstein, *Ambiguous Legacy: The Left in American Politics* (New York: New Viewpoints, 1975), pp. 75, 77, 79; Prickett, "Communists and the Communist Issue," p. 455; Jeremy Brecher, *Strike!* (San Francisco: Straight Arrow Books, 1972), p. 257; for similar views see Stanley Aronowitz, *False Promises: The Shaping of American Working Class Consciousness* (New York: McGraw-Hill, 1973), pp. 241–245.

24. Earl Browder, *The People's Front* (New York: International Publishers, 1938), pp. 148–149.

25. Max Gordon, "The Communist Party of the Nineteen-thirties and the New Left," *Socialist Revolution* (January-March 1976), 19-20.

26. U.S., Congress, House, Committee on Education and Labor, *Amendments to the National Labor Relations Act.* Vol. 3, 80th Cong., 1st sess., 1947, pp. 1426-1430.

27. David Montgomery, "Spontaneity and Organization: Some Comments," *Radical America* (November-December 1973), 76.

28. William Weinstone to Roger Keeran (July 27, 1979).

29. Len DeCaux, *Labor Radical From Wobblie to CIO: A Personal History* (Boston: Beacon Press, 1970), p. 245; Notes on an interview with Lee Pressman in the Daniel Bell Collection (Tamiment).

30. Foster, *History of the Communist Party of the United States*, p. 351; Henry Kraus, *The Many and the Few: A Chronicle of the Dynamic Auto Workers* (Los Angeles: Plantin Press, 1947); Mortimer, p. 113.

31. Glazer, p. 84; for a discussion of Communist popular culture in the 1930s see *Cultural Correspondence* (Spring 1978), 78-101; A.B. Magill and Henry Stevens, *The Peril of Fascism: The Crisis of American Democracy* (New York: International Publishers, 1938); George Seldes, *Facts and Fascism* (New York: In Fact, 1943).

32. Those not previously mentioned: John Williamson, *Dangerous Scot: The Life and Work of an American "Undesirable"* (New York: International Publishers, 1969); Al Richmond, *A Long View from the Left: Memoirs of an American Revolutionary* (Boston: Houghton Mifflin, 1973); Shannon, p. 376.

33. Peter Friedlander, *The Emergence of a UAW Local, 1936-1939: A Study in Class and Culture* (Pittsburgh: University of Pittsburgh Press, 1975), pp. xxix, xxxii.

## II. THE AUTO WORKERS UNION

1. William E. Leuchtenburg, *The Perils of Prosperity, 1914-1932* (Chicago and London: University of Chicago Press, 1938), p. 186; Robert S. Lynd and Helen M. Lynd, *Middletown: A Study in Modern American Culture* (New York: Harcourt, Brace & World, 1956), p. 253; Sinclair Lewis, *Babbitt* (New York and Scarborough, Ontario: New American Library, 1961), p. 23; Irving Bernstein, *The Lean Years: A History of the American Worker, 1920-1933* (Boston: Houghton Mifflin, 1966), pp. 179-180; Victor Reuther, *The Brothers Reuther and the Story of the UAW* (Boston: Houghton Mifflin, 1976), pp. 41-42

2. Frank Marquart, *An Auto Worker's Journal: The UAW from Crusade to One-Party Union* (University Park and London: Pennsylvania State University Press, 1975), p. 38.

3. Theodore Draper, *The Roots of American Communism* (New York: Viking Press, 1966) pp. 176-281; Robert K. Murray, *Red Scare: A Study in National Hysteria, 1919-1920* (New York, Toronto, London: McGraw-Hill, 1964), pp. 210-262; William Preston, Jr. *Aliens and Dissenters: Federal Suppression of Radicals, 1903-1933* (Cambridge, Mass.: Harvard, 1963), pp. 221, 332; Ruthenberg quoted by Draper, p. 198; Communist Party Program and Communist Labor Party Programs quoted by Draper, p. 185.

4. William Z. Foster, *History of the Communist Party of the United States* (New York: International Publishers, 1952), pp. 164-193; Theodore Draper, *Roots*, pp. 164-281, 311-344.

5. Robert W. Dunn, *Labor and Automobiles* (New York: International Publishers, 1929), pp. 13, 21–22; James Weinstein, *The Decline of Socialism in America, 1912–1925* (New York and London: Monthly Review, 1967), pp. 96, 116–117; Draper, *Roots*, pp. 158, 164–167, 182–184, 210–211; Max Eastman, "The Chicago Conventions," *Liberator* (October 1919) quoted by Irving Howe and Lewis Coser, *The American Communist Party: A Critical History, 1919–1957* (Boston: Beacon Press, 1957), p. 39.

6. Dunn, pp. 18, 186–187; Oral History Interview of Lester Johnson (WSU), pp. 6, 22; William P. Mavell, "History," *Spark Plug* (February 10, 1917); William P. Mavell, "History," *Auto Worker* (May 1919).

7. Oral History Interview of Arthur Rohan (WSU), pp. 18, 34; "Editorial," *Auto Worker* (December 1919); *Spark Plug* (February 10, 1917); *Auto Worker* (May, June, July, September, October, and December 1919); William A. Logan, "The Onward March," *Auto Worker* (May 1919); John S. Martin, "The I.W.W.," *Auto Worker* (October 1919); "Socialists Nominate Old Friend of Auto Workers," *Auto Worker* (June 1920).

8. "Leftwingers," *Auto Worker* (August 1919); William A. Logan, "Our Government," and August Claessens, "'M'ass' Action of the R-R-R-Revolutionary Prowling Terriers," *Auto Worker* (November 1919).

9. Dunn, pp. 187–191; Interview with Phil Raymond, Detroit, July 26, 1971; "News From the Locals," *Auto Worker* (May, June, and July 1919; March 1920); Arthur Rohan, "Latest News of the New York Strike," *Auto Worker* (February 1920).

10. Testimony of Thomas C. Wilcox in U.S., Congress, House, Special Committee on Communist Activities in the United States, *Investigation of Communist Propaganda, Hearing Before a Special Committee to Investigate Communist Activities in the United States of the House of Representatives*, Part IV, Vol. 1. 71st Cong., 2nd sess., 1930, pp. 120–121; Foster Rhea Dulles, *Labor in America: A History* (New York: Thomas Y. Crowell, 1949), pp. 230–246; Dunn, p. 9.

11. Dunn, pp. 191–192; Oral History Interview of Lester Johnson (WSU), pp. 26–27; Gordon Cascoden, "Michigan Workers Walloped by Depression and Reaction," *Auto Worker* (January 1921); "General Organizers' Reports," *Auto Worker* (January 1921); "Local News," *Auto Worker* (April 1921); Ben Blumenberg, "Detroit Notes," *Auto Worker* (August 1921).

12. "Saved Again," *Auto Worker* (February 1922); "Another Redskin Bites the Dust," *Auto Worker* (May 1922).

13. Solon DeLeon, ed., *The American Labor Who's Who* (New York: Hanford Press, 1925), pp. 180–181; Oral History Interview of Lester Johnson (WSU), pp. 12–14; Oral History Interview of Phil Raymond (WSU), p. 2

14. "The Conference for Progressive Political Action," "Exposing the 'Reds,'" and William A. Logan, "Labor's Political Problem," *Auto Worker* (January 1923).

15. Draper, *Roots*, p. 373; Interview with Phil Raymond, Detroit, July 26, 1971.

16. "Workers' Party Members Join Auto Workers," *Auto Worker* (April 1924); Oral History Interview of Arthur Rohan (WSU), p. 23.

17. Theodore Draper, *American Communism and Soviet Russia: The Formative Period* (New York: Viking, 1961), pp. 153–163, 186–194; "Composition of the Party (By Districts)," *Party Organizer* (December

1927), 15; Jack Stachel, "Our Factory Nuclei," *Party Organizer* (May-June 1928), 5–10; "Ohio Nuclei in Large Factories," *Party Organizer* (March-April 1928), 13–14; Vera Buch Weisbord, *A Radical Life* (Bloomington: Indiana University Press, 1977), pp. 100–136, 146–147.

18. Vera Buch, "The Functioning of a Detroit Shop Nucleus," *Party Organizer* (July-August 1928), 14–15; Draper, *American Communism,* p. 193; Weisbord, pp. 147–148.

19. Rebecca Grecht, "Factory Newspapers," *Party Organizer* (December 1927), 16; "Issuing Shop Papers," *Party Organizer* (February 1930), 9–10.

20. Dunn, p. 194; *Ford Worker* (April 1926); *Investigation of Communist Propaganda,* Part IV, Vol. 1, p. 193.

21. *Fisher Body Worker* (October 1926); *Ford Worker* (May and October 1926); *Dodge Worker* (November 1926).

22. William E. Chalmers, "Labor in the Automobile Industry;" (Ph.D. dissertation, University of Wisconsin, 1932), p. 285; *Ford Worker* (April, October, and November 1926; June and July 1927); *Dodge Bros. Workers' News* (August 1926); *Dodge Worker* (July 1927); *Fisher Body Worker* (August 1927).

23. A Ford Shop Nucleus Organizer, "The Ford Worker," *Party Organizer* (April 1927), 9–10; *Ford Worker* (June and September 1926); Statement of the Employers' Association of Detroit in Robert Dunn Papers (WSU); Dunn, p. 194.

24. Robert L. Cruden, "What the Workers Think," *Labor Age* (April 1929), 10; Reinhold Niebuhr, "Ford's Five-Day Week Shrinks," *Christian Century* (June 9, 1927), 713–714.

25. Marquart, pp. 33–35.

26. Lois Rankin, "Detroit Nationality Groups," *Michigan History Magazine* (Spring 1939 [written ca. 1931]), 129–205; *Michigan Worker* (November 6, 1932).

27. *Daily Worker* quoted by Draper, *American Communism,* p. 118; "Labor Day," *Auto Worker* (September 1924).

28. Oral History Interview of Lester Johnson (WSU), p. 12; "Strikes Must Be Authorized," *Auto Worker* (May 1924); William A. Logan, "Why Put the Cart Before the Horse," *Auto Worker* (August 1924); *Workers' Bulletin* (August 1926).

29. "Program for the Automobile Industry" (July 21, 1926), in the Earl Browder Papers (Syracuse University); Oral History Interview of Lester Johnson (WSU), pp. 12–15; Oral History Interview of Phil Raymond (WSU), p. 1; Interview with Phil Raymond, Detroit, July 26, 1971.

30. Oral History Interview of Lester Johnson (WSU), pp. 12–15; Oral History Interview of Arthur Rohan (WSU), p. 23; Oral History Interview of Phil Raymond (WSU), p. 1; Interview with Phil Raymond, Detroit, July 26, 1971.

31. Interview with Phil Raymond, Detroit, July 26, 1971; *Auto Workers News* (March 15, 1930); *Detroit News* (March 8, 1932); *Daily Worker* (February 4, 9, 1933); *Auto Workers News* (May, July, and August 1929); notes on YCL in Henry Kraus Papers (WSU).

32. William Z. Foster, "Organizing the Unorganized," *Labor Herald* (July 1923), 11–12; "Program for the Automobile Industry" (July 21, 1926) and "Trade Union Committee of C. E. C." (May 23, 1927), in Earl Browder Papers (Syracuse University).

33. Bernstein, pp. 84, 97–107; Dulles, pp. 241–258.

34. International Association of Machinists, *Proceedings of the Seventh Convention* (Washington, D.C., 1924), p. 188; Metal Trades Department of the American Federation of Labor, *Proceedings of the Eighteenth Annual Convention* (Detroit, 1926), p. 16.

35. Draper, *American Communism*, pp. 223–224; American Federation of Labor, *Report of the Proceedings of the Forty-Sixth Annual Convention* (Washington, D.C., 1926), pp. 40, 171–173; "Can Labor Capture Detroit?" *New Republic* (October 27, 1926), 261–262.

36. Draper, *American Communism*, pp. 215–217; David M. Schneider, *The Workers' (Communist) Party and American Trade Unions* (Baltimore: John Hopkins Press, 1928); Interview with Phil Raymond, Detroit, July 26, 1971; William Z. Foster, "Organize the Unorganized," *Labor Herald* (July 1923), 11–12; James P. Cannon, "The Bolshevization of the Party," *Workers' Monthly* (November 1924), 36, Earl Browder, editorial, *Workers' Monthly* (November 1924), 15; A. Losovsky, "Struggle for Unity in the World Labor Movement," *Workers' Monthly* (December 1924), 59; William Z. Foster, "The American Federation of Labor Convention," *Workers' Monthly* (January 1925), 107; *Ford Worker* (October and November 1926; June 1927); 1926 Report of AWU in Robert Dunn Papers (WSU).

37. William Green, "Communist Internationale," *American Federationist* (November 1926), 1305–06; 1926 Report of AWU in Robert Dunn Papers (WSU).

38. William Chalmers to [Florence] Thorne (August 16, 1927) in William Chalmers Papers (WSU); John Love, "Detroit a Sterile Field for Organized Labor," *Annalist* (November 12, 1926), 620–631; Dunn, pp. 176–180; James O. Morris, *Conflict Within the AFL: A Study of Craft Versus Industrial Unionism, 1901–1938* (Cornell University: Ithaca, N.Y., 1958), pp. 57–61.

39. William F. Dunne, "Surrender Raised to a System," *Communist* (November 1927), 417; William Z. Foster, "Capitalist Efficiency 'Socialism,'" *Communist* (March 1928), 169–171.

40. Reinhold Niebuhr, "How Philanthropic Is Henry Ford?" *Christian Century* (December 9, 1926), 1516–17; Niebuhr, "Ford's Five-Day Week Shrinks," *Christian Century* (June 9, 1927), 713–714; Ben Lifschitz, "Who Will Organize the Auto Workers?" *Daily Worker* (August 25, 1928).

41. Oral History Interview of Phil Raymond (WSU), p. 23; Chalmers, pp. 291–292.

42. *Auto Workers News* (May and June, 1927).

43. *Auto Workers News* (July, September, October, and December 1927; March and December 1928; June, July, September, and November 1929; March 15, 1930).

44. *Auto Workers News* (May, June, October, and December 1927; March, June, and October 1928; June, August, and October 1929); Interview with Phil Raymond, Detroit, July 26, 1971; Oral History Interview of Lester Johnson (WSU), p. 25; "A Chink Raises the Ante," *Auto Worker* (October 1921); *Auto Worker* (September and November 1922).

45. James Steele, *Conveyor* (New York: AMS Press, 1976); Dunn, p. 173; notes on *Auto Workers News* in Robert Dunn Papers (WSU); Oral History of Phil Raymond (WSU), p. 22; Chalmers, p. 308; Robert L. Cruden, "While Packard Prospers . . . ," *Daily Worker* (February 8, 1929).

46. Robert L. Cruden, "No Loitering: Get Out Production," *Nation* (June 12, 1928).

47. Harry Bennett (as told to Paul Marcus), *We Never Called Him Henry* (New York: Fawcett Publications, 1951), pp. 14–15, 32–34; Phillip Bonosky, *Brother Bill McKie: Building the Union at Ford* (New York: International Publishers, 1953), p. 13; Bernstein, p. 74.

48. Chalmers, p. 308, Platform of AWU, 1929 in Robert Dunn Papers (WSU); Interview with Phil Raymond, Detroit, July 26, 1971.

49. Oral History of Interview of John W. Anderson (WSU), p. 2; Oral History Interview of Frank Marquart (WSU), pp. 2–3; Chalmers, pp. 278–279, 212; Robert Cruden, "While Packard Prospers . . . ," *Daily Worker* (February 8, 1929).

50. Oral History Interview of Phil Raymond (WSU), p. 20; Oral History Interview of Frank Marquart (WSU), pp. 2–3.

51. Dunn, pp. 197–200; Chalmers, pp. 226–228, 231, 309–310; *Auto Workers News* (October 1926; July, October, and November 1927; March and August 1928; March, April, May, June, July, and August 1929); *Workers' Bulletin* (August 1926); *Fisher Body Workers' Bulletin* (August, October, and November 1926; October 1927); *Fisher Body Worker* (July 1927); *Dodge Worker* (August 1927); "Report of General Secretary-Pro Tem [of AWU, 1928]" in Robert Dunn Papers (WSU); Ben Lifschitz, "The Flint Strike and Its Lessons," *Daily Worker* (August 24, 1928); Phil Raymond, "Auto Union Lays Plans to Organize Industry," *Auto Workers Union* (August 20, 1929).

52. William Green to Paul Smith (June 17, 1929) in William Green Papers, quoted by Bernstein, p. 143; Interview with Phil Raymond, Detroit, July 26, 1971.

53. Nathan Glazer, *The Social Basis of American Communism* (New York: Harcourt, Brace & World, 1961), p. 115; *Party Organizer* (March-April 1928), 9–12.

54. "Report of the General Secretary Pro Tem" [1928], in Robert Dunn Papers (WSU); "Minutes of the Conference on Organization of the Auto Workers" [Detroit, January 13, 1929], in Robert Dunn Papers (WSU); William Z. Foster, "Organizing the Automobile Workers," *Labor Unity* (February 1929), 2–5; *Auto Workers News* (February 1929; August 20, 1929; September 1929).

### III. WORK OR WAGES: ORGANIZING THE UNEMPLOYED

1. William E. Leuchtenburg, *The Perils of Prosperity, 1914–1932* (Chicago & London: University of Chicago Press, 1972), pp. 179–186; Matthew Josephson, "Detroit: City of Tomorrow," *Outlook* (February 13, 1929) in Melvin G. Holli, ed., *Detroit* (New York and London: New Viewpoints, 1976), pp. 162–170.

2. Robert W. Dunn, *Labor and Automobiles* (New York: International Publishers, 1929), pp. 101–112; Irving Bernstein, *The Lean Years: A History of the American Worker, 1920–1933* (Boston: Houghton Mifflin, 1960), pp. 254–255; Beulah Amidon, "Toledo: A City the Auto Ran Over," *Survey* (March 1, 1930), 672; Mauritz A. Hallgren, "Bankers and Bread Lines in Toledo," *Nation* (April 6, 1932), 359–397; Bruce Bliven, "No Money, No Work," *New Republic* (November 19, 1930), 12–14.

3. Bernstein, pp. 255, 300–301; Bliven, 12–14; Helen Hall, "When

Detroit's Out of Gear," *Survey* (April 1, 1930), 9–14, 51–54; Beulah Amidon, "Detroit Does Something About It," *Survey* (February 15, 1931), 540–542; *New Republic* (November 25, 1931), 29–30.

4. Hall, 51–52; William H. Chafe, "Flint and the Great Depression," *Michigan History* (Spring 1969), 225–229.

5. Mauritz A. Hallgren, "Grave Danger in Detroit," *Nation* (August 3, 1932), 99; *Detroit News* (August 22, 1931); Clayton Fountain, *Union Guy* (New York: Viking Press, 1949), pp. 34–37.

6. Bernstein, pp. 314–321; Robert L. Cruden and Robert W. Dunn, "How the Crisis Hit the Auto Workers," *Communist* (March 1932), 230–238; *Auto Workers News* (February and March 15, 1930); Hall, 9–14; "Detroit Feels the Punch," *Survey* (June 15, 1931), 299–300; Wyndham Mortimer, *Organize! My Life as a Union Man* (Boston: Beacon Press, 1972), p. 51.

7. Theodore Draper, *American Communism and Soviet Russia: The Formative Period* (New York: Viking, 1960), pp. 284–290, 300–314; "Extracts from the Theses of the Sixth Comintern Congress on the International Situation and the Tasks of the Communist International" and "Programme of the Communist International Adopted at Its Sixth Congress," in Jane Degras, ed., *The Communist International, 1919–1943: Documents* (London, New York, Toronto: Oxford University Press, 1960), II, pp. 455–462, 471–526.

8. William Z. Foster, *From Bryan to Stalin* (New York: International Publishers, 1937), pp. 195–220; Theodore Draper, "Communists and Miners, 1928–1933," *Dissent* (Spring 1972), 371–373; William Z. Foster, "Capitalist Efficiency 'Socialism,'" *Communist* (March 1928), 173; Draper, *American Communism and Soviet Russia*, pp. 405–431; Jay Lovestone, "Some Immediate Party Problems," *Communist* (July 1928), 433.

9. *Auto Workers News* (April 1929; December-January and March 15, 1930); "Plans to Organize Industry," *Auto Workers News* (August 20, 1929); "Special Report of Trade-Union Unity League Cleveland Convention," in U.S., Congress, House, Special Committee on Communist Activities in the United States, *Investigation of Communist Propaganda, Hearings Before a Special Committee to Investigate Communist Activities in the United States of the House of Representatives*, 71st Cong., 2nd sess., 1930, Part IV, Vol. 1, p. 218; Phil Raymond, "Report on Automobile Industry" [*ca.* 1930] in Henry Kraus Papers (WSU); Minutes of Auto Workers' Union Conference in Detroit, March 8, 1930 in Henry Kraus Papers (WSU).

10. Jack Stachel, "Organization Report to the Sixth Convention of the Communist Party of the U.S.A.," *Communist* (April 1929), 180–186; Theodore Draper, *American Communism and Soviet Russia* (New York: Viking, 1960), p. 430; J.B.S. Hardman, "Communism in America," *New Republic* (August 27, 1930), 34–37; letter from the Comintern, "To the Central Committee CPUSA," *Party Organizer* (June-July 1930), 2–5; "General Registration of the Party Membership," *Party Organizer* (September-October 1931), 7–9; Earl Browder, "Approaching the Factories as Insiders and Not as Outsiders," *Party Organizer* (May-June 1932), 4–5; "Our Unemployed Comrades," *Party Organizer* (November-December 1932), 48.

11. "Organization Work in Detroit," *Party Organizer* (March-April

1928), 9–12; John Williamson, "Some Burning Problems of Organization," *Communist* (June 1930), 522–523; "Shop Paper Statistics," *Party Organizer* (May-June 1932), 45–46.

12. Daniel J. Leab, "'United We Eat': The Creation and Organization of Unemployed Councils in 1930," *Labor History* (Fall 1967), 300–303; Carl Winter, "Unemployment Struggles of the Thirties," *Political Affairs* (September-October 1969), 54–59; Interview with Phil Raymond, Detroit, July 26, 1971.

13. Foster, *From Bryan to Stalin* p. 226; Len DeCaux, *Labor Radical: From the Wobblies to CIO: A Personal History* (Boston: Beacon Press, 1970), p. 167; Bernstein, pp. 426–427; *Daily Worker* (February 12, 1930); *Investigation of Communist Propaganda, Part IV, Vol. 1, pp.* 110–112, 131–132.

14. Phillip Bonosky, *Brother Bill McKie: Building the Union at Ford* (New York: International Publishers, 1953), p. 56; "Work for the *Daily Worker*," *Party Organizer* (March 1930), 12–13.

15. Foster, *From Bryan to Stalin*, p. 227; Bernstein, p. 427; *Daily Worker* (March 7, 1930); *New York Times* (March 7, 1930); *Detroit Free Press* (March 7, 1930); *Detroit News* (March 7, 1930); *Investigation of Communist Propaganda*, Part IV, Vol. 1, p. 273; Caroline Parker to the editor, *Nation* (April 30, 1930), 518.

16. Bernstein, p. 427; *Daily Worker* (March 7, 1930); *New York Times* (March 7, 1930); *Milwaukee Journal* (March 7, 1930); *Milwaukee Sentinel* (March 7, 1930); *Detroit Free Press* (March 7, 1930); *Flint Daily Journal* (March 7, 1930); *Investigation of Communist Propaganda*, Part IV, Vol. 1, pp. 110–111, 131–132, 183.

17. *Flint Daily Journal* (March 7, 1930); *Investigation of Communist Propaganda*, Part IV, Vol. 1, pp. 2–3.

18. *Investigation of Communist Propaganda*, Part IV, Vol. 1, pp. 110–112, 131–132, 183; *Detroit Free Press* (March 7, 1930).

19. *New York Times* (March 7, 1930); *Nation* (March 12, 1930), 284–285; Bernstein, pp. 427–428; *Detroit Labor News* (March 7, 1930); *Flint Daily Journal* (March 7, 1930); *Detroit Free Press* (March 8, 1930).

20. "Notes of the Month," *Communist* (April 1930), 291; Moissaye J. Olgin, "From March Sixth to May First," *Communist* (May 1930), 417–419; Earl Browder, "Preparing for the Seventh Party Convention," *Communist* (May 1930), 441; Louis Adamic, *My America* (New York, London: Harper & Brothers, 1938), pp. 93–94.

21. Interview with Phil Raymond, Detroit, July 26, 1971; interview of Arthur McPhaul, Detroit, August 21, 1971; *Investigation of Communist Propaganda*, Part IV, Vol. 1, pp. 233, 292; *Detroit News* (August 21, 22, 1931).

22. Leab, 308–309.

23. Hallgren, "Detroit's Liberal Mayor," 526–28; Nydia Barker, "Unemployed Work," *Party Organizer* (January 1932), 3–5; Hallgren, "Grave Danger in Detroit," 99–101.

24. Edmund Wilson, "Detroit Motors," *New Republic* (March 25, 1931), 145–150; Bonosky, p. 62; Adamic, p. 68; *Detroit News* (August 21, 22, 1931); Earl Browder, "'Fewer High-Falutin' Phrases, More Simple Every-Day Deeds—Lenin', *Communist* (January, 1931), 16.

25. "Killed for Asking," *New Force* (March-April 1932), 7; Paul F. Douglass, *Six Upon the World: Toward an American Culture for an Industrial Age* (Boston: Little, Brown and Co., 1954), p. 92.

26. Bonosky, pp. 71–82; *New York Times* (March 8, 9, 1932); *Detroit Free Press* (March 8, 9, 1932); *Detroit News* (March 8, 9, 1932); *Daily Worker* (March 8, 9, 10, 14, 21, 22, 28, 1932); *Detroit Labor News* (March 11, 1932); Harry Bennett (as told to Paul Marcus), *We Never Called Him Henry* (New York: Fawcett, 1951), pp. 90–94; Charles E. Sorensen, *My Forty Years With Ford* (New York: Norton, 1956), pp. 254–256; Bernstein, 432–435; Keith Sward, *The Legend of Henry Ford* (New York: Rhinehart, 1948), pp. 231–242; Maurice Sugar, "Bullets—Not Food—For Ford Workers," *Nation* (March 23, 1932), 333–335; *New Force* (March-April, 1932).

27. Bonosky, p. 81; *Detroit Free Press* (March 8, 9, 1932); *Detroit News* (March 8, 9, 1932); *Daily Worker* (March 8, 9, 10, 1932).

28. *Detroit Free Press* (March 9, 1932); Sharts quoted by the *Detroit Free Press* (March 14, 1932); *Detroit News* (March 9, 10, 1932); *Detroit Times* (March 9, 10, 1932); *Daily Worker* (March 10, 14, 1932).

29. M. Palmer, "Organizational Lessons Learned from Bloody Monday-Mobility," *Party Organizer* (March-April 1932), 20; Hallgren, "Grave Danger in Detroit," 101; Bonosky, pp. 83–87; Oakley Johnson, "After the Dearborn Massacre," *New Republic* (March 30, 1932), 172–174; *New York Times* (March 13, 1932); *Daily Worker* (March 10, 14, 1932); *New Force* (March-April, 1932); *Detroit Free Press* (March 12, 13, 1932); *Detroit News* (March 12, 13, 1932); Robert L. Cruden, "Bloody Monday at Ford's," in Robert Dunn Papers (WSU).

30. Mauritz Hallgren, "Detroit's Liberal Mayor," *Nation* (May 13, 1931), 526–28; Tony, "Experiences in Recruiting and Building New Young Communist League Units Immediately After the Ford Massacre," *Party Organizer* (April-May, 1932), 18–20; "Comparative Results of Recruiting in First Nine Months of 1932 and 1933," *Party Organizer* (October 1933), 16–17; "Why a Recruiting Drive Now," *Party Organizer* (September-October 1932), 1–4.

31. Bernard Karsh and Phillip L. Garman, "The Impact of the Political Left," in Milton Derber and Edwin Young, eds., *Labor and the New Deal* (Madison: University of Wisconsin Press, 1957) p. 82.

32. Charles R. Walker, "Down and Out in Detroit," in Charles A. Beard, ed., *America Faces the Future* (Boston and New York: Houghton Mifflin Co., 1932), pp. 70–85; Hallgren, "Grave Danger in Detroit," 101; Wilson, "Detroit Motors," 149.

33. I. Amter, "More Leadership in the Struggle for Unemployed Insurance," *Party Organizer* (May-June 1933), 18–21; "Work Among Unemployed," *Party Organizer* (August-September 1933), 66–69; "Resolution on the Application of the Open Letter by Section One Conference, Detroit District," *Party Organizer* (August-September 1933), 91–94.

## IV. THE BRIGGS STRIKE

1. William Z. Foster, *From Bryan to Stalin* (New York: International Publishers, 1937), pp. 216–219; *Auto Workers News* (September 1929 and March 15, 1930).

2. "Self-Criticism Must Be Followed By Correction," *Party Organizer* (February 1932), 7–8; J. M. "Rooting the Party in the Shops, Systematic Work in the Factory Brings Results," *Party Organizer* (February 1932), 5–6; J. B. "Proper Attention Brings Results," *Party Organizer* (March-April 1932), 11–12; "Shop Paper Reviews," *Party Organizer* (Au-

gust 1931), 18–20; "Shop Paper Reviews," *Party Organizer* (September-October, 1932), 19–20; John Schmies, "Organizing in Ford's," *Labor Unity* (July 1932), 15.

3. See Chapter II for a description of unemployment activity; *Daily Worker: Special Detroit Election Campaign Edition* [1930] in Henry Kraus Papers (WSU); "On Making Contacts," *Party Organizer* (May 1931), 13–14; U. S., Congress, House, Special Committee to Investigate Communist Activities in the United States, *Investigation of Communist Propaganda, Hearings Before a Special Committee to Investigate Communist Activities in the United States of the House of Representatives*, Part I, Vol. 1, 71st Cong., 2nd sess., 1930, p. 18.

4. Sidney Fine, *The Automobile Under the Blue Eagle* (Ann Arbor: University of Michigan Press, 1963), pp. 65–66; William E. Chalmers, "Labor in the Automobile Industry" (Ph.D. dissertation, University of Wisconsin, 1932), pp. 211–225; Robert Cruden, "Flint Strikes Fire," *Labor Defender* (August 1930), 165; *Flint Journal* (July 1–12, 1930); *New York Times* (July 4, 6, 1930); U. S., Congress, House, Special Committee on Communist Activities in the United States, *Investigation of Communist Propaganda, Hearings Before a Special Committee to Investigate Communist Activities in the United States of the House of Representatives*, Part IV, Vol. 1, 71st Cong., 2nd sess., 1930, pp. 5–13, 17–18.

5. "Concentration—A Means of Winning the Workers in the Key Industries," *Party Organizer* (February 1933), 5; "The Shop—A Center of Mass Activity," *Party Organizer* (February 1933), 1–4; Earl Browder, "Approaching the Factories as Insiders and Not as Outsiders," *Party Organizer* (May-June 1932), 4; John Schmies, "Organizing in Ford's," *Labor Unity* (July 1932), 15–16; William Weinstone to Roger Keeran (July 27, 1979).

6. John Schmies, "Organizing in Ford's," *Labor Unity* (July 1932), 15; J. M. [John Mack?], "Rooting the Party in the Shops, Systematic Work in the Factory Brings Results," *Party Organizer* (February 1932), 5–6. "Shop Paper Reviews," *Party Organizer* (September-October 1932), 19–20; "Will the Comrades Explain?" *Party Organizer* (September-October 1932), 22–23; "Shop Paper Statistics," *Party Organizer* (May-June 1932), 45–46; Robert Alperin, "Organization in the Communist Party, U.S.A., 1931–1938" (Ph.D. dissertation, Northwestern University, 1959), pp. 307, 309.

7. J. B. "Proper Attention Brings Results," *Party Organizer* (March-April 1932), 11–12.

8. Mack, "Learn to Answer Questions Asked by Shop Workers," *Party Organizer* (May-June 1932), 8–10; "Why a Recruiting Drive Now?" *Party Organizer* (September-October 1932), 4.

9. Robert Cruden, "Bloody Monday at Ford's," [1932] in Robert Dunn Papers (WSU); Jack Stachel, "The Strikes in the Auto Industry," *Labor Unity* (March 1933), 4; "Safeguarding the Party—II," *Party Organizer* (April 1931), 6–7; Max Salzman, "Methods of Agitation Among Ford Workers," *Party Organizer* (January 1934), 19–20; "Build the Party and the Unions in the Factory," *Party Organizer* (November-December 1932), 3.

10. "Memo on the Briggs Manufacturing Company" in Robert Dunn Papers (WSU); "Why Auto Body Workers Are [More] Militant than Other Auto Production Workers" (unpublished manuscript, 1933) in Joe Brown

Papers (WSU); newspaper clippings on Briggs profits in Joe Brown Papers (WSU).

11. Robert Dunn, *Labor and Automobiles* (New York: International Publishers, 1929), p. 138; Sidney Fine, *The Automobile Under the Blue Eagle* (Ann Arbor: University of Michigan Press, 1963), pp. 27–28; Mayors Fact Finding Committee quoted by Fine, p. 28; *Detroit Labor News* (January 27, 1933); "Strikers and Workers" (leaflet) in Joe Brown Papers (WSU); Oral History Interview of John W. Anderson (WSU), pp. 3–4.

12. Phil Raymond, "The Briggs Auto Strike Victory," *Labor Unity* (March 1933), 21–23; John Schmies, "The Lessons of the Briggs Auto Strike—How It Was Organized," *Daily Worker* (January 30, 1933); Samuel Romer, "The Detroit Strike," *Nation* (February 15, 1933), 167–168; Interview with Phil Raymond, Detroit, July 26, 1971; Joe Brown, "Strike at Brigg's Vernor Highway Plant" in Joe Brown Papers (WSU).

13. Joe Brown, "Re the Strikes in Detroit Auto Industry—the Status of Auto Workers Union" in Joe Brown Papers (WSU); Romer, 167–168; "Developing Shop Work in Detroit," *Party Organizer* (July 1933), 10–14; *Detroit Labor News* (January 27, 1933).

14. *Daily World* (February 9, 1933); Oral History of Phil Raymond (WSU), 17–18; Interview with Phil Raymond, Detroit, July 26, 1971; Henry Kraus, *The Many and the Few: A Chronicle of the Dynamic Auto Workers* (Los Angeles: Plantin Press, 1947), pp. 34–35.

15. *New York Times* (February 8, 9, 1933); *Daily World* (February 14, 1933); "Re the Strikes in Detroit Auto Industry—the Status of Auto Workers Union in" and "Hudson Motor Car Company Strike" in Joe Brown Papers (WSU); "Developing Shop Work in Detroit," *Party Organizer* (July 1933), 13.

16. *Auto Workers News* (January 27, 1933); Romer, 167–168; "Briggs Strike" in Joe Brown Papers (WSU); "To All Auto Workers—Employed and Unemployed" (leaflet, 1933), in Joe Brown Papers (WSU); Interview with Phil Raymond (January 1933), in Henry Kraus Papers (WSU).

17. Fine, pp. 28–29; Briggs Company statement, the Fact Finding Committee and Pilkington quoted by Fine, pp. 28–29; Connolly quoted by *New York Times* (January 31, 1933).

18. Ford quoted by *New York Times* (January 28, 1933); Romer, 167–168; *Detroit Free Press* (January 30, 1933); *Daily Worker* (January 31, 1933).

19. "Briggs Strike" in Joe 8rown Papers (WSU); Statement of Earl Bailey and E. Paul Gouzer (March 20, 1933), in Joe Brown Papers (WSU).

20. Interview of Frank Cedervall, Madison, Wisconsin, November 1, 1971; Oral History Interview of Leon Pody (WSU), pp. 4–16; Oral History Interview of John W. Anderson (WSU), pp. 6–18; "'I.W.W. Leadership is Strikebreaker in Auto Struggles,' An article in the Daily Worker by Phillip Raymond [sic], October 17, 1933" in Joe Brown Papers (WSU); *Detroit Labor News* (February 3, 1933); "Developing Shop Work in Detroit," *Party Organizer* (July 1933), 10–14; Fine, p. 29.

21. Romer, 167–168; *New York Times* (February 2, 1933); *Daily Worker* (February 2, 1933).

22. "'I.W.W. Leadership is Strikebreaker in Auto Struggles' . . ." in Joe Brown Papers (WSU); "Developing Shop Work in Detroit," *Party Organizer* (July 1933), 10–14; *Detroit News* (January 27, 1933); Interview of

Phil Raymond (January 1933), in Henry Kraus Papers (WSU); strike committee quoted by Detroit *Times* (January 31, 1933) and *Daily Worker* (January 30, 1933).

23. *New York Times* (February 2, 9, 1933); Detroit *Free Press* (February 2, 1933); *Detroit Labor News* (March 17, 1933).

24. Detroit *Free Press* (January 30, 1933); Briggs official quoted by *Free Press* (January 31, 1933); *New York Times* (February 2, 1933); *Detroit Labor News* (February 3, 1933); Interview with Phil Raymond, Detroit, July 26, 1971.

25. "'I.W.W. Leadership is Strikebreaker in Auto Struggles' . . ." in Joe Brown Papers (WSU); "Briggs Strike" in Joe Brown Papers (WSU); Interview of Frank Cedervall, Madison, Wisconsin, November 1, 1971; Oral History Interview of John W. Anderson (WSU), pp. 6–18.

26. Andrew Overgaard, "Lessons of the Detroit Automobile Strike," *Daily Worker* (March 3, 1933); Jack Stachel, "The Struggles in the Auto Industry," *Labor Unity*; "Briggs Strikers" (AWU leaflet, February 2, 1933), in Joe Brown Papers (WSU); *Detroit Labor News* (February 17, 1933); *New York Times* (February 7, 1933); "'I.W.W. Leadership is Strikebreaker in Auto Struggles' . . ." in Joe Brown Papers (WSU).

27. Oral History Interview of Leon Pody (WSU), p. 11; *Daily Worker* (February 14, 1933).

28. "Developing Shop Work in Detroit," *Party Organizer* (July 1933), 10–14; "Building Party During Strikes," *Party Organizer* (August-September 1933), 37–40.

29. "Greater Tempo Needed in Party Recruiting," *Party Organizer* (May-June 1933) 7; "Comparative Results of Recruiting in First Nine Months of 1932 and 1933," *Party Organizer* (October 1933), 16–17; "Developing Shop Work in Detroit," *Party Organizer* (July 1933), 10–14.

30. "Re the Strikes in Detroit Auto Industry—the Status of Auto Workers Union in" in Joe Brown Papers (WSU).

## V.   TOWARD AN INTERNATIONAL
## INDUSTRIAL UNION OF AUTO WORKERS (I)

1. A. J. Muste, *The Automobile Industry and Organized Labor* (Baltimore, Maryland: Christian Social Justice Fund Inc., 1936), p. 29; *United States Statutes at Large 1888–1937* quoted by Irving Bernstein, *The New Deal Collective Bargaining Policy* (Berkeley and Los Angeles: University of California Press, 1950), p. 37.

2. *Daily Worker* (June 27, 1933); *Michigan Worker* quoted by Sidney Fine, *The Automobile Under the Blue Eagle* (Ann Arbor: University of Michigan Press, 1963), p. 40.

3. Earl Browder, "Why an Open Letter to Our Party Membership?" *Communist* (August 1933), 710, 713, 716.

4. Fine, p. 40.

5. Fine, pp. 44–74; Phil Raymond, "The Auto Code—The Infamous 'Merit' Clause," *Labor Unity* (November 1933), 21–22.

6. Bruce Minton and John Stuart, *Men Who Lead Labor* (New York: Modern Age Books, 1937), pp. 3–29; Saul Alinsky, *John L. Lewis: An Unauthorized Biography* (New York: Putnam's, 1949), p. 67; Benjamin Stolberg, *The Story of the CIO* (New York: Viking Press, 1938), pp. 10–11.

7. Edward Levinson, *Labor On the March* (New York and London:

Harper, 1938), p. 60; Stolberg, p. 158; Fine, pp. 60, 142–143, 150; *Daily Worker* (June 22, 1933).

8. Fine, pp. 187–188; *Daily Worker* (September 20 and October 11, 1933).

9. Fine, pp. 85–95; Carl Mydans, "Why Ford Workers Strike," *Nation* (October 25, 1933), 482–483; *New York Times* (September 28, 30, 1933); *Daily Worker* (September 28, 29, 30; October 3, 5, 6, 9, 10, 11, 16; December 23, 1933); *Auto Workers News* (January 13, 1934).

10. Fine, pp. 208–209; *Daily Worker* (November 8, 13, 17, 23, 1933); *Auto Workers News* (February 25, 1934); "The Nash Strike in Kenosha, WI." *Party Organizer* (January 1934), 21–25.

11. Fine, pp. 194–202; *Daily Worker* (November 20, 1933).

12. Fine, pp. 142–163; Irving Bernstein, *Turbulent Years: A History of the American Worker, 1933–1941* (Boston: Houghton Mifflin, 1971), pp. 95–96.

13. Harry Dahlheimer, *A History of the Mechanics Educational Society of America from Its Inception in 1933 Through 1937* (Detroit: Wayne University Press, 1951), pp. 1–4, 47; Fine, pp. 42, 173.

14. Dahlheimer, pp. 4–13; Fine, pp. 163–171; *New York Times* (September 19, 29, October 31, 1933); *Daily Worker* (September 25, 26, 28, 29, October 2, 11, 14, 16, 18, 28, 31, November 3, 6, 7, 1933).

15. McCracken quoted by Fine, p. 175; Joe Brown, "The MESA: Tool and Die Makers Organize and Strike" (unpublished manuscript, 1937) in Joe Brown Papers (WSU); *Daily Worker* (September 25, October 14, 1933); "Mass Meeting," "Call for Action," "Chevrolet Production Workers" (AWU leaflets) in Joe Brown Papers; Fine, p. 168.

16. Interview of John Anderson, Tampa, June 18, 1974; Dahlheimer, pp. 18–37; *Daily Worker* (April 21, 27, May 5, 8, 17, 1934).

17. *Daily Worker* (September 28, 29, October 11, 1933); Brown, "The MESA . . ."; "Statement of Communist Party on Tool and Diemakers Strike" in Joe Brown Papers.

18. Fine, pp. 166–167; Brown, "The MESA . . ."; *Daily Worker* (October 14, 16, 18, 1933).

19. Fine, pp. 170–171; Dahlheimer, pp. 4–13; Brown, "The MESA . . ."; "Statement of Communist Party on Tool and Diemakers Strike."

20. Joe Brown, untitled manuscript on the situation in the auto industry, *ca.* 1933 and Brown, "The MESA . . ." in Joe Brown Papers.

21. John Schmies, "The Open Letter and Our Tasks in the Detroit District," *Communist* (October 1933), 990; AWU Membership 1934 in Henry Kraus Papers (WSU); "Directives on Work Within the A. F. of L. and Independent Trade Unions," *Communist* (Janauary 1934), 113–115.

22. "Directives on Work Within the A. F. of L. and Independent Trade Unions," *Communist* (January 1934), 113–115.

23. Fine, pp. 213–218.

24. *Auto Workers News* (March 10, 24, 1934); "Wed., 9 a.m. is the Time. Strike!" (AWU leaflet) in Joe Brown Papers.

25. Fine, pp. 218–225; Levinson, p. 62.

26. *Daily Worker* (March 26, 27, 1934); *Auto Workers News* (April 7, 1934); "Reject the Sell-out" and "The Truth About the Washington Agreement" (AWU leaflets to Dodge, Chevrolet, Briggs Highland Park, Graham Paige and Hudson workers, March 1934) in Joe Brown Papers; *Red Motor* (June 1934) and *Sparkplug* (May 1934) in Henry Kraus Papers; *Ternstedt Worker* (ca. April 1934) in Joe Brown Papers.

27. Mathew Smith, "Militant Labor in Detroit," *Nation* (May 16, 1934), 560–562; Maurice Sugar to Frank Martel (March 27, 1934) in Wayne County AFL-CIO Papers (WSU); Oral History Interview of Leonard Woodcock (WSU), p. 6; Interview of Henry and Dorothy Kraus, Paris, June 19, 1972.

28. Fine, pp. 205–206, 220, 239–244, 259–283.

29. Fine, pp. 242–243; *Daily Worker* (April 6, 1934); *Ternstedt Worker* (ca. April 1934) in Joe Brown Papers.

30. Fine, pp. 274–277.

31. Fine, p. 276; Oral History of A. J. Muste (Columbia); Daniel Bell, *Marxian Socialism in the United States* (Princeton, N.J.: Princeton University Press, 1967), pp. 173–174; John Williamson, *Dangerous Scot: The Life and Work of an American 'Undesirable'* (New York: International Publishers, 1969), p. 104; *Daily Worker* (June 18, 1934).

32. Williamson, pp. 104–105; John Burns, "The Lessons of the Auto-Parts Strike in Toledo," *Party Organizer* (July 1934), 8–15.

33. Fine, pp. 275–278; Burns, 8–9; Pollock quoted by Art Preis, *Labor's Giant Step* (New York: Pioneer Publishers, 1964), pp. 21–22; Howard quoted by Bernstein, *Turbulent Years*, p. 221.

34. Fine, pp. 277–279; A. J. Muste, "The Battle of Toledo," *Nation* (June 6, 1934), 639–640; Louis F. Budenz, "Strikes Under the New Deal," in Alfred M. Bingham and Selden Rodman, ed., *Challenge to the New Deal* (New York: Falcon, 1934), pp. 102–103; *Daily Worker* (May 24, 25, 26, 1934); Burns, 10–15.

35. Fine, pp. 279–280; *Daily Worker* (May 28, 1934); Williamson, *Dangerous Scot*, p. 105.

36. Fine, pp. 280–283; William Green to Otto Brach (May 28, 1934) in AFL Papers (State Historical Society of Wisconsin); Bernstein, *Turbulent Years*, pp. 226–229; Otto Brach to William Green (June 5, 1934) in AFL Papers; *Daily Worker* (June 6, 1934).

37. Wyndham Mortimer, *Organize! My Life as a Union Man* (Boston: Beacon Press, 1971), pp. 1–53; Williamson, *Dangerous Scot*, p. 101.

38. Mortimer, pp. 54–61; *Daily Worker* (August 7, November 14, 1933).

39. Mortimer, pp. 61–63; John Nagy, "The Hungarian Language Movement Is Turning Toward the Shops," *Party Organizer* (May 1935), 11–14; *Red Motor* (June 1934-March 1935) in Henry Kraus Papers.

40. Mortimer, pp. 61–68; Williamson, *Dangerous Scot*, p. 101; Fine, pp. 211–212; *Auto Workers News* (March 10, 1934); George Lehman to William Green (February 27, 1934) and William Green to George Lehman (February 27, 1934) in AFL Papers.

41. "Organizational Status of the Party," (1934) in Earl Browder Papers (Syracuse University).

42. Marjorie R. Clark, "The AFL and Organization in the Automobile Industry," in *Essays in Honor of Jessica Blanch Peirotte* (Berkeley: University of California Press, 1935), p. 79.

43. Fine, p. 176; Oral History Interview of Leon Pody (WSU), pp. 17–22; Oral History Interview of John W. Anderson (WSU), pp. 21–23; Interview of Frank Cedervall, Madison, November 1, 1971.

44. David A. Shannon, *The Socialist Party of America: A History* (Chicago: Quadrangle, 1967), pp. 185, 216, 236–241; "Report of the State Secretary [of the SP]" (June 5, 6, 1937) in Lawrence and Dorothy Van

Camp Papers (WSU); untitled manuscript on the situation in the auto industry [ca. 1933] in Joe Brown Papers.

## VI. TOWARD AN INTERNATIONAL INDUSTRIAL UNION OF AUTO WORKERS (II)

1. Sidney Fine, *The Automobile Under the Blue Eagle* (Ann Arbor: University of Michigan Press, 1963), pp. 293–296; *Auto Workers News* (February 1934).

2. Fine, pp. 296–297; *Detroit News* (June 24, 1934); *New York Times* (June 24, 1934); *Auto Workers News* (July 21, 1934); "First National Conference of United Automobile Workers Federal Labor Unions Held in Detroit, Mich. June 23 and 24, 1934" [Minutes], in AFL Papers (SHSW).

3. "An Open Letter to the Delegates of the National Conference of Federal Auto Locals of the A.F. of L." [June 23, 1934], in Joe Brown Papers (WSU).

4. Fine, pp. 296–297; *Daily Worker* (June 28, 1934); Kushley's background in *Detroit Saturday Night* (April 24, 1937).

5. "First National Conference of United Automobile Workers Federal Labor Unions Held in Detroit, Mich. June 23 and 24, 1934" [Minutes]; Fine, p. 298; *Daily Worker* (June 25, 28, 30, 1934).

6. "First National Conference of United Automobile Workers Federal Labor Union Held in Detroit, Mich. June 23 and 24, 1934" (Minutes); *Daily Worker* (June 26, 1934); Fine, p. 299; Wyndham Mortimer, *Organize! My Life As A Union Man* (Boston: Beacon Press, 1971), pp. 69–71.

7. Charles K. Beckman Oral History Interview (WSU); Mortimer, pp. 76–78; Interview with Henry and Dorothy Kraus, Paris, June 19, 1972; John Williamson, *Dangerous Scot: The Life and Work of an American 'Undesirable'* (New York: International Publishers, 1969), p. 101; Minutes of Cleveland Rank and File Meetings, July 10, 1934-January 1935 in Henry Kraus Papers (WSU). The only existent copies of the *United Auto Worker* are in the possession of the Library of Congress, which was unable to locate the collection during the course of my research.

8. "Cleveland Conference for an International Union of All Automobile and Auto Parts Workers in the American Federation of Labor" (August 18, 1934) in Henry Kraus Papers; Mortimer, p. 77; *Daily Worker* (August 22, 1934); "Statement and Call of the Rank and File Conference of Federal Auto Locals on the Movement for an International Industrial Union" (August 1934), in Henry Kraus Papers.

9. *Daily Worker* (August 20, 1934); Green to the Officers and Members of the AFL (September 11, 1934), in Wayne County AFL-CIO Collection (WSU); National Council quoted by Jack Skeels, "The Background of UAW Factionalism," *Labor History* (Spring 1961), 164.

10. *Auto Workers News* (October 1934); *Daily Worker* (September 18, October 16, 1934); Bud Simons Oral History Interview (WSU), pp. 13–14; Mortimer, pp. 77–79; Williamson, p. 101; Fine, pp. 303–304.

11. Collins quoted by Fine, p. 304; American Federation of Labor, *Proceedings of the 54th Annual Convention* (Washington, D.C., 1934), pp. 214–215, 586–587, 593; Rose Pesotta, *Bread Upon the Waters* (New York: Dodd, Mead, 1945), p. 228; Dillon quoted by Skeels, 162; Fine, pp. 300, 318.

12. "Minutes of Flint, Michigan Conference of United Auto and Parts

Workers Federal Labor Union—November 10th—1934," and "Resolution" [adopted by the Flint Conference, November 10, 1934] in Henry Kraus Papers; *Daily Worker* (November 15, 1934).

13. *Auto Workers News* (July 21, 1934); Samuel Romer, "The Place of Labor in the Auto Industry," *Nation* (April 4, 1934), 379–380; Fine, p. 181; Nathan Glazer, *The Social Basis of American Communism* (New York: Harcourt, Brace & World, 1961), p. 115; William Z. Foster, *History of the Communist Party of the United States* (New York: International Publishers, 1952), pp. 303–304, 320–321.

14. *Machinists Monthly* (November 1934), 523; "Motion of Vice President Lewis" [to AFL Executive Council, January 1935], in John L. Lewis Papers (United Mine Workers Headquarters); T.N. Taylor to F.J. Dillon (December 8, 1934), in William Chalmers Papers (WSU); "Call to Conference on January 26, 1935 . . .", in AFL Papers; Paul Smith to William Green (January 9, 1935), in AFL Papers.

15. *Daily Worker* (January 9, 1935); McKinnon quoted by Mortimer, pp. 82–83 and *Daily Worker* (January 9, 1935).

16. "Minutes of Detroit Conference" (January 26, 1935) in Henry Kraus Papers; *Daily Worker* (January 28, 30, 1935); Fine, pp. 404–405; Mortimer, p. 79.

17. Mortimer, p. 64; Fine, pp. 385–386, 339–340, 407; Marjorie Clark, "The AFL and Organization in the Automobile Industry," in *Essays in Honor of Jessica Blanch Pierotto* (Berkeley: University of California Press, 1935), pp. 85–86, 91–92, 100; United Automobile Workers of America, *Proceedings of the First Constitutional Convention* (Detroit, 1935), p. 29; J. Raymond Walsh, *C.I.O.–Industrial Unionism in Action* (New York: W.W. Norton, 1937), pp. 103–111; Irwin Klibaner, "The Origins of the United Automobile Workers" (Masters thesis, University of Wisconsin, 1969), pp. 128–129; summary of Henderson report by Clark, pp. 97–99.

18. *Daily Worker* (February 2, 25, 1935); Skeels, 164; Fine, pp. 382–384; "Build Your Union" (Communist Party leaflet, February 1935), in Joe Brown Papers.

19. Clark, p. 96; Fine, pp. 387–393; Green quoted by Fine, p. 385.

20. Fine, pp. 395–400; Resolution of Federal Labor Union 18384 (May 24, 1935), in AFL Papers.

21. James Wilson to William Green (May 13, 1935), Francis Dillon to William Green (June 11, 1935), and William Green to William F. Siefke (June 19, 1935) in AFL Papers; "Automobile" (results of survey by Green of auto federal labor unions, July 12, 1935) in AFL Papers; Fine, p. 405; *Daily Worker* (March 1, 5, 12, 1935).

22. "Minutes of the National Conference of the Progressives in the United Automobile Workers' Union Affiliated to the American Federaion of Labor, Held in Cleveland, June 29th and 30th, 1935," in Henry Kraus Papers.

23. Roy S. Barkdall to William Green (August 16, 1935), R. Lee Guard to Francis Dillon and Paul Smith (August 19, 1935), Francis Dillon to R. Lee Guard (August 20, 1935) in AFL Papers; Phillip Bonosky, *Brother Bill McKie: Building the Union at Ford* (New York: International Publishers, 1953), p. 118; John North had been the leader of the AWU at Hayes in Grand Rapids, *Auto Workers News* (August 18, 1934); the names of the Communists, Communist sympathizers and Progressives appear in

the *Proceedings of the First Constitutional Convention* except for Henry Kraus who appears in the official portrait and William Weinstone mentioned by the *Daily Worker* (August 31, 1935); *Detroit News* (August 26, 1935).

24. "Statement of the Progressive Delegates to the Convention of the United Automobile Workers Union" (August 28, 1935) in Henry Kraus Papers.

25. *Proceedings of the First Constitutional Convention*, pp. 11–19; *Daily Worker* (August 27, 1935).

26. *Proceedings of the First Constitutional Convention*, pp. 27–31.

27. *Proceedings of the First Constitutional Convention*, pp. 35–44; Skeels, 166; Mortimer, pp. 84–87; *Daily Worker* (August 28, 1935); *Detroit News* (August 27, 28, 1935); *New York Times* (August 28, 1935).

28. *Proceedings of the First Constitutional Convention*, pp. 60–67; *Daily Worker* (August 30, 31, September 2, 1935); *Detroit News* (August 29, 30, 1935); Mortimer, pp. 84–87; James O. Morris, *Conflict Within the AFL: A Study of Craft Versus Industrial Unionism, 1901–1938* (Ithaca: Cornell University Press, 1958), pp. 202–203.

29. *Proceedings of the First Constitutional Convention*, pp. 68–71; *Daily Worker* (August 31, 1935); Mortimer, pp. 86–87.

30. Mortimer, pp. 88–89; *Daily Worker* (September 2, October 7, 1935).

31. Cyrus L. Sulzberger, *Sitdown with John L. Lewis* (New York: Random House, 1938), pp. 49, 52–53; Saul Alinsky, *John L. Lewis: An Unauthorized Biography* (New York: Putnam's, 1949), pp. 49–51, 62–78; Len DeCaux, *Labor Radical: From the Wobblies to CIO: A Personal History* (Boston: Beacon Press, 1970), pp. 207–209; Mortimer, pp. 91–92.

32. American Federation of Labor, *Report of Proceedings of the Fifty-Fifth Annual Convention* (Washington, D.C., 1935); pp. 523–524, 534–542.

33. American Federation of Labor, *Report of Proceedings of the Fifty-Fifth Annual Convention*, pp. 726–729; Alinsky, pp. 75–77; Mortimer, pp. 91–93, and DeCaux, pp. 210–217, describe Lewis's actions at the convention approvingly.

34. Alinsky, pp. 80–81; Walter Galenson, *The CIO Challenge to the AFL: A History of the American Labor Movement, 1935–1941* (Cambridge: Harvard University Press, 1960), pp. 1–6; press release by Committee for Industrial Organization (November 10, 1935), in Henry Kraus Papers; John L. Lewis to William Green (November 23, 1935), in AFL Papers; John Brophy, *A Miner's Life* (Madison: University of Wisconsin Press, 1964), pp. 250–255; Edward Levinson, *Labor on the March* (New York: Harper, 1938), pp. 104–120.

35. Alinsky, pp. 79–80, 115; DeCaux, pp. 219–220; DeCaux recalls that when he was hired by John Brophy as Publicity Director of the CIO, that DeCaux "told him frankly that I had close sympathies with the Communists, had many friends among them, and associated myself with them in a number of ways, though not organizationally," DeCaux, p. 220; Brophy, pp. 258–260; Earl Browder, "The American Communist Party in the Thirties," in Rita Simon, ed., *As We Saw The Thirties* (Urbana: University of Illinois Press, 1967), p. 231.

36. Bernard Karsh and Phillip L. Garman, "The Impact of the Political Left," in Milton Derber and Edwin Young, eds., *Labor and the New*

*Deal* (Madison: University of Wisconsin Press, 1957), p. 104; Sulzberger, p. 54; Bruce Minton [Richard Bransten] and John Stuart, *Men Who Lead Labor* (New York: Modern Age Books, 1937), p. 108; Max Kampelman, *The Communist Party vs. the C.I.O.: A Study in Power Politics* (New York: F.A. Praeger, 1957), p. 16.

37. Fine, pp. 422–423; *Daily Worker* (November 22, 1935); "Summary of the Motor Products Strike," in Henry Kraus Papers; Dillon quoted in "Summary of the Motor Products Strike"; letter of Automotive Workers Fraction (November 23, 1935), in Henry Kraus Papers; leaflet of the Progressive Auto Workers Club entitled "The Motor Products Strike Situation" (December 1935), in Henry Kraus Papers; Skeels, 167–170.

38. Mortimer, pp. 96–97; Hall quoted by Mortimer, p. 97

39. Fine, p. 89; Skeels, 170–171; *Daily Worker* (March 22, 1936, April 28, 1936).

40. United Automobile Workers Union, *Proceedings of the Second Convention of the International Union* (South Bend, 1936), pp. 6–9, 10–24, 26–29; George Blackwood, "The United Automobile Workers of America, 1935–1951" (Ph.D. dissertation, University of Chicago, 1951), pp. 50–52; Fine, pp. 425–426; Oral History Interview of Carl Haessler (WSU), p. 4; Oral History Interview of Roy Speth (WSU), pp. 13–15.

41. United Automobile Workers Union, *Proceedings of the Second Convention* (South Bend, 1936), pp. 71–77; Fine, p. 426; Blackwood, p. 52.

42. United Automobile Workers Union, *Proceedings of the Second Convention* (South Bend, 1936), pp. 96–97, 159, 161–162, 190, 203, 253–255; Harry Dahlheimer, *A History of the Mechanics Educational Society in Detroit from Its Inception in 1933 through 1937* (Detroit: Wayne State University Press, 1951), pp. 36–37; Earl Browder, *What Is Communism?* (New York: Vanguard Press, 1936), pp. 112–127; Joe Brown to Edward Wieck (May 19, 1936), in Edward Weick Papers (WSU).

43. An "independent observer" quoted by Blackwood, p. 52.

44. Georgi Dimitroff, *The United Front: The Struggle Against Fascism and War* (New York: International Publishers, 1938), pp. 9–93; Institute of Marxism-Leninism, Central Committee of the C.P.S.U., *Outline History of the Communist International* (Moscow: Progress Publishers, 1971), pp. 371–387; "Report of the Central Committee to the Ninth National Convention of the Communist Party, U.S.A., June 24, 1936," in Earl Browder, *The People's Front* (New York: International Publishers, 1938), pp. 22–42.

45. Oral History of Carl Haessler (WSU), pp. 4–5; Interview of Carl Haessler, Detroit, July 25 and August 1, 1975; United Automobile Workers Union, *Proceedings of the Second Convention* (South Bend, 1936), pp. 124–135, 232; Oral History of Nat Ganley (WSU), p. 17; Blackwood, p. 53.

46. United Automobile Workers Union, *Proceedings of the Second Convention* (South Bend, 1936), pp. 162, 253–255, 265; Blackwood, p. 54; Germer quoted by Galenson, p. 131; Irving Howe and B.J. Widick, *The UAW and Walter Reuther* (New York: Random House, 1949), p. 53.


VII.  THE SIT-DOWN STRIKES

1. United Automobile Workers of America, *Proceedings of the Second Annual Convention* (South Bend, 1936), p. 161; *Detroit News* (May 2, 1936); *Daily Worker* (May 2, 1936); William Z. Foster, *Industrial*

*Unionism* (1936) reprinted in a shortened form in William Z. Foster, *American Trade Unionism: Principles and Organization, Strategy and Tactics, Selected Writings* (New York: International Publishers, 1970), p. 210.

2. Homer Martin: Bruce Minton [Richard Bransten] and John Stuart, *Men Who Lead Labor* (New York: Modern Age Books, 1937), pp. 216–217; John Brophy, *A Miner's Life* (Madison: University of Wisconsin Press, 1964), pp. 268–269; J. Raymond Walsh, *C.I.O.–Industrial Unionism in Action* (New York: W. W. Norton, 1937); Len DeCaux, *Labor Radical: From the Wobblies to CIO: A Personal History* (Boston: Beacon Press, 1970), pp. 250–252; Oral History Interview of Frank Marquart (WSU), p. 30; Interview of Carl Haessler, Detroit, July 25, 1971; Oral History Interview of Lee Pressman (Columbia), pp. 56, 336; Brophy quoted in Joe Brown to Edward Wieck (January 24, [1938]) in Edward Wieck Papers (WSU). For a more favorable view of Martin than the above sources supply, see Benjamin Stolberg, *The Story of the CIO* (New York: Viking Press, 1938), *passim*. Wyndham Mortimer: Wyndham Mortimer, *Organize! My Life as a Union Man* (Boston: Beacon Paperback, 1972), *passim*; Henry Kraus, *The Many and the Few: A Chronicle of the Dynamic Auto Workers* (Los Angeles: Plantin Press, 1947), pp. 19–20; DeCaux, p. 254; Oral History Interview of Lee Pressman (Columbia), p. 56; Interview of Carl Haessler, August 1, 1971; Interview of Henry and Dorothy Kraus, Paris, June 19, 1972; Sidney Fine, *Sit-down: The General Motors Strike of 1936–1937* (Ann Arbor: University of Michigan Press, 1969), pp. 78–79; John P. Frey testimony before the Dies Committee in U.S., Congress, House, Special Committee on Un-American Activities. *Investigation of Un-American Propaganda Activities in the United States, Hearings Pursuant to H. Res. 282,* 75th Cong., 3rd sess., 1938, I, p. 103.

3. Mortimer, pp. 103–104.

4. Fine, *Sit-down*, pp. 106–108; Bob Travis to Adolph Germer (October 28, 1936) in Henry Kraus Papers (WSU); Irving Bernstein, *Turbulent Years: A History of the American Worker, 1933–1941* (Boston: Houghton Mifflin, 1971), p. 516. Jerold S. Auerbach, *Labor and Liberty: The La Follette Committee and the New Deal* (Indianapolis and New York: Bobbs-Merrill, 1966), pp. 112–113.

5. Kraus, p. 25; Bernstein, p. 520; Mortimer, p. 104.

6. Kraus, pp. 16–18; Bernstein, pp. 518, 521–522; Fine, *Sit-down*, p. 109; Oral History Interview of Bud Simons (WSU), p. 19; Mortimer, pp. 105–106; Wyndham Mortimer to the International Executive Officers (September 27, 1936), in Homer Martin Papers (WSU); Michael S. Clinasmith, "The Black Legion: Hooded Americanism in Michigan," *Michigan History* (Fall 1971), 243–262.

7. Kraus, pp. 16–17; Mortimer, pp. 110, 113, 118, 127; Interview of William Weinstone, New York, November 27, 1971; Interview of Henry and Dorothy Kraus, June 19, 1972; A. Allen, "Party Building in Auto," *Party Organizer* (June 1937), 10–15; Oral History Interview of Bob Travis (University of Michigan—Flint); Oral History Interview of Bud and Hazel Simons (University of Michigan—Flint); Oral History Interview of Mr. and Mrs. Michael Evanoff (University of Michigan—Flint).

8. Mortimer, pp. 105, 107; Kraus, pp. 17, 20; Mortimer's open letters to Flint auto workers, July 10, 17, 24, 31; August 12; September 29; October 6, 15; November 3, 10, 1936, in Henry Kraus Papers.

9. Kraus, 18–19, 39; Mortimer, pp. 110–111; Fine, *Sit-down*, p. 110

10. Kraus, pp. 27-30, 71; Bernstein, p. 522; Fine, *Sit-down*, p. 93; Mortimer, pp. 114, 116-118; Homer Martin to Wyndham Mortimer (March 24, 1936), in Homer Martin Papers.

11. Minton and Stuart, p. 218; Kraus, pp. 31-32; Mortimer, pp. 116-117; Fine, *Sit-down*, pp. 91-92; Oral History of Lee Pressman (Columbia), pp. 55-56; Interview of William Weinstone, November 27, 1971; *Detroit News* (August 9, 1954); Oral History Interview of Carl Haessler (WSU), pp. 14-15.

12. William Z. Foster, "Strike Movement in Mass Production Industries: Methods of Organization Vital to Winning Strike," *Daily Worker* (January 5, 1937); Bob Travis to Adolph Germer (October 28, 1936), Travis to Fred Peiper (October 19, 1936), Travis to Kenneth Cole (October 21, 1936), Travis to Wyndham Mortimer (October 22, 1936), in Henry Kraus Papers; Kraus, p. 39; Fine, *Sit-down*, pp. 113-114.

13. Fine, *Sit-down*, pp. 114-115, 222; Kraus, pp. 62-69; Saul Alinsky, *John L. Lewis: An Unauthorized Biography* (New York: Putnam's, 1949), p. 109. For LaFollette Committee activites later in the strike, see DeCaux, p. 267; *Daily Worker* (January 8, 11, 1937); Auerbach, pp. 167-169.

14. Kraus, pp. 38, 41-55; Fine, *Sit-down*, pp. 116-117; Mortimer, p. 118; Oral History Interview of Bud Simons (WSU), pp. 20-22; Adolph Germer to John L. Lewis (November 20, 1936), George Addes to Adolph Germer (December 19, 1936), in Adolph Germer Papers (SHSW).

15. Fine, *Sit-down*, pp. 122-129; Henry W. Ehrmann, *French Labor From Popular Front to Liberation* (New York: Oxford University Press, 1947), pp. 38-42; Maurice Neufeld, *Italy: School for Awakening Countries* (Ithaca, N.Y.: New York State School of Industrial and Labor Relations, 1961), pp. 377-379; Oral History Interview of Rudy Miller (University of Michigan—Flint); Oral History Interview of Bud and Hazel Simons (University of Michigan—Flint).

16. International Union, United Automobile Workers of America, "Executive Board Minutes, November 20-December 5, 1936" in Henry Kraus Papers; Fine, *Sit-down*, pp. 129-130; *Midland Flash*, in Adolph Germer Papers; *Strike Edition of Midland Flash* (December 1936), in Henry Kraus Papers; Clyde Morrow testimony in *Investigation of Un-American Propaganda Activities*, II. p. 1493; "Midland Steel Stay-in Effects Chrysler Shutdown," press release (December 2, 1936), in Henry Kraus Papers; Oral History of Nat Ganley (WSU), pp. 1-10; John P. Frey testimony in *Investigation of Un-American Propaganda Activities*, I. p. 125; Mortimer, pp. 120-122; *Daily Worker* (December 23, 1936); *Strike Edition of the Midland Flash* (December 1936), "Midland Steel Strikers Learn the Truth" (leaflet), "An Old Trick that Won't Work" (leaflet), in Henry Kraus Papers; Interview of Henry and Dorothy Kraus, June 19, 1972.

17. Fine, *Sit-down*, pp. 131, 208, 97, 131-133, 207; Bernstein, pp. 558-559; Merlin D. Bishop, "The Kelsey Hayes Sit-in Strike" (1936), in Oral History of Merlin D. Bishop (WSU); *Daily Worker* (December 15, 1936); Ralph Knox testimony in *Investigation of Un-American Propaganda Activities*, II, p. 1532; Richard Eager testimony in *Investigation of Un-American Propaganda Activities*, III, pp. 2325-2333; Oral History of Nat Ganley (WSU), p. 19; Phillip Bonosky, *Brother Bill McKie: Building the Union at Ford* (New York: International Publishers, 1953), pp. 135-140, 146; transcript of an interview with Bill McKie in Nat Ganley Papers

(wsu); Murray Kempton, *Part of Our Time: Some Ruins and Monuments of the Thirties* (New York: Simon and Schuster, 1955), pp. 261–298. For a copy of the Reuther letter and the story of the controversy surrounding it, see Ralph de Toledano, "The Walter Reuther Story," *American Mercury* (May 1953), 5–7; an official of the Communist Party who asked to remain anonymous was one source of information on Reuther's brief flirtation with the Communist Party; another source was Carl Haessler, a close advisor of Reuther in the later 30s and editor of the *West Side Conveyor*, the paper of Reuther's Local 174, Interview of Carl Haessler, July 25, 1971; additional evidence of Reuther's membership in the CP in Martin Glaberman, "A Note on Walter Reuther," *Radical America* (November-December 1973), 113–117.

18. William Z. Foster, "Strike Movement in Mass Production Industries: Methods of Organization Vital to Winning Strikes," *Daily Worker* (January 9, 1937); Bernstein, pp. 522–523; Mortimer, p. 124.

19. Bernstein, pp. 522–523; Fine, *Sit-down*, pp. 134–136; Mortimer, pp. 120–121; Kraus, pp. 70–73.

20. Fine, *Sit-down*, pp. 141–143; Kraus, pp. 82–85; Bernstein, pp. 524–525; Mortimer, pp. 124–126; *Daily Worker* (December 31, 1937); Oral History of Charles Beckman (wsu), pp. 6–8, 21; Frank Winn to Wyndham Mortimer (December 25, 1936), John Soltis to Wyndham Mortimer (December 28, 1936), in Henry Kraus Papers; Haessler describes Miley as a leftist in interview of Carl Haessler, July 25, 1971; Clayton Fountain, *Union Guy* (New York: 1949) describes Beckman as a CP-liner; John Williamson, *Dangerous Scot: The Life and Work of an American "Undesirable"* (New York: International Publishers, 1969), pp. 106–107; Oral History Interview of Rudy Miller (Univeristy of Michigan—Flint).

21. Interview of William Weinstone, November 27, 1971.

22. Kraus, pp. 86–89; Fine, *Sit-down*, pp. 144–146; Bernstein, pp. 524–526, 828; *Daily Worker* (December 31, 1936); Mortimer, pp. 126–127; Oral History of Clayton Johnson (wsu), pp. 3–4; Oral History Interview of Bud Simons (wsu), pp. 23–25, 28–30.

23. William Z. Foster, "Strike Movement in Mass Production Industries: Toward a Peoples Front—Historic Tasks Are Facing Progressive Labor Leaders," *Daily Worker* (January 14, 1937).

24. "The Work of the Party During Strike Struggles," *Party Organizer* (February 1937), 2–3; Interview of Carl Haessler, July 25, 1971 and August 1, 1971; Williamson, p. 108; "Auto Strike Section," *Daily Worker* (January 16, 20, 27, February 3, 1937); T.G. "How an Auto Shop Unit Functions," *Party Organizer* (August 1937), 12–14; John Williamson, "A General Motors Shop Branch: Before and After the Strike," *Party Organizer* (June 1937), 15–16; A. Allen, "Party Building in Auto," *Party Organizer* (June 1937), 10–11; Devitt quoted by Fine, pp. 171–172; Fisher No. 1 strike committee minutes quoted by Kraus, p. 92.

25. William Z. Foster, "Strike Movement in Mass Production Industries: Methods of Organization Vital to Winning Strike," *Daily Worker* (January 11, 1937); Alinsky, p. 113, 117; Kraus, p. 121; Fine, *Sit-down*, pp. 190–191, 226, 229, 263, 284, 334; John M. Barringer testimony in *Investigation of Un-American Propaganda Activities*, II, p. 1687.

26. Interview of Carl Haessler, August 1, 1971; Interview of William Weinstone, November 27, 1971; "The Work of the Party During Strike Struggles," 3; Allen, 10–11; Reuther quoted by Fine, *Sit-down*, p. 222.

27. William Weinstone, "The Great Auto Strike," *Communist* (March

1937), 221; Statement of the Central Committee of the Communist Party, "The Great Battle for Unionism," *Daily Worker* (January 16, 1937); "Radio Broadcast . . . over station CKLW, Windsor . . . delivered by Wyndham Mortimer" (January 20, 1937) in Adolph Germer Papers; William Weinstone, "Militia—For Whom? Against Whom?" *Daily Worker* (January 16, 1937).

28. Allen, 10–13; strike committee quoted by Allen, 11; Simon quoted by Fine, p. 162; William Weinstone, "The Great Auto Strike," 225; Clyde Morrow report of a Weinstone speech to District 7 of CP in Detroit about March 10, 1937 in *Investigation of Un-American Propaganda Activities,* II, p. 1496; William Weinstone, "Some Things for the Auto Workers to Think About," *Daily Worker* (February 3, 1937); John Williamson, "A General Motors Shop Branch: Before and After the Strike," 15–16; W. W. Weinstone, "Recruiting Among Trade Unionists," *Party Organizer* (August 1937), 15–18.

29. Hy Fish to Ben Fischer (September 2, 1937) and Ben Fischer to Herbert Zam (September 13, 1938), in Daniel Bell Collection (Tamiment Library); Thomas quoted by Fine, p. 220; Norman Thomas, "Politics and Strike in Auto," *Socialist Call* (January 2, 1937); Frank N. Trager, "Auto Strikers Take Offensive," *Socialist Call* (February 6, 1937); Weinstone, "The Great Auto Strike," 227; James Oneal to Adolph Germer (February 10, 1937), in Adolph Germer Papers.

30. "Stay-in Strikes Challenge Capitalism," *Socialist Call* (January 2, 1937); Norman Thomas, "At the Front," *Socialist Call* (January 30, 1937); Krzycki speech reported in the *Socialist Call* (February 13, 1937); Thomas speech reported in the *Socialist Call* (February 20, 1937); William Z. Foster, *From Bryan to Stalin* (New York: International Publishers, 1937), pp. 305–306.

31. Daniel Bell, *Marxian Socialism in the United States* (Princeton, N.J.: Princeton University Press, 1967), Frank Trager, "The Battle for Industrial Unionism," *Socialist Call* (January 23, 1937); "What Means the Stay-In?" *Socialist Call* (January 23, 1937); Frank Trager, "Danger of Forced Auto Arbitration," *Socialist Call* (January 30, 1937); William Z. Foster, "Strike Movement in Mass Production Industries: Mine and Rail Unions Must Back Steel—Foster," *Daily Worker* (January 8, 1937); "G.M. Gangster Rule in Flint," *Daily Worker* (January 13, 1937); Statement of the Central Committee of the Communist Party, "The Great Battle For Unionism"; "Two Blows Aimed at Auto Strike," *Daily Worker* (January 9, 1937); for Communist approval and disapproval of various actions of Roosevelt and Murphy see *Daily Worker* (January 14, 15, 23, 27, 30, 1937).

32. William Z. Foster, *What Means the Strike in Steel?* (February 1937) reprinted in William Z. Foster, *American Trade Unionism,* p. 221; Fine, *Sit-down,* pp. 200–201, 221; Brophy, pp. 257–259, 267–273; Alinsky, pp. 105–147; Oral History Interview of Adolph Germer (WSU), pp. 25–30; Lorin L. Cary, "Adolph Germer: From Labor Agitator to Labor Professional" (Ph.D. dissertation, University of Wisconsin, 1968), pp. 107–112; Genora Johnson, "Women's Brigade Gives Aid to Auto Strikers" and Mary Hillyer, "Genora Johnson," *Socialist Call* (February 13, 1937); *Sunday Worker* (January 24, 1937); Weinstone, "The Great Auto Strike," 226.

33. Clyde Morrow testimony reporting on speech of Weinstone in *Investigation of Un-American Popaganda Activities,* II, p. 1496; Fine, *Sit-*

*down*, pp. 116, 221; Interview of William Weinstone, November 27, 1971; Interview of Henry and Dorothy Kraus, June 19, 1972; Kraus, pp. 32–39; William H. Lawrence, "There's Music Inside—and Plenty of Discipline," *Daily Worker* (January 11, 1937); Oral History Interview of Bud Simons (WSU), *passim;* Mortimer, pp. 127–128; Adolph Germer to John Brophy (October 25, 1937), in Adolph Germer Papers.

34. William Z. Foster, "Strike Movement in Mass Production Industries: Methods of Organization Vital to Winning Strike," *Daily Worker* (January 9, 1937); William Weinstone, "The Great Auto Strike," 225; John Williamson, "A General Motors Shop Branch: Before and After the Strike," 15–16; A. Allen, "Party Building in Auto," 10; Fine, *Sit-down*, pp. 156–177; Kraus, pp. 93–96; Robert Morss Lovett, "A G.M. Stockholder Visits Flint," *Nation* (January 30, 1937), 123; William H. Lawrence, "There's Music Inside and Plenty of Discipline"; Charles Walker, "Flint Faces Civil War," *Nation* (February 13, 1937), 175; Hy Fish, "A Date with the Striking Auto Workers in Fisher Body Plant No. 1," *Socialist Call* (February 13, 1937); *Daily Worker* (January 16, 1937).

35. Fine, *Sit-down*, pp. 169, 171–174; William Weinstone. "The Great Auto Strike," 225.

36. William Z. Foster, "Strike Movement in Mass Production Industries: Methods of Organization Vital to Winning Strike," *Daily Worker* (January 11, 1937); *Daily Worker* (January 20, 27, 1937).

37. Interview of Henry and Dorothy Kraus, June 19, 1972; newspaper clipping on Dorothy Kraus in Bud and Hazel Simons Papers (WSU); Fine, pp. 200–201; Rose Pesotta, *Bread Upon the Waters* (New York: Dodd, Mead, 1944), pp. 237–239; Kraus, pp. 93, 98.

38. William Z. Foster, "Strike Movements in Mass Production Industries: Methods of Organization Vital to Winning Strike"; *Daily Worker* (January 11, 16, 27, 1937).

39. DeCaux, pp. 8–10, 18, 26–27, 36–123, 250; Brophy, p. 258.

40. Oral History Interview of Carl Haessler (WSU), *passim;* Interview of Carl Haessler, July 25, August 1, 1971; DeCaux, pp. 123, 269; Carl Haessler, "The Auto Union Shifts into High," *New Masses* (January 19, 1937), 6–7 and "Behind the Auto Strike," *New Masses* (February 2, 1937), 3–5.

41. Oral History Interview of Lee Pressman (Columbia), *passim;* DeCaux, pp. 256, 262–263; Fine, *Sit-down*, p. 222; Brophy, p. 260; Bernard Karsh and Phillip L. Garman, "The Impact of the Political Left," in Milton Derber and Edwin Young, eds., *Labor and the New Deal* (Madison: University of Wisconsin Press, 1957), p. 109.

42. Oral History of R. J. Thomas (Columbia), Vol. 5, p. 1; Interview of Phil Raymond, Detroit, July 26, 1971; *Michigan Worker* (November 6, 1932); *Daily Worker* (July 24, 1936); Interview of Carl Haessler, July 25, 1971; Interview of William Weinstone, November 27, 1971; Fine, *Sit-down*, p. 222; Bernstein, p. 501.

43. Davidow quoted by Kraus, p. 112; William Z. Foster, "Strike Movement in Mass Production Industries: Strong Relief Apparatus— Mass Defense Activity Are Essential to Strikers"; *Daily Worker* (January 12, 1937); Kraus, pp. 112–114; Adolph Germer's Diary (1937) in Adolph Germer Papers; Bernstein, p. 528; Oral History Interview of Lee Pressman (Columbia), pp. 53–55, 58–60; Oral History Interview of Adolph Germer (WSU), p. 27; Fine, *Sit-down*, pp. 193–195; Alinsky, pp.

113–116; *Daily Worker* (January 5, 6, 7, 1937). Cyrus L. Sulzberger, *Sit Down with John L. Lewis* (New York: Random House, 1938), pp. 72–73.

44. Fine, *Sit-down*, pp. 165, 187–190; Kraus, pp. 114–116, 122–124, 173; Travis quoted by *Daily Worker* (January 26, 1937); Simon's order book quoted by Kraus, p. 150; Simons quoted by Fine, p. 296.

45. Fine, *Sit-down*, pp. 1–13; Kraus, pp. 125–145; Bernstein, pp. 529–530; Mortimer, pp. 129–130; Oral History of Victor Reuther (WSU), pp. 14–15; Oral History of Carl Haessler (WSU); *Daily Worker* (January 17, 1937); Testimony of Captain Edwin H. Hughes of Flint Police Department in *Investigation of Un-American Propaganda Activities*, II, *passim*.

46. Flint Alliance: Fine, *Sit-down*, pp. 187–190; Kraus, pp. 115–120; *Daily Worker* (January 8, 9, 16, 19, 1937); Abortive truce: Fine, *Sit-down*, pp. 248–254; Kraus, pp. 154–166; Alinsky, pp. 122–123; Brophy, pp. 269–270; Bernstein, pp. 533–534; *Daily Worker* (January 16, 18, 19, 1937).

47. Fine, *Sit-down*, pp. 254–260, 305; Kraus, pp. 173–178; *Daily Worker* (January 20, 1937).

48. Kraus, pp. 183–188; Fine, *Sit-down*, pp. 197–198, 210–215, 261–262; Bernstein, p. 525; *Daily Worker* (January 26, 27, 28, 29, 30, 1937); Claude E. Hoffman, *Sit-down in UAW Local 663, Anderson, Indiana* (Detroit: Wayne State University Press, 1968), pp. 47–67; Oral History of Victor Reuther (WSU), pp. 17–25.

49. Kraus, pp. 189–226; Fine, *Sit-down*, pp. 266–271, 398; Bernstein, pp. 537–540; Irving Howe and B. J. Widick, *The UAW and Walter Reuther* (New York: Random House, 1949), pp. 58–59; Pesotta, pp. 244–245; Brophy, p. 271; Kermit Johnson's account of the capture of Chevy 4 in *Searchlight*, paper of UAW Local 659 in Flint (February 11, 1959) reprinted in Art Preis, *Labor's Giant Step* (New York: Pioneer Publishers, 1964), pp. 57–60; Interview of Carl Haessler, July 25, 1971; William Weinstone, "The Great Auto Strike," 217; John Monarch, "How the Union Took Chevrolet Plant No. 4," *Socialist Call* (February 13, 1937); *Daily Worker* (February 2, 1937).

50. Fine, *Sit-down*, pp. 272–274, 301; Mortimer, pp. 138–139; Kraus, pp. 220–226; Alinsky, p. 137.

51. Fine, *Sit-down*, pp. 234–235, 239–240, 262–264; 274–276; Bernstein, p. 537; Mortimer, pp. 130–131; Maurice Sugar, "Is the Sit-Down Legal?" *New Masses* (May 6, 1937), 19–20; *Daily Worker* (February 2, 1937); Testimony of Paul V. Godola in *Investigation of Un-American Propaganda Activities*, II, pp. 1674–80; J. Woodford Howard, Jr., "Frank Murphy and the Sit-down Strikes of 1937," *Labor History* (Spring 1960), 103–140.

52. Kraus, pp. 231–232.

53. Kraus, p. 233; Sulzberger, pp. 77–79; Fine, *Sit-down*, pp. 278–279; Howe and Widick, pp. 60–61.

54. Kraus, pp. 233–237; Fine, *Sit-down*, pp. 279–281; photographs of demonstration on February 3 in Walter Lindner, *The Great Flint Sit-down Strike Against General Motors, 1936–1937* (Brooklyn: Progressive Labor Party Pamphlet, n.d.), p. 114, reprinted from an article in *Challenge* (February-March 1967), 90–123.

55. Fine, *Sit-down*, pp. 281–283, 292–293, 297, 301; Kraus, pp. 241–247; *Daily Worker* (February 5, 1937).

56. Fine, *Sit-down*, pp. 285–306; Bernstein, pp. 541–549; Kraus, pp.

263–285; Mortimer, pp. 131–141; DeCaux, pp. 249–253; Alinsky, pp. 133–139; Sulzberger, p. 81; Oral History of Lee Pressman (Columbia), pp. 59, 70, 73; Oral History of Ed Hall (wsu), p. 25.

57. Fine, *Sit-down*, pp. 311–312; Kraus, pp. 286–293; Mary Heaton Vorse, *Labor's New Millions* (New York: Modern Age Books, 1938), pp. 89–90; *United Automobile Worker* (February 25, 1937); Brophy, p. 272; Williamson, p. 109; Pesotta, pp. 251–255.

58. Fine, *Sit-down*, pp. 310–311; Weinstone, "The Great Auto Strike," 225; testimony of John P. Frey in *Investigation of Un-American Propaganda Activities*, I, pp. 255–256; DeCaux, p. 256; Alinsky, p. 125; Davidow and Mortimer quoted by Fine, p. 221.

59. Mortimer, pp. 145–146; Bernstein, p. 551; *Investigation of Un-American Propaganda Activities*, II, p. 1606; Walter Galenson, *The CIO Challenge to the AFL: A History of the American Labor Movement, 1935–1941* (Cambridge: Harvard University Press, 1960), p. 150; Melvyn Dubofsky and Warren Van Tine, *John L. Lewis: A Biography* (New York: Quadrangle, 1977), p. 271; Lamont quoted by Staughton Lynd, "The United Front in America: A Note," *Radical America* (July-August 1974), 32.

60. Max Gordon, "The Communist Party of the Nineteen-thirties and the New Left," *Socialist Revolution* (January-March 1976), 18–19; F, "We Must Bring the Party out in the Open," *Party Organizer* (April 1938), 6–8; Bill Allen, "The Work of a Detroit Section," *Party Organizer* (June 1938), 9–12; *Spotlight* (March 1937), Chrysler CP shop paper in Adolph Germer Papers; Nathan Glazer, *The Social Basis of American Communism* (New York: Harcourt, Brace & World, 1961), p. 115; W.W. Weinstone, "Recruiting Among Trade Unionists," *Party Organizer* (August 1937), 15–18; A. Allen, "Party Building in Auto," *Party Organizer* (June 1937), 14; *Investigation of Un-American Propaganda Activities*, I, II, III, *passim*; affidavit of Fred Durrance (February 24, 1939), in Homer Martin Papers.

## VIII. FACTIONALISM

1. Max Kampelman, *The Communist Party vs. The C.I.O.: A Study in Power Politics* (New York: Frederick A. Praeger, 1957), p. 73; David J. Saposs, *Communism in American Unions* (New York: McGraw-Hill Book Co., Inc.), p. 128. Irving Howe and B. J. Widick, *The UAW and Walter Reuther* (New York: Random House, 1949), pp. 72–81.

2. In their brief references to these events both Edward Levinson and James Prickett are near the mark when they describe Communist behavior as "self-effacing" and "self-effacing affability." Edward Levinson, *Labor on the March* (New York: Harper Brothers Publishers, 1938), p. 282; James R. Prickett, "Communism and Factionalism in the United Automobile Workers, 1939–1947," *Science and Society* (Summer 1968), 260.

3. U. S., Congress, House, Special Committee on Un-American Activities, *Investigation of Un-American Propaganda Activities in the United States, Hearings Pursuant to H.Res. 282*, 75th Cong., 3rd sess., 1938, I, II, III, *passim*; A. Allen, "Party Building in Auto," *Party Organizer* (June 1937), 14; affidavit of Fred Durrance (February 24, 1939), in Homer Martin Papers (wsu); Nathan Glazer, *The Social Basis of American Communism* (New York: Harcourt, Brace & World, 1961), p. 115; W.

W. Weinstone, "Recruiting Among Trade Unionists," *Party Organizer* (August 1937), 15–18; John Williamson, "Recruiting in Ohio," *Party Organizer* (August 1937), 38–41.

4. Earl Browder, *The People's Front* (New York: International Publishers, 1938), p. 67; Earl Browder, "The Communists in the People's Front," *Communist* (July 1937), 604–607; William Z. Foster, "Political Leadership and Party Building," *Communist* (July 1937), 645; Albert Maltz, *The Underground Stream* (Boston: Little, Brown, 1940), p. 111.

5. Irving Bernstein, *Turbulent Years: A History of the American Worker, 1933–1941* (Boston: Houghton Mifflin Co. Sentry Edition, 1971), pp. 508–509, 555–557; Jay Lovestone, "The People's Front in America," *Workers Age* (April 16, 1968); Jay Lovestone, "The Major Issue Facing Our National Convention," *Workers Age* (May 1, 1937); Interview of Bert Cochran, New York City, November 24, 1971 *New York Times* (November 28, 1937); Defense Briefs, parts I and II, on behalf of Wyndham Mortimer, *et al.* (July-August 1938) in Henry Kraus Papers (WSU); Interview of Lee Pressman in Daniel Bell Collection (Tamiment).

6. J. R. Walsh, *C.I.O.—Industrial Unionism in Action* (New York: W. W. Norton, 1937), pp. 126–129; Bernstein, pp. 551–554; Al Richmond, *A Long View from the Left: Memoirs of an American Revolutionary* (Boston: Houghton Mifflin, 1973), pp. 241–243; A. Allen, 11–12; Joe Brown, "UAW Strike Against Chrysler Corp.," in Joe Brown Papers (WSU).

7. Earl Browder, "The Communists in the People's Front," 610; William Z. Foster, "Political Leadership and Party Building," 644; William Weinstone, "Chrysler Pact Step Forward in Union Advance, Says Weinstone," *Daily Worker* (April 8, 1937).

8. Jack Skeels, "The Development of Political Stability Within the United Auto Workers Union," (Ph.D. dissertation, University of Wisconsin, 1957), pp. 37, 42; William H. McPherson, *Labor Relations in the Automobile Industry* (Washington, D.C.: Brookings Institution, 1940), pp. 61–62; *United Automobile Worker* quoted by Walter Galenson, *The CIO Challenge to the AFL: A History of the American Labor Movement, 1935–1941* (Cambridge: Harvard University Press, 1960), pp. 153–154; *United Automobile Worker* quoted by Skeels, p. 44; *New York Times* (April 3, 1937).

9. Oral History Interview of Tracy Doll (WSU), pp. 26–27; Joe Brown to Edward Wieck (February 2, 1938), in Edward Wieck Papers (WSU).

10. Communist Party of Michigan, press release (April 5, 1937), in Adolph Germer Papers; *Daily Worker* (April 8, 1937); "Review of the Month," *Communist* (May, 1937), 349.

11. *Detroit News* (April 2, 1937) clipping in Henry Kraus Papers; [Henry Kraus,] *Flint a True Report*, pamphlet issued by Local 156 in the summer of 1937, 5–9, notes from the minutes of Local 156 (1937), in Henry Kraus Papers; Wyndham Mortimer and Ed Hall press release (July 1937), in Henry Kraus Papers; Interview of Bert Cochran, New York, November 24, 1971.

12. George D. Blackwood, "The United Automobile Workers of America, 1935–51," (Ph.D. dissertation, University of Chicago, 1952), p. 85; *Flint Journal* (July 6, 1937), in Henry Kraus Papers; Homer Martin to Henry Kraus (March 29, 1937), Henry Kraus to General Executive Board (April 27, 1937), George Addes to Henry Kraus (April 28, 1937), Robert Travis to Adolph Germer (May 17, 1937), in Henry Kraus Papers; Oral

History Interview of Victor Reuther (WSU), pp. 25–26; *Socialist Call* (July 17, 1937); Homer Martin to Victor Reuther (May 7, 1937), (July 14, 1937), (July 28, 1937) and Victor Reuther to Ed Hall (April 5, 1937), in Victor Reuther Papers (WSU); Adolph Germer to John L. Lewis (July 7, 1937), in John L. Lewis Papers (United Mine Workers Headquarters); Joe Brown to Ed Wieck (February 2, 1938), in Edward Wieck Papers.

13. Report of CP Political Buro meeting of April 18, 1937 in *Investigation of Un-American Propaganda Activities*, I, pp. 252–255; Robert Travis statement (July 14, 1937), in Henry Kraus Papers; Henry Kraus to General Executive Board (April 25, 1937), in Henry Kraus Papers; Hy Fish to Frank Trager (July 13, 1937) a copy of this letter is in the writer's possession; Joe Brown to Edward Wieck (February 2, 1938), in Edward Wieck Papers.

14. William H. McPherson and Anthony Luchek, "Automobiles," in Harry A. Mills, ed., *How Collective Bargaining Works* (New York: Twentieth Century Fund, 1945), p. 584; "Program of the Martin-Frankensteen Progressive Caucus ..." [1937], in Henry Kraus Papers; Skeels, pp. 46–47; Oral History Interview of Carl Haessler (WSU), pp. 29–30; *Business Week* (August 21, 1937), 26–31.

15. Oral History Interview of R. J. Thomas (Columbia), Vol. III, p. 25; Oral History Interview of Carl Haessler (WSU), pp. 28–30; Oral History Interview of Frank Marquart (WSU), pp. 8–9, 11–12; Frank Winn quoted by Galenson, pp. 152–153; "For a United Democratic Union" (program of the Unity caucus, 1937), in Henry Kraus Papers; Oral History Interview of Nat Ganley (WSU), pp. 17–18; B. K. Gebert, "The Convention of 400,000," *Communist* (October, 1937), 893.

16. United Automobile Workers of America, *Proceedings of the Third Annual Convention of the International Union United Automobile Workers of America* (Milwaukee, 1937), pp. 125–130, 164–165, 184–187, 206–210, 218, 224–228, 260–265, 282, 285–286; Skeels, pp. 48–54; Galenson, pp. 155–157; *Socialist Call* (September 4, 1937); Blackwood, pp. 90–93; Oral History Interview of Wyndham Mortimer (WSU), p. 52; B. K. Gebert, "The Convention of 400,000," 896–902.

17. Letters of the leaders of the Unity caucus to their supporters (March 9, 16, 24, 30, April 7, 1938), in Henry Kraus Papers; Skeels, pp. 56–60; *Flint Journal* (September 18, 1937), *Detroit Free Press* (September 16, 1937), *Detroit News* (October 19, 1937), clippings in Henry Kraus Papers; Adolph Germer to John Brophy (October 28, 1937), in Adolph Germer Papers (SHSW); Wyndham Mortimer to John Brophy (September 29, 1937), in Henry Kraus Papers.

18. *Detroit Times* (September 17, 1937), *Flint News Advertiser* (September 24, 1937), *Detroit News* (October 19, 1937), clippings in Henry Kraus Papers; *New York Times* (September 30, 1937); Mortimer, pp. 118–120, 154; Skeels, p. 56; Wyndham Mortimer to John Brophy (September 29, 1937) and Wyndham Mortimer to John L. Lewis (October 22, 1937), in Henry Kraus Papers; Adolph Germer to John Brophy (October 25, 1937), in Adolph Germer Papers; James Nelson to John L. Lewis (August 4, 1938), in John L. Lewis Papers (United Mine Workers Headquarters).

19. Homer Martin to Employees of the International Union (September 1, 1937) and Homer Martin to Victor Reuther (September 28, 1937), in Victor Reuther Papers; Skeels, pp. 55–57; Blackwood, pp. 94–95; Oral

History Interview of John W. Anderson (WSU), pp. 33, 78–79; Oral History Interview of Carl Haessler (WSU), pp. 32–33; Oral History Interview of Stanley Nowak (WSU), pp. 1–3, 18–19; Joe Brown to Edward Wieck (February 2, 1938), in Edward Wieck Papers; Homer Martin to All Local Union and All Organizers and Representatives (October 8, 1937), William B. Mason to Homer Martin (October 19, 1937), "In Reply to President Martin," a statement of Ternstedt Bargaining Committee (October 19, 1937), in Henry Kraus Papers; Carl Haessler, "Martin's Gunplay Brings UAW Strife into Spotlight," *Federated Press* (October 1, 1937), in Henry Kraus Papers; *Daily Worker* (October 5, 1937).

20. McPherson and Luchek, p. 584; [Jay Lovestone] to Homer Martin (August 3, 1937), in Homer Martin Papers (WSU); Oral History Interview of George Addes (WSU), p. 19; *Investigation of Un-American Propaganda Activities*, I, p. 253; B. K. Gebert, "The Convention of 400,000," 892.

21. McPherson and Luchek, p. 585; Galenson, p. 157; [Jay Lovestone] to Homer Martin (August 3, 1937), in Homer Martin Papers; Jay Lovestone to W. Jett Lauck (November 24, 1937 and January 15, 1938), in W. Jett Lauck Papers (WSU); UAW press release of letter to William S. Knudsen (September 1937) in Henry Kraus Papers; Wyndham Mortimer speech (January 1939) in Henry Kraus Papers; Carl Haessler, "Auto Workers Spurn GM Agreement," *Federated Press* (November 22, 1937), in Henry Kraus Papers; Robert Travis Report on the First Peace Meeting (December 15, 1937), in Henry Kraus Papers.

22. Blackwood, pp. 98–99; *Socialist Call* (December 25, 1937); Oral History Interview of George Addes (WSU), p. 24; *Daily Worker* (January 15, 1938, February 5, 1938); *New York Times* (February 4, 1938); "Lenin and Collective Security," *Communist* (January, 1938), 26; *Daily Worker* (February 5, 1938); Wyndham Mortimer to John Brophy (March 20, 1938), in Henry Kraus Papers.

23. *Socialist Call* (February 26, March 26, April 2, April 10, April 17, May 7, 1938); Joe Brown to Edward Wieck (January 1, 1938), in Edward Wieck Papers; William Z. Foster, *Communist* (June 1938), 509–512; Instructions of John Williamson to Cleveland Shop and Industrial Branches in *Workers Age* (June 4, 1938); Len DeCaux, *Labor Radical: From the Wobblies to the CIO: A Personal History* (Boston: Beacon Press, 1970), p. 316; Interview of William Weinstone, November 27, 1951; Interview of William McKie (undated), in Nat Ganley Papers; Oral History Interview of Nat Ganley (WSU), p. 18; Oral History Interview of R. J. Thomas (Columbia), Vol. IV, p. 20.

24. Oral History Interview of George Addes (WSU), pp. 21–23, 25–26; Irving Howe and B. J. Widick, *The UAW and Walter Reuther* (New York: Random House, 1949), p. 150; Oral History Interview of Richard Frankensteen (WSU), pp. 45–46; Interview of Carl Haessler, Detroit, July 25, 1971; Oral History Interview of Frank Marquart (WSU), pp. 30–31; Joe Brown to Ed Wieck (April 10, 1938), in Edward Wieck Papers; Wyndham Mortimer to John Brophy (March 20, 1938), in Henry Kraus Papers; "A Pastor Losing His Flock," (report on local elections dated March 24, 1938), in Henry Kraus Papers; *Workers Age* (June 25, 1938); Francis J. Michael testimony in proceedings of trial of Wyndham Mortimer *et al.* (1938), pp. 30–32, in Henry Kraus Papers; Galenson, pp. 159–160; *Daily Worker* (April 25, 1937); Skeels, pp. 64–65; "Confidential Report of the Socialist Party on the Inner Situation in the Auto Union" (June 7, 1938),

in Henry Kraus Papers; William Weinstone to Roger Keeran (May 6, 1977); Adolph Germer to John L. Lewis (July 17, 1938), in John L. Lewis Papers.

25. Joe Brown to Edward Wieck (April 19, 1938) in Edward Wieck Papers; *Workers Age* (June 18, 1938); Skeels, p. 65; resolutions adopted at June 8, 1938 Executive Board meeting, in Henry Kraus Papers; Edward Levinson, "The CIO in Crisis," *Nation* (July 2, 1938), 11–14; Galenson, p. 163; Homer Martin Press release (July 25, 1938), in Henry Kraus Papers.

26. Galenson, p. 163; Blackwood, pp. 102–105; opening statement by Larry Davidow (July 27, 1938), in Henry Kraus Papers; Homer Martin to Richard Frankensteen, *et al.* (June 24, 1938), in Henry Kraus Papers; "Defense Brief" (July 1938) and "Defense Brief, Part II" (July-August 1938), in Henry Kraus Papers; Press Release by Jay Lovestone (August 5, 1938), in W. Jett Lauck Papers; Mortimer, p. 161; Transcript of phone conversation between Bill Munger and Jay Lovestone (August 3, [1937]) in Daniel Bell Collection (Tamiment).

27. Ed Hall, Wyndham Mortimer, *et al.* to Officers and Members of UAW (June 23, 1938) and "Locals Demanding Reinstatement of 5 Officers" (July 1938), in Henry Kraus Papers; Matthew Josephson, *Sidney Hillman, Statesman of Labor* (Garden City, N.Y.: Doubleday, 1952), p. 457; Galenson, p. 163; *Daily Worker* (September 8, 16, 1938); Blackwood, pp. 106–107.

28. Skeels, pp. 85–90; Galenson, pp. 166–168.

29. Skeels, pp. 89–94; Blackwood, p. 109; Galenson, pp. 166–168; Oral History Interview of George Addes (WSU), p. 26.

30. Oral History Interview of R. J. Thomas (Columbia), Vol. IV, pp. 28–29; Vol V, pp. 12–13; Mortimer, p. 162; Interview of William Weinstone, New York City, November 27, 1971; Oral History Interview of Carl Haessler (WSU), p. 39; Oral History Interview of Lee Pressman (Columbia), pp. 338–339; DeCaux, pp. 316–317; Howe and Widick, p. 150; United Automobile Workers of America, *Proceedings of the Special Convention* (Cleveland, 1939), pp. 444, 600–601.

31. Oral History Interview of Wyndham Mortimer (WSU), pp. 60–61; Oral History Interview of Carl Haessler (WSU), p. 39; Interview of Carl Haessler, Detroit, July 25, 1971; Oral History Interview of Lee Pressman (Columbia), p. 338; DeCaux, pp. 316–317; Oral History Interview of George Addes (WSU), pp. 29–32; *Proceedings of the Special Convention*, p. 322; Frank Emspak, "The Break-up of the Congress of Industrial Organizations (CIO), 1945–1950" (Ph.D. dissertation, University of Wisconsin, 1972), p. 28.

32. Wyndham Mortimer, *Organize! My Life as a Union Man* (Boston: Beacon Paperback, 1972), p. 163; Interview of Henry Kraus, Paris, June 19, 1972; DeCaux, pp. 316–317; Richmond, pp. 238–239, 241, 243; William Weinstone, "'Labor Radical'—An Insider's Story of the CIO," *Political Affairs* (May 1971), 51; James R. Prickett, "Communism and Factionalism in the United Automobile Workers, 1939–1947," *Science and Society* (Summer 1968), 259–260; *Proceedings of the Special Convention*, pp. 600–601; Oral History Interview of Nat Ganley (WSU), p. 21; Oral History Interview of R.J. Thomas (Columbia), Vol. V, p. 12.

33. Emspak, p. 28; Galenson, pp. 171–172; Prickett, pp. 259–260; Oral History Interview of Nat Ganley (WSU), pp. 22–23; *Socialist Call* (April 29, 1939); *Daily Worker* (April 7, 1939); G. K. Gebert, "The Auto

Workers Forge Unity at the Cleveland Convention," *Communist* (May 1939), 439–440.

34. Robert Alperin, "Organization in the Communist Party, U.S.A., 1931–1938" (Ph.D. dissertation, Northwestern, 1959), pp. 304, 325, 330; Roy Hudson, "The Path of Labor's United Action," *Communist* (October 1939), 935; Gebert, "The Auto Workers Forge Unity," 438–440; Richmond, pp. 243–245; Interview of William Weinstone, New York, November 27, 1971; Oral History Interview of Wyndham Mortimer (WSU), p. 60; Mortimer, p. 164; Oral History Interview of Bob Travis (Univeristy of Michigan—Flint).

35. Tucker Smith to Norman Thomas (October 8, 1937) in Norman Thomas Papers (New York Public Library); Gus Tyler to Gerry Allard (ca. January-February 1938), in Daniel Bell Papers (Tamiment Library).

36. Ben Fischer to Herbert Zam (March 17, 1938), Ben Fischer, "Auto League Report #1" (June 7, 1938), Ben Fischer to Art McDowell (June 16, 1938), Ben Fischer to Gus Tyler (June 18, 1938), Ben Fischer to Zam, Tyler [*et al.*] (November 10, 1938), in Daniel Bell Papers (Tamiment Library); Tucker Smith to Paul Porter (ca. November 28, 1938), Norman Thomas to Tucker Smith (February 9, 1939), in Norman Thomas Papers (New York Public Library).

## IX. THE NATIONAL DEFENSE STRIKES

1. George D. Blackwood, "The United Automobile Workers of America, 1935–51" (Ph.D. dissertation, University of Chicago, 1952), p. 127; Walter Galenson, *The CIO Challenge to the AFL: A History of the American Labor Movement, 1935–1941* (Cambridge: Harvard University Press, 1960), pp. 172–176.

2. Oral History Interview of Richard Frankensteen (WSU), p. 43: Oral History Interview of R. J. Thomas (Columbia), Vol. III, p. 33; Oral History Interview of John W. Anderson (WSU), p. 34; Jean Gould and Lorena Hickok, *Walter Reuther, Labor's Rugged Individualist* (New York: Dodd, Mean, 1972), p. 143; Eldorous L. Dayton, *Walter Reuther: The Autocrat of the Bargaining Table* (New York: Devin-Adair, 1958), p. 143; Fred J. Cook, *Walter Reuther* (Chicago: Encyclopedia Britannica Press, 1963), p. 129; Len DeCaux, *Labor Radical: From the Wobblies to CIO: A Personal History* (Boston: Beacon, 1970), pp. 258–260.

3. Daniel Bell, *Marxian Socialism in the United States* (Princeton: Princeton University Press, 1967), p. 179; Oral History Interview of Frank Marquart (WSU), pp. 11–14; Oral History Interview of Leonard Woodcock (WSU), pp. 15, 20; Oral History Interview of Tracy Doll (WSU), p. 37; Oral History Interview of John W. Anderson (WSU), p. 32, 34; Oral History Interview of Carl Haessler (WSU), p. 41.

4. Adam B. Ulam, *Stalin: The Man and His Era* (New York: Viking Press, 1973), pp. 504–535; Alan Bullock, *Hitler: A Study in Tyranny* (New York: Harper & Brothers, 1952), pp. 485–488.

5. Al Richmond, *A Long View From the Left: Memoirs of an American Revolutionary* (Boston: Houghton Mifflin, 1973), p. 283; Molotov quoted by William Z. Foster, *History of the Communist Party of the United States* (New York: International Publishers, 1952), pp. 374–375; Foster, *History of the Communist Party*, pp. 387–388; John Williamson, *Dangerous Scot: The Life and Work of an American "Undesirable"* (New

York: International Publishers, 1969), pp. 142–143; Irving Howe and Lewis Coser, *The American Communist Party: A Critical History, 1919–1957* (Boston: Beacon Press, 1957), pp. 387, 390; Ulam, pp. 513–535.

6. Howe and Coser, pp. 390–391; Williamson, pp. 142–143; Foster, *History of the Communist Party*, p. 387; William Z. Foster, "The Trade Unions and the War," *Communist* (October 1940), 897–900.

7. Foster, *History of the Communist Party*, pp. 392–393; Williamson, p. 143; Earl Browder, *The Way Out* (New York: International Publishers, 1941), p. 84.

8. Joel Seidman, *American Labor From Defense to Reconversion* (Chicago: University of Chicago Press, 1953), pp. 21, 23–24; Earl Browder, "The American Communist Party in the Thirties," in Rita J. Simon, ed., *As We Saw the Thirties* (Urbana: University of Illinois Press, 1967), p. 244; Foster, *History of the Communist Party*, p. 386.

9. International Union, United Automobile Workers of America, *Proceedings of the Fifth Annual Convention* (St. Louis, 1940), pp. 110, 112–114; *Daily Worker* (August 1, 3, 4, 1940).

10. *Proceedings of the Fifth Annual Convention of the International Union*, pp. 292–293, 295–299, 301–303; Oral History Interview of Victor Reuther (WSU), p. 43; *Daily Worker* (August 4, 1940); *Call* (August 10, 1940).

11. *Proceedings of the Fifth Annual Convention of the International Union*, pp. 426, 428, 431–433, 436–440; Blackwood, pp. 144–145.

12. Oral History Interview of Nat Ganley (WSU), p. 23; *Call* (August 10, 1940); *Daily Worker* (August 6, 1940); Galenson, pp. 177–178; Blackwood, p. 146.

13. Benjamin Stolberg, "Inside Labor," *American Mercury* (August 1941), 180; Max Kampelman, *The Communist Party vs. The C.I.O.: A Study in Politics* (New York: F. A. Praeger, 1957), pp. 26–27; Louis Budenz, *This Is My Story* (New York: McGraw-Hill, 1947), p. 201.

14. Wyndham Mortimer, *Organize! My Life as a Union Man* (Boston: Beacon Paperback, 1972), pp. 166–173; Oral History Interview of Nat Ganley (UAW), p. 23; Clayton Fountain, *Union Guy* (New York: Viking Press, 1949), p. 145; *Daily Worker* (November 16, 20, 22, 23, 24, 25, 26, 27, 1940); *United Automobile Worker* (December 1, 15, 1940); Seidman, p. 43.

15. "The Case of Harold Christoffel," [n.d.] in Nat Ganley Papers (WSU); Blackwood, pp. 170–172; Testimony of Harold Christoffel in U.S., Congress, House, Committee on Education and Labor, *Amendments to National Labor Relations Act, Hearings*, 80th Cong., 1st sess., 1947, pp. 2094–2097; *New York Times* (March 2, 4, 26, 27, 28, 1941); U.S., Congress, House, Committee on Naval Affairs, *Preliminary Report of the Committee on Naval Affairs, House of Representatives, Investigating the Naval Defense Program*, House Report No. 1634, 77th Cong., 2nd sess., 1942, pp. 106–107; *Daily Worker* (January 23, 30; March 1, 11, 27, 28, 1941); James R. Prickett, "Communism and Factionalism in the United Automobile Workers, 1939–1947," *Science and Society* (Summer 1968), 260–261; Seidman, pp. 43–44.

16. *Daily Worker* (March 29; April 1, 2, 3, 8, 1941); *Sunday Worker* (March 30, 1941); Blackwood, p. 172; *New York Times* (March 30, 1941); *United Automobile Worker* (May 1, 1941).

17. *United Automobile Worker* (April 1, 1941); *New York Times* (March 28, 1941); Walter Reuther in International Union, United Automobile Workers of America, *Proceedings of the 1941 Convention* (Buffalo, 1941), p. 94.

18. *New York Times* (April 17, 1941); Seidman, p. 45; *Daily Worker* (June 10, 1941); Foster, "The Trade Unions and the War," 896–900.

19. Mortimer, pp. 175, 179, 183; *Daily Worker* (June 7, 1941).

20. Prickett, "Communism and Factionalism in the United Automobile Workers, 1939–1947," 261–263; James Prickett, "Fifty Cents an Hour: A Re-examination of the 1941 North American Strike" (Los Angeles: Plantin Press, 1973), pp. 2–4; Oral History Interview of Richard Frankensteen (WSU), p. 53; Mortimer, pp. 177–179; *Proceedings of the 1941 Convention*, pp. 426, 430; Elmer Freitag and Walter Wiitanen to Fellow Workers (June 20, 1941), in Carl Haessler Papers (WSU); *United Automobile Worker* (June 1, 1941).

21. *Daily Worker* (March 21, June 6, 1941); Elmer Freitag and Walter Wiitanen to Fellow Workers (June 20, 1941) in Carl Haessler Papers (WSU); Prickett, "Fifty Cents an Hour," pp. 10, 13–16; Oral History Interview of Elmer Freitag (WSU), pp. 8–12.

22. *Los Angeles Times* and Harold Ickes quoted in Prickett, "Fifty Cents an Hour," pp. 15–16.

23. Prickett, "Fifty Cents an Hour," pp. 16–17, *Proceedings of the 1941 Convention*, pp. 432–433; Oral History Interview of Richard Frankensteen (WSU), pp. 54–55; 84–85; *New York Times* (June 9, 1941); Mortimer, p. 183; Oral History Interview of Lew Michener (WSU), pp. 27–29; *Daily Worker* (June 13, 1941); Oral History Interview of Elmer Freitag (WSU), p. 16.

24. Prickett, "Fifty Cents an Hour," pp. 17–18; *United Automobile Worker* (July 1, 1941); *Daily Worker* (June 9, 10, 1941); Elmer Freitag and Walter Wiitanen to Fellow Workers (June 20, 1941) in Carl Haessler Papers (WSU).

25. Prickett, "Fifty Cents and Hour," p. 20; Matthew Josephson, *Sidney Hillman: Statesman of American Labor* (Garden City: Doubleday, 1952), pp. 544–546; Blackwood, p. 167; Mortimer, pp. 184–186; *Daily Worker* (June 12, 1941); *Sunday Worker* (June 15, 1941); William Z. Foster, "Lessons of the Inglewood Strike," *Daily Worker* (June 17, 1941); Seidman, p. 48; *Proceedings of the 1941 Convention*, p. 421.

26. William Allen, "Many Years of Effort Lie Back of Ford Victory," *Daily Worker* (April 21, 1941); Phillip Bonosky, *Brother Bill McKie: Building the Union at Ford* (New York: International Publishers, 1953), *passim*; "Bil Allan [sic] Monday, June 14" [n.d., transcript of an interview with William Allen] in Nat Ganley Papers (WSU); *Ford Worker* (June 30, 1937); *Ford-Dearborn Worker* (March and May 1938) in Henry Kraus Papers (WSU); Oral History Interview of John W. Anderson (WSU), p. 101.

27. Keith Sward, *The Legend of Henry Ford* (New York: Rhinehart, 1948), pp. 373–407; Seidman, pp. 46–47; "Bil Allan [sic] Monday, June 14," [n.d., transcript of an interview with William Allen] in Nat Ganley Papers (WSU); Gallo: *United Automobile Worker* (March 1, 1941) and *Detroit News* (August 9, 1954).

28. *Daily Worker* (January 25, 27, February 21, 26, March 2, April 5, 10, 1941); Joseph R. Starobin, *American Communism in Crisis, 1943–1957* (Cambridge: Harvard University Press, 1972), p. 30; Untitled tran-

script of an interview with LeBron Simmons (n.d.) in the Nat Ganley Papers (wsu).

29. Seidman, pp. 46–47; Sward, pp. 404–407; *United Automobile Worker* (April 15, 1941); *Daily Worker* (February 21, 26, April 2, 3, 4, 5, 6, 1941).

30. Seidman, pp. 46–47; Sward, pp. 416–423; *United Automobile Worker* (April 15, July 1, 1941); *Sunday Worker* (June 22, 1941).

31. *Daily Worker* (June 23, 1941); Executive Committee Statement in Williamson, p. 144; Roy Hudson, "Labor's Great Responsibilities and Possibilities," *Communist* (August 1941), 687.

32. Hudson, "Labor's Great Responsibilities and Possibilities," 687; Seidman, p. 51; *Daily Worker* (June 27, 1941); *Sunday Worker* (July 6, 1941); Fountain, pp. 144, 148.

33. *Proceedings of the 1941 Convention*, pp. 53, 80–85, 94–97, 108, 115, 117, 303–327, 573–574; Oral History Interview of Carl Haessler (wsu), p. 85.

34. *Proceedings of the 1941 Convention*, pp. 243–259, 268, 401–446, 457, 754–757.

35. *Proceedings of the 1941 Convention*, pp. 683–711.

36. Prickett, "Communism and Factionalism in the United Automobile Workers, 1939–1947," 265; Jack Skeels, "The Development of Political Stability Within the United Auto Workers Union" (Ph.D. dissertation, University of Wisconsin, 1957), p. 150.

37. Travis: *Daily Worker* (June 11, 1941); La Motte: *Sunday Worker* (August 17, 1941); Mortimer: Mortimer, pp. 187–191; Wyndham Mortimer to R. J. Thomas (June 9, 1942) and R. J. Thomas to Wyndham Mortimer (June 15, 1942), in R. J. Thomas Papers (wsu).

## X. EVERYTHING FOR VICTORY

1. Joel Seidman, "Labor Policy of the Communist Party During World War II," *Industrial and Labor Relations Review* (October 1950), 69; Irving Howe and B. J. Widick, *The UAW and Walter Reuther* (New York: Random House, 1949); Art Preis, *Labor's Giant Step: Twenty Years of the CIO* (New York: Pioneer Publishers, 1964); Bert Cochran, *Labor and Communism: The Conflict that Shaped American Unions* (Princeton: Princeton University Press, 1977), p. 220.

2. John Williamson, *Dangerous Scot: The Life and Work of an American "Undesirable"* (New York: International Publishers, 1969), p. 144; Earl Browder, "The Strike Wave Conspiracy," *Communist* (June 1943), 483–494; Joel Seidman, *American Labor from Defense to Reconversion* (Chicago: University of Chicago Press, 1953), pp. 79–80; Murray quoted by Nelson Lichtenstein, "Industrial Unionism Under the No-Strike Pledge: A Study of the CIO During the Second World War" (Ph.D. dissertation, University of California, Berkeley, 1974), pp. 235–236; Lichtenstein, pp. 236–256, 267–271; International Union, United Automobile, Aircraft, and Agricultural Implement Workers of America, *Proceedings of the Seventh Convention* (Chicago, 1942), pp. 62–65; Oral History of Nat Ganley (Wayne State University [WSU]), p. 25.

3. William Z. Foster, *American Trade Unionism: Principles and Organization, Strategy and Tactics: Selected Writings* (New York: International Publishers, 1970), p. 289; William Z. Foster, "The Struggle

Against Revisionism," *Political Affairs* (September 1945), 786; Elizabeth Hawes, *Hurry Up, Please, It's Time* (New York: Reynal & Hitchcock, 1949), pp. 84-85.

4. Thomas E. Linton, *An Historical Examination of the Purposes and Practices of the Education Program of the United Automobile Workers of America—1936-1959* (Ann Arbor: Malloy Lithoprinting, Inc., 1965), pp. 97-100; Clayton W. Fountain, *Union Guy* (New York: Viking Press, 1949), p. 160.

5. Linton, pp. 101-154.

6. Linton, pp. 109-114, 125-154.

7. Earl Browder, *Victory—and After* (New York: International Publishers, 1942), p. 19; Anna Long, "Women Workers After the War," *Political Affairs* (March 1945), 260; Elizabeth Gurley Flynn, "The New Role of Women in Industry," *Communist* (April 1943), 355; Hawes, pp. 15, 16, 39, 44, 133.

8. Jervis Anderson, *A Philip Randolph. A Biographical Portrait* (New York: Harcourt Brace Jovanovitch, 1973), p. 253; James W. Ford, "The Negro People Unite for Victory," *Communist* (July 1943), 643; Earl Browder, *Victory—and After*, pp. 90-91; "Negro Digest Poll: Have Communists Quit Fighting for Negro Rights?" and William L. Patterson, Benjamin A. Davis, Jr., and James W. Ford in "Roundtable: Have Communists Quit Fighting for Negro Rights?" *Negro Digest* (December 1944), 56-70.

9. Alfred M. Lee and Norman D. Humphrey, *Race Riot* (New York: Dryden Press, 1943), pp. 88-97; B. J. Widick, *Detroit: City of Race and Class Violence* (Chicago: Quadrangle Books, 1972), pp. 88-98; auto worker quoted by Widick, p. 94.

10. Philip S. Foner, *Organized Labor and the Black Workers, 1619-1973* (New York and Washington: Praeger Publishers, 1974), pp. 255-258; Widick, pp. 93-112.

11. International Union, United Automobile, Aircraft, and Agricultural Implement Workers of America, *Proceedings of the Eighth Convention* (Buffalo, 1943), pp. 370-371; "Rope and Faggot Figures," *Negro Digest* (December 1944), 70.

12. *Proceedings of the Eighth Convention*, pp. 370-398, 414-421.

13. Linton, pp. 110, 127-129, 147-148, 153; Hawes, pp. 65-66, 211-212.

14. Lichtenstein, pp. 386-387; Roy Hudson, "The Party Recruiting Campaign in Michigan," *Communist* (April 1943), 342-344; Interview of Art McPhaul, Detroit, August 21, 1971; Martin Halpern, "The 1941 Strike at the Ford Motor Company" (unpublished paper in the possession of the author, 1974).

15. Seidman, *American Labor From Defense to Reconversion*, p. 107; Edwin E. Witte, "Wartime Handling of Labor Disputes," *Harvard Business Review* (Winter 1947), 169-177; N. V. Sivachev, *Government and Labor in the USA During World War II* (Moscow: Moscow Univeristy Press, 1974), pp. 360-374.

16. Seidman, *American Labor From Defense to Reconversion*, pp. 129, 135, 275-276; National War Labor Board, *The Termination Report*, vol. 1 (Washington: U.S. Government Printing Office, 1945), p. 1159 and vol. 2, pp. 845-847, 938; Witte, 184.

17. Sivachev, pp. 375-376.

18. Lichtenstein, pp. 368–370, 393–397; William Z. Foster, *History of the Communist Party of the United States* (New York: International Publishers, 1952), pp. 411–412; Earl Browder, *Production for Victory* (New York: Workers Library, 1943) and *Wage Policy in War Production* (New York: Workers Library, April 1943); *Fountain*, p. 159; Nat Ganley to *Detroit News* (June 3, 1943), in Nat Ganley Papers; C. G. "Pop" Edelen, *Production with Incentive Pay*, in Nat Ganley Papers (WSU).

19. Lichtenstein, pp. 401–403, 406, 415–417; Howe and Widick, p. 115.

20. Lichtenstein, pp. 406, 413, 422–423, 431–440; Fountain, p. 161.

21. Lichtenstein, pp. 267–271, 429–441; Oral History of Clayton Johnson (WSU), p. 22.

22. Howe and Widick, p. 115; Lichtenstein, pp. 413–417.

23. Frank Cormier and William J. Eaton, *Reuther* (Englewood Cliffs, N.J.: Prentice Hall, 1970), pp. 209–210; Executive Board of Local 155, "Open Letter to Secretary-Treasurer George Addes and Board Member Richard Leonard" (September 1, 1943), in Wellman-Ganley Papers (WSU); *New York Times* (October 7, 8, 9, 1943); *Proceedings of the Eighth Convention*, pp. 370–391.

24. *Detroit News* (May 9, 1943) quoted by Howe and Widick, pp. 116–117; Oral History of Nat Ganley (WSU), pp. 26–40; Lichtenstein, pp. 382–387, 431.

25. U.S. Department of Labor, Bureau of Labor Statistics, *Impact of the War on the Detroit Area*, Industrial Area Study No. 10 (July 1943), p. 2; "Industrial Disputes," *Monthly Labor Review* (May 1943), 694; Ed Jennings, "Wildcat! The Wartime Strike Wave in Auto," *Radical America* (July-August 1975), 85.

26. Jennings, 102; *Impact of the War on the Detroit Area*, pp. 36–37; Hawes, p. 44.

27. "Strikes in 1943," *Monthly Labor Review* (May 1944), 934; "Strikes and Lockouts in 1955," *Monthly Labor Review* (May 1945), 961–964; U.S., Congress, House, *Wartime Record of Strikes and Lockouts 1940–45*, compiled by Rosa Lee Swafford, 79th Cong., 2d sess., 1946 (Washington, D.C.: Government Printing Office, 1946), p. 2; Romney and Thomas quoted by Jennings, 84, 93.

28. Jennings, 85, 88–89; *Wartime Record of Strikes and Lockouts 1940–45*, pp. 9–13.

29. *Daily Worker* quoted by Seidman, "Labor Policy of the Communist Party During World War II," 62–63; *United Automobile Worker* (March 1, 1945); *Wartime Record of Strikes and Lockouts 1940–45*, pp. 16–17, 31; Foster, *History of the Communist Party of the United States*, p. 411.

30. Interview of Irwin Baur, Detroit, August 11, 1971; Oral History of Max Shachtman (Columbia), pp. 31–394, 403; Interview of Marty and Jesse Glaberman, Detroit, August 4, 1971; Lichtenstein, pp. 380–381; *Rank and Filer* (January, February, and April, 1945); *Proceedings of the Eighth Convention*, p. 409; Lichtenstein, pp. 614–616.

31. International Union, United Automobile, Aircraft and Agricultural Implement Workers of America, *Proceedings of the Ninth Convention* (Grand Rapids, 1944), pp. 147–235; Frank Marquart, *An Auto Worker's Journal: The UAW From Crusade to One-Party Union* (University Park and London: Pennsylvania State University Press, 1975), p. 105.

32. Communist leaflet quoted by James R. Prickett, "Communists and the Communist Issue in the American Labor Movement, 1920–1950" (Ph.D. dissertation, University of California, Los Angeles, 1975), p. 274; UAW Committee to Uphold the No-Strike Pledge, "Straight Talk About Our No-Strike Pledge" (leaflet, 1945), in Nat Ganley Papers; *Rank and Filer* (January, February, and April, 1945).

33. Interview of Saul Wellman, Detroit, July 21, 1971; *Proceedings of the Eighth Convention*, p. 409; *Rank and Filer* (January, February, and April, 1945).

34. Earl Browder, *Teheran: Our Path in War and Peace* (New York: International Publishers, 1944), pp. 12–13, 66, 71; Earl Browder, "Teheran—History's Greatest Turning Point," *Communist* (January 1944), 3–8; Joseph R. Starobin, *American Communism in Crisis, 1943–1957* (Cambridge: Harvard University Press, 1972), pp. 54–59, 68; "Decisions of the National Committee of the Communist Party," *Communist* (February 1944), 107; Eugene Dennis, "Postwar Labor-Capital Cooperation," *Political Affairs* (May 1945), 415–422.

35. Hawes, p. 43; Oral History of Nat Ganley (WSU), pp. 33–34; Interview of Art McPhaul (August 21, 1971).

36. Nathan Glazer, *The Social Basis of American Communism* (New York: Harcourt Brace & World, 1961), p. 115; Roy Hudson, "The Party Recruiting Campaign in Michigan," *Communist* (April 1943), 342–347; John Williamson, "The Organizational and Educational Tasks of Our Party," *Communist* (October 1943), 932; Hawes, pp. 42–43; Linton, pp. 97–100; Fountain, p. 160.

37. John Williamson, "The CPA—Our Most Indispensable Weapon," *Political Affairs* (January 1945), 49–54; John Williamson, "The Reconstitution of the Communist Party," *Political Affairs* (September 1945), 805; John Williamson, "For a Mass Marxist Party of the Working Class," *Political Affairs* (March 1946), 225, 232–233.

38. Oral History of Nat Ganley (WSU), pp. 40–41.

## XI.   REUTHER AND REACTION, 1946–1949

1. *Daily Worker* (September 23, 1945 and March 17, 1946); Barton Bernstein, "Walter Reuther and the General Motors Strike of 1945–46," *Michigan History* (September 1965), 262–265; *Time* (December 3, 1945), 21; *New York Times* (March 25, 1946).

2. "Finish Fight?" *Time* (December 3, 1945), 19–22; Herbert Brean, "Walter Reuther," *Life* (November 26, 1945), 113–124; "Reuther: F.O.B. Detroit," *Fortune* (December 1945), 149–151, 280–288.

3. *Daily Worker* (March 14, 15, 17, 19, 1946); *New York Times* (February 24, 1946); *Time* (December 3, 1945), 21; *Business Week* (February 23, 1946), 108.

4. "Minutes Special Session, International Executive Board, Detroit Michigan, February 22–24, 1946," in UAW Executive Board Meeting Collection (WSU); *Daily Worker* (March 2, 15, 23, 1946).

5. Richard Ward, "The Role of the Association of Catholic Trade Unionists in the American Labor Movement" (Ph.D. dissertation, University of Michigan, 1958), pp. 56–61, 68; "Constitution of the ACTU—Detroit" (adopted July 15, 1938) and *ACTist Bulletin* (August 25, 1938) in Association of Catholic Trade Unionists—Detroit Collection (WSU); Frank

Emspak, "The Association of Catholic Trade Unionists and the United Automobile Workers" (Masters thesis, University of Wisconsin, 1968), pp. 6, 11–12, 44–45, 48–49.

6. Oral History of Al Leggat (WSU), pp. 61–62; Emspak, pp. 66–68; *Fortune* quoted by Ward, pp. 142–143; Oral History of Carl Haessler (WSU), p. 264.

7. James R. Prickett, "Communists and the Communist Issue in the American Labor Movement, 1920–1950" (Ph.D. dissertation, University of California, Los Angeles, 1975), pp. 280–282; Bert Cochran, *Labor and Communism: The Conflict That Shaped American Unions* (Princeton, N.J.: Princeton University Press, 1977), p. 252; "Finish Fight?" *Time* (December 3, 1945), 19–22; Herbert Brean, "Walter Reuther," *Life* (November 26, 1945), 113–124; "Reuther: F.O.B. Detroit," *Fortune* (December 1945), 149–151, 280–288; Interview of Harold Christoffel, Oconomowoc, Wisconsin, June 27, 1974.

8. *Daily Worker* (April 7, 1946); Frank Emspak, "The Break-up of the Congress of Industrial Organizations (CIO), 1945–1950" (Ph.D. dissertation, University of Wisconsin, 1972), pp. 72–73; *New York Times* (March 22, 31, 1946); United Automobile Aircraft and Agricultural Implement Workers of America (UAW-CIO), *Proceedings of the Tenth Convention* (Atlantic City, New Jersey, 1946), pp. 234–235.

9. *New York Times* (March 31, 1946).

10. Clancy Sigal, *Going Away* (New York: Dell, 1970), pp. 309, 311, 314–315.

11. Joyce and Gabriel Kolko, *The Limits of Power: The World and United States Foreign Policy, 1945–1954* (New York: Harper & Row, 1972), pp. 29–46; Walter LaFeber, *America, Russia, and the Cold War, 1945–1966* (New York, London, Sydney: John Wiley and Sons, 1967), pp. 21–56; Baruch quoted by Eric Goldman, *The Crucial Decade—and After: America, 1945–1960* (New York: Vintage Books, 1960), p. 60; Peter H. Irons, "American Business and the Origins of McCarthyism: The Cold War Crusade of the United States Chamber of Commerce," in Robert Griffith and Athan Theoharis, eds., *The Specter: Original Essays on the Cold War and the Origins of McCarthyism* (New York: Franklin Watts, 1974), pp. 78–89.

12. David Caute, *The Great Fear: The Anti-Communist Purge Under Truman and Eisenhower* (New York: Simon and Schuster, 1978), pp. 26–28, 55–56, 85, 268–275, 350, 447; Earl Latham, *The Communist Controversy in Washington: From the New Deal to McCarthy* (New York: Atheneum, 1969), pp. 365–366; Irons, pp. 78–89; Chamber of Commerce of the United States, *Communist Infiltration in the United States* (Washington, D.C., 1946), *Communists Within the Government* (Washington, D.C., 1947), and *Communists Within the Labor Movement* (Washington, D.C., 1947); Donald F. Crosby, "The Politics of Religion: American Catholics and the Anti-Communist Impulse," in Griffith and Theoharis, pp. 20–38; Frank Marquart, *An Auto Worker's Journal: The UAW from Crusade to One-Party Union* (University Park and London: Pennsylvania State University Press, 1975), p. 156.

13. Interview of Saul Wellman, Detroit, July 21, 1971; Testimony of Richard Franklin O'Hair, Walter Scott Dunn, Bereniece Baldwin, Elesio Romano, and Shelton Tappes in U.S., Congress, House, Committee on Un-American Activities, *Communism in the Detroit Area.* 82d Cong., 2d

sess., 1952, pp. 2713–2756, 2778–2798, 2926–2958, 3035–3091, 3117–3145; Testimony of Witness X, Beatrice Churchill, and Herbert H. Donnelly in U.S., Congress, House, Committee on Un-American Activities, *Investigation of Communist Activities in the State of Michigan.* 83rd Cong., 2d sess., 1954, pp. 5487–5511; 5515–5564; 5680–5701.

14. Testimony of Richard Franklin O'Hair, Walter Scott Dunn, Bereniece Baldwin, Elesio Romano, and Shelton Tappes, pp. 2713–2756, 2778–2798, 2926–2958, 3035–3091, 3117–3145; most of the Communists listed served as delegates to the 1946 UAW convention, see United Automobile, Aircraft and Agricultural Implement Workers of America, *Proceedings of the Tenth Convention* (Atlantic City, 1946), pp. 344, 360, 374, 412, 414, and 444; Irving Richter to Roger Keeran (July 20, 1978); Sigal, p. 328.

15. "Minutes Regular Session, International Executive Board . . . Chicago, Illinois, April 16–26, 1946," pp. 6–7, 105–109, 118–130 and "Minutes Special Session, International Executive Board . . . Cleveland, Ohio, June 4–5, 1946," pp. 57–63 in UAW Executive Board Meeting Collection (WSU); Oral History of Al Leggat (WSU), pp. 66–68; *Daily Worker* (April 2 and 9, 1946); *New York Times* (March 31 and April 1, 1946); Emspak, "The Break-up of the Congress of Industrial Organizations (CIO), 1945–1950," pp. 77–78.

16. Irving Richter to Roger Keeran (July 20, 1978); Joel Seidman, *American Labor from Defense to Reconversion* (Chicago: University of Chicago Press, 1953), p. 164; *Daily Worker* (February 7, 1945); "Minutes of Special Session, International Executive Board . . . Cleveland, June 4–5, 1946," pp. 58–63; *Wage Earner* (May 24 and 31, June 7, 1946).

17. Michael Parenti, *The Anti-Communist Impulse* (New York: Random House, 1969), pp. 91–101; *Daily Worker* (January 6, 1947).

18. *United Automobile Worker* (December 1946 and April 1947); Kim Sigler, Testimony in U.S., Congress, House, Committee on Un-American Activities, *Investigation of Un-American Propaganda Activities in the United States.* 80th Cong., 1st sess., 1947, pp. 309–326; Walter Reuther, "How to Beat the Communists," *Colliers* (February 28, 1948), 11, 44–49.

19. "Fourth Quarterly Meeting Minutes, International Executive Board . . . Louisville, Kentucky, March 17–29, 1947," in UAW Executive Board Meeting Collection (WSU), pp. 37–39, 103–105, 155–161; *Detroit News* (June 16, 1946); *Wage Earner* (May 24 and 31, June 7, 1946); Congressman Louis C. Rabaut, Extension of Remarks in U.S., Congress, House, *Appendix to the Congressional Record.* 79th Cong., 1st sess., 1946, vol. 92, pt. 11, p. A3525; *The Bosses' Boy: A Documentary Record of Walter Reuther* (Detroit, 1947), in Nat Ganley Papers (WSU), p. 20.

20. "Fourth Quarterly Meeting Minutes, International Executive Board . . . Louisville, Kentucky, March 17–29, 1947," pp. 155, 162–186; Irving Richter to Roger Keeran (July 20, 1978).

21. "Special Meeting Minutes, International Executive Board . . . Detroit, Michigan, April 22–28, 1947," in UAW Executive Board Meeting Collection (WSU), pp. 197a–225.

22. "Statement by Nat Ganley" (February 1947), in Nat Ganley Papers (WSU); "Labor's Communists Come Under Fire," *Life* (March 24, 1947), 31; *Daily Worker* (February 25 and April 5, 1947).

23. *Business Week* (January 4, 1947); *Daily Worker* (November 25, 1946).

24. Cochran, pp. 166–173; Thomas W. Gavett, *The Development of*

*the Labor Movement in Milwaukee* (Madison: University of Wisconsin Press, 1965), pp. 180–181; Interview of Harold Christoffel, Oconomowoc, Wisconsin, June 27, 1974.

25. U.S., Congress, House, Committee on Education and Labor, *Amendments to the National Labor Relations Act, Hearings before the Committee on Education and Labor.* 80th Cong., 1st sess., 1947, vol. 3, p. 1386 and vol. 4 pp. 2024–2033, 2047–2049; *Newsweek* (November 11, 1946), pp. 32–34; *Daily Worker* (June 2, 1947); George Seldes, *Facts and Fascism* (New York: In Fact, 1943), pp. 139–156.

26. Gavett, pp. 190–191; *Amendments to the National Labor Relations Act, Hearings before the Committee on Education and Labor,* vol. 4, pp. 2025–2030, vol. 5, pp. 2994–2997.

27. *Milwaukee Journal* and *Milwaukee Sentinel* articles summarized in *Amendments to the National Labor Relations Act, Hearings before the Committee on Education and Labor,* vol. 3, p. 1344; Affidavit of Hugh W. Swofford, Janaury 23, 1950, in Nat Ganley Papers; *Communists Within the Labor Movement,* p. 17; *Newsweek* (November 11, 1946), 32–34; *New York Times* (November 26, 1946).

28. "UAW-CIO Views on the Issues in the Allis-Chalmers Strike" (transcript of radio program on WTMJ Milwaukee, November 17, 1946) in Local 248 Collection (WSU): Gavett, p. 192; *Daily Worker* (November 28, 1946).

29. *Wage Earner* (January 3 and 10, 1947); A report by R.J. Thomas to the membership on the Allis-Chalmers strike (February 7, 1947), in Nat Ganley Papers; "Third Quarterly Meeting Minutes, International Executive Board . . . New York, New York, December 9–18, 1946," pp. 9–15, 18–19, 53–55 in UAW Executive Board Meeting Collection (WSU); *New York Times* (January 29, 1947).

30. U.S., Congress, House, Committee on Un-American Activities, *Hearings Regarding Communism in Labor Unions in the United States.* 80th Cong., 1st sess., 1947, pp. 1–60.

31. *Amendments to the National Labor Relations Act, Hearings before the Committee on Education and Labor,* vol. 3, pp. 1335–1487; *Daily Worker* (February 25, 1947).

32. *Amendments to the National Labor Relations Act, Hearings before the Committee on Education and Labor,* vol. 4, pp. 2049–2078.

33. *Amendments to the National Labor Relations Act, Hearings before the Committee on Education and Labor,* vol. 4, pp. 1973–2049, 2079–2142 and vol. 5, pp. 3603–3623; *New York Times* (July 24, 1947).

34. *Amendments to the National Labor Relations Act, Hearings before the Committee on Education and Labor,* vol. 3, pp. 1346, 1424–1435 and vol. 4, pp. 1982, 1987, 1989, 1998, 2009, 2011, 2096, 2109, 2111; Interview of Harold Christoffel, Oconomowoc, Wisconsin, June 27, 1974.

35. Interview of Harold Christoffel, Oconomowoc, Wisconsin, June 27, 1974; Buse in *Amendments to the National Labor Relations Act, Hearings before the Committee on Education and Labor,* p. 2013; *Wage Earner* (January 10, 1947); "Third Quarterly Meeting Minutes, International Executive Board . . . New York, New York, December 9–18, 1946," in UAW Executive Board Meeting Collection (WSU), pp. 16–18, 73–75.

36. Clancy Sigal, *Going Away* (New York: Dell, 1970), p. 332; Philip Taft and Philip Ross, "American Labor Violence: Its Causes, Character, and Outcome," in Hugh D. Graham and Ted R. Gurr, *The History of Vio-*

*lence in America: A Report to the National Commission on the Causes and Prevention of Violence* (New York, Toronto and London: Bantam Books, 1970), pp. 281–395.

37. Seymour Martin Lipset, *Political Man: The Social Bases of Politics* (Garden City, N.Y.: Anchor Books, 1963), pp. 387–436; Burton H. Hall, ed., *Autocracy and Insurgency in Organized Labor* (New Brunswick, N.J.: Transaction Books, 1972), pp. 1–79; *Amendments to the National Labor Relations Act, Hearings before the Committee on Education and Labor*, vol. 3, pp. 1442–1457; *Hearings Regarding Communism in Labor Unions in the United States*, pp. 24, 32, 39, 46, 49–50; Gavett, pp. 92–94.

38. *Daily Worker* (March 17, 18, 20, 24, 25 1947, July 24, 1947, November 26, 1947, December 2, 1947); *New York Times* (July 24, 1947, March 4 and 6, 1948, October 4, 1948, February 7 and 24, 1950, March 15, 1950); Gavett, p. 194.

39. Emspak, "The Break-up of the Congress of Industrial Organizations (CIO), 1945–1950," p. 169; "Fifth Quarterly Meeting International Executive Board . . . June 9–13, 1947, Chicago, Illinois," pp. 147–164 in UAW Executive Board Meeting Collection (WSU).

40. "Special Session International Executive Board . . . June 20, 1947, Detroit, Michigan," pp. 1–58 in UAW Executive Board Meeting Collection (WSU); *Wage Earner* (July 4, 25, 1947); Oral History of John W. Anderson (WSU), p. 132; Haessler quoted by Emspak, p. 169; Sigal, p. 330.

41. Fred A. Hartley, Jr., *Our New National Labor Policy: The Taft-Hartley Act and the Next Steps* (New York: Funk & Wagnalls Company, 1948), pp. 39–40; Emspak, "The Break-up of the Congress of Industrial Organizations (CIO), 1945–1950," pp. 172–173; *United Automobile Worker* (November 1947); *Daily Worker* (November 9, 1947).

42. Emspak, "The Association of Catholic Trade Unionists and the United Automobile Workers," p. 96.

43. Walter Reuther, "Report to the Membership," *United Automobile Worker* (September 1947); Walter Reuther to All Members, UAW-CIO (October 6, 1947), in Nat Ganley Papers (WSU); Charles G. Givens, "Asleep at the Ringside," *New Republic* (November 10, 1947), 10.

44. *The Bosses' Boy: A Documentary Record of Walter Reuther* (Detroit, 1947), in Nat Ganley Papers (WSU); *FDR* (June 5, September 25, October 9, November 1, 1947); Interview of Carl Haessler, Detroit, July 25, 1971; Irving Richter to Roger Keeran (July 20, 1978); *Daily Worker* (November 27, 1947); *Worker* (June 27, 1948).

45. United Automobile, Aircraft and Agricultural Workers of America (UAW-CIO), *Proceedings of the Eleventh Convention* (Atlantic City, New Jersey, 1947), pp. 8, 17, 38–44, 77–110, 128, 135–136, 174–175, 202; *Newsweek* (November 17, 1947), 29 and (November 24, 1947), 28–29.

46. *New York Times* (November 15, 1947); *Newsweek* (November 24, 1947), 29; *Business Week* (November 15, 1947), 92–94; *New Republic* (November 24, 1947), 32.

47. Oral History of John W. Anderson (WSU), p. 136; Matthew Ward, *Indignant Heart* (New York: New Books, 1952), p. 151; *Daily Worker* (December 2, 1947); Oral History of Carl Haessler (WSU), pp. 185–186, 214–228; *Progressive Unity Caucus* (1949) in Vertical File Collection (WSU); United Automobile, Aircraft and Agricultural Implement Workers of America (UAW-CIO), *Proceedings Twelfth Constitutional Convention*

(Milwaukee, 1949), pp. 261–277; Jack Stieber, *Governing the UAW* (New York and London: John Wiley and Sons, 1962), pp. 14–15.

48. Frank Cormier and William J. Eaton, *Reuther* (Englewood Cliffs, N.J.: Prentice Hall, 1970), pp. 241–254; *New York Times* (December 1, 1947); *Daily World* (February 21, 1974); Irving Richter to Roger Keeran (July 20, 1978); Interview of Irving Richter, Albany, New York, June 1, 1978.

49. *New York Times* (December 2, 1947); *Proceedings Twelfth Constitutional Convention*, pp. 245–254; Interview of John Anderson, Tampa, Florida, June 18, 1974; Oral History Interview of Russell Leach (WSU), pp. 1–2, 19–29; Stieber, p. 138; Gerry Weeks, "Reuther in the Saddle," *New Republic* (July 18, 1949), 10.

50. *Daily Worker* (February 10, 1948); Testimony of Lee Romano, Shelton Tappes, and Archie Acciacca in *Communism in the Detroit Area—Part 2*, pp. 3035–3091, 3117–3145, and 3190–3201; *Detroit News* (February 1, 1948); *Detroit Free Press* (February 10, 1948); *Michigan CIO News* (February 13, 1948); Bill McKie to the General Council and Membership of Local 600 UAW-CIO (February 16, 1948), in Nat Ganley Papers (WSU).

51. John Williamson, "Why Reuther Won in UAW," *Daily Worker* (November 26 and 27, 1947); Saul Wellman, "The Party and the Trade Unions," *Emphasis* [December 1947], in Nat Ganley Papers (WSU); "A Critical Review of Party's Work in Auto," *Worker* (June 27, 1948).

52. Williamson, "Why Reuther Won in UAW"; Wellman, "The Party and the Trade Unions"; "A Critical Review of Party's Work in Auto."

53. *Spotlight* (issued by Communist auto workers, June and December 1949) in Vertical File Collection (WSU).

54. Wyndham Mortimer to Nat Ganley (April 9, 1956), in Nat Ganley Papers (WSU).

55. Gil Green, *What's Happening to Labor* (New York: International Publishers, 1976), p. 9; Peggy Dennis, *The Autobiography of an American Communist: A Personal View of a Political Life* (Westport and Berkeley: Lawrence Hill & Co., 1977), pp. 184–218; Joseph Starobin, *American Communism in Crisis, 1943–1957* (Cambridge, Mass.: Harvard University Press, 1972), pp. 195–223; *Communism in the Detroit Area Party* (1952); *Investigation of Communist Activities in the State of Michigan* (1954); U.S., Congress, Senate, Subcommittee to Investigate the Administration of the Internal Security Act and Other Internal Security Laws of the Committee on the Judiciary, *Scope of Soviet Activity in the United States*. 85th Cong., 1st sess., 1957.

# INDEX